The History of Beads

Harry N. Abrams, Inc., Publishers, New York

The History of Beads

from 30,000 B.C. to the Present   Lois Sherr Dubin

Original Photography by Togashi

For Ted
who understood

Project Director: MARGARET L. KAPLAN
Editor: CHARLES MIERS
Designer: ANA ROGERS
Maps and Line Drawings: LEA CYR

Library of Congress Cataloging-in-Publication Data

Dubin, Lois Sherr.
   The history of beads, from 30,000 B.C. to the present.

   Bibliography
   Includes index.
   1. Beads—History.   I. Title.
GT2250.D83   1987   391′.7   87-1428
ISBN 0-8109-0736-4

Times Mirror Books

Printed and bound in Japan

Measurements: a bead's length is given as the length of
the perforation; its diameter is the bead's width mea-
sured perpendicular to the perforation.

Maps appear on pages 23, 35, 50, 58, 67, 94, 103, 128,
148, 155, 183, 195, 228, 255, and 270

HALF-TITLE PAGE:
An ivory shibayama-*technique* ojime *(slide fastener) from
nineteenth-century Japan, depicting a proud cockerel and
his hen. Inlaid with mother-of-pearl, horn, and lacquer.
Diameter, 1.7 cm. Private collection*

PAGES 4–5:
*Tibetan beads, typical of the shapes and materials worn by
most Himalayan peoples. Turquoise, amber, and coral are
believed to be imbued with protective powers. Turquoise
bead: length, 5.1 cm. Collection Ivory Freidus and Tambaran
Gallery, New York*

Contents

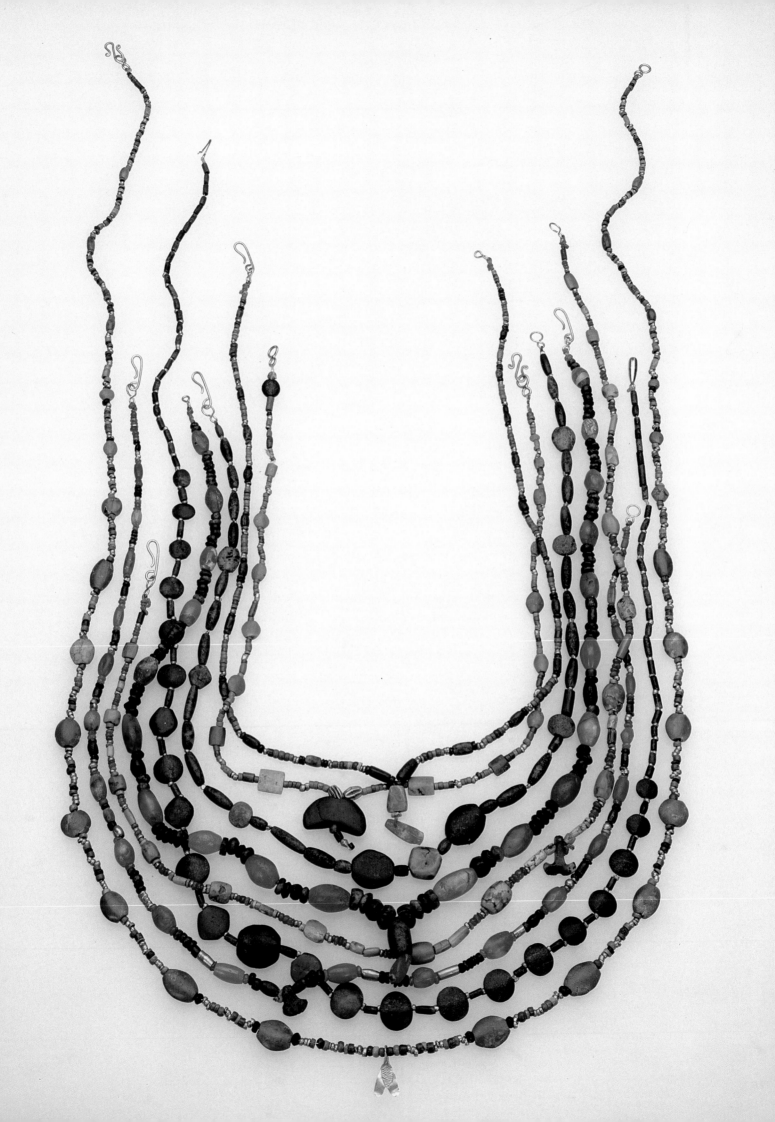

Foreword

Beads were probably the first durable ornaments humans possessed, and the intimate relationship they had to their owners is reflected in the fact that they are among the most common items unearthed from ancient graves. In the past, as today, men, women, and children adorned themselves with beads. In tribal cultures still, certain beads are often worn from birth until death and then are buried with their owner for the afterlife. Abrasion due to daily wear alters the surface features of beads, and if they are buried for long the effects of corrosion can further change their appearance. Thus, beauty is imparted to the bead both by use and the effects of time. When one looks at a bead, it is hard not to think about who previously owned it and how far through time and distance it has traveled to reach its current destination.

Besides their wearability, either as jewelry or incorporated into articles of attire, beads possess the desirable characteristics of every collectible: they are durable, portable, available in infinite variety, and often valuable in their original cultural context as well as in today's market. Pleasing to look at and touch, beads come in shapes, colors, and materials that almost compel one to handle them and to sort them.

Beads are such intriguing objects that one must ask the basic questions of what, where, when, and how whenever an interesting bead is encountered. They are miniature bundles of secrets waiting to be revealed: their history, technology, cultural context, economic role, and ornamental use are all points of information one hopes to unravel. Even the most mundane beads may have traveled great distances and been exposed to many human experiences. For example, in the eighteenth and nineteenth centuries many glass beads were shipped from Venetian and Bohemian factories to African destinations and then were traded through middlemen before reaching their tribal owners.

A collection of lapis lazuli, turquoise, carnelian, agate, and gold beads recently recovered from archaeological sites in northern Afghanistan, believed to date between 2200 and 1600 B.C. These beads resemble in quality, form, and materials those of the same period from Mesopotamia. Their minute scale—as many as forty to an inch have been recorded—is associated with wealth, since it was necessary to waste considerable raw material in their fabrication.

The gold fly amulet (at center of the bottom necklace) has both Sumerian and Egyptian origins, appearing in burials at Ur and in royal Egyptian jewelry of the Twelfth Dynasty (1991–1786 B.C.). Gold fly: Length, 1.5 cm. Private collection

During the past two to three decades they have been sold again to bead traders for reexport to the Western world. They were always treated as valued personal adornments, until economic conditions and changing cultures caused them to be sold to a new, appreciative market of Western museums and collectors.

These special attractions of beads contribute to the uniqueness of bead research. While often regarded as the "small change of civilizations," beads are a part of every culture, and they can often be used to date sites and to designate the degree of mercantile, technological, and cultural sophistication. While beads have been and are studied by scholars trained in many different academic fields, the bead expert is often self-trained and sometimes without formal schooling. (This is a trend that is perhaps more pronounced today, although Horace C. Beck and W. G. N. van der Sleen, the spiritual fathers of contemporary bead researchers, were both self-trained.)

The bead researcher concentrates on a single category of artifacts, regardless of their origins in time or space. Yet, like the ethologist, the researcher of beads must gather information from many diverse fields. In addition to having to be a generalist while specializing in what many regard as a very narrow field, the researcher is faced with the problem of primary materials that have little or no documentation. Many ancient beads are from looted sites, and beads of ethnographic interest often are separated from their original cultural context. Furthermore, the bead enthusiast is also a missionary of knowledge, trying to enlighten the vast majority of people who are ignorant of the beauty, charm, and fascinating history that characterize these small, perforated artifacts.

Until now, there has been no comprehensive book on beads that adequately presents all aspects of their story. This book, a five-year labor of love and frustration for the author, who enlisted the cooperation of over thirty-five museums and numerous individuals, covers the cultures of the world in which beads proliferated. Richly illustrated with specially commissioned photographs, the volume also contains a unique time line of bead history. Over two thousand individual specimens are shown in their chronological and geographic contexts. Such an ambitious undertaking has never been attempted before. This feature alone will be of immense aid and interest to both amateur and expert bead connoisseurs. Cognizant of the enormity of the field and the constant flow of new information on beads, the author has presented this work in the hope of generating discussion and feedback from readers around the world. She encourages comments, corrections, and additions that she might incorporate into future editions.

Since beads have been a constant and primary part of jewelry throughout history, those with an interest in personal adornment will find Lois Dubin's book rewarding, not only for her history of tribal and ancient ornaments, but also for her coverage of the exciting renaissance of beads in contemporary jewelry. Today, beads are being combined and shaped into aesthetically dynamic jewelry and are being made of materials and techniques that are in themselves expressing new artistic and technological dimensions. As was the case in so many ancient and tribal cultures, the ordinary is again being used in extraordinary ways by artists and craftsmen.

—Robert K. Liu

Acknowledgments

I can always remember loving beads. My interest and appreciation for them started as a young girl and intensified when I spent considerable amounts of time visiting various countries as a professional landscape architect. Having little money and moving frequently, I found beads were the ideal objects to collect and wear. Besides, they were beautiful and studying them seemed to bring me closer to the cultures with which I came into contact. Whenever possible, I gleaned information about beads from museums, books, and dealers.

An exciting discovery occurred during the summer of 1974, when my sister Lynn brought me the first copy of *The Bead Journal* (now *Ornament* magazine), a quarterly publication of ancient and ethnic beads. Published in Los Angeles by Robert K. Liu, the magazine provided the first scholarly forum for the exchange of information on beads.

It was not, however, until I visited Kenya in 1982 that it became obvious to me how beads served as much more than adornment. I was deeply moved by observing both the women and men of the Maasai, Turkana, and Samburu tribes in their colorful beaded attire. It was obvious they use beads to create a visually powerful communication system, an insight previously explored by anthropologist Herbert Cole in an article for *The Bead Journal* ("Artistic and Communicative Values of Beads in Kenya and Ghana"). After many evenings in Kenya spent discussing beads, the leaders of our trip, Jill and Roger Caras, suggested I write a book on the subject. Although I am not a writer nor, for that matter, a scholar, historian, anthropologist, archaeologist, jeweler, or linguist— any one of these qualifications would have been extraordinarily helpful—I decided to tackle this formidable task. My goal was to create a comprehensive and visually stimulating book that would synthesize the most important information known about beads

A Yoruba diviner's bag from late nineteenth- or early twentieth-century Nigeria, used to carry ritual accessories. The six cylinders in the strap are bead-covered corncobs. Height, 125.7 cm. Collection Ruth and Paul Tishman, New York

from twelve world regions and examine the roles beads play in their cultural contexts.

A book with such a quantity and diversity of information—over thirty thousand years of bead history—was only possible with the help of many knowledgeable people: museum curators, gallery owners, archaeologists, anthropologists, bead specialists, collectors, and photographers. I derived enormous pleasure from visiting bead connoisseurs in museums, galleries, and private homes; individuals who gave me free access to their often extensive collections. I want to thank these people for their patience and generosity in allowing me to select the beads illustrated in this book.

I particularly wish to thank Carol A. R. Andrews and James Putnam of the Department of Egyptian Antiquities, Leslie Goulding and Dennis Plummer of Western Asiatic Antiquities, and Geff Cooper of Photographic Services at the British Museum; Priscilla Price at the Corning Museum of Glass; Paul Taylor and Chang-su Houchins at the Smithsonian Institution; Conrad Graham at the McCord Museum; Doris Dohrenwend at the Royal Ontario Museum; Ghazy A. R. Sheikh at the National Museums of Kenya; Cynthia Nakamura at the Denver Art Museum; and Anibal Rodriguez at the American Museum of Natural History. Robert Dyson of the University Museum kindly granted permission to photograph the Ur jewelry. The community of bead scholars whose published work greatly influenced this book includes Jamey D. Allen, Horace Beck, Peter Francis, Jr., Kenneth Kidd, Alastair Lamb, Robert K. Liu, and W. G. N. van der Sleen. I also thank Dr. Michael Heide, who wrote the Chevron beads section.

I also had the benefit of helpful suggestions from specialists who reviewed parts of the manuscript. Jamey D. Allen, Esin Atil, Raymond Bushell, Jill Claster, Derek Content, Doris Dohrenwend, David Ebbinghouse, Andre Emmerich, Peter Francis, Jr., Anita Gumpert, Chang-su Houchins, Ronald Mason, Michael Meister, Barbara Robertson, and Roy Sieber each read draft chapters. Kate Fitzgibbons and Andy Hale helped with the chronology of central Asian beads. Jamey D. Allen checked all the glass bead manufacturing techniques on the Bead Chart and wrote the Glossary. Peter Francis, Jr., both critiqued the maps and supplied valuable information on beads.

For welcoming me into their galleries and permitting the photography of special artifacts, I thank Stephen Paul Adler, Collector's Edition, New York; Robin Beningson, Antiquarium Gallery, New York; Lisa Bradley and the late Bryce Holcombe, Pace Gallery, New York; Byzantium Gallery, New York; Jim Camp, J. Camp Gallery, New York; Julie Schafler Dale, Julie: Artisian's Gallery, New York; Audrey Friedman, Primavera Gallery, New York; Cynthia Gofre, Bamboula, New York; Albert Gordon and Suzanne Bach, Tribal Arts Gallery, New York; Wolf Hunger, Sac Frères, London; Arthur King, Arthur King Gallery, New York; Margaret and Joe Knopfelmacher, Craft Caravan, New York; Edward Merrin, Edward Merrin Gallery, New York; and Sylvia Pine, Uniquities, New York. At Andre Emmerich Gallery, New York, Catherine Jalayer and my dear friend Andre Emmerich were generous contributors to the book from its inception. Maureen Zarember of Tambaran Gallery, New York, gave freely of her knowledge and telephoned whenever a wonderful new object appeared in her gallery. Henry Anavian, who was extraordinarily generous in lending beads from his personal collection as well as from Sumer Gallery, New York, spent many hours organizing beads for the Bead Chart and provided invaluable historical information. Derek Content was extremely generous in providing a wealth of highly original insights and sharing his glorious beads. Sachi Wagner of Midori Gallery, Coconut Grove, Florida, coauthor of the *ojime* section in Chapter 8, traveled to California to select *ojime* for the book. Robert Ebendorf and Ivy Ross led me to several contemporary beadmakers, whose work is represented in the last chapter. An indication of the popularity of beads is reflected in the numbers of beads reproduced in the book that come from private collections. I am most grateful to Ivory Freidus for allowing us to publish her remarkable collection of ethnographic beads and beadwork. It would be a lesser book without Ivory's beads.

For help in organizing various phases of the manuscript over the past four years, I am deeply indebted to several people: Marc Rabun, who worked with me for over two years; Richard Eger and Kim Honig, who assisted in my initial presentation to Harry N. Abrams (Richard also critiqued several chapters); Ann-Marie Cunningham, who helped me organize and write the manuscript in its early stages; and Joan Gregg and Beth Pacheco, wonderful editors and friends. Delores Schapiro gave up a summer vacation and many weekends to work on the Bead Chart. Her eye contributed immeasurably to the chart's aesthetic appeal. Charles Donaldson was the "curator" of slides for the Bead Chart, a task admirably accomplished. Lea Cyr is responsible for the wonderful maps and illustrations, and Lea Cyr and Michael Guran for the map designs.

Many photographers contributed to the book: Alexander Marshack was extremely generous in supplying photographs and information, and I particularly wish to thank Barry Howard for his photographic help during the past three years. Above all, I am indebted to Togashi, who took the majority of the book's photographs. An artist of outstanding talent, Togashi spent hours laying out arrangements and capturing the appropriate spirit of each bead or piece of adornment. In many cases, other photographers were inspired by viewing his work. I also wish to thank Bob and Kim Reed from Reed Photo Art in Denver, who prepared the excellent assemblies for many plates and the Bead Chart.

Conversations with friends provided the inspiration for many of the ideas expressed on these pages. Kitty and Carl Becker, Rona Bross, Dr. Robert Bross, Esther Gushner, Diane Love, Sasha Nowicki, Betty and Bill Ruder, Rosalie Wolff, and Adele Santos were helpful advisers. In addition, David Goldberg gave me much emotional support, and goldsmith Nina Safdie was a frequent source of useful suggestions. My office staff at Luis F. Villa/Lois Sherr Associated, Frances Chamberlain, Maryanne Connelly, and Elizabeth Kennedy, were very supportive. For over thirty years my partner, Luis F. Villa, was a constant source of stimulating discussions about how things are made. Donna Sue Campbell was a marvel of organization during the final months of writing and revisions.

At Harry N. Abrams, Inc., a truly fine publisher, I wish to thank Margaret Kaplan, Senior Vice-President and Executive Editor, to whom I made my initial presentation; Samuel N. Antupit, Vice-President for Art and Design, who both discovered Togashi and helped to give the book its exquisite graphic concept; Ana Rogers, who designed the book with grace and talent; Heidi Colsman-Freyberger, who thoughtfully checked facts on the maps and in parts of the text; and Charles Miers, my excellent and meticulous editor, who not only pulled together all aspects of this complex undertaking but also made innumerable contributions that improved the book in every way.

My mother, Shirley "Kohalan" (Evening Star) Sherr, a lover of beads since her days as a campfire girl, when she wove glass bead necklaces in Indian patterns, and my sister and brother-in-law, Lynn Sherr and Larry Hilford, gave continual and much appreciated support to the book. My father, Louis Sherr, who often subsidized his daughter's bead addiction, would, I believe, have been pleased with this result.

Lastly, I am grateful to Stuart Struever for his editorial advice, encouragement, and help in all aspects of the book during its final two years. His anthropological expertise helped me to develop perspectives that are reflected in the discussions of beads in a number of chapters. Stuart's guidance immeasurably strengthened the book's content.

—L.D.

Introduction: Why a Book on Beads

Westerners tend to think of beads as adornment. In fact, we confine ourselves for the most part to draping them around our necks. Yet, through the centuries, beads have functioned as more than jewelry. They are kaleidoscopic, combined and recombined in an astonishingly wide range of materials; they express social circumstances, political history, and religious beliefs.

Beads are small, colorful, symmetrical, and often quite beautiful. They are frequently standardized, inexpensive units that can be arranged in almost endless configurations. They can be seen not only in the familiar forms of necklaces and bracelets but also on anklets, headbands, and headdresses. Beadwork is used in West Africa on altar mantles, garments for royal statues, and coverings for kingly stools. In ancient Asia, beads were scattered like seeds beneath temples to induce bountiful harvests, and among the Kogi of Colombia beads are part of ritual offerings to insure the future of newly built houses. In the Philippines, the practice of placing two beads in a cup at wedding ceremonies still binds marriages. Beads are worn to communicate status almost everywhere and were even used in North America to cement political alliances.

Beads have frequently been enlisted as symbolic repositories of sacred knowledge, been deemed to have curative powers, served as the fee for passage to the afterlife, and used as prompters to insure the proper conduct of ritual and prayer. Beads have been the medium of exchange in barter and the standard units of value in market systems. From the seventeenth to the nineteenth century, Europeans exchanged glass beads for beaver pelts in North America, for spices in Indonesia, and for gold, ivory, and slaves in Africa. Beads so often mirror the culture of which they are a part that they tell us a great deal about the social, political, economic, and religious lives of the people who have made and worn them.

A collection of etched carnelian beads from Parthian to Sasanian period sites in Iran, dating from 249 B.C. to A.D. 642. The bead with rectangular patterns in the upper right corner may be older. Lower left bead: length, 3.2 cm. Collection Derek Content, Houlton, Maine

17

The ways in which beads are used helps to define a particular group's concept of beauty. Both the selection of individual beads and the combinations and assemblages are informative. In some societies, beauty can even be rewarded by beads: an attractive East African Maasai woman will be courted with beads, and the accumulation of beads in itself will enhance her beauty.

The History of Beads: From 30,000 B.C. to the Present examines beads in twelve areas, not in an attempt to be encyclopedic but rather to identify certain features and patterns that are important to the story of beads. Different facets of the bead story are emphasized in each area. In North America, for example, the impact of European trade on the indigenous bead culture of the Great Lakes and Plains Indians is stressed. By contrast, in the chapter on India the pervasive role beads play in all aspects of life, secular and sacred, and the extraordinary continuity in beadmaking technology over the past four thousand years are the overriding concepts.

There are several perspectives from which beads might be looked at, but this book attempts to observe them primarily from cultural and historical viewpoints, to understand their importance in the lives of people through the history of a region and to account for the striking similarities and differences in bead culture between geographic areas and historical eras.

A combination of qualities makes beads especially interesting artifacts to study. They first appear with the advent of modern man, *Homo sapiens*, at least forty thousand years ago, and probably have been made and used by every culture in the world since then. Because beads are often made of durable materials, and because they have always been treated as important personal possessions and therefore not infrequently taken to the grave with their owners, they are well represented in the archaeological record. The great variety of materials, forms, and technology used to create finished beads, together with their portability and their natural prominence as adornment, renders them ideal vehicles for conveying a complex range of cultural information.

Beads and the raw materials to make them have been important trade items for millennia. Discovering the origins of finished beads, as well as bead styles and technologies, and tracing their subsequent travels provide an interesting picture of intercultural relations. The movement of beadmakers, bead technology, bead styles, and beads themselves are each complicated stories. A major task in bead research is identifying which combination of these processes accounts for the spread of bead knowledge at a particular time and place.

An important issue that recurs throughout bead history is the impact of trade on indigenous decorative styles. Over the centuries, cultures have expressed their own decorative styles in locally made beads. However, the sudden importation of quantities of inexpensive finished beads through newly created trade partnerships frequently changed both the role beads played in the recipient culture and the decorative styles produced thereafter.

Almost every society has had the minimum technology necessary to produce beads of one raw material or another. In fact, the technical sophistication of bead manufacturing often mirrors the general technological level of the society. Throughout history, beads have frequently been one of the first items produced by societies experimenting with new technologies. When bronze and iron were first worked by craftsmen, for example, they were often employed to make weapons, tools, and beads at the same time. As soon as glass was invented, it was used to make beads. Moreover, beads were always popular trade items, and the more technologically sophisticated cultures traded their finished products to less advanced peoples. Tracing the diffusion of beads thus affords us a view of the broader history of technology.

While this book seeks to explain similarities and differences in bead culture in terms of historical factors, it also recognizes certain universal features of beads and the handling of them that appear to cut across cultural differences. In the chapters that follow, broad commonalities in the creation of beaded adornment are identified that express certain basic human needs.

Although beads are typically described as small balls perforated for stringing, the earliest beads were generally tubular, barrel-, and disk-shaped, reflecting the limitations of technology and availability of raw materials. Once the technical capacity developed to make spheres, they became the most common bead shape for thousands of years thereafter. The appeal of spheres supersedes cultural differences. Moreover, sphere-shaped beads should be thought of as small sculptures: they are whole and perfect. In a perplexing world, this simple, familiar shape has visual and tactile completeness, which is reinforced when several beads are joined together to form a circlet. It is perhaps through the use of rosaries, circlets of prayer beads, that people have achieved their most profound and complete relationship with beads.

We must look for primal causes in the wearing of beads. Some psychiatrists trace bead adornment to feelings of security connected with the eye and sight. Joan Mowat Erikson, author of *The Universal Bead*, suggests:

> The eyes may be a basic clue to the elemental power of rounded objects. . . . It is with the eyes that mother and child communicate before speech develops, and the meeting of the eyes serves as an adjunct to speech whenever language fails. . . . We begin life with this relatedness to eyes; we are protected by seeing, we feel secure when there is light. Eyes have been described as shining, laughing, dancing, glowing, glaring, gleaming—like beads—and are, like beads, colored blue, green, gray, brown, and golden.[1]

The "eye bead," a common bead type that resembles the form of an eye, was created in many early cultures and continues to be made today. Eye beads were used to meet people's age-old need for protection against malevolence—the "evil eye." Eye beads became "eyes that can see in all directions" and thereby served as protective amulets against the evil eye.[2] Inexorably, the viewer is drawn to look at eye beads, but because of their realism, they disturb rather than charm, and therefore encourage the viewer to look away from them and the vulnerable throats they encircle.

Psychiatrist Robert Bross, on the other hand, believes that touch, not sight, is the primary sense for an infant. He suggests that the passion for beads may be connected to the longing for the tactile pleasures associated with breast-feeding and the nipple. Whether or not we accept his arguments, the power of beads is such that there must be hidden within them some meaning essential to us all.

This volume will give the reader only an idea of the range of human creativity that has been applied to beads. It is a sampling of what people have done with this universal object, but it is hoped that the reader will come away with a sense of how deeply embedded the manufacture and use of beads have become in human society. Beads are tools by which people convey information to other people, while reminding the wearer of his or her own commitment to a set of beliefs and principles. They have been significant to people from Neolithic Asia to twentieth-century New York. They are and have always been used to state basic relationships to life and the supernatural. People have used beads to organize and symbolize their world. They have been guideposts in human relationships and expressions of innermost feelings. Perhaps the reader will identify with a particular segment of the bead story, thus prompting an exploration of the meaning of beads, not only in history, but in his or her life as well.

The Beginnings

While the first evidence of culture is manifested in simple stonecutting tools that were made in East Africa 1.5 million years ago, the earliest known beads are associated with Neanderthal man. They were discovered at La Quina, an archaeological site in France, and have been dated to approximately 38,000 B.C., at about the time *Homo sapiens* populations were replacing the Neanderthals and developing new and more complex cultures.[1] The La Quina beads, which predate the earliest known figurative art (engravings on mammoth tusks) by about 5,000 years, are made from grooved animal teeth and bones and were worn as pendants. They are unique to the Neanderthal period, however, and few in number. It is not until the earliest phase of the Upper Paleolithic period in western Europe—known as the Châtelperronian period (c. 31,000 B.C.)—that beads appear in quantity and as creations of modern man. Although beads have been found with fossil bones and other cultural remains in archaeological discoveries throughout the world (including India, China, Korea, Africa, and Australia), most of these finds involve no more than a few, simply made bead forms. Only in the Upper Paleolithic sites of Europe and Russia and in the Upper Cave of Zhou-kou-dian in China have large numbers of beads been excavated.

The European and Russian sites are concentrated in five major regions, including western Europe (southern France and northern Spain), the Mediterranean (Italy and eastern Spain), central Europe (Czechoslovakia, Germany, and Austria), and Russia (the upper Ukraine and central Siberia). The evidence from these sites suggests that beads really made their appearance as part of a significant evolutionary development in culture some 33,000 years ago.

Basic subsistence requirements played a central role in human evolution during

1. *An extraordinary assemblage of Upper Paleolithic beads of various fossilized shell species from the East Gravettian site of Pavlov in present-day Czechoslovakia, c. 28,000 B.C. By this time, most beads were perforated rather than grooved, indicating increased technical facility. Length, 35 cm. Moravske Muzeum, Brno, Czechoslovakia*

21

2. *Breast-shaped ivory bead of the East Gravettian culture from Dolni Vestonice, Czechoslovakia, c. 28,000 B.C. The Gravettian culture also produced bone, ivory, and stone "Venus" figurines with oversize breasts, belly, buttocks, and thighs. Both the Venus figurines and this bead capture an inner vision of fertility and motherhood. The bead, part of a necklace of similar beads, is one of the earliest known figurative art objects. Length, 3.2 cm. Moravske Muzeum, Brno, Czechoslovakia*

the Ice Age. Modern man evolved in Europe and Asia during a comparatively cold phase of the late Ice Age (when the climate shifted back and forth between bitter cold and warm periods). With the onset of a dry climate that necessitated animals to migrate to sources of water and vegetation about 45,000 to 40,000 years ago, people's search for food intensified. Simultaneously, herds became concentrated and larger. Hunting was a dangerous business, made safer and more productive by hunters cooperating in large bands. Hunting bands gathered near game concentrations in sheltered valleys and at narrow passes during seasonal migrations, employing sophisticated drive-hunting techniques.[2]

Social mechanisms developed that organized people into large multiband groups held together by the bonds of kinship and marriage and the shared requirements of large-scale hunting. Rituals developed to define and reinforce cohesive relationships among the larger groups of individuals and to teach and sanctify the many more complex rules of behavior required by increased group size. This led to even more densely settled communities with greater populations. It is within this context that art and adornment—and beads—had their beginnings.[3]

Concurrent with the appearance of *Homo sapiens* populations is the arrival of an elaborate structure of symbolism. The most spectacular expressions of this development are the famous ritualistic cave paintings of southwestern France and northern Spain, as well as a few remarkably sophisticated assemblage of carvings used in ceremonies and adornment.

At Grotte du Renne, a cave at Arcy-sur-Cure in France that dates to 31,000 B.C., one of the earliest caches of beads was found: a group of fox, hyena, wolf, reindeer, bear, and marmot teeth clearly grooved and notched for hanging from some sort of necklace. With them was a fossilized crinoid stem with a center hole.[4] Beads made of fossil shells, including marine species from the Mediterranean, have been found in a range of occupation levels in the limestone rock-shelter of Abri Pataud in southwestern France. They date from 30,000 to 19,500 B.C. Some have natural holes, but most were grooved and pierced for suspension.[5]

More sophisticated bead craftsmanship developed during the Gravettian and Aurignacian periods (30,000–18,000 B.C.), at about the same time the first European cave paintings and carvings appeared. Grooving ornaments gave way to perforation: pieces of bone and ivory were ground into definite bead shapes and decorated with incisions.[6] Important bead discoveries from this period have been made at the sites of Dolni Vestonice and Pavlov in Czechoslovakia. These beads were part of the material possessions of a culturally advanced, mammoth-hunting society that produced a rich array of bone tools, as well as necklaces with beads of animal teeth, shells, and pebbles. Some of the beads were carved in the shape of female breasts and torsos and were probably associated with rituals for increasing fertility (plates 2–3). Fired-clay animal figurines, dating to 23,500 B.C.—the oldest ceramic objects known—were also excavated at Dolni Vestonice.[7]

The early beads reflect the sophisticated mentality of Upper Paleolithic people, who were able to develop abstract forms and symbols that increased their capacity to cope with an often hazardous environment. Beads were self-conscious expressions of prowess in hunting. They also symbolized people's need for spiritual assistance (and protection) in obtaining resources that they found difficult but necessary to have. They were talismanic, made from by-products of the hunt: bone, teeth, tusks, and shells. By wearing parts of the animal's body, the wearer and creator of the beads gained a measure of control over its spirit. The appearance of jewelry can also be associated with

The Beginnings:
Archaeological Discoveries of Beads,
38,000 B.C. to 10,000 B.C.

RUSSIA

Arcy-sur-Cure
Pekarna- *Sungir*
Abri Pataud *Dolni Vestonice*
Pavlov
La Quina
Petersfels *Mezhirichi*
La Bastide *Grimaldi*

Krasnyi
Mal'ta

Ikhen-gung
Gurnai

Zhou-kou-dian
Turubong *Chŏmmal*

Ushki

CHINA

Haua Fteah

INDIA

AFRICA

Poona
Kurnool

AUSTRALIA

Devil's Lair

▲ Archaeological Sites
Mentioned in Chapter
and Notes.

TOP: 3. *Necklace of lignite or jet (a hard form of coal) beads shaped as female buttocks, made by Magdalenian craftsmen, from Petersfels, East Germany, c. 13,000 B.C. Similar abstract shapes were also engraved on stones. The beads appear to have been used in ceremonies involving female mythology. Center bead: length, 4.4 cm. Hegau Museum, Sengen, East Germany*

BELOW: 4. *Late Upper Paleolithic beads of the Magdalenian culture, from Pekarna, Czechoslovakia; c. 13,000 B.C. They are made of animal teeth and waterworn pebbles. By this period, bow drills and abrasives were used to perforate stone. Necklace: diameter, 30 cm. Moravske Muzeum, Brno, Czechoslovakia*

the growing need for personal identity when the human population expanded and large-scale communities evolved 30,000 to 20,000 years ago.

The late Upper Paleolithic era (17,000–10,000 B.C.) witnessed an elaborate development both in the design of individual beads and in the ways in which beads were combined.[8] In France, the Magdalenian culture, which produced some of the most famous cave paintings, is known also for beautifully crafted beads. In southern France, for example, a human burial at Barma Grande, near Grimaldi, was found with a necklace of three parallel rows of fish vertebrae, *Nassus* shells, and stag canine teeth arranged symmetrically.[9]

Beads were used as grave offerings in Russia at this time. The grave of two young boys excavated at Sungir, 130 miles northeast of Moscow, "suggests that either the boys were very important, or that the peoples of Sungir 23,000 years ago had very elaborate ideas of an afterlife. The boys—one seven to nine years old, the other twelve or thirteen—were laid out in a line, skull to skull. Both had been dressed from head to toe in clothing decorated with ivory beads carved from mammoth tusks and they wore bracelets and rings of the same materials."[10] In another ocher-covered grave at Sungir,

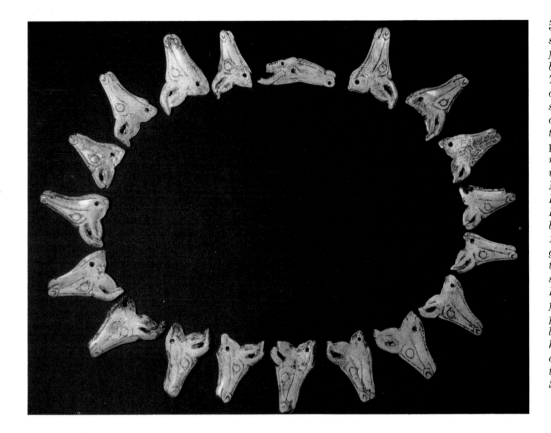

a man was buried "laden with beads, a headband of carved mammoth ivory and the teeth of Arctic foxes."[11]

In Siberia, a number of spectacular late Upper Paleolithic bead finds have been made. At the Ushki Lake site in Kamchatka, graves from 12,000 to 11,000 B.C. were discovered containing pendants and numerous stone beads that evidently had been sewn onto the clothing of the deceased. Ostrich eggshell beads dating to the same period were found at Krasnyi, near Irkutsk. And at Mal'ta, also near Irkutsk, an infant burial dated 12,500 B.C. yielded spatula-shaped, engraved bone beads.[12]

Upper Paleolithic beads have been found at several localities in India,[13] China,[14] and Korea.[15] In Africa, the earliest known beads are from 10,000 B.C. and were found in Haua Fteah in Libya. They are disk-shaped and made of ostrich eggshell.[16] At Devil's Lair, a small limestone cave in southwestern Australia, three beads of kangaroo bone were found that were made between 13,000 and 10,000 B.C. The beads have rounded edges and were strung on kangaroo sinew less than one millimeter in diameter.[17] In the Americas, the only bead contemporary with the European and Asian Upper Paleolithic is a single bead of hardened calcium carbonate found at Tule Springs, Nevada, and estimated to have been made in 11,000 B.C.[18]

This wide-ranging evidence suggests there was an explosion of symbolic expression rendered in ceremonial paraphernalia and personal adornment, including beads, between 33,000 and 12,000 years ago, immediately following the emergence of modern man's increased cognitive powers and his new capacities for making cultural objects. It corresponds also with *Homo sapiens*'s emergence throughout the world, often in environments previously uninhabited, and with the development of new and more complex modes of human organization, including ritual behavior, which were an essential part of peoples' increasingly successful strategies for coping with the natural world.

The use of symbols in ritual activity and in personal adornment began with the

Neanderthals between 70,000 and 40,000 years ago. Bear skulls were arranged in patterns around graves, and burials were sprinkled with red ocher and accompanied by offerings of food, tools, and fresh flowers. The idea of an afterlife, that something human lives on, required symbols of permanence that would remain intact at the grave after the completion of the rituals. The first adornment was probably made of perishable berries and seeds, but with the discovery of more durable materials, such as bone, shell, and stone, and ways of working with them, beads became one of these symbols.

Something began in Neanderthal times and dramatically increased with the emergence of *Homo sapiens* to bring about an increasing self-consciousness and desire for adornment. Early *Homo sapiens* quite possibly used cosmetics (such as red ocher for rouge) and wore great quantities of jewelry, including clothes decorated with rows of beads, jet pendants, ivory bracelets, and necklaces of pierced animal teeth, vertebrae, and shells.[19]

Beads are therefore among the earliest evidence of abstract thinking. They could not kill an animal or provide warmth, but they could render in material form concepts of prestige, prowess, protection, and beauty. Beads were a conscious effort at self-beautification, reflecting modern man's ability to visualize himself and enhance his appearance through the creation of relatively uniform, valued, and displayable forms. Man's concern with his effectiveness as a hunter had a particularly important influence on adornment. After eating the flesh of the mammoth, reindeer, bison, and horse, Upper Paleolithic people crafted ornaments from the bones, horns, and skin. Ornaments made from parts of the animal were thought to imbue the wearer with the animal's courage and strength. By transforming parts of the animal skeleton—reshaping, carving, and engraving bones—their intrinsic magic was enhanced. To be effective, certain of these transformed objects had to be attached to the owner. Tying them together probably seemed the most obvious solution. Thus, the bead was conceived.

The stringing together of many beads, as opposed to wearing a single one, occurred at a very early date (at least 28,000 B.C.) and suggests a deep primal belief that "more is better." If one bead provided protection against life's real or imagined threats or helped to identify the status of individuals associating in groups too large to know everyone by sight, a bead necklace accomplished the task tenfold.

The elaborate ibex-bone necklace composed of head-shaped beads shown in plate 5, dated to between 11,000 and 10,000 B.C., speaks of a sophisticated, flourishing hunting society that prized beautifully decorated artifacts and enjoyed rich symbolism. Both miniature animal sculptures and the grand cave art had magical and religious significance connected with the seasons of game and the chase. They were associated with rituals that organized the hunter's life. It may be significant that the ibex bead necklace was carved toward the close of the Magdalenian period, at the same time that the cave paintings of animals reached their greatest degree of sophistication. As the glaciers retreated and the herds became smaller, this artistic outpouring suggests one last ritualistic effort to restore the abundance of times past.[20]

The fine quality of the carved ibex beads shows the technological prowess of late Paleolithic artists. Working with ivory and bone required highly specialized tools, and their availability predetermined the complexity and often the shape of crafted objects people could conceive and make. Central to understanding human cultural development is the knowledge of how artisans used tools to extend their thinking and dexterity.

To work flexible, organic materials such as bone, antler, and ivory—raw materials readily available as by-products of the hunt—a special kind of tool was required. That tool was the burin. Its strong, sharply beveled edge or point was well-adapted to cut, incise, and shape other materials. It differed from most other Paleolithic stone tools in that it was not used to kill animals or cut meat, but rather to manufacture other tools. It was also used to carve miniature sculptures that served as ritual paraphernalia and items of adornment, such as the ibex beads.

Beads were shaped by chipping, grinding, and polishing, then perforated by turning a sharp-pointed stone tool. The earliest beads were comparatively thin-walled shells or teeth, easy to pierce. The proliferation of disk-shaped beads in early cultures probably indicates that they were easy to form and perforate. A stone tool can engrave, but it cannot gouge for any length of time before its point becomes dull. By 16,000 B.C., a technology using abrasives was devised to drill pebbles, fossils, and other hard materials. Drilling thin stones was probably accomplished with bits of flint or chert and palm-rotated hand drills. For thicker stones, bow drills were made of hollow bone and filled with an abrasive of sand or crushed stone. Later, craftsmen developed a technique to bore larger beads by drilling halfway through from opposite ends, with the holes meeting at the center of the bead. Their awareness that it was actually the abrasive and not the drill that effectively ground away the stone marked an important cognitive advance.

The earliest materials used for beads came from the immediate environment and included seeds, berries, coal, and other vegetal matter, as well as shells and animal bone. The creation of Upper Paleolithic stone beads was the beginning of the search through the mineral world for variously colored materials that could be shaped and drilled for beads. Early investigations for potential materials anticipate the established trade patterns of later cultures. Indeed, there is evidence of trade in bead materials at the cave site of Patne in India. In a context dating to 23,000 B.C., a bead made of marine shell was found at least 367 miles from its ocean source.[21] In the excavation of dwellings at Mezhirichi, southeast of Kiev in western Russia, Soviet archaeologists uncovered seashells of 15,000 years ago that were imported from 400 to 500 miles away, as well as amber that is believed to have been traded in from distant sources.[22] Marine shells used in beadmaking were brought to the Upper Cave of Zhou-kou-dian in about 16,000 B.C. from sources between 93 and 218 miles away.[23]

The glorious artistic creations of the late Paleolithic Magdalenian culture, so closely related to the existence of the large animals, ended when the glaciers began to retreat in approximately 10,000 B.C. As the climate warmed up, plant life that was dependent on cold, glacial conditions and was the major food source for large herds of reindeer, horses, and bison survived only in the north. With their food sources gone, the great herds moved north or vanished.

As temperate forests replaced the glaciers, there was a shift to a new way of life, known as the Mesolithic era. The wider range of plant and animal life that evolved with the milder climate had a dramatic impact on cultural activities, including the development of adornment. Upper Paleolithic peoples had adapted to a way of life centered on hunting a specialized group of migratory mammals. Focusing on these large and dangerous herd animals controlled every aspect of people's existence. Community structure, rituals, art, and jewelry reflected this intense concern with a limited range of animals.

In the new temperate landscape, resources were abundant and dispersed over large areas. With a wide variety of plants, shellfish, and smaller, nonmigratory animals available, people no longer had the same dramatically singular relationship to their environment. Whereas the function of jewelry and beads had been intimately connected with hunting prowess in Upper Paleolithic communities, Mesolithic people had a ritual life of a totally different character. Their society chose not to develop beads and other forms of adornment.

Antiquity: From Neolithic Times to the Roman Empire

In western Asia between 8000 and 6500 B.C., the foundations were laid for what is known as the Neolithic Revolution. It was during this period that people first made the transition from nomadic food-gatherers to settled food-producers—an extremely important advance that led to the establishment of permanent settlements. Village life, in turn, encouraged the accumulation of material possessions and stimulated trade. Moreover, the ability to store surplus food allowed time for craft specialization.

Civilization did not develop in one specific area in western Asia: at least three (and possibly more) centers are now known to have existed in Turkey, Iraq, and Iran. The wild ancestors of some of the modern world's most important agricultural staples—including wheat, barley, pigs, sheep, and goats—thrived on the hilly flanks of the Taurus Mountains of southern Turkey and the Zagros Mountains northeast of the Tigris River, in present-day Iraq and Iran. During the eighth millennium B.C., human populations gradually domesticated these plants and animals. The Neolithic Revolution then spread from these regions into the Levant and northern Greece.

Villages sprang up where people were harvesting plants and raising animals. Realizing the limited agricultural potential of growing crops in the rocky hills, people gradually introduced domesticated plants into the lower floodplains, where the soil was rich, but the rainfall scanty. It was with the invention of irrigation systems that river valley societies in Mesopotamia (present-day northern Syria and Iraq), India, and Egypt evolved into sophisticated, complex city-states.

Settled village life was one of the predominant characteristics of Neolithic society. Stone and mud-brick dwellings were built, providing the first permanent forms of architecture. An unprecedented level of craftsmanship also flourished: the first examples

6. *A group of early western Asian stone beads made of hard stones (predominantly quartz minerals), including agate, rock crystal, sard, carnelian, and jasper, c. 4000–2000 B.C. Also shown are beads of lapis lazuli, breccia, steatite, fossilized shell (top left), and fossilized coral (middle left).*

During this period, beads were often made with the same techniques employed to create stone weapons and tools— flaking or rough grinding on abrasive blocks. Final shaping and polishing was done with abrasives made of flint chips, sand, or clay slurry. The similarity of shapes between all early beads in the region probably reflects the use of similar technologies. Fossilized shell: length, 4.9 cm. Collection Derek Content, Houlton, Maine

of weaving and pottery and a proliferation of bead forms are associated with Neolithic times. In the later phases of the period, as of 3500 B.C., metal weapons and tools came into use alongside traditional stone implements. (This was a technological advance that led to man's next phase of development, the Bronze Age.) Of great significance for the study of beads was the expansion of long-distance trade between the rapidly evolving, agriculturally intensive civilizations of the Mediterranean and the mountain cultures of western Asia. The uneven distribution of the regions' resources created networks of commercial relations that united these societies and encouraged the exchange of cultural artifacts.

Made of scarce, durable, and easily recognizable raw materials to which commercial value could be easily assigned, and produced in small, standardized, and readily portable sizes, beads became a major commodity for traders. The demand for exotic and rare materials to be used for adornment helped to establish trade networks in western Asia and the Mediterranean at a very early date. By 6500 B.C., there were strong and far-reaching interchanges. Butterfly-shaped beads of imported agate and serpentine as well as other forms of beads made of Sinai turquoise and Mediterranean cowrie shells are recorded at Abu Hureyra, in today's Syria.[1] At Çatal Hüyük, one of the world's first towns and a prosperous Anatolian trading center on the central plains of Turkey, beads of Mediterranean coral dating to 6000 B.C. have been discovered. In the Mediterranean, necklaces of imported carnelian beads were worn by Neolithic people on the island of Cyprus.[2]

Sophisticated systems of commerce evolved by the fourth millennium B.C. in which beads and bead materials often played an important role. Beads of lapis lazuli, a beautiful blue stone with numerous amuletic properties attributed to it, were a great favorite of the Sumerians of southern Mesopotamia during the third millennium B.C. Lapis was mined in the ancient Afghan region Badakhshan, fifteen hundred miles away. While the Sumerians exercised no political control over Afghanistan's production centers or the trade routes traversing the rugged Iranian plateau, supplies of lapis were guaranteed by independent middlemen located at centers on the plateau, such as Shahr-i Sokhta and Tepe Hissar.

At Shahr-i Sokhta, large numbers of finished and unfinished beads and beadmakers' tools, dating from 2600 to 2400 B.C., have been found by archaeologists. A great amount of lapis lazuli waste was also discovered. It has been determined, however, that this was not a beadmaking center for Sumer but primarily an intermediate stop where pure lapis was separated from the worthless limestone cortex. The lapis was then shipped from Iran (later Persia) to Mesopotamia in the form of small blocks. This preprocessing of the raw material at a midway point allowed significant savings in transportation costs and also shows how trade stimulated technology.[3]

The early Greeks of Mycenae, who established trading contacts with the Bronze Age cultures in the Baltic, exchanged copper and bronze implements for rare amber, with which they made beads. In effect, they extended their technical expertise to the less developed European regions while absorbing new materials and forms of adornment. Eventually, large quantities of glass beads would be carried thousands of miles by the ancient Phoenician and Roman seafaring civilizations.

Throughout antiquity, raw materials were traded more often than finished beads. A system developed of rural areas in Europe and western Asia supplying luxury materials to the urban centers, where craftsmen congregated under the aegis of wealthy patrons. Using the most advanced technology, they created beads in the latest styles. A corollary to this pattern is that finished beads were traded usually by more technically advanced cultures to less advanced ones.

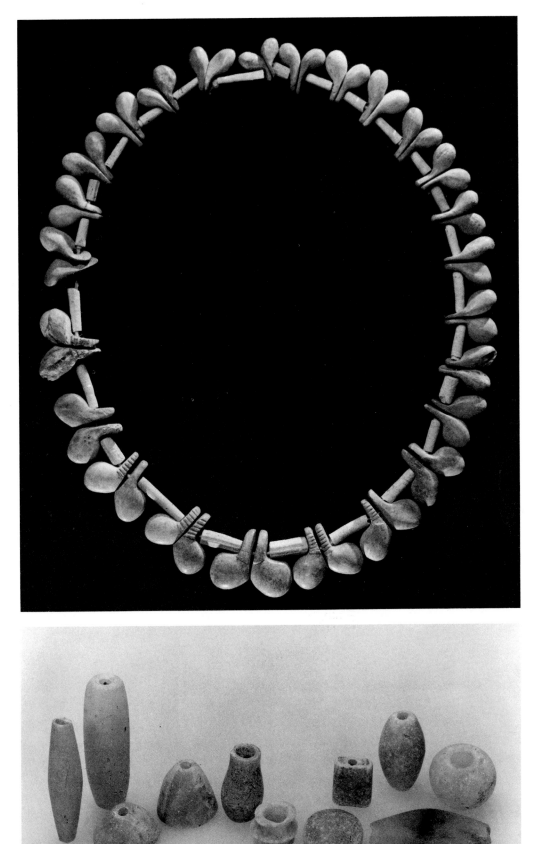

TOP: 8. *A necklace of dentalium (a mollusk with a thinly pointed shell) and breast-shaped beads of bone, made by the Natufians, the original inhabitants of the Jordan River valley. One of the earliest examples of Neolithic beadmaking, this is from the site of El-Wad, c. 10,000– 8000 B.C. Length, 18 cm. Israel Department of Antiquities, Israel Museum, Jerusalem*

BOTTOM: 9. *Beads of alabaster (gypsum), a soft mineral easily carved with tools of flint, wood, and bone. Although this collection is from northern Syria, the shapes and wide perforations are typical of western Asian and Egyptian beads from the fifth to the third millennium B.C. Far left bead: length, 5 cm. Collection Henry Anavian, New York*

Moving easily through the cultural landscape, beads transmitted stylistic concepts as well as production techniques from one society to the next. Beads demonstrating intricate craftsmanship were particularly prized. This is true, for example, of the complex mosaic, or "millefiore," glass forms invented in Mesopotamia about 1500 B.C.[4] These mosaic glass beads were refined by the Syrians and Egyptians during Roman times and traded as far north as Scandinavia. Over the seven thousand to eight thousand years between the rise of the Neolithic village and the fall of the Roman Empire (A.D. 476), the strong political and cultural relationships between the peoples of western Asia, Egypt, and the Mediterranean were maintained. Hubs of power frequently shifted, as city-states and empires flourished and declined. During moments of prominence, however, each civilization sustained an artistic center that influenced the surrounding region. When a town's political fortunes veered downward, the craftsmen relocated, either willingly or by force, and took their styles, techniques, and secrets with them.

Neolithic Beads in Western Asia

Beads are among the commonest objects recovered from Neolithic sites in western Asia. Since people were interred with valued possessions, the inclusion of large quantities of beads in numerous burials points to their importance within ancient societies. Archaeological evidence also indicates that beads were produced in all shapes and sizes from a very early date. Between 10,000 and 8000 B.C., the Natufians of the Jordan River valley had made beads from stone, shell, and bone (plate 8). Beads of native copper, serpentine, and malachite have been excavated at Çatal Hüyük, which was founded in 6250 B.C. Seventh- and sixth-millennium B.C. sites in Afghanistan, Iran, Syria, and Mesopotamia have yielded beads made of basalt, limestone, steatite, obsidian, ivory, and occasional examples of the harder agates and carnelian.

Neolithic western Asian craftsmanship was generally quite primitive. Typical bead forms included disks, cylinders, barrels, and flattened rhomboids, shapes that were easily created with available tools and limited technology. Irregularly shaped shell and stone beads were often little more than lumps of raw material pierced for suspension.

Most Neolithic bead materials were locally available, while some shells and obsidian were imported. The early use of Anatolian obsidian for western Asian beads occurred during a period when trade was largely confined to utilitarian materials and objects. Most imported obsidian was used to make knife blades. Its employment in bead-

River Valley Civilizations—Mesopotamia, Egypt, Indus Valley :
Distribution of Beads and Bead Materials,
c. 2500 to 1600 B.C.

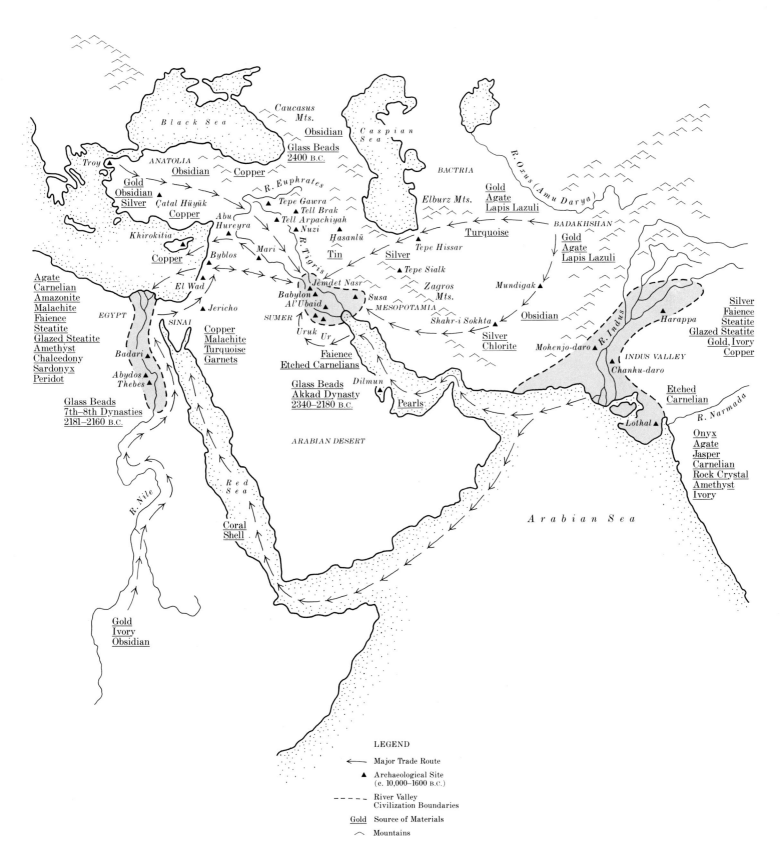

Caucasus Mts.

Black Sea

Caspian Sea

Obsidian
Glass Beads 2400 B.C.

BACTRIA

R. Oxus (Amu Darya)

Troy

ANATOLIA

Obsidian   Copper

Gold
Obsidian
Silver
Çatal Hüyük
Copper

Abu Hureyra

R. Euphrates

Tepe Gawra
Tell Brak
Tell Arpachiyah
Nuzi

Hasanlū

Elburz Mts.

Gold
Agate
Lapis Lazuli

BADAKHSHAN

Turquoise

Gold
Agate
Lapis Lazuli

Khirokitia

Byblos

Mari

R. Tigris

Tin

Tepe Hissar

Silver

Mundigak

El Wad

Tepe Sialk

Zagros Mts.

Jemdet Nasr

Silver
Faience
Steatite
Glazed Steatite
Gold, Ivory
Copper

Agate
Carnelian
Amazonite
Malachite
Faience
Steatite
Glazed Steatite
Amethyst
Chalcedony
Sardonyx
Peridot

EGYPT

SINAI

Jericho

Babylon
Al'Ubaid

Susa

MESOPOTAMIA

Shahr-i Sokhta

Obsidian

Harappa

R. Indus

Mohenjo-daro

INDUS VALLEY

Copper
Malachite
Turquoise
Garnets

SUMER

Uruk *Ur*

Silver
Chlorite

Badari

Faience
Etched Carnelians

Chanhu-daro

Abydos
Thebes

Glass Beads
Akkad Dynasty
2340–2180 B.C.

Dilmun

Pearls

Etched
Carnelian

R. Narmada

Glass Beads
7th–8th Dynasties
2181–2160 B.C.

Lothal

Onyx
Agate
Jasper
Carnelian
Rock Crystal
Amethyst
Ivory

ARABIAN DESERT

R. Nile

Red Sea

Coral
Shell

Arabian Sea

Gold
Ivory
Obsidian

LEGEND

⟵ Major Trade Route

▲ Archaeological Site
(c. 10,000–1600 B.C.)

- - - River Valley
Civilization Boundaries

<u>Gold</u> Source of Materials

⌒ Mountains

ABOVE: 16. *A First Dynasty ivory bead in the shape of a* serekh, *a rectangular frame with bottom paneling similar to the decorative features on Old Kingdom doors and the facades of early brick tombs. The falcon, Horus, sits atop the* serekh. *Excavated at Abydos in Egypt and dated to about 3000 B.C. Length, 1.6 cm. British Museum, London*

ABOVE RIGHT: 17. *Egyptian beads from the Predynastic and Early Dynastic periods, 3200–2700 B.C. Top to bottom: (1) copper, carnelian, glazed steatite, and shell beads; (2) steatite, lapis lazuli, garnet, shell, and carnelian beads; (3) mixed stone beads, including carnelian turquoise, and steatite; (4) quartz, lapis lazuli, carnelian, and shell beads; (5) glazed green steatite and carnelian beads with carnelian drop pendant. The use of glazed steatite was a way of producing less expensive colored stones. Bottom pendant: length, 2 cm. British Museum, London*

making was secondary and probably occurred only when there were enough flakes left over from the knife-manufacturing process. A black, glassy volcanic substance, obsidian was durable, decorative, and rare—ideal properties for beads.

In wealthy societies, however, there was a wide-ranging luxury trade by 4200 B.C. At Tepe Gawra, an important northern outpost of the Mesopotamian 'Ubaid culture that was closely connected with the early trading, beads of turquoise, amethyst, beryl, gold, electrum, and lapis lazuli have been found.[5] While the beads were fashioned at Tepe Gawra, the gold and electrum came from Iran or Anatolia, the turquoise from Iran, and the lapis lazuli from Afghanistan.

Beads played an important role in early organized religion. At the temple site of Tell Brak in eastern Syria (Jemdet Nasr period, c. 3000 B.C.), over one hundred thousand beads, mostly tiny disks of glazed faience, steatite, and shell, were embedded in gray mud bricks used to construct the sacred Eye Temple platform (the temple was named after numerous Eye Goddess figurines excavated there). Neolithic people customarily consecrated a temple area by sowing it with beads or mixing beads into the mud used for foundation bricks. This ritual, symbolically analogous to sowing a field with seed, was intended to bring prosperity to the temple, which was also a repository of the city's wealth.[6]

One can only speculate on the circumstances that produced the earliest western Asian beads. While Neolithic agriculture involved the whole community in subsistence activities for most of the year, the winter months provided some leisure time for farmers to make crafts. Later, more complex societies supported non-food-producing specialists, including full-time craftsmen. The appearance of specialists is one of the distinguishing characteristics of the transition from autonomous local villages of the Neolithic period to large-scale, regional cultures with towns and cities.

Mesopotamia Between 4000 and 3000 B.C., three of the earliest centers of civilization based on intensive agriculture developed in the river valleys of Mesopotamia, Egypt, and India. These were hierarchical societies with an upper strata of merchant, priestly, military, and royal classes in whose collective hands wealth was concentrated. One way in which social differences were reflected was the display of adornment, including beads. Indeed, for the first time, the role of beads as status symbols equaled or surpassed their ritual or magical functions. The dual function of beads as amulets and status symbols is a prevailing theme of their history throughout most of western Asia, Egypt, and the Mediterranean in ancient times.

Mesopotamian and Egyptian priests and kings employed full-time jewelers, and through their patronage beadmaking technology developed rapidly. The degree of prestige attached to a necklace depended not only on its craftsmanship, but on the use of rare and precious materials. To obtain not only the basic necessities of life, but these scarce minerals, metals, and marine products as well, trade routes spanning great distances developed into an important part of these civilizations' commercial activities.

Egypt had within its boundaries most of the natural resources used in beadmaking; Mesopotamia, however, had none of the appropriate materials. Gold probably came to the Tigris and Euphrates valleys from the mountains of Anatolia or Iran, carnelian and agate from India and Afghanistan, and lapis lazuli from Afghanistan. Lapis, the one stone important to Egyptian jewelry not found inside its borders, reached the Nile Delta via Mesopotamia.

By 2500 B.C., beads produced for Sumerian royalty in the city-state of Ur in southern Mesopotamia were of superb craftsmanship, employing sophisticated goldsmithing techniques for granulation and filigree (plates 10–11 and 14). Fluted melon beads were crafted in gold and lapis lazuli. The products of Sumerian jewelers spread into the less-developed cultures of western Asia and into Anatolia, the probable source of the jewelers' gold. Sumerian jewelry techniques also traveled to southern Greece and Crete, where gold beads in related styles appear at slightly later dates.[7] The path of a distinctive four-spiraled bead style can be traced from its origin in Sumer or Iran about 2500 B.C. through its metamorphosis (of materials and form) along this same Mediterranean route (plate 29).

The importance of Sumerian and Mesopotamian jewelry and beadmaking and its direct or indirect influence on the adornment of subsequent cultures in western Asia and the Mediterranean cannot be overemphasized. Indeed, most techniques practiced by jewelers today were known to the ancient Sumerian goldsmiths. With the dissolution of the Sumerian Empire about 1600 B.C., the techniques developed by Sumerian smiths were passed on to Babylonian craftsmen in northern Mesopotamia.

Glass and glass beads also appear to have a western Asian and possibly Sumerian origin. The earliest examples are from Mesopotamia, dating to the Akkad dynasty (2340–2180 B.C.),[8] and from the Caucasus region in present-day Russia.[9] Large numbers (over eleven thousand) of artistically beautiful glass beads, made by a wide range of manufacturing methods and dating before the site's destruction in 1400 B.C., have been excavated from the Hurrian settlement of Nuzi, located 130 miles north of Baghdad in present-day Iraq.[10]

Egypt One of the most stable civilizations of antiquity established itself along the Nile shortly after the emergence of Mesopotamia. While the economic and social organization of dynastic Egypt generally resembled that of Sumer, geography created important differences. Egypt, unlike Mesopotamia, had relatively clearcut, defensible borders. In addition, the Nile, Egypt's major transportation route, was easily navigated, allowing its rulers to control shipping. By regulating all major movements of goods and people, the Egyptian kings possessed the means for effective rule.[11] Furthermore, Egypt was rich in the precious metals and minerals needed for subsistence and luxury items. These factors provided security and insulated Egyptian life from foreign influences. Consequently, there is a marked conservatism to Egyptian art and jewelry. The styles and techniques developed in early Egypt changed relatively little from early dynastic to Ptolemaic times (c. 3100–30 B.C.) and seem particularly consistent when compared with the variations in western Asian adornment.

No other civilization, however, manufactured such an enormous variety of beads in so many different materials. They were not only used for necklaces but were also attached to linen and papyrus backings to make belts, aprons, and sandals. Beadwork originated in Old Kingdom Egypt about 2200 B.C. A spectacular early example is the belt of Prince Ptah-Shepses, which was covered with a beadwork band. The beads were made of gold and semiprecious stones and were threaded with a gold wire. During the Middle Kingdom (2133–1786 B.C.), ceremonial beaded aprons contained multicolored faience and white shell beads. In the New Kingdom (1650–1085 B.C.), a great variety of beadwork objects was put in the tomb of King Tutankhamen (d. 1352 B.C.)—included were broad collars, sandals decorated with a beadwork flower pattern, and a ceremonial garment of bead bands and bead netting. Some of the objects seemed to have been used during the king's lifetime. During the Late Period (1085–332 B.C.), however, beadwork materials were prepared mainly for funerary purposes (plate 25). Egyptian beadwork was produced by a special technique that threaded single beads together, rather than using a bead loom. Beadwork bands and figures were the main products made by this method (plate 26).[12]

Virtually everyone in ancient Egypt, from predynastic to Ptolemaic times, wore

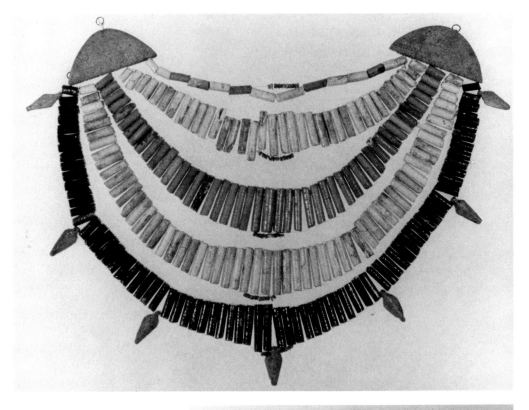

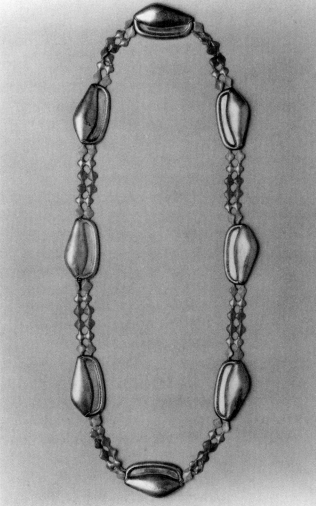

TOP: 19. *A broad wesekh collar with five rows of beads, semicircular terminal spacers, and pendants, all of faience. The introduction of spacers, to keep multiple-layered necklaces hanging properly, became an important component of Middle Kingdom (2133–1786 B.C.) jewelry. Excavated at Deir-el-Bahari (near Thebes), Egypt. Length (outer row), 41.6 cm. British Museum, London*

BOTTOM: 20. *A girdle of cast gold cowrie shell effigy beads and carnelian, lapis lazuli, and green feldspar beads simulating acacia seeds. Each hollow gold shell effigy contains a pellet, making the girdle sound like a rattle when the wearer moves.*

Dating to the Twelfth Dynasty (1991–1786 B.C.), the girdle belonged to Princess Si-Hathor-Yunet from Lahun. The Middle Kingdom was a period of sophisticated aesthetics in Egyptian history, and jewelry produced then has an elegant, unified style. Length, 84 cm. Metropolitan Museum of Art, New York

OVERLEAF: 21. *Lunar pectoral with necklace of carnelian, lapis lazuli, feldspar, and gold beads and a lotus blossom counterpoise. This is a striking example of the three basic components in Egyptian jewelry—pectoral, beaded necklace, and counterpoise—unified into a single design. Even the beaded tassels hanging from the counterpoise acted as amulets, protecting the wearer from behind. This piece was worn by King Tutankhamen and buried in his tomb at Thebes, c. 1352 B.C. Pectoral: width, 11.8 cm. Cairo Museum*

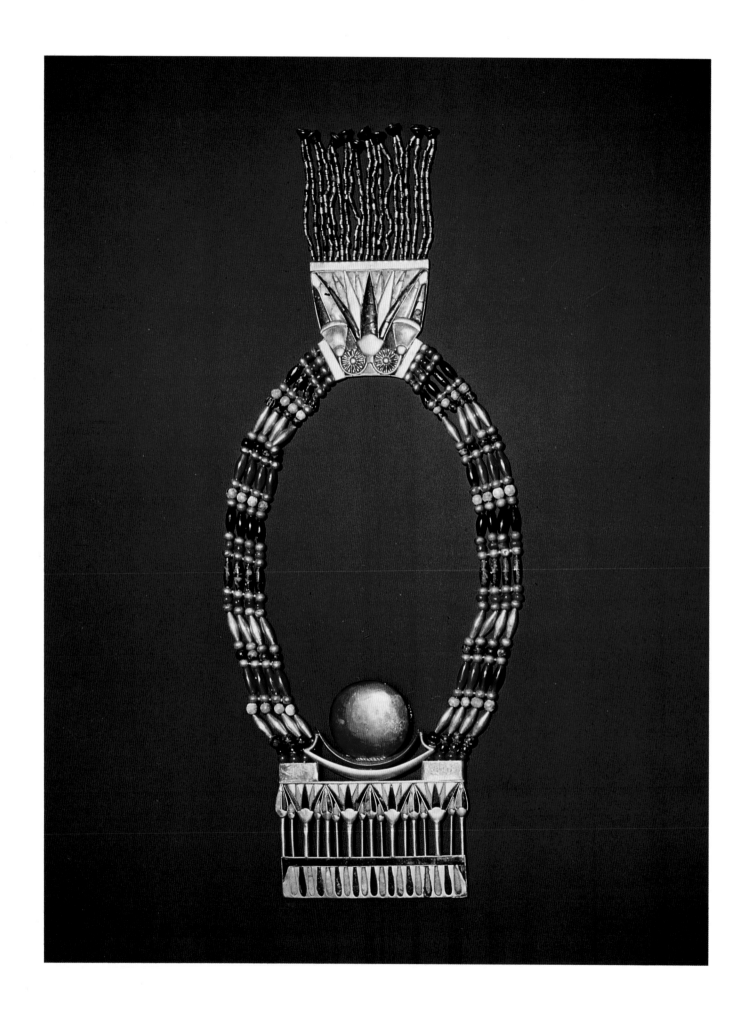

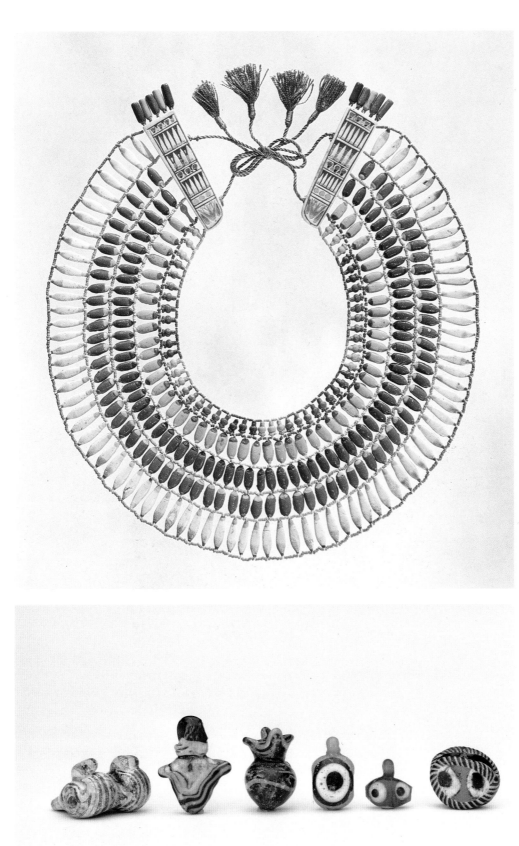

ABOVE: 22. *An example of New Kingdom bead production. Effigy lotus seedpods in carnelian, gold, lapis lazuli, and feldspar, with tiny carnelian and gold spacer beads. Typical carnelian lotus pod: length, 1.5 cm. British Museum, London*

LEFT: 23. *Collar of faience beads depicting cornflowers, dates, lotus seed-pods, and petals in a pattern derived from garlands of real flowers. Faience bead collars were frequently supplied as favors to guests at banquets. This necklace typifies the technical brilliance of the faience and glass jewelry of the Amarna period (1379–1362 B.C.). It has been suggested that the uniquely gay and joyful quality of Amarna period art and jewelry reflects the sudden appearance of outside influences — possibly attributable to Minoan artists who may have fled to Egypt after the fall of Crete. Excavated from the tomb of Tutankhamen at Thebes. Diameter, 31 cm. Metropolitan Museum of Art, New York. Rogers Fund*

BOTTOM: 24. *A collection of New Kingdom sand-core glass beads from the Amarna period. Far right eye bead: diameter, 1.5 cm. Collection Henry Anavian, New York*

41

TOP: **25.** *Egyptian bead-work represents some of the earliest known examples of beadwork in the world and dates back to the Old Kingdom (2686–2181 B.C.). Here, a net of protective blue faience beads covers the mummy of Takheb-khenem, daughter of the "Gatekeeper of the Temple of Amun." Beaded funerary nets were a characteristic feature of the New Kingdom, resulting in the production of millions of "mummy beads." Twenty-sixth Dynasty (664–525 B.C.). British Museum, London*

RIGHT: **26.** *Egyptian winged-scarab bead-work: a scarab beetle with outstretched wings symbolized the rising sun. Composed of small faience disk beads threaded together, bead-work figures of this kind were not made for their own sake but formed part of the beaded shroud placed over a mummy. Length, 22.2 cm. British Museum, London*

beads. While the famous treasures of Tutankhamen include dazzling examples of the beads of Egyptian royalty, simple strings of shell, stone, and faience (a type of ceramic with a quartz sand body and colored glaze) have been found in even the poorest of burial sites. The Egyptian word *sha* means "luck" and *sha-sha* means "bead," suggesting that beads were thought to have amuletic or protective properties, which explains the Egyptian custom of using beads to cover almost every article of clothing and every part of the body. The Egyptians also believed that to insure comfort in the afterlife, the dead must be surrounded with the paraphernalia of daily life. Quantities of beads were buried with their owner, the choice of materials depending on the family's wealth. Occasionally, delicately beaded funereal pieces were also included.

As in Mesopotamia, beads were worn by both men and women in Egypt and were depicted on statues of the gods. Although numerous stones were available to the Egyptians (amethyst became very popular in the Middle Kingdom), certain metals and stones were favored, especially gold, carnelian, lapis lazuli, and turquoise. A stone's color almost certainly had particular talismanic value to the Egyptian lapidary and his clients and therefore determined its popularity. Green turquoise or feldspar symbolized the earth's fertility and was considered the color of new life; red carnelian was the color of blood, symbolizing life; while lapis lazuli, the "heavenly stone," resembled the sky.[13] The use of other stones often reflected recent discoveries. The popularity of garnet beads in the Middle Kingdom may have been due to abundant sources of the mineral in Sinai during that period. Since garnets occur in nature in the form of dodecahedral crystals and are frequently detached from their matrix, after which they weather into rounded stones, it required very little work to turn them into beads.[14]

In reliefs and paintings, lapidaries and metalsmiths are shown working side by side in ateliers under the supervision of a chief jeweler. The various materials and phases of beadmaking were divided into specialties according to skill. Separate guilds existed for goldsmiths, faience workers, stone carvers, bead threaders, and eventually glassmakers. The art of beadmaking reached a high point during the Middle Kingdom, when extraordinarily fine stone beads were made in minute sizes and in large sizes with very long perforations. In both types, it is theorized that the holes were drilled first, and afterward the beads were ground down to the desired thickness.[15]

Egyptian jewelers frequently used large numbers of beads of one stone to form blocks of color. Opaque stones were preferred, and repetitious patterns employing multiple strands of a small variety of stone beads were common. The *wesekh*—a broad collar with many beaded strands separated by spacer beads to keep multilayered necklaces hanging properly—was in use by the Fourth Dynasty (2613–2494 B.C.).[16] From the beginning of the Middle Kingdom, the *wesekh* became a characteristic form and almost an essential item of dress. Its visually impressive size and large quantities of precious materials undoubtedly indicated the power and prestige of its wearer. The Egyptians understood that spacers—perforated bars of bone, ivory, wood covered with gold leaf, faience, glass, or metal placed at intervals along the strands—were flexible ornamental bands that kept the beads in position. The integration of spacers as part of a necklace's total design concept was frequently masterful. At first simple in execution, they later became elaborate individual units (plate 19).

The greatest number of Egyptian beads were made of faience, an inexpensive substance generally considered to be the forerunner of true glass, although glass was used earlier in glazed steatite beads of Badarian-period Egypt (5500–3800 B.C.; Bead Chart 417). Invented in either Mesopotamia or Egypt by 4000 B.C., faience was the first mass-produced synthetic material to simulate precious stones such as turquoise and lapis lazuli. The development of faience and eventually glass satisfied the desire of the general populace to wear beads that emulated the precious stones of the wealthy.

Although glass beads are known by the Seventh and Eighth Dynasties (c. 2181–c. 2160 B.C.), they were first manufactured for a large commercial market beginning in Egypt about 1400 B.C.[17] The New Kingdom, especially the later phases of the Eighteenth Dynasty (c. 1350 B.C.), is generally considered to be the world's first great glassmaking epoch. The earliest glass, an exotic material, was made for use by the pharaohs and their courts, although it eventually became available to wealthier commoners. The proximity of Egyptian glass factories to the palaces at Thebes, Amarna, and Shurak attests to the royal patronage of glassmaking.

During the New Kingdom, glass beads began to replace precious and semiprecious stones. The Egyptians favored deeply colored opaque glass, since it more closely resembled lapis lazuli and turquoise. Early Egyptian glass beads are carefully finished and have luminous colors. Frequently, they were made by quite complex techniques (plate 24).

The elegance and restraint of Middle Kingdom designs gave way in the New

27. Glazed spacer beads were developed to spread out the layers of beads in collar necklaces. At first simple in design, they later became elaborately designed individual units. This Egyptian spacer bead, c. 1050–750 B.C., depicts the figures of the god Horus the child and Horus the warrior with prisoners. Length, 4.5 cm. British Museum, London

43

28. *Agate, jasper, and carnelian beads purported to have been excavated near the Amu Darya River, the legendary "Oxus of empires," in northeastern Afghanistan. All the beads of this group, particularly the rhomboidal or lenticular agates, are of the finest quality. Note that the bead forms are beautifully shaped according to the natural banding of the stone. These beads have almost exact counterparts among artifacts discovered in the royal tombs at Ur (2600–2100 B.C.).*

Rhomboidal beads date to 7000 B.C. at Çatal Hüyük, Anatolia. Agates of this fine quality, however, are documented at only a few archaeological sites: Ur (Mesopotamia), Tepe Hissar (Iran), and Mundigak (Afghanistan). Their distribution may be related to the far-reaching third-millennium trade in lapis lazuli or to trade in etched beads between Mesopotamia and the Indus Valley.[IV] Inside necklace, center bead: length, 3.5 cm. Private collection

Kingdom to a more exuberant style. Forms such as flowers, leaves, and buds were directly copied from nature in both glass and faience. Faience, which had originated as simple tubes and disks in limited colors, became particularly plentiful. Complex shapes were developed and new colors supplemented the familiar blues and greens. Collars of faience beads, imitating woven floral garlands, were particularly popular at Amarna, the capital city of Akhenaten and Nefertiti from 1379 to 1362 B.C. (plate 23).

A decline in glassmaking skills occurred in Egypt after the Nineteenth Dynasty ended (c. 1200 B.C.), and glass virtually disappeared after the fall of the New Kingdom (1085 B.C.). It was revived in Ptolemaic times, during the fourth century B.C., when Alexander the Great founded Alexandria, a cosmopolitan center with international trading links. Glass reputedly produced in Alexandria through the early Roman period included some of the most beautiful and complex beads ever made.

The Indus Valley

Two great cities, Mohenjo-daro and Harappa, and numerous smaller towns prospered on the banks of the Indus River and its tributaries between 2500 and 1500 B.C. Although some aspects of this civilization paralleled those of Mesopotamia and Egypt, notably the architecture and jewelry, little is known of its historical development or why it disappeared. Contact existed between the Indus Valley civilization and Mesopotamia, as seen

in the quantities of etched carnelian beads with similar shapes and white patterns found at both Ur and Mohenjo-daro. The source of manufacture is not certain, but it was most probably the Indus Valley (plate 13).[18]

Afghanistan Ancient Afghanistan was a major supplier of both raw materials and beautifully made stone beads, a fact as much related to the mineral wealth of its mountains as to its geographic location. Surrounded by Iran, India, China, and Russia, trade routes between these countries passed through Afghanistan, making it an important transmitter of materials and culture and a strategic intermediary between East and West.[19] Historically underrated as a source of bead craftsmanship, Afghanistan was considerably more than a source of raw materials. Many beads excavated there and attributed to the third and second millennia B.C. have exact counterparts among the artifacts recovered from the royal tombs of Ur (plates 10–11 and 28). Because these beads are found in such quantity in Afghanistan, it is reasonable to assume they were manufactured locally.

The great beadmaking era in Afghanistan ended about 1600 B.C., a date synchronous with the decline of the Babylonian Empire. As trade to the south dwindled, both the incentives and the economic structures supporting beadmaking seem to have disappeared.

TOP: 30. *Breast beads from Aegina, 1700–1600 B.C. These beads, in the form of a right hand holding a woman's breast, are of Minoan workmanship and were found in a tomb of Cretans who presumably had lived on the island of Aegina. The image of a naked woman holding her breast had a long history in western Asia, where it was associated with fertility goddesses. Mesopotamian and Egyptian influences are evidenced in the combination of gold, carnelian, and lapis lazuli beads of homogeneous shapes and sizes within a single necklace. Typical bead: length, 1.5 cm. British Museum, London*

RIGHT: 31. *To the Mycenaeans, glass was an exotic, treasured material. Flat, molded blue glass relief beads like these were mass-produced in the region of Mycenae from 1400 to 1150 B.C. They were identical to gold relief beads that were made in the same steatite molds. As gold became scarce, glass was used with increasing frequency. In addition to the architectural volute motif shown in relief on these beads, countless stylized designs inherited from the Minoans were used, including shapes of plants, flowers, fish, shells, and animals. Typical bead: length, 2.6 cm. Corning Museum of Glass, Corning, New York*

Crete, Mycenae, and Cyprus

By 2000 B.C., a lively commerce was established between western Asia, Egypt, and the Mediterranean. Sea travel developed as an alternative to hazardous and expensive land journeys. Along with grain, tin, copper, and precious stones, stylistic concepts and technical knowledge were also transmitted from culture to culture.

On the island of Crete, Minoan beads show the influence of both Egypt and the western Asian civilizations. Granulation, filigree, and repoussé techniques were introduced to Crete from western Asia by 2000 B.C. By 1700 B.C., all three methods had been mastered and effectively adapted to Minoan tastes. The Minoans were inspired by the forms of plants, animals, and sea creatures, which they interpreted in their art with enormous originality.[20]

With the fall of Knossos, the capital of Crete, about 1400 B.C., the center of Minoan culture moved to Mycenae on mainland Greece, a transition that is clearly reflected in Mycenaean beads. A variety of pendants and beads made of gold, stone, and glass, often identical to those from Crete, were commonly found in excavated Mycenaean sites. "Relief" beads are the most characteristic ornament of Minoan-Mycenaean jewelry (plate 31). Consisting primarily of stylized representations in shallow relief of marine and plant life, as well as occasional architectural and religious subjects, the beads were initially stamped out of sheet gold. The finest examples were decorated additionally with granulation and enamel. Using the same steatite molds, counterparts of these beads were also made in dark blue glass to imitate lapis lazuli. The early glass relief beads were possibly valued equally with the gold beads, as glass was a rare and

exotic material. With the decline of the Mycenaean civilization (c. 1150 B.C.), the manufacture of relief beads only in glass appears to reflect the dwindling supply of gold.[21]

The Mycenaeans, who wore large quantities of beads made from a variety of materials, were famed sailors and traders. The presence of amber beads in seventeenth-century B.C. Mycenaean shaft graves indicates they traded with the Baltic region. The source of this amber has been identified as Jutland, the Danish peninsula. It reached Mycenae via the famed amber routes that crossed Europe from the Baltic to the northern coast of the Adriatic Sea. Greek ships were used for the final stage of the southern voyage, possibly accounting for the great concentration of amber beads along the west coast of the Peloponnisos.[22] The dispersion throughout Spain, England, southern France, and Hungary of the segmented faience bead, manufactured in Egypt around 1400 B.C., has also been attributed to Mycenaean enterprise and is considered indicative of their far-reaching importance as major bead traders (Bead Chart 8).[23]

It is not surprising that beads from Cyprus are a mixture of Minoan-Mycenaean, Syrian, and Egyptian elements,[24] since Cyprus was a convenient halfway point for traders sailing between the Aegean countries and western Asia. Another factor that contributed to the importance of Cyprus in Mediterranean history was its wealth of copper (the Latin word is *cuprius*). Mycenaeans, attracted to Cyprus for the copper, used harbor towns on the eastern and southern coasts of the island to trade with western Asia.

A developed civilization had evolved in Cyprus between 7000 and 6000 B.C. Most information from that period is derived from Khirokitia, a settlement of approximately 4,500 inhabitants, who practiced weaving and made beads from dentalium shells and imported carnelian as early as 5800 B.C. By 1900 B.C., faience beads were found along with pottery of various origins, suggesting overseas trade with Egypt and the Levant. The design of Cypriot gold beads of the late Bronze Age (1300–1200 B.C.) was strongly influenced by the trade relationship between Cyprus and Mycenae, clearly seen in a jewelry cache uncovered at Enkomi (plate 32). These foreign exchanges had lasting effects on the people and their adornment.

The Phoenicians and the Mediterranean:
Distribution of Beads and Bead Materials,
c. 1250 to 30 B.C.

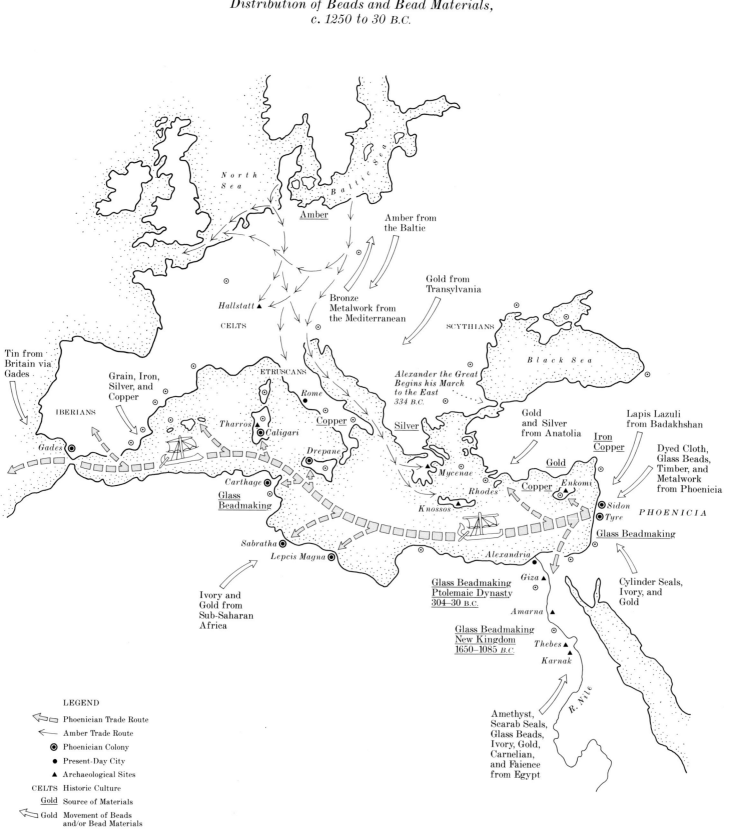

North Sea

Baltic Sea

Amber

Amber from the Baltic

Gold from Transylvania

SCYTHIANS

Hallstatt ▲

CELTS

Bronze Metalwork from the Mediterranean

Black Sea

Tin from Britain via Gades

Alexander the Great Begins his March to the East 334 B.C.

Grain, Iron, Silver, and Copper

ETRUSCANS

Rome

Copper

Silver

Gold and Silver from Anatolia

Lapis Lazuli from Badakhshan

IBERIANS

Tharros

Caligari

Drepane

Gold

Iron Copper

Dyed Cloth, Glass Beads, Timber, and Metalwork from Phoenicia

Gades

Copper

Enkomi ▲

Sidon

Tyre PHOENICIA

Carthage

Glass Beadmaking

Rhodes

Mycenae ▲

Knossos ▲

Glass Beadmaking

Sabratha

Lepcis Magna

Alexandria

Cylinder Seals, Ivory, and Gold

Ivory and Gold from Sub-Saharan Africa

Glass Beadmaking Ptolemaic Dynasty 304–30 B.C.

Giza ▲

Amarna ▲

Glass Beadmaking New Kingdom 1650–1085 B.C.

Thebes ▲

Karnak ▲

R. Nile

Amethyst, Scarab Seals, Glass Beads, Ivory, Gold, Carnelian, and Faience from Egypt

LEGEND

⟸ Phoenician Trade Route

← Amber Trade Route

◉ Phoenician Colony

● Present-Day City

▲ Archaeological Sites

CELTS Historic Culture

Gold Source of Materials

⟸ Gold Movement of Beads and/or Bead Materials

⊙ Archaeological Finds of Phoenician Core-Formed Glass Beads

Etruria The exact origin of the Etruscans has long been an enigma. It is likely their ancestors entered Italy from Asia Minor in the ninth century B.C.; by the third century B.C., they were assimilated into the Roman Empire.

Etruria's intensive commercial activities and affluent society were based on its ready access to iron, copper, zinc, and tin ores. Together with manufactured metal objects, their raw materials were exchanged for Eastern luxury products made of gold, silver, and ivory. Trade with western Asia and Greece brought the Etruscans into contact with important Orientalizing influences in the eighth and seventh centuries B.C., resulting in the formation of a distinctive Etruscan style that incorporated Syrian, Phoenician, Iranian, and Greek elements. Etruscan tomb frescoes illustrate a thriving aristocratic class whose noblewomen dressed elegantly and sported the famed Etruscan jewelry—among the finest in the ancient world.

Etruscan beads are known for technical perfection. While some of their technical knowledge came from the Phoenicians, the Etruscans were jewelry innovators in their own right. They developed, for example, a technique of granulation using amber to affix tiny droplets of gold on a piece of jewelry to enhance its beauty.[25] To satisfy their love of color, the Etruscans often combined Phoenician polychrome glass beads with gold beads (plate 37).

Iran Ancient Iran was home to one of the most geographically expansive civilizations of the ancient Near East. Unlike the Egyptian and Mesopotamian civilizations, which retained a relatively consistent artistic unity throughout their histories, Iran hosted a mixture of artistic styles; the result of a wide range of political and geographic influences. Caravans crossing the highlands from Badakhshan to Sumer not only brought lapis lazuli, but kept Iranian craftsmen in touch with the latest technical achievements of Mesopotamian and Babylonian goldsmiths and Indian and Afghan beadmakers. The resulting stylistic diversity is illustrated in the variously shaped beads of glazed frit, antimony, copper, bronze, amber, carnelian, shell, stone, glass, and incised bone found at one site—Ḥasanlū—in northwest Iran. (The beads date from 1350 to 800 B.C.) Exquisite granulated gold beads were made in Iran by at least 1000 B.C. (plate 40), and a wide variety of stone beads, particularly the banded agates, enjoyed great popularity in all periods of Iranian history.

Greece and Persia For three hundred years after the decline of Mycenae in 1150 B.C., Greece was a poor region, and little jewelry was produced. By 850 B.C., Greek contacts with western Asia and the East resumed. Once again, beautifully crafted gold jewelry was made in Greece at Knossos and the great city-states of Corinth and Athens. Although some beads created at this time resemble earlier Mycenaean styles, their presence appears not to reflect a continuity of tradition among Greek craftsmen but instead was due to a reintroduction of Greek designs and techniques by immigrant Phoenician goldsmiths.[26] By 650 B.C., many Greeks had settled in Syria, Egypt, and Palestine and brought with them ideas that were absorbed by the local populace. However, in the next century, the Achaemenids in Iran established themselves as a military and commercial power under Cyrus II (589–525 B.C.). He built an obscure tribe into a major power—the legendary Persian Empire , which stretched from Libya to northern Afghanistan and the Indus Valley.

By 480 B.C., the Persians and Greeks began to compete for the same territories, but dissension among the Greek states allowed the Persians to conquer most of Asia Minor and Egypt. During the mid-fourth century B.C., the Greek ruler Philip II of Macedonia reunited some of the land lost to the Persians. The Achaemenid leadership, weakened by internal strife, was slow to respond, and by 334 B.C., at the age of twenty-two,

TOP: 38. *Bronze wine jug bead, representing a sacred Minoan motif, recovered from tombs near Potidaea, Macedonia, c. 800–700 B.C. These beads have also been found made of gold in early Minoan sites (2000–1700 B.C.). Length, 3.8 cm. British Museum, London*

ABOVE: 39. *Bronze wine jug bead, from Potidaea, Macedonia, c. 800–700 B.C. Length, 2.6 cm. British Museum, London*

Philip's son, Alexander the Great, began his march through Asia. His campaigns extended into Persia, Bactria, India, and Egypt. Alexander's eastern conquests transformed both the Persian and Greek worlds, as he captured vast territories of the former Persian Empire. In turn, Greece was increasingly exposed to Egyptian, western Asiatic, and northern Indian cultural influences.

The cultural cross-fertilization had a particularly strong impact on Greek adornment. The Persian treasure of Emperor Darius III, captured by Alexander's soldiers, included remarkable jewelry that proved to be a rich source of new design motifs and increased the Greeks' use of inlaid stones, glass, enamel, and pearls. Furthermore, gold, in short supply in Greece after the collapse of Mycenae and during the great age of the city-states (500–400 B.C.), flowed back into the country. Alexander's wars brought his armies into contact with all of the world's known gold mines, and thereafter gold was widely used in Grecian coinage, jewelry, and tomb furnishings. Alexander's empire also brought Mediterranean civilization into direct contact with Far Eastern artistic tra-

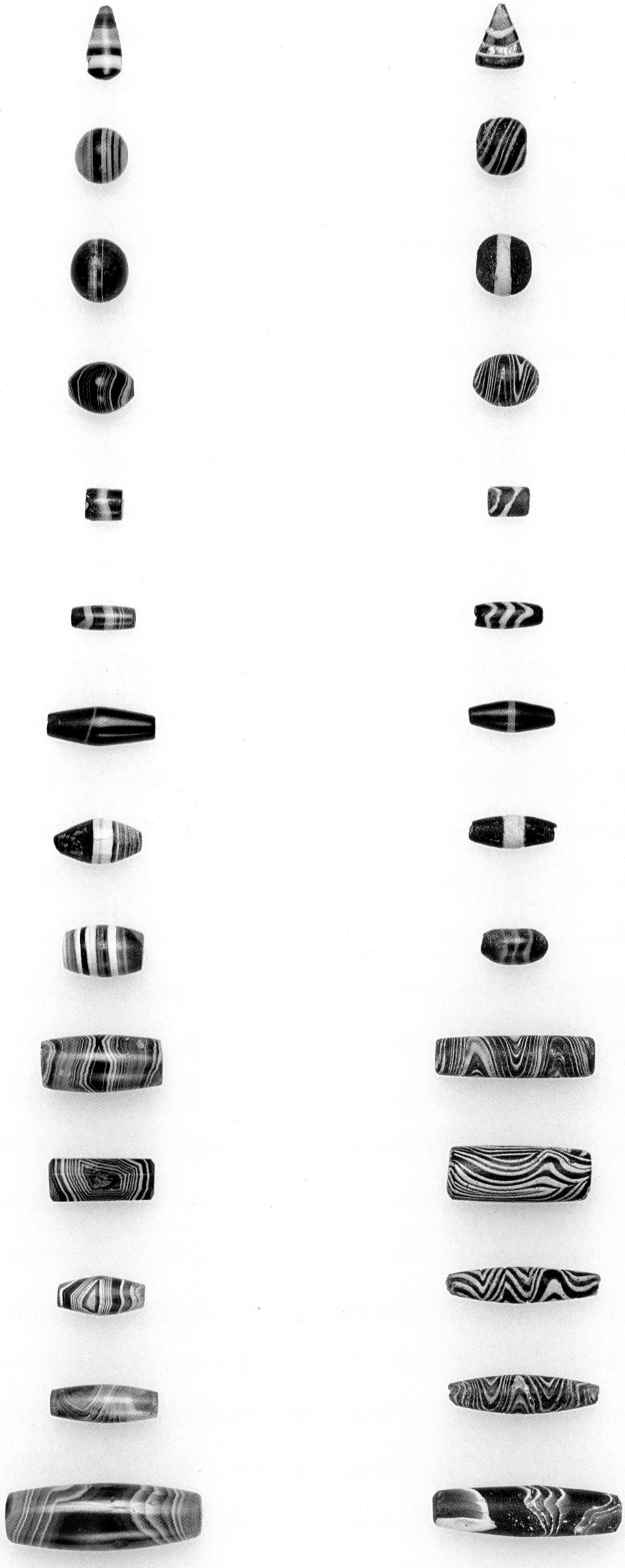

ditions, and a period of extraordinarily beautiful Greek jewelry followed. The richness of their beads is indicative of the prosperity that Hellenistic Greece enjoyed (plate 41).

In Persia, the Achaemenid dynasty was followed by the rule of the Parthians (249 B.C.–A.D. 226), who traded with both the Roman Empire and the Chinese Han dynasty, earning a fortune as middlemen in the silk trade. Many Western motifs were incorporated into their culture, and large quantities of Roman and Parthian stone and glass beads have been found throughout present-day Iran (plate 42).

Stone beads of hard and rare materials were time-consuming to make, expensive, and available only to the wealthy. Yet, the continuing spread of civilization invited an interest in fashion and adornment among increasing numbers of people. Attractive and affordable beads were in demand. The glazing of steatite and rock crystal in fourth-millennium B.C. Egypt was an early solution, but only with the invention of faience and the subsequent manufacture of glass was it possible to imitate precious stones in quantity and at low cost. While the manufacturing and trading of glass beads on a truly global scale commenced with the Romans, a major production site for Hellenistic glass beads was recently uncovered on the island of Rhodes. The discovery of debris from a glass factory there proved the island was an important manufacturer of beads during the late third or early second century B.C. Over ten thousand glass beads were excavated. Made by folded, drawn, pressed, wound, and ground techniques, they included melon, heart, biconical, bipyramidal, spherical, and cylindrical shapes and pendants (Bead Chart 407). Also found were about two hundred gold-in-glass beads in long and short cylinders and spherical forms, providing a very early provenance for these beads. Additionally, there were large quantities of eye beads and numerous more unusual varieties, including dolphin shapes, spacers, spools, and cubes, in all colors and in mosaic, opaque, and translucent glass.[27]

The Roman Empire

The Romans emerged from a small second-millennium B.C. enclave near Rome to become the dominant power in the Mediterranean and Europe until their empire's collapse in A.D. 476. By A.D. 100, Rome's territories extended from Armenia and Assyria in the east to Germany and Britain in the north and Mauritania and Egypt in the south.

Rome's artistic language was largely derived from the preceding Hellenistic period. Its jewelry melded the Eastern taste for colored stones with the Etruscan use of surface-decorated gold, favoring colors and gold that enhanced one another. Originally, jewelry was a luxury disapproved of in Rome, but by the first century B.C., this penchant for austerity had disappeared, and for hundreds of years thereafter, rings, necklaces, and other jewelry commonly adorned Romans.

The vastness of the empire and its extensive trade networks accommodated the wealthy with a wide variety of beads made from precious materials. Pearls and coral from the Persian Gulf and emeralds from Egyptian mines near the Red Sea were made into necklaces and earrings (plates 43 and 44). Trade with northern Europe brought Whitby jet from England and amber from the Baltic. With improved navigational methods, Roman mariners surpassed their Mediterranean predecessors, reaching India, Burma, and Sri Lanka (Ceylon): major sources for rubies, sapphires, and garnets.[28] The old Hellenistic workshops of Alexandria and Antioch, and Rome itself, were the primary centers of production for imperial Roman jewelry, while glass beads were made in numerous locations throughout the empire. Moreover, most craftsmen working within Rome had emigrated from the Eastern provinces.[29]

Roman Glass Beads

The Roman period, New Kingdom Egypt, and the era of Islamic dominance in the Mediterranean (c. A.D. 600–1400) are generally considered the three great periods of ancient glassmaking. The terms "Roman" and "Roman-period" glass are used to describe glass production from 100 B.C. to A.D. 400 within the boundaries of the Roman Empire, including factories in Syria, Egypt, Italy, Switzerland, the Rhineland, France, and England. Everywhere the Romans went they brought glass beads to trade. Produced in a large range of colors, patterns, and frequently complex techniques, Roman-made glass beads were widely coveted (plates 50–53). Exchanged as far north as Scandinavia, and as far east and south as China, Korea, Iran, Syria, Mali, and Ethiopia, quantities of Roman-period glass beads have been found in each of these countries, frequently raising the question of where they were originally manufactured because of their similar patterns and manufacturing techniques.

46. *Iridescent green, blue, and gold Roman glass beads, 100 B.C.– A.D. 200. Glass of this period has less color and more transparency than earlier varieties, due to the contemporary taste for translucent precious stones. The second necklace from the bottom is Egypto-Roman and is made of faience disk beads with a glass Eye of Horus, the important Egyptian funerary amulet. The overall greenish blue tinge of Roman glass comes from iron impurities in the sand used in making the glass. Bottom necklace, center bead: diameter, 2 cm. Private collection*

After Alexander's conquests, the practice of glassmaking appears to have moved from the interior of Egypt to Hellenistic Alexandria, where exquisite mosaic glass was manufactured from 300 B.C. to A.D. 100. (Yet, despite the city's reputation as the ancient center of the luxury glass industry, no glassmaking factory has ever been found in Alexandria.) About 100 B.C., glassmakers in Sidon and Tyre on the Lebanese coast competed with the Alexandrians in producing beautiful glass beads. Eventually, craftsmen from both centers migrated to new locations within the Roman provinces, setting up factories and disseminating techniques and forms.

During the first century B.C., core forming, a glass manufacturing technique long in use, went out of style. Newly invented larger furnaces with hotter fires were capable of creating a more fluid glass, affecting bead shapes and their patterns. Furthermore, glass's constituents (sand, alkali, and coloring agents) were refined, subsequently producing purer glass. The invention of the blowpipe, reputedly in Sidon, completely modernized the glass industry by increasing the level of production and opening the way

for still further new techniques, forms, and decorative styles. Although the blowpipe was not directly relevant to glass beadmaking, since few beads were blown (the great majority were still produced by winding and the newly introduced drawn techniques), the combined result of all these innovations under Roman guidance was the growth of glassmaking into a large-scale industry. More glass was made in the first century A.D. than in the previous fifteen hundred years.[30] Because the material was widely obtainable, relatively inexpensive, and no longer reserved for the elite, everyone could now afford to wear beads.

While beads manufactured in the European provinces during the late Roman period were generally of poorer quality than those of earlier times, glassworks along the east coast of the Mediterranean and within the Byzantine and Sasanian empires continued to produce finely crafted and styled beads, providing a link between Rome and the Islamic era, the last great period of ancient glass beadmaking.

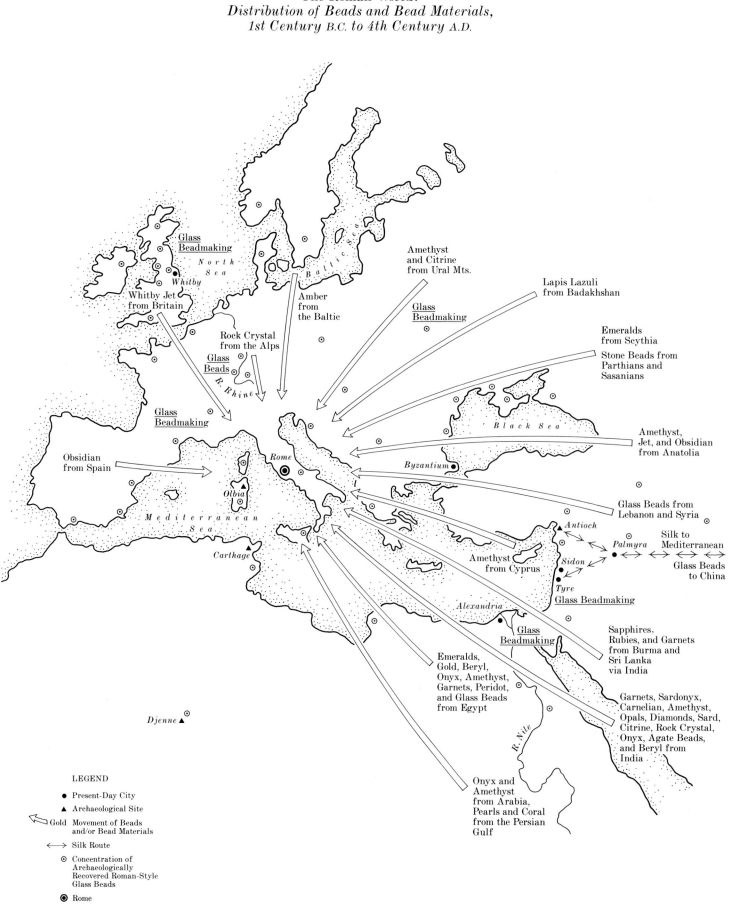

The Roman World:
Distribution of Beads and Bead Materials,
1st Century B.C. to 4th Century A.D.

Glass Beadmaking

North Sea

Whitby

Whitby Jet from Britain

Amethyst and Citrine from Ural Mts.

Baltic Sea

Amber from the Baltic

Glass Beadmaking

Lapis Lazuli from Badakhshan

Rock Crystal from the Alps

Glass Beads

R. Rhine

Glass Beadmaking

Obsidian from Spain

Rome

Olbia

Black Sea

Byzantium

Emeralds from Scythia

Stone Beads from Parthians and Sasanians

Amethyst, Jet, and Obsidian from Anatolia

Glass Beads from Lebanon and Syria

Antioch

Palmyra

Silk to Mediterranean

Glass Beads to China

Mediterranean Sea

Carthage

Amethyst from Cyprus

Sidon

Tyre Glass Beadmaking

Alexandria

Glass Beadmaking

Sapphires, Rubies, and Garnets from Burma and Sri Lanka via India

Emeralds, Gold, Beryl, Onyx, Amethyst, Garnets, Peridot, and Glass Beads from Egypt

Garnets, Sardonyx, Carnelian, Amethyst, Opals, Diamonds, Sard, Citrine, Rock Crystal, Onyx, Agate Beads, and Beryl from India

R. Nile

Djenne

Onyx and Amethyst from Arabia, Pearls and Coral from the Persian Gulf

LEGEND

● Present-Day City

▲ Archaeological Site

Gold   Movement of Beads and/or Bead Materials

⟷ Silk Route

⊙ Concentration of Archaeologically Recovered Roman-Style Glass Beads

◉ Rome

Northern, Central, and Western Europe from Neolithic Times to the Bronze Age

Farming developed in temperate Europe several thousand years after its origins in western Asia. Agriculture spread into Europe from Anatolia, reaching Scandinavia and the British Isles about 4000 B.C. A tin-bronze metallurgy industry emerged in the Balkans by 3000 B.C., giving rise to increased trade and the beginnings of wealth. Burial sites of wealthy chieftains have yielded metal weapons and tools, as well as beads of copper, bronze, faience, and amber. The oldest known copper ornaments in prehistoric Europe are disk beads made from the copper carbonate minerals azurite and malachite, which have been found at the site of Lepenski Vir in southeast Yugoslavia dating from 6000 to 4500 B.C.[31]

The European Bronze Age is contemporaneous with the Minoan-Mycenaean civilization (1800–1150 B.C.). The exchange of finished copper and bronze implements from the southern Mediterranean for Baltic amber, coveted for adornment, was an integral part of the cultural growth of Europe's northern regions.

Bronze Age beads from western and northern Europe are frequently of imported materials, including Egyptian faience and glass and Baltic amber. In Wessex, a center of early Britain, blue and green faience beads, possibly from New Kingdom Egypt, have been excavated from more than thirty graves (Bead Chart 8).[32] Beads from Gilchorn in Scotland and Lough Gur in Ireland resemble those of the Egyptian Eighteenth Dynasty (1567–1320 B.C.).[33] It is not a coincidence that Egyptian faience bead production reached its peak at the same time that faience beads were being widely dispersed throughout Europe. Irish gold copies of segmented faience beads were found as far east as central Germany.[34] Faience may also have been produced locally.

Baltic amber collars with trapezoidal plaques used as spacers to separate rows of

Mosaic Glass Beads Mosaic glass beads of the Hellenistic and Roman periods (300 B.C.–A.D. 400) were made with techniques initially used in the earliest days of glassmaking. Archaeological evidence points to the invention of mosaic glass in western Asia.[x] Mosaic glass reappeared in Egypt (Alexandria) and Syria only after the fourth century B.C. and declined after the first century A.D. It had a final renaissance in Venice about 1500.

Artistically crafted mosaic glass beads, also called millefiore ("thousand flowers"), are the product of great technical expertise. The fine detail of the beads was achieved by laying a bundle of preformed colored glass rods in parallel rows so that the cross-section of the bundle had a pattern. The glass was then heat-softened and stretched, fusing the canes together. This miniaturized the design, but the cross-sectional pattern remained unchanged.

BOTTOM : 50. *Mosaic face beads — miniature masterpieces of ancient glassmaking. The fine detail achieved on beads typically less than one-half inch in diameter was astonishing. Note the eyes with pupils, the skin tones, and women wearing tiny bead necklaces. Top left bead: diameter, 1.2 cm. Private collection.* RIGHT : 51. *A mosaic glass bead of remarkable complexity—identified with the skills of Alexandrian glassmakers. The bead was constructed by fusing 18 plaques involving 4 different designs (a lion and 3 views of a lotus blossom). Each plaque is formed from 18 to 25 separate rods of glass, thus the bead represents the assemblage of nearly 350 individual parts. Length, 1.7 cm. Private collection.* ABOVE RIGHT : 52. *Mosaic glass bars from which beads could be easily manufactured were an important trade commodity in the Roman world. Thin slices of a bar, as shown here, were cut with a metal blade and abrasive sand. These slices were then pierced for beads. By distributing the bars, complex mosaic glass was made available to less sophisticated glass industries. It was not unusual for merchants separated by thousands of miles to order glass ingots from a common supplier. As a result, mosaic glass beads of similar patterns were found throughout the empire. 100 B.C.–A.D. 100. Length, 3.7 cm. Corning Museum of Glass, Corning, New York.* NECKLACE : 53. *A wide variety of mosaic and other patterned glass beads interspersed with small carnelians and blue glass cornerless cubes. Beads shown date from the Phoenician through early Islamic periods (c. 400 B.C.–A.D. 900). Center bead: diameter, 1.9 cm. Private collection*

spheres are found in excavations in Denmark and Wiltshire in England, and similarly designed necklaces made of jet are frequently found in Scottish cist burials. The best-known source for jet in the ancient world was located near Whitby in England, and Whitby jet was highly praised. Quantities of it found their way to Italy via the tin trade routes during the days of the Roman Empire (plate 56).

The Iron Age to the Roman Empire

The late Bronze Age peoples of central Europe cremated their dead, placing the ashes in pottery vessels that were buried in "urnfields." Out of these communities, which have been characterized by their urnfield cemeteries, emerged Europe's first iron-using culture, the Hallstatt (700–450 B.C.), who are recognized as the forerunners of the Celts. The Hallstatt, named by archaeologists for an Austrian site near Salzburg, was a culture whose wealth derived from local salt and copper deposits. Over one thousand graves have been excavated at Hallstatt, many rich in amber, bronze, and glass beads. They also contain examples of the torque, the most characteristic item of Celtic adornment.

From the time of their emergence about 600 B.C., the Celts, identified as a culture rather than with a particular region, were important international traders. By 200 B.C., they established manufacturing and distribution centers called *oppida* (after the Latin for "towns"), where specialized products, including Roman amphorae and amber and glass beads, were merchandised. The first century B.C. seems to have been the most active period in the oppida, and many different beads were imported into Britain at this time.[35]

The manufacture—or perhaps just the importation—of glass beads in Europe dates to the late second or early first millennium B.C. The first glass beads were undecorated, but thereafter quantities were produced within various centers throughout the Mediterranean, central Europe, and Russia that had decorative eyes and spirals believed to possess magical or protective properties (plates 54 and 55). It is thought that the beads with raised spiral eyes were produced in Celtic workshops between 200 and 1 B.C.

In Britain, the earliest glass beads were imported by the late second millennium. Between 500 and 100 B.C., Iron Age beads, associated on the Continent with the Celts, appear in large numbers. Between 300 B.C. and A.D. 1, glass beads were probably manufactured in Britain that reused glass imported from Europe. By A.D. 100, most of the typical Roman-period beads are found in Britain, including those of gold-in-glass, cornerless cubes, and melons (Bead Chart 19).[36]

platelike spacer beads separating elongated barrel forms has parallels with amber beads of the same date in England, Denmark, and Mycenae. The bracelet is from Pen-y-Bonc, Scotland, 1800–1400 B.C. British Museum, London

TOP LEFT: 57. A bronze bracelet with a classic Celtic blue glass and white spiral bead. The torque, or neckring, is considered the most identifiable item of Celtic jewelry. Most torques were made of locally produced bronze. The Celts loved beads, which they used for bracelets and torques. This bracelet is from the Hallstatt site, 400–300 B.C. Bead: diameter, 1.2 cm. British Museum, London

TOP RIGHT: 58. Bronze torque with spiral-engraved bead elements designed into it. These bead derivations are traceable to actual blue-and-white glass beads used on earlier neckrings. This type of torque was worn by noblewomen in Champagne. From Avon Fontenay, France, 300–200 B.C. Diameter, 15.5 cm. British Museum, London

LEFT: 59. A bronze torque incorporating cast melon beads. An outstanding example of British decorative design, this collar represents the final integration of torque and bead in Celtic art. From Lochar Moss, Dumfrieshire, Scotland, A.D. 1–100. Diameter, 16.5 cm. British Museum, London

Europe: The Late Roman Empire to the Renaissance

A network of bead manufacturers who shared stylistic and technical methods existed in Europe, western Asia, and the Mediterranean while the Roman Empire flourished. With the dissolution of the empire, however, the major centers of beadmaking were replaced by numerous smaller, local workshops that obtained their ideas and primary materials from a variety of sources, including Persia, Egypt, and regions of Europe settled by the Celts. As traditional beadmaking links were severed, beads with highly localized characteristics developed.

Throughout the history of the Roman Empire, its frontiers were almost continuously assailed by marauding bands seeking booty from the wealthy, civilized world. In addition, there was the constant pressure of groups from central and western Asia who were forced from their own lands by tribes farther east and gradually migrated to the fertile regions of Europe. Asian tribes who invaded western Europe during the fourth century A.D., a time known as the Migrations Period, found a fragmented society with internal political and social problems, neither strong enough to hold them at bay nor flexible enough to absorb them into the Roman system. In the next century, the overwhelming numbers of these nomadic people finally brought about the collapse of imperial power in the West. The remaining power of the Roman Empire was then vested entirely in its eastern capital, Constantinople.

European beads from the late Roman Empire to the beginning of the Renaissance reflect the wide social and historical divisions of the period. Beads of gold and precious or semiprecious stone adorned the elite, Byzantine nobility, Europe's feudal rulers, and officials of the Christian church. Clay, amber, stone, and glass beads were worn by migratory and settled tribal people and by common folk of the indigenous populations.

60. *Necklaces made from stone and glass beads excavated about 1900 from a large Frankish burial field in the German village of Niederbreisig, located on the west bank of the Rhine. Found with a number of other Roman artifacts in a series of tombs, the beads have been dated to the fourth to the seventh century A.D. Although some of the beads were probably produced locally, the face bead on the top necklace (right side) was from the Roman period, made in Syria or Egypt. The turquoise green melon beads, Frankish favorites, were inspired by Roman prototypes. Typical necklace length, 75 cm. Metropolitan Museum of Art, New York. Gift of J. Pierpont Morgan, 1917*

Wealthy, urban Romans did not favor glass beads, which they considered "barbaric" decorations. This was particularly true after the beginning of the Christian Era, when quantities of glass beads made through newly discovered mass-production techniques became affordable to the populace at large. As artistic activity was transferred to Constantinople from Rome, the empire's jewelers continued to make beads primarily from precious metals and stones, usually in styles characteristic of earlier Roman jewelry.

However, in numerous central and northern European regions that had once been provincial Roman glassmaking centers, glass beads never ceased being made and worn. During the era of the great migrations, colorful and eye-catching beads of gold and garnet or amber and glass were donned by tribesmen. As the tribes settled and in some cases forged their own empires, regional styles of glass beadmaking developed, particularly in areas that already had a glassmaking tradition.

The Byzantine Empire

By 330 A.D., Emperor Constantine I (306–337) moved his capital from Rome to the city of Constantinople (present-day Istanbul), an action that eventually divided the empire into eastern and western realms. Located on the site of Byzantium, a former Greek colony, Constantinople subsequently grew into a political, cultural, and religious center of international importance from the fourth until the eleventh century.

A geographic meeting point of the Occident and the Orient, Constantinople's ideal location helped it to become a major trading and artistic center. The Byzantine Empire reached its political and economic zenith during the sixth century A.D. International commerce prospered: fleets of ships sailed to Cornwall in England, while beautiful gold coins minted by Emperor Justinian I (483–565) and his successors found their way as far afield as Sweden, China, and Zanzibar.[1] A wealth of materials, including gold, garnets, rubies, emeralds, sapphires, pearls, and ivory flowed into Constantinople from India, Burma, southern Russia, and Africa.

The luxurious jewelry of Constantinople was famous and admired throughout the world. The Byzantine emperors had inherited not only the great historic lands of Greece, western Asia, Egypt, parts of Russia, and North Africa, but also the finely developed skills of their artists and artisans, many of whom were drawn to Constantinople by its wealth and concentration of patrons. Consequently, art and jewelry of the period reflected two major styles: one based on the classical Greek and Roman legacy, which epitomized formal elegance; the other derived from the more abstract and robust two-dimensional forms of western Asia and the Far East. Neither style ever completely dominated Byzantine jewelry; they coexisted or reemerged in new configurations.[2] By the sixth century, Byzantine adornment was rich, ornate, and colorfully intricate, a distinctive synthesis of both Hellenistic and Persian elements.

The most complete record of the Byzantine royal court wearing luxurious beaded jewelry is found on mosaics that decorate the church of San Vitale in Ravenna. (In 402, Ravenna officially became the capital of the western Roman Empire. From the late sixth century to 751, it was the seat of the governor of Byzantine Italy. Its capture by the Lombards in 751 finished Byzantine power in Italy.) The portraits of the prosperous, "apostle-like" Emperor Justinian and the Empress Theodora made in 547 convey the regal, highly stylized splendor of their court:

> The imperial diadem, the sign of the ruler's dignity in the time of Constantine was then still a ring of jewels. Under Justinian, elaborate strings of beads were added. This can be seen in the portrait of his wife, Theodora, in

Europe: *Constantinople and the Migrations Period,*
c. A.D. 330 to 1400

VIKINGS
c. 800–1000

Staraja Ladoga
▲ *Glass Beadmaking*
c. 700–1000

● *Novgorod*
Baltic Amber
Beadworking
to 12th C.

Helgö,
Birka ▲

<u>Amber</u>

VIKINGS
c. 800–1000

GOTHS

▲ *Paviken*

Ribe ▲

N o r t h
S e a

B a l t i c
S e a

<u>Amber</u>
● *Königsberg*

R. Dvina

Amber,
Ivory, and Furs
from Russia and
Scandinavia to
Western Asia
c. 800–1100

Whitby ▲

York ▲

Hedeby ▲

<u>Glass</u>
<u>Beadmaking</u>

R. Vistula

R. Dnieper

<u>Silver</u>
<u>Gold</u>

<u>Glass</u>
<u>Beadmaking</u>

R. Elbe

R. Rhine

<u>Garnet</u>

● *Kiev*
Glass Beadmaking
c. 975–1200

HUNS

● *Trier* <u>Agate</u>

LOMBARDS
5th C.

OSTROGOTHS

Settled Tribes:
<u>Beads of Gold, Glass,</u>
<u>Garnet, and Amber,</u>

VISIGOTHS 270

R. Danube

Black Sea

La Seube ▲

● *Venice*

● *Ravenna*

<u>Callaïs</u>

<u>Jet</u>

Silver from
Persia and
Carnelian Beads
from India to
Scandinavia via
Muslim Traders
c. 800–1100

■ *Constantinople*

Rome

Sardis
▲ *Glass Beadmaking*
c. 400–600

<u>Coral</u>

M e d i t e r r a n e a n
S e a

● *Sidon*
● *Tyre*

Glass Beads
from Sidon,
Tyre, and
Egypt to
Scandinavia
and Europe

Agate Beads and
Garnets from India,
Onyx and Carnelian Beads
from Yemen and India,
Pearls from the Persian Gulf,
Rubies, Emeralds, and
Sapphires from Burma
and Sri Lanka, and
Ivory from Africa
to Constantinople

LEGEND

○ Concentration of
Archaeologically
Excavated Glass Beads

● Present-Day City

▲ Archaeological Site and
Glass Beadmaking
and/or Distribution Center

Gold Movement of Beads
and/or Bead Materials

<u>Gold</u> Source of Materials

Tribal Migrations
—··— Goths
——— Vikings
—·— Ostrogoths
– – – Visigoths
····· Huns
——— Lombards

the mosaics at San Vitale in Ravenna. She wore a magnificent ring of precious stones and beads round her head, from which several strings of beads hung right down to her chest, resembling strands of hair which had been frozen miraculously into precious jewels.[3]

The mosaics are an important source of information, especially since the custom of burying jewelry with the dead was banned by the church. In practice, however, the edicts were not strictly enforced: the Merovingians, among other tribes, continued to place beads in graves even after their conversion to Christianity.

There is no clear separation in technique between late Roman and early Byzantine jewelry beadmaking following the division of the empire in 395. Polychrome jewelry continued to be popular. Beads made from precious stones, such as sapphires and ame-

thysts, were cut in cabochon shapes and strung on gold links with naturally cut emerald crystals and pearls (plate 61). Beads of metal or glass were frequently used as spacers to separate gold coins, for example, that had been mounted as pendants.[4] Filigree and granulation, techniques used by the Romans, continued to be practiced. A new technique, *Opus interrasile*—cutting through a thin sheet of metal in order to produce an openwork pattern—grew in use (plate 63).

Byzantine and Migrations Period jewelers had many techniques and design motifs in common, but their work also differed in several major ways. Craftsmen from both traditions shared a love for color, best expressed in their combination of metals, colored stones, and glass. Migrations Period artisans tended to employ sturdy forms, perhaps because beads were worn abundantly by every member of the tribal societies. In contrast, Byzantine jewelry was worn primarily by the elite. Pieces were designed for a more sedentary life-style and employed a greater use of precious metals and stones, rarely using glass. Tribal jewelers were more dependent than their Byzantine counterparts on whatever raw materials happened to be locally available. Constantinople, on the other hand, was the hub of a vast trade network that allowed access to a very wide range of raw materials, even if only a few specific materials were selected for jewelry.

Although the tribal cultures also developed influential lapidary approaches, in-

64. *A fifth-century A.D. necklace of gold and inlaid garnet polyhedral (ten-faceted) beads found near Olbia in southern Russia and undoubtedly worn by a high-ranking tribal aristocrat. The technique of inlaying garnet in complex cloison cells was perfected in western Europe during the Migrations Period. The garnet was probably imported from India, suggesting that even nomadic horsemen engaged in long-distance trade for luxury goods. Center bead: diameter, 0.95 cm. Walters Art Gallery, Baltimore*

laying garnet-with-gold (the origin of the technique was probably India, via Persia and Egypt), for example, Byzantine goldsmiths preferred enamel cloisonné (the fusing of multicolored enamels within small cells, or cloisons, to produce a mosaiclike effect). Whereas inlaid garnet-and-gold beads were frequently worn by the elite among the settled and migratory tribes, enamel cloisonné was in fact rarely used for Byzantine beads (plate 64).

Byzantine beads typically were made of precious metals and stones. Along with goldsmiths and other artists, glassmakers had moved to Constantinople from the former Roman provinces, but no definite records exist of their having made beads; only their mosaic tiles and vessels remain. Glass historian Gustavus Eisen mentions that Roman-style gold-in-glass beads were manufactured there in the fourth and fifth centuries, and he also describes a necklace of mosaic glass disks set in gold that he attributes to Constantinople craftsmen.[5] Most glass beads used in early Byzantine jewelry were probably imported from the beadmaking centers of Egypt and Syria. Closer to home, Sardis, in western Turkey, was a glass beadmaking site during early Byzantine times.[6]

By the fourth century, a glass bead industry also existed in Europe. During the first centuries of the Christian Era, immigrant glassmakers from the East (Alexandria and Syria) had established glass workshops in the western Roman provinces of Italy, France, and the Rhineland. Local industries grew out of these early Roman glassworks and supplied beads to their provincial rulers and the export market from at least A.D. 200 to 800. It is quite possible that some beads produced in the European provinces reached Constantinople. Later Byzantine glass beads (made both in the East and West) had similar shapes and patterns to earlier Syrian and Egyptian glass but were often less technically accomplished (Bead Chart 486).[7]

Early in the fourth century, Emperor Constantine allied himself with Christianity, thus paving the way for it to become the empire's official religion. The toleration of Christianity was accompanied by the manufacture of a variety of religious symbols. During the fourth century, the cross and molded-glass amulets representing drops of sacred blood, fish, doves, and faces of Christ were incorporated into necklaces as "amulets in the round." Although later burials rarely included Christian adornment, in the early days of imperial Christianity religious amulets and beads were still interred with the deceased. Two distinctive types of glass beads, called the "Vision of Constantine" and the "Road to Golgotha," were generally found in tombs in Syria and near Jerusalem, the spiritual center that gained increasing importance with the spread of Christianity.[8] By the seventh century, Byzantine jewelry was almost a complete synthesis of Christian symbols and Eastern forms, and the cross had become a popular motif (plate 63).

As the age of classical antiquity came to an end, and its aesthetic values were increasingly rejected by the Christian church's "low opinion of the sensual world," new religious attitudes influenced the wearing of jewelry. Although warned that they should love "not precious stones but the sacred," Byzantine nobility continued to adorn themselves with jewels.[9] They incorporated Christian symbols into their adornment but otherwise generally ignored the church's dictum, apparently heeding the call of materialism over spirituality.

The successful tribal (or "barbarian") invasions of the fifth century and the settlement of Germanic and Slavic peoples within the Roman Empire open a new chapter in Western history. By the seventh century, Muslim Arab conquests of western Asia and North Africa and the eventual migration of the Slavs into the Balkans severed the last links between Constantinople and the West.

Between the eleventh and the fourteenth century, a series of wars known as the Crusades were undertaken by European Christians to recover the Holy Land from the Muslims. In 1204, the knights of the Fourth Crusade, under pressure from the rulers of Venice, who had been eyeing Byzantine riches for centuries, were diverted from their original course and conquered Constantinople, which had been ruled by Macedonian emperors since 864. In the years that followed, the city's wealth was plundered and its jewelry was often melted down; consequently, few examples of Byzantine goldsmiths' work can still be seen.

After the fall of Constantinople to the Turks in 1453, and its incorporation into the Ottoman Empire, the influence of Byzantine jewelers continued only in pockets of the former empire, namely Greece and southern Russia.[10] Byzantine traditions, however, did not entirely die out. A necklace made in sixteenth-century Venice (and currently at the Museo Poldi-Pezzoli in Milan) is composed of enameled gold and filigree beads and shows that Byzantine practices were continued in Europe.[11]

The Migrations Period and the United Tribes

As the Mediterranean framework of the Roman world dissolved, power and influence shifted north of the Alps. Europe began to develop new "Romano-Germanic" civilizations, whose peoples had been on the continent's periphery only a few centuries earlier.[12] The Migrations Period commenced with the rise of the Huns, led by Attila (c. 406–453). The Huns entered eastern Europe from central Asia, crossing the Volga River about 370 and expanding their borders to the south and west until they were defeated in France by the Romans in 451. In their wake, they had unsettled the Teutonic tribes that lived in the regions through which they passed, causing a series of migrations and subsequent wars among tribes north of the Black Sea, in western Russia and eastern Europe, which continued until the tenth century.

From the fourth to the eighth century, powerful seminomadic tribes occupied most of southwest Europe, forming feudal societies that ruled a divided continent. The major tribes were the Visigoths in Spain, the Ostrogoths in eastern Germany and Aus-

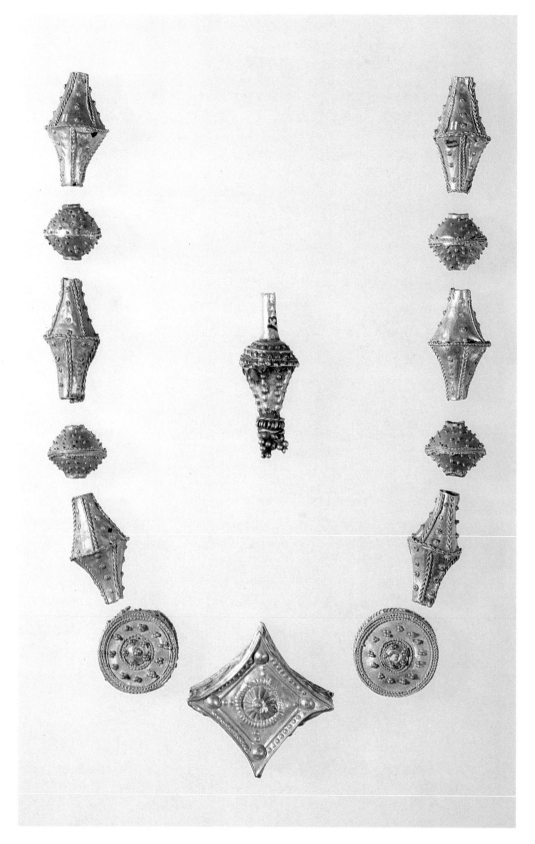

ABOVE: 65. *A unique sixth- to seventh-century* A.D. *inlaid garnet and lapis lazuli bead, made in two parts by a master Anglo-Saxon jeweler. Length, 3.3 cm. Ashmolean Museum, Oxford, England*

RIGHT: 66. *Gold filigree and finely granulated beads made in Denmark about* A.D. *100–200, using techniques probably introduced by the Romans. The beads were found in a peat bog in 1783. Typical biconical bead: length, 2.4 cm. National Museum of Copenhagen*

tria, the Vandals in North Africa, the Franks in western Germany, the Lombards in northern Italy, and the Angles and Saxons in England.

Adornment was very important to these people. Although each group produced their own styles of jewelry, reflecting specific tribal traditions, their adornment shared several common characteristics. Due to a long history of nomadic life, few possessions other than jewelry accompanied their journeys. Personal adornment was therefore portable wealth and a "badge of rank" used for decorating themselves as well as their horses.[13] The migratory life meant that jewelry had to be practical, well constructed, and compact, without too many protruding ends that could catch onto woolen tunics or capes. To be seen, it had to be bold in design, large, and colorful. For these reasons, beads, worn by both men and women, played an important role in of their jewelry.

Color was a dominant factor in most decoration of the Migrations Period. The inlaying of shaped garnets in gold cloisons—*verroterie cloisonné*—was a specialty of the period, often giving the finished bead the brilliant and mysterious appearance of a miniature stained glass window whose supports were made of gold rather than lead.[14] Inlaying was also practiced with lapis lazuli, glass, and enamel, and the techniques of filigree and granulation were sometimes used (plates 64 and 65). The intensive use of color and the extensive covering of surfaces with ornamental detail were designed to reflect light and to call attention to the wearer—priorities for jewelry meant to be noticed.

Migrations Period adornment evolved from many cultures, and the tendency to absorb and transform the styles and techniques of other cultures was a continuing feature of this jewelry.[15] A polychrome style was developed in the fourth century by Ostrogoth and Visigoth goldsmiths who worked near the Black Sea and were influenced by Greco-Roman and Eastern jewelry techniques and styles. In this region, as early as the fourth century B.C., Greek methods had been synthesized with the art of the Scythians and Sarmatians, migrant tribes with remarkable aesthetic traditions who lived between the Danube and the Don rivers from the fourth century B.C. to the second century A.D. Trade with Roman colonies north of the Black Sea also allowed the tribes to organize trading connections with India, through which they acquired garnets and other stones needed for their adornment. By the time of the Hun attacks, in the mid-fifth century A.D., most Germanic tribes had a rich and established jewelry tradition characterized by sophisticated geometries and abstract designs.[16] During the seventh century, the polychrome technique was refined into exquisite forms by the Anglo-Saxon jewelers in Britain (plate 65).

Beads of clay, amethyst, amber, and glass were worn by all of the tribes, generally in combinations that were strung or linked with pendants. Bead materials varied as new territories were conquered. The production of colorful glass beads flourished under the Merovingians (500–751), a Frankish dynasty, whose territories encompassed the Rhineland, where numerous glass workshops previously had been established by the Romans (plate 60). Merovingian jewelry was marked by the decline of classical traditions, and by the rise of the new abstract and brilliantly ornamental style of the tribes.[17]

The Franks, the first migrant people to accept Christianity, were the most powerful and important of all the successors of Rome, and their kingdom dominated western Europe from the late fifth to the early ninth century. Frankish glassmakers, although basically inspired by Roman designs, also developed their own styles, some of which imitated Celtic beads known from La Tène and Hallstatt fifteen hundred years earlier. The Franks not only copied Celtic patterns but also wore Celtic beads on their necklaces and carried slivers of La Tène glass.[18] Having recovered these objects from

ancient Celtic burial grounds, the Franks probably regarded them as protective amulets. Other beads were distinctively Merovingian, including ones with bright yellow lines embedded in a terra-cotta red background (Bead Chart 32).[19] Due to their acceptance of Christianity and the church's edicts forbidding grave deposits, beads slowly disappeared from Frankish burials during the seventh and eighth centuries.[20]

The history of glass beads in medieval Europe (800–1400) following the decline of the Merovingian dynasty is not clear. Archaeologists and historians continue to fill in the gaps, but the evidence is slim and is still not very well understood.[21] Glass beadmaking in the Roman tradition did survive, however, in various parts of Europe despite the destruction of the western empire and the subsequent turmoil of the Migrations and early medieval periods. Production continued in pockets of the Rhineland, Italy, and France, and gradually spread into central, eastern, and northern Europe, including Russia, and the Balkans.[22] Potash lime glass, made from local wood ashes rather than imported soda, is characteristic of central European glass and started to replace Roman and western Asian soda glass by the late eleventh century.[23]

After the twelfth century, glass beads do not appear to have been produced in Europe in quantity or quality until the fifteenth century, when Venice became the glassmaking center of the Western world.

The Vikings

The final phase of European migrations involved the Vikings. The region constituting the present-day countries of Denmark, Sweden, and Norway was among the most stable in Europe. Located so far north that they escaped invasions, these countries, however, were not isolated. During the second millennium B.C., Scandinavians were actively involved in the Baltic amber trade, manufacturing beads as well as exporting the raw material in exchange for metal ores not locally available. Although outside the Roman sphere, the Scandinavians

traded with the Romans for metal, pottery, and glass. Gold collars found in Scandinavia dating to the fourth century B.C. show decorative motifs influenced by Scythian, Etruscan, and Celtic art. Techniques of filigree and granulation seen in gold beads that date from the second and third centuries were probably introduced by Roman intermediaries during the first century A.D.

By A.D. 800, the Scandinavians were a seafaring people who raided and traded in northern, western, and eastern Europe. They acquired riches from the Eastern world, settled in Greenland, discovered America, and served as mercenaries at the court of Byzantium.[24]

A major impetus for the Viking raids and commerce was the acquisition of precious materials for adornment. Silver was particularly coveted; a major supply was garnered in the form of coins from the East when contact was established with Arab traders. Great quantities of silver were exported to western and northern Europe by the Vikings to replace the exhausted supplies of Byzantine gold.[25] Indian carnelian beads also entered Scandinavia via Islamic traders, while etched carnelians from Iran went north into Russia in exchange for furs and wax. Amber apparently traveled south along this same route.[26] Ivory walrus tusks and furs from the arctic regions of Scandinavia and Russia were staples the Vikings exchanged for precious materials.

Beads, along with pottery, nails, and knives, are the most common objects found in pre-Christian Viking graves. This has caused bead historian Johan Callmer to observe that Viking beads were directly related to social status, since almost without exception, they occur in the graves of wealthier Vikings. Typically, the beads are silver, amber, carnelian, rock crystal, and glass (plate 68). Some of the beads were made locally; others were imported.[27]

Beadmaking workshops have been excavated in southwest Scandinavia at several sites where flourishing towns existed in the ninth and tenth centuries and served as international marketplaces and import-export centers. Carnelian and crystal may have been imported to the town of Hedeby both as raw materials for manufacturing into beads and as finished products. There is also evidence of specialized amber workshops, where the amber debris shows that it was cut, carved, and turned using many of the techniques for working jet and bone.

Glass beads were made at the towns of Helgö and Paviken. Glass shards at Helgö as well as monochrome and mosaic glass rods found at nearby Birka and Ribe were all imported, suggesting that beadmakers on the southwestern periphery of Scandinavia worked at least in part with glass brought in from other areas.[28] Most Viking glass beads, however, were imported. Glass beads have been uncovered from graves in a variety of shapes, including spheres, tubes, melons, and cornerless cubes. The techniques they used include gold-in-glass, or gold sandwich, and mosaic, or millefiore, glass in both opaque and translucent colors.[29] It appears that glass beads found in Scandinavian Viking sites have many origins, which is not unexpected, given the far-ranging activities of the Viking sailors and warriors. Some possibly were passed down as heirlooms or obtained as loot; others may have been manufactured in distant western Asia and entered Scandinavia either during the days of trade with the Romans or in the ninth century, when contact was established with Arab traders along the Volga River in Russia.

The Vikings forged strong links between themselves and northern and eastern Europe. Their remarkable ships and nautical abilities took them into many distant waterways, including the rivers of France and the British Isles. Glass beadmaking occurred in most of the regions they traveled to, and it seems logical to assume that beads accompanied the Vikings on their homeward voyages. The Vikings frequently settled where they traded. Beads have been excavated at York, in England, and other Viking colonial outposts, indicating their far-flung trading activities.

Beads from the Coppergate excavation at York include amber, jet, and glass examples. The glass beads range from large, multicolored objects to small seed beads that were probably sewn onto clothing. A cowrie shell bead from the Red Sea may show there was contact between the Vikings at York and western Asians or Egyptians.[30]

Some glass bead types that were widely distributed throughout Scandinavia suggest production areas existed close to northwest Europe, in Marseilles, northern Italy, or the Rhine Valley. Other Viking beads closely resemble eastern European products, particularly the beads of Bohemia. The Vikings had direct contacts with all of these areas.[31]

A distinctive mosaic glass bead found outside the Roman Empire and concentrated in Scandinavia is of particular interest. This bead (plate 67), examples of which have been found in Scandinavian archaeological contexts dating from A.D. 300 to 400, is also known from Viking sites that date from 800 to 1000. Some of the beads recovered from the earlier period include unique mosaic glass faces with Byzantine-style royal helmets. The technical complexity of the beads suggests they were originally manufactured in workshops somewhere within the Roman Empire.[32]

The Middle Ages

During the Middle Ages (A.D. 600–1400), the use of jewelry was considered a pagan custom and was discouraged by the church. The simplicity of medieval dress was generally accompanied only by a brooch at the neck, a belt buckle, and finger rings. Beads of ivory, jet, coral, wood, gemstones, and precious metals were used primarily for rosaries. By the late fourteenth century, however, as rosaries and cruciforms became more popular and ornate, they were worn as necklaces, and their decorative function apparently rivaled their religious significance.

Medieval jewels, including beads, were talismanic and intended to bring supernatural benefits to the wearer. Paganism was generally abandoned in the regions as Christianity spread, although superstitions persisted for a long time and many magical practices were incorporated into Christianity. Materials were selected for their amuletic value, and stones were used that were considered to have protective powers: amethyst prevented drunkenness, coral strengthened the heart, and emeralds combated epilepsy. Crystal was regarded as the symbol of purity.

Certain areas were famed for working specific materials into beads. Novgorod, in Russia, was an important trading city which, until the Mongolian invasions of the twelfth century, produced most of the Baltic amber beads. Trebnitz, in Bohemia, was known for garnets cut into beads. Venice, according to Columbus's later descriptions, was a pearl-processing center. The agates of southern Germany (which would eventually result in the establishment of a famed bead industry at Idar-Oberstein) were beginning to be exploited: the first written notice of them was in 1375, and there were already beadmaking guilds by 1451.[33]

With few exceptions, European beadmaking was a decentralized cottage industry from the Roman period until the end of the Middle Ages. With rising prosperity in fifteenth-century Europe—due to sophisticated banking and trading networks, and the beginning of global exploration—glass beadmaking reappeared as an important art and industry. In Venice, many of the old Roman glass techniques were rediscovered, and beadmaking took its place alongside the great arts of the Renaissance.

Prayer Beads

All night she spent in bidding of her bedes,
And all the day in doing good and Godly deeds.
—Edmund Spenser
The Faerie Queene

Prayer beads are commonly associated with the Middle Ages (A.D. 600–1400) and Roman Catholicism. Their use, however, is universal and predates the Christian Era. Christianity, in fact, was the last of the major religions to employ prayer beads in an important ritualistic role. Even today, the religions of nearly two-thirds of the world's population utilize some form of prayer beads.

The word *bead* is derived from the Anglo-Saxon *bidden* ("to pray") and *bede* ("prayer"). During the medieval period, when jewelry was discouraged by the church, rosaries were acceptable as convenient portable devices for counting prayers. Their purpose was to assist the worshiper in accurately repeating from memory the correct number of prayers and incantations required by his faith.

The rosary is only one of several ancient ways used to count prayers. The earliest means involved counting on fingers or shifting pebbles from one pile to another as the prayers were recited. These unwieldy methods were replaced by tying knots on a cord: the strings of prayer beads probably evolved from strings of knots. The Greek Orthodox church still employs a knotted rosary, the *kombologion*. One of the oldest forms of the rosary in Europe is a thong of leather sewn into a circlet, with bone rings attached like scales to the spine of a fish. The rings were turned over as prayers were counted. This form of rosary, known from eighth-century graves, was still in use in southern Germany in the nineteenth century.[1]

70. *A Buddhist* mala. *The 108 disk-shaped prayer beads are made from the bones of a lama (holy man). The dividers and retaining beads are coral, and the tassels are silk. The satin ribbon is partially covered with Tibetan writing. The two counters, each with ten silver beads, terminate in thunderbolt pendants (*djore*). Several hundred years old, this mala belonged to Lama Kunga Rinpoche of the Ngor monastery. Length (side to top center bead), 40 cm. Collection Ivory Freidus*

ABOVE LEFT: 71. A chaplet of sixty-six rudraksha beads made from the seeds of a small tree unique to Java. Often worn as a necklace by followers of the Hindu god Siva, rudraksha are perhaps the earliest form of prayer beads. The natural surface of each seed is rough with grooves, symbolizing the austere life required for the worship of Siva. The five lines typically incised on each seed represent Siva's five faces. Typical bead: diameter, 2 cm. Plates 71–72: collection Ravi Kumar

ABOVE RIGHT: 72. A chain of 108 silver prayer beads, usually carried by a follower of the Jain sect of Hinduism. Length, 29 cm

The use of beads to count prayers appears to have originated with the Hindus in India. Sandstone sculptures of the Sunga and Kushan periods (185 B.C.–A.D. 320) portray Hindu sages holding rosaries.[2] It is possible, however, they were used even earlier by the Hindu cult of Siva or, according to legend, by Sakyamuni (c. 563–483 B.C.), the founder of Buddhism. One account places the rosary's origin in the sixth century B.C. when Sakyamuni paid a visit to King Vaidurya, a recent Buddhist convert. Assisting the king in his new faith, "Sakya directed him to thread 108 seeds of the Bodhi tree [*Ficus religiosa*] on a string, and while passing seed by seed between his fingers to repeat a certain formula meaning 'Hail to the Buddha, the Law, and the Congregation' at least two thousand times a day."[3] Later, Buddhists in Tibet, China, and Japan used rosaries, as did Muslim Persians and Arabs.

Christians may have first learned about the concept of the rosary from the Arabs, either as a result of the Crusaders' experiences in the Holy Land or through its introduction into Spain by eighth-century Muslim invaders. More likely, the Christian rosary evolved independently in western Europe (first, possibly in Ireland) as the church developed more sophisticated rituals and its practitioners had an increasing number of prayers to count. Many church members were illiterate; using beads as a counting device insured that each prayer was repeated the prescribed number of times.

Although the number, arrangement, and materials of prayer beads are different with each religion, there are shared concepts that link the beads of the major faiths. Symbolic associations are frequently made between flowers (particularly the rose) and gardens and prayer beads. The name for prayer beads in Tibet and India is the Sanskrit word *mala*: it means "garden," "garland of flowers," and "necklace of beads." The oldest name for Hindu prayer beads is *japamala*: "muttering chaplet." But *japamala* also means "rose chaplet," presumably because the beads were made of rolled petals from the flower rose of Sharon (*Hibiscus syriacus*).[4] The Roman Catholic rosary has a rich historical relationship with rose garlands and rose gardens. In contemporary Italy, a *coronario* makes both flower wreaths for funerals and prayer beads.

While the quantities of beads used in rosaries differ from religion to religion (and even between various sects of a single faith), multiples of three predominate the iconography of rosaries, reflecting the significance of the number in prayers and even fundamental doctrines—the Buddhist triad (Buddha, the doctrine, and the community), for example, or the Roman Catholic Trinity (the Father, Son, and Holy Ghost). The Buddhist rosary, and the Hindu rosary from which it was derived, have 108 beads; the Muslim, 99; and the Roman Catholic, 150. In addition to their practical purpose, rosaries have intellectual, social, psychological, and aesthetic significance. Highly sensual, inviting continual handling, they were sometimes an ascetic's only material possession. Healing powers have been attributed to rosaries, as well as the power to exorcise evil spirits and ward off lightning. Certain materials, such as agate, were almost universally talismanic; their use as religious beads provided double protection. Coral beads were associated with the prevention of ailments of the blood. In many medieval paintings, the Christ Child is shown wearing or holding a coral rosary.[5]

Beginning in ancient times, prayers have been recited in cycles. Countless ceremonies exist in which a circle is used to join people together, to create a sense of place, and to "protect what is within; to keep out what is dangerous or to concentrate force."[6] There are also ageless associations with the cycles of life, as well as annual, seasonal, and daily cycles. Symbolizing cycles of prayer, rosaries form closed circlets or chaplets. Whether the circle is large or small, it usually has either a terminal bead or tassel marking the beginning and end of the prayer cycle. Markers of a different shape or size occur at intervals among the counting beads, providing the user with a place to pause and rest.

The rosary's circular form has different levels of religious and psychological meanings. In meditation, the circle centers the mind in contemplation: "One uses prayer beads, ringing oneself in." Meditation involves establishing a space, a circle, and focusing attention within it, thus concentrating energy. Writing about introspection, Saint Augustine admonished the faithful: "God is a circle whose center is everywhere." He prescribed "[returning] within yourself, for it is in the inward man that truth dwells." The solitary, thoughtful manipulation of prayer beads enhances this contemplative state of mind, and the repetitious handling of the beads helps the worshiper concentrate on spiritual needs. As prayers are said, a closed circuit is created: words are spoken, fingers move, and ears listen.[7]

The meditative state induced by repeating prayers while holding beads plays a great role in Eastern religions. The Eastern worshiper suspends thinking during meditation in contrast to the Westerner, who is encouraged to think while reciting prayers. Another difference between the beads' role in Eastern and Western religions is in the handling of the actual rosaries. In the East, prayers are counted by moving the string in one hand; in the West, rosaries are usually held in both hands.[8] This has an interesting parallel with the frequent use of assymetry in the aesthetics of the East, while the West so often stresses symmetrical balance.

Throughout the centuries, the elaborate craftsmanship of prayer beads often

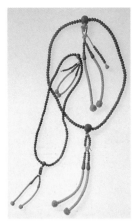

ABOVE: 73. *The* sho-zoiki jiu-dzu *are prayer beads used by all Japanese Buddhist sects. Each composed of 112 plum wood beads of equal size, these two rosaries are split into two groups of larger parent beads called the "father" and "mother" beads. Length (either), 180 cm. National Museum of Natural History, Smithsonian Institution, Washington,* D.C.

RIGHT: 74. *A Buddhist* mala *composed of 108 disk-shaped beads of human bone, inlaid with turquoise, coral, amber, pearl, and lapis lazuli. One retaining bead and three large divider beads of jade, turquoise, carnelian, and coral separate the* mala *into four sections of 27 beads each. The circlet ends in a* djore, *indicating the beginning and the end of the prayer cycle. There are no counters. Skull beads, like other Tibetan ritualistic objects of human bone, were meant to impress upon the devotee the transient nature of human existence.[1] Length, 72.4 cm. Collection Franyo Schindler, New York*

TOP: **75.** *Islamic prayer beads (subha) from Cairo, consisting of ninety-nine round olivewood beads divided into three sections by two vase-shaped marker beads. The marker beads, placed after the thirty-third and sixty-sixth beads, allow the devotee a respite from counting prayers. The ends of the cord pass through a spindle-shaped terminal bead, known as the "leader," which indicates that one has "come into" the circle of prayer. The cords finally go through two smaller beads, terminating in a tassel. Because evil spirits are believed to dislike fringed objects, the tassel keeps away the evil eye. Length, 101.6 cm. National Museum of Natural History, Smithsonian Institution, Washington, D.C.*

LEFT: **76.** *Islamic coral prayer beads inlaid with silver, probably made in Istanbul during the nineteenth century. Length, 146 cm. Collection Franyo Schindler, New York*

83

stands in stark contrast to the concepts of simplicity they were meant to enhance. Attempting to make the beads' appearance conform with spiritual values has led to interesting interpretations. A bead authority notes: "One may feel, as Lady Godiva did in the eleventh century, that it is fitting to count one's prayers on jewels for they are being offered to God. Or one may feel that a wretched sinner like oneself should not presume to offer prayers on any but the plainest beads."[9] It has been difficult to keep luxury out of religion. The custom of prominently displaying prayer beads led to their elevation as objects of social status as well as piety. Rarely does the village priest carry the same beads as an archbishop, or a poor devotee the same as a wealthy one. The most common materials for rosaries throughout the world are wood, glass, and plastic. But museums display ones made of every known precious material, including gold, silver, emeralds, rubies, diamonds, coral, jet, crystal, alabaster, pearls, and lapis lazuli. There are also rosaries of amber, ebony, marble, ivory, jade, mother-of-pearl, enamel, and porcelain. French royal inventories in 1380 listed rosaries of enameled gold encrusted with jewels, and medieval Córdoba was famous for its prayer beads made of gold.

Primarily in reaction to these excesses, Protestants do not use prayer beads. The leaders of the Reformation protested the self-indulgence and blatant materialism of the medieval church. As a result, Protestant doctrines stress moderation, minimize ritual, and tend to reject what are considered displays of material extravagance, including prayer beads. The founders of Protestantism stressed literacy and encouraged individual interpretation of the Scriptures. John Calvin, the great Reformation theologian, said that each person in the reformed church should be able to read the creed for himself. This meant that prayers were not to be memorized in set circular formulas, and therefore aids, such as beads, were not needed.

Judaism also excludes prayer beads. Its history emphasizes the rejection of paganism. Beads were considered magical and therefore pagan. Talismanic beads are generally considered a device to win the beneficence of the gods, and traditionally Jews do not speak to God through intermediaries. Furthermore, since counting prayers on beads served no ethical purpose, Judaism never accorded the custom any significance.[10]

Hindu Beads

Prayer beads are central to the life of many Hindus. Prayers are repeated along with the names of favorite gods for hours daily, causing one nineteenth-century observer to note that "the pious Hindu…computes his daily prayers as if they were so many rupees added to his capital stock in the bank of heaven."[11] Two basic types of prayer beads (*mala*) correspond to the two major Hindu cults of Siva and Vishnu. For at least a thousand years, the devotees of Siva have carried rosaries of *rudraksha*, beads made from the seeds of the tree *Eleaocarpus ganitrus* (plate 71). Vishnu rosaries consist of 108 beads made from tulsi, the holy basil *Ocimum sanctum*. It has been suggested that the continued importance of wooden prayer beads in India parallels a preference for wood in the construction of religious buildings.[12]

Buddhist Beads

Originating in India about 500 B.C., Buddhism reached China in the first century A.D., Korea about the beginning of the fourth century, Japan in the sixth, and Tibet in the eighth. As Buddhism became the established religion in these countries, it was influenced by the diverse cultures with which it came into contact. Unlimited tolerance is an essential principle of Buddhism, a concept reflected in the various forms and materials of its prayer beads. This can be seen, for example, by comparing Tibetan Buddhist beads (plates 70 and 74) with those from Japan (plate 73). Differences exist in the elaboration of form, the number and types of pendants and tassels, the spacing beads, and the materials—the Japanese, regardless of their social status, have tended to use wood, while wealthy Tibetans preferred amber and coral or human bone.

Buddhism adopted rosaries from the Hindus. The rosary, an important part of a Buddhist monk's attire, usually consists of 108 smooth beads, corresponding to the number of mental conditions or sinful desires that can be overcome by recitation with the beads. Although monks use full chains of 108 beads, rosaries carried by lay people often consist of only 30 or 40 beads.

Favored beads are carved from the wood of the sacred bo tree, a species of fig (*Ficus religiosa*). The use of beads for meditation and attainment of a mystical state through repetition of prayer has its widest application in Buddhism, particularly in the Himalayan region, where they are still a familiar part of life.

Tibet

In old Tibet, nearly everyone carried or wore prayer beads of wood, shell, amber, semi-precious, or precious stones. The materials differed according to the owner's taste and wealth, and depended too on the devotee's sect and the deity worshiped. The most highly prized beads were made from the bones of a lama (plate 74).

In old Tibetan rosaries, 3 beads of different sizes and materials were used to divide the full rosary of 108 round or disk beads into four groups of 27 each. At the point where the two ends of the string came together, 3 large retaining beads were included to indicate the completion of a round or circuit of prayer. These last beads symbolize the triad of Buddha, the doctrine, and the community.[13] Attached to the main string were usually two strands of 10 smaller beads. Known as the "number keepers" or counters, these act like a miniature abacus, keeping track of the number of times the user recites his prayers or mantra. The counter strings generally terminate with two small pendants, called the *djore* and *drilbu*. The *djore* (a representation of the conventionalized thunderbolt of Indra) is the single circuit string, while the *drilbu* (a tiny bell) marks every ten repetitions. In addition to these conventions, it is common to find personal odds and ends, such as tweezers or keys, attached to the rosaries.[14]

China, Korea, and Japan

Prayer beads were never very widespread in China. Under Manchu rule (1644–1912), however, Buddhist prayer beads, modeled after those from Tibet, became fashionable with the ruling hierarchy and quite elaborate. Called "court chains," they were used in China primarily for status symbols rather than prayer. In Korea, where Buddhism was the official state religion until banned by the Yi dynasty (1392–1910), rosaries were quite an important part of religious rituals. Korean rosaries typically have 110 beads, whereas most Buddhist rosaries use 108. The 2 extra beads are large: one is decorated with a swastika and located at the beginning of the strand; the other is plain and placed in the middle. A devotional treatise entitled "The Classic of the Rosary" is displayed as a poster on the walls of Korean Buddhist temples. "The Classic" shows a rosary and explains its numerous uses.[15]

Among the Japanese, prayer beads were also an important component of both social and religious life. The beads were carried by monks and lay citizens to funerals and other ceremonial events. All teahouses had a hook on the wall for hanging the beads; an important or unusual set gave prestige to the teahouse.[16]

The Buddhist rosary took on unique forms in Japan, with different sects exhib-

ABOVE: *77. The rose, the embodiment of beauty, mystery, and perfection in Roman times, became a spectacular Christian symbol. "Rosary" is derived from* rosarium, *meaning "rose garden."*

RIGHT: *78. Jan van Eyck.* The Virgin of the Fountain. *1439.*

In an enclosed rose garden with a fountain (the "water of life"), the Virgin cradles the Christ Child, who is holding coral prayer beads. The matching color of the coral beads and the roses establishes their connection. This is perhaps the earliest known work showing the relationship between prayer beads and rose gardens. Although the scene was painted at least fifty years before the term "rosary" was officially in use by the church, the association between beads and roses was obviously recognized in Flanders.[11] Koninklijk Museum voor Schöne Kunsten, Antwerp

TOP: 79. *A carved box-wood prayer bead made in Flanders about 1500. It usually served as a terminal bead to a one-decade paternoster. The exquisite carving juxtaposes scenes from the life and death of Christ. In the upper sphere, the Nativity, the Adoration of the Magi, and the Annunciation of the Shepherds; in the lower sphere, the Crucifixion. Diameter, 5.4 cm. Metropolitan Museum of Art, New York*

BOTTOM: 80. *A fifteenth-century rosary of hollow agate beads, each of which opens, revealing a scene in enameled gold. The rosary illustrates the elaborate materialism of the late medieval period, a source of controversy within the church. Length, 51 cm. Musée National du Louvre, Paris*

81. *The Langdale Rosary, a fifteenth-century enameled gold English rosary consisting of fifty "Ave beads," six lozenge-shaped paternoster beads, and a suspended gold pendant. Each bead is hollow and decorated with depictions of saints in niello. The rosary belonged to the Yorkshire family of Langdale. It is possibly the oldest existing rosary in Protestant Europe, since most rosaries were destroyed during the Reformation. Typical bead: length, 1.25 cm. Victoria and Albert Museum, London*

iting various numbers and arrangements of beads. The most widely used was the *sho-zoiki jiu-dzu*, a strand of 112 beads (plate 73). *Jiu-dzu* shops, often located at pilgrimage stops, advertised their sacred wares by hanging huge wooden rosaries outside the store. A set of prayer beads that had been blessed over the incense smoke of a respected temple was highly valued by its owner.

Wood was the preferred material for Japanese Buddhist rosaries. Cherry, rose, plum, carved and smoothed peach, ebony, and mahogany were all used. Walnut shells, cherry pits, and the nuts of the bead tree (*Melia azedarach*) were also popular.

Islamic Beads

The Muslims probably derived the concept of prayer beads from the Buddhists. When this happened, however, is uncertain. Called *subha*, meaning "to exalt," the Islamic rosary has ninety-nine counting beads in addition to an elongated terminal one, known as the *Iman* or "Leader," "pillar," or "minaret" (plate 75).

The counting beads are used to recite the ninety-nine attributes of God the Holy, the Mighty, the Forgiver, and so forth. The one hundredth bead is reserved for saying the name of God, *Allah*. Devotional phrases recited on the prayer beads include the *tah-mid*, "God be praised," and the *tahlit*, "There is no deity but God." Great stock is put into uttering the one hundred names of God and chanting the formulas. A prophet said, "There are ninety-nine names of God, and whoever recites them shall enter into Paradise," and "Whoever recites the *tasbih* and the *tahmid*, a hundred times morning and evening, will have all his sins forgiven."[17] Ultraorthodox, conservative Muslims were, at the time of the prayer beads' appearance, opposed to them. During the thirteenth century, Ibn al-Hajj complained that the exaggerated use and esteem of the *subha* was contrary to the primitive simplicity of Islam.[18] Islamic beads are often made of wood, including acacia, olivewood, ebony, sycamore, and sandalwood. Materials such as bone, ivory, coral, amber, carnelian, agate, lapis lazuli, and glass have also been used. In Mogul India (1526–1756), pearls, rubies, emeralds, and sapphires were the beads of the court.[19] Beads of date pits from the sacred cities of Mecca and Medina are revered. Mecca is a huge bead emporium, and a vast array of beads imported from all over the world are sold there. Wooden beads that have been dyed red and immersed in water from the holy well of Zemzem are taken away from Mecca by pilgrims who have made the hajj, or pilgrimage, to the sacred Muslim city.[20]

Roman Catholic Rosaries

Different theories exist about the origin of the Christian rosary. Seventh-century graves have disclosed strings of beads twisted around the deceased's hands, a custom still followed in parts of Italy and Japan. Saint Rosalia (742–814), a relative of Emperor Charlemagne's, was reported to have been found buried with a string of little beads that ended in a cross. These beads were probably talismanic rather than counting devices.[21]

The use of beads for saying prayers began in medieval European monasteries almost a thousand years ago. Often illiterate and unable to understand Latin, Christian laity were unable to sing or recite the psalms. Instead, they were given a set of 150 prayers to say, and they used beads to aid in counting.

Most information on European rosaries comes from medieval wills. The earliest mention of a string of beads being used to count prayers occurs in England. The eleventh-century bequest of Lady Godiva to the Monastery of Coventry involves "a circlet of gems which she had threaded on a string in order that by fingering them one by one, as she successively recited her prayers, she might not fall short of the exact number."[22]

In the mid-sixteenth century, however, Pope Pius V decreed that the rosary had been invented by Saint Dominic (1170–1231). While there is little historical evidence supporting the claim, a series of popes have approved the tradition, and today the Dominicans are officially in charge of making rosaries.[23] The number of beads in a typical Catholic rosary has remained constant since the middle of the sixteenth century. A chaplet of 150 small beads is divided into "decades" (groups of 10 beads) by 15 larger beads. The decade system corresponds to the ten fingers, the original method of counting. A pendant, comprised of 1 large and 3 small beads and terminating in a cross, is usually attached to the chaplet.

The 150 beads, known as the "Ave beads," correspond to the number of psalms and are used for reciting the Hail Mary prayer. A decade of Aves, counted on the small beads, is followed by a Paternoster (the Lord's Prayer), for which a larger bead is used. This is followed by the Gloria ("Glory be to God"). The fifteenth Paternoster is counted on the retaining bead, used to close the loop or chaplet. Each of the fifteen decades represents a subject, or "mystery," in the lives of Christ and Mary, which are divided into five joyful, five sorrowful, and five glorious mysteries. The division of the rosary into three sets of five decades, known as "The Three Fifties," allows prayers to be recited on the more commonly used smaller chaplets. The number three, which is a basic component of rosary iconography, has a complex history dating back to early Ireland. It is related to the trefoil of the shamrock, the national symbol of Ireland.[24]

By the late Middle Ages, men and women wore rosaries around their necks, like bandoliers across their chests, or on belts. Rosaries were often clasped in the hands or twisted around the forearm. By the fourteenth century, they were essential possessions as objects of both devotion and adornment. A chronicle of the city of Biberach, dated 1530 to 1540, relates that everyone "carried a paternoster or else was taken not to be a Christian. It was a badge of religion, and therefore of respectability."[25]

By the thirteenth century, makers of rosaries, called "paternosters," had formed guilds that specialized in beads of a particular material. There were paternosters who worked only in amber, and others who specialized in precious stones, metal, or glass. The most common rosaries were those of wood and glass, while beads of amber, agate, and particularly coral were valued for their protective attributes. In the Mediterranean region, the coral of southern Italy and the Tunisian coast was extremely popular for rosary beads. The wealthy owned beads of gold, silver, and precious stones. The elaborate quality of many rosaries became an ongoing subject of controversy. As early as 1261, the Dominicans were forbidding lay brothers to "give themselves airs by using excessively grand beads." In the middle of the fourteenth century, an Augustinian canon of Osnabrück outlawed the wearing of coral rosaries around the neck.[26]

Royalty was not impeded by such limitations. In 1380, a listing of the jewelry of King Charles V of France records nineteen rosaries made of "rose-tinted amber, coral with pearls for markers, gold beads, jet beads with eleven gold crosses, black coral and pearls, coral alternating with beads of silver, and gold beads of Damascus work which were filled with musk." The widow of Cesare Borgia, Charlotte d'Alhret, who died in 1514, had rosaries interspersed with enameled pierced-gold beads for holding scent. It has also been recorded that Mary, Queen of Scots, was beheaded in 1587 while wearing a necklace of pomander beads.[27]

The first descriptions of musk-filled pomanders in the shape of rosary beads stem from inventories of the fourteenth century. Pomanders, often of enameled gold and set with precious stones, were shaped as balls, hearts, or pomegranates. The carved hollow bead shown in plate 79 may have been used as a pomander. The fashion for wearing scented rosaries was utilitarian as well as aesthetic. In late medieval Europe, musk, cloves, and myrrh, which were commonly placed in the pomanders, were considered to offer protection against the plague.[28]

To control the extravagances, a series of monastic and municipal laws were enacted in which monks were not permitted to wear beads around their neck. Carrying certain beads was permitted, and wearing beads in the belt denoted membership in certain religious orders.

One of the most interesting aspects of the Christian rosary is the history of its name, derived from *rosarium* ("rose garden").[29] Since classical times, the rose has been universally beloved. Its form, fragrance, and color symbolize beauty, mystery, love, and perfection. Aphrodite wore rose perfume and a crown of roses, while the Muses wore garlands of roses and thyme. The ancient Romans associated roses with success and festivity: victorious warriors returning from battle were greeted with roses. In Christianity, the red rose symbolizes Christ's blood and the purity of the Virgin Mary. Originating in the concept of the Paradise Gardens of Persia (with obvious biblical roots in the Old Testament's Garden of Eden), the cloistered rose garden became an essential part of medieval architecture; a secluded, high-walled courtyard filled with fragrant roses. The rose garden was an ideal place for meditation and prayer. Collections of medieval prayers and hymns were bound into books called *rosaria* ("flower gardens").

By the middle of the fifteenth century, rose gardens, rose garlands, and rosaries were associated with the Virgin Mary and the Christ Child in paintings and in the illustrations of rosary books (plate 78). Religious paintings of the period are often set in rose gardens, under rose arbors, or near a rosebush. Angels and the Christ Child are seen wearing or holding rosaries.

It is unclear at what point the word meaning "a garden of roses" was transformed into "a string of beads used to count prayers." Nonetheless, the spiritual identity of roses was extended to beads, which came to symbolize a permanent garden of prayer called the rosary.

Worry Beads

Visitors to present-day Greece, Turkey, or the Middle East see men and women holding "worry beads." At business meetings in Saudi Arabia, businessmen discuss transactions involving millions of dollars while fingering strings of beads. If questioned, people will deny the beads have any special meaning. However, since there are usually thirty-three beads on the string with a vase-shaped retaining bead ending in a tassel, they are probably derived from both Christian and Islamic prayer beads. Worry beads, like prayer beads, are made in a great many materials—plastic, glass, olive pits, wood, amber, ivory, and semiprecious stones—catering to various owners' wealth and status. Their primary function as a release for tension provides a security that may, in fact, be subconsciously spiritual.

The secularization of worry beads demonstrates the range of religious and social values associated with rosaries. The arrangement and number of beads, their size and materials, and the way they are worn communicate a great deal of historical, spiritual, and social information. Above all, prayer beads articulate the universal human need for personal adornment. Religious beads, symbolizing piety and fulfilling a practical purpose, could be made of the simplest materials. Yet to fulfill the apparently necessary expressions of social status, prayer beads have been made from a variety of rare and precious materials. However, they are primarily an organizing device, coordinating the fingers, voice, and ears. If used in the prescribed manner, they offer "something to hold onto."[30]

The World of Islam

The art of Islam spans nearly fourteen centuries, three continents, and a wide range of cultures. The Islamic faith originated in seventh-century Arabia with the teachings and revelations of the Prophet Muhammad and quickly spread to Africa, Asia, southeastern Europe, and China.

Despite this vast geographic expanse, a long, tumultuous history, and the significant cultural differences that Islam encompasses, its art has retained a distinct identity. In each area to which Islam spread, local traditions were integrated with Islamic motifs to create new modes of expression. Although great differences exist from region to region, strong underlying iconographic concepts unify much of the artistic output. As craftsmen were able to move freely through Islam's many countries, they concentrated in regions or urban centers with important intellectual communities and politically powerful patrons—in cities such as Damascus, Baghdad, Isfahan, Constantinople, Córdoba, Timbuktu, and Cairo. New styles and techniques were constantly integrated into existing regional traditions, thus creating the overriding characteristic of Islamic art—a unity in diversity.[1]

This dynamic was reinforced by vigorous commercial activity. Islamic merchants became a vital force in international trade. Caravan routes and maritime networks linked Islam's mercantile centers with Scandinavia, Africa, China, and India, resulting in a remarkable diffusion of Islamic styles, techniques, materials, and products. Mosaic glass beads found in ninth- to eleventh-century Viking sites in Sweden and Denmark, for example, strongly suggest Syrian or Egyptian influence and perhaps even origin (Bead Chart 366).

Many regions that became part of the Islamic world already had long histories of

82. *Glass beadmaking flourished in the Islamic world from A.D. 700 to 1400. Adopting manufacturing techniques from earlier Egyptian and Roman practices and using traditional Islamic designs, Egyptian and western Asian craftsmen fashioned great quantities of glass beads. Theirs was the last great phase of ancient glassmaking. This early Islamic necklace of combed, marvered, and gold-in-glass beads has concentric circular beads resembling designs of Christian amulets from Syria that appeared after A.D. 400.[1] Length, 51 cm. Metropolitan Museum of Art, New York*

The World of Islam:
Distribution of Beads and Bead Materials,
A.D. 600 to 1400

Baltic Amber
to Iran

Amber

Glass Beads,
Glass Ingots,
Carnelian, and Silver
from Middle East
to Scandinavia
800–1100

Venice

Black Sea

Constantinople

SPAIN

Toledo

Córdoba

Coral

Tangier

Algiers

Tunis

Tripoli

Mediterranean Sea

MOROCCO

SAHARA

Alexandria

Cairo

Cairo Local:
Beads of:
Coral, Ivory
Pearls, Cowries
Glass 10th C.;
Lapis Lazuli
Rock, Crystal
Amethyst, Onyx
Turquoise
Carnelian
Glass 12th C.

Gold and Ivory
to Europe

Timbuktu

Agadez

R. Niger

AFRICA

TURKEY

Jet

R. Euphrates

R. Tigris

Pearls

Damascus

Sidon, Tyre

Jerusalem

Glass Beadmaking

Baghdad

Isfahan

SUMER

Carmana

Turquoise
Copper

ARABIA

Dilmun

Gold

R. Nile

Mecca

Onyx
Carnelian

Red Sea

YEMEN

OMAN

Silver,
Turquoise,
and Etched
Carnelians
to Russia

R. Amu Darya

Glass Beadmaking
c. 1400

Samarkand

IRAN

Kabul

Turquoise

R. Indus

Lapis Lazuli
from Badakhshan
to Islamic World

R. Ganges

INDIA

Chlorite
Peridot

Cambay

R. Narmada

Agate
Carnelian

▲ *Limodra*

Agate and
Carnelian
Beads

to
S.E.
Asia

Glass
Beads

Pearls

SRI LANKA

Rubies
Spinel
Sapphire

Ivory,
Rubies,
Pearls, and
Onyx to Oman
10th C.

to Cairo

to
East
Africa

Indian Ocean

Glass
Beads
from
Cairo to
Sub-Saharan
Africa

Glass Beads
from Middle East
to Southeast Asia

Gold and
Ivory from
Africa to
Europe and
Middle East

Balas Rubies (Afghanistan),
Coral (Mediterranean),
Pearls (Gulf of Mannar),
Rubies (Sri Lanka),
Quartz Crystal,
Garnets, Emeralds,
Carnelian, and
Cat's-Eye (India),
to China 14th C.

LEGEND

Gold   Source of Materials

Gold   Movement of Beads
       and/or Bead Materials

●   Present-Day City

▲   Archaeological Site:
    Beadmaking and/or
    Distribution Center

←→   Trans-Saharan Trade
     Routes

◉   Bead Emporium

94

trading and cultural exchange. For millennia, finished beads and their raw materials had moved over sea and caravan routes into the Arabian peninsula, home to some of the earliest western Asian civilizations. In the Arabian Gulf, Bahrain served as a trading post between the cities of Mesopotamia and the Indus Valley. Quantities of beads have been found on the island of Bahrain, the site of the ancient city of Dilmun, which had established trade links with the Sumerians of southern Mesopotamia by 2500 B.C.[2]

A vast array of bead materials was traded within Islamic lands, particularly from the tenth through the fourteenth century. Between A.D. 900 and 1000, Cairo became an important center for beadmakers, who imported, processed, and traded coral, pearls, cowrie shells, and African ivory. Cairene artisans also made and exported silver, bronze, and glass ornaments, including beads. By the twelfth century, beads of lapis lazuli from Badakhshan, turquoise from Kirman and Nishapur, as well as rock crystal, amethyst, carnelian, and glass, were all so common in Cairo that they suffered price cuts. Only fine onyx from India and Yemen maintained its value at this time. Mecca was also a great center for buying and selling prayer beads of materials from around the world.[3]

The medieval Muslims were accomplished mariners. From the tenth to the fourteenth century, they shipped agates from western Asia to Mecca, Cairo, and Alexandria, from where they were dispersed throughout the Islamic world. Traders carried agate and glass beads from the Red Sea to the east coast of Africa, establishing permanent outposts in which beads were traded for ivory. At this time, Islamic ships carried Ceylonese rubies, Indian carnelian, emeralds, and garnets, and pearls, coral, and cat's-eye to China, where they were fabricated into beads. Marco Polo recorded that at Baghdad, pearls from India (and presumably the Arabian Gulf) were drilled and exported to Europe in great numbers.[4]

The manufacture of Islamic glass beads was the last important phase of traditional western Asian glass beadmaking. The Islamic world included many regions in which significant artistic styles and glass manufacturing techniques had already evolved, notably Egypt, Mesopotamia, Syria, the Levant, and Sasanian Persia. Although Islamic craftsmen developed their own glassmaking aesthetics, their repertory was built upon the pre-Islamic traditions. Recalling technical and stylistic concepts that originated nearly four thousand years earlier in Mesopotamia and Egypt, fine Islamic glass beads were primarily derived from Roman Period beads made after the division of the empire in the late fourth century A.D. Islamic glass beads developed their own distinctive dragged and trailed, feathered, festooned, and folded patterns. Glass beadmaking centers of note were in Egypt, Syria, and the Levant. Recent archaeological excavations in the Jewish quarter of the Old City of Jerusalem uncovered evidence of a glass workshop that produced vessels at various times between A.D. 661 and 1250, but it is not clear if beads were also part of their production.[5]

Islam is an all-encompassing religion: faith is the center of a Muslim's life, and religious principles guide all endeavors, including art and design. To prevent idolatry, Islamic art has remained primarily abstract and symbolic, consistently avoiding pictorial representations of the divine. Four basic patterns of decoration are used: geometric, floral, and calligraphic designs, and stylized animal and human figures. This "language of decoration" provided a unified framework of imagery within which Islamic craftsmen have had considerable freedom of expression. Islamic design is rich and intricate, but details were rarely isolated ends in themselves. The artists' highest priorities, whether in carpets, tiles, furniture, or beads, are the beauty of overall design and harmony of color.[6]

83. *A faceted glass cornerless-cube bead ground or cut by lapidary methods in the seventh-century A.D. Length, 2.7 cm. Private collection*

ABOVE: 84. *Faceted lapis lazuli beads made in Iran between the ninth and the sixteenth century* A.D. *Craftsmen in early medieval Islamic countries, especially Iran, developed faceting in tandem with their interest in polyhedral forms. Mathematics was considered an integral part of art, reflecting the underlying geometric patterns in nature. Faceting stones into polyhedral forms articulated that relationship. Second bead from right: length, 2.1 cm. Collection Henry Anavian, New York*

RIGHT: 85. *A necklace of opaque black wound-glass beads, probably made in Iran between* A.D. *900 and 1300, with typical geometric and arabesque lines in repetitive patterns. Largest bead: diameter, 3.2 cm. Corning Museum of Glass, Corning, New York*

Within the Islamic world, beads serve as status symbols, portable wealth, and amulets. Amulets were worn primarily by women and children, who were thought to require more protection than men: nowhere is the eye bead worn more often to avert the evil eye than in Arab countries. Men wear the *subha*, a strand of thirty-nine or ninety-nine prayer beads corresponding to the ninety-nine "beautiful names" of Allah. The Koran refers to stars as "beads of the sky."[7] Stars (like beads) are bright and shining "heavenly eyes" which offer protection by lighting up the darkened skies.[8]

It has generally been true throughout Islamic history that an individual's wealth determines which materials will be used for his or her beads. In Islamic lands today, the choice of jewelry usually distinguishes townspeople from poorer villagers and nomads. Urban women tend to wear gold and precious stones, while women who live in the countryside, such as the Bedouin, wear chain and beaded necklaces of brass, silver, copper, and glass. In the past, wood, ivory, amber, semiprecious and precious stones like carnelian, lapis lazuli, turquoise, and agate were all expensive and equally favored for their talismanic value. Turquoise, *fayruz* in Arabic, means "lucky stone" and is believed to protect the wearer from poison, reptile bites, and diseases of the eye; by changing color—after exposure to heat and sunlight, turquoise frequently changes color—it warns of the approach of death.[9] Throughout western Asia, wearing carnelian jewelry is thought to repel evil and offer protection against the envious. Its great popularity among Muslims is said to stem from the fact that Muhammad himself wore a ring set with carnelian that he used as a seal.[10] Lapis lazuli beads were common in children's jewelry. Fashions have also governed the choice of beads: in Iran during the eleventh and twelfth centuries, glazed white quartz was particularly in demand.[11]

The role of beads in Islamic cultures may well have been enhanced by the importance accorded to circles and spheres in medieval Islamic thought. The Koran, Islam's holy book, emphasizes the relationship between the visible world and underlying reality, a philosophy that encouraged the exploration of relationships between design principles and mathematics. Muslims consider mathematics an integral part of art and believe that geometric patterns underlie all natural phenomena. For the Muslim, "The circle is the primary cosmological symbol, one of wholeness and unity."[12] By the twelfth century, Arab mathematicians, exploring theoretical geometry and the philosophy of Platonic solids, discovered that all regular and semiregular forms are based on the sphere. From the basic circle and a hexagonal arrangement of tangential circles of the same radius surrounding it, three primary shapes emerge: the triangle, the hexagon, and the square. During the tenth, eleventh, and twelfth centuries, artisans, particularly, Iranians, fas-

ABOVE LEFT: 86. *Similar in design to a Moorish architectural column, this cylindrical gold bead from sixteenth-century Spain is set with emeralds and rubies. Gold filigree scrolls serve as cloisons for white, green, blue, and violet enamel. Openwork filigree balls decorate the ends. This bead possibly served as a cassolette for scent.*[11] *Length, 5.2 cm. Hispanic Society of America, New York*

ABOVE MIDDLE: 87. *An unusual late Islamic gold bead from eighteenth-century Morocco, set with emeralds and rubies (or garnets). Length, 2.49 cm. Metropolitan Museum of Art, New York*

ABOVE RIGHT: 88. *Gold openwork filigree beads with granulation, a combination of techniques perfected by Syrian and Egyptian artisans in the tenth and eleventh centuries A.D. The openwork filigree has been constructed without additional support. These beads exemplify the Islamic artistic ideal of balancing pure geometry with flowing, organic forms. Biconical bead: length, 5 cm. Metropolitan Museum of Art, New York*

cinated by the ideas of the sphere as the minimal unit of design, developed a whole family of patterns based on a five- and ten-part division of the circle. In accordance with these principles, polyhedral beads were developed by faceting spheres into hexagons and octagons. The practice of grinding stones into complex geometric forms also indicates that bead craftsmen had learned of the natural crystalline structure of the stones they were working.[13]

The use of gold and silver filigree patterns superimposed over spherical beads was another technique used by Islamic artisans to make complex geometric forms. The art of filigree reached a high level of technical and aesthetic perfection among medieval Islamic smiths, which permitted the manufacture of strong, lightweight hollow forms that required less gold. Gold polyhedral beads were often "filigree illusions," in that wires and tiny granulated balls were adhered to the surface of a hollow gold or silver bead, so that the edges of the resulting polygons hid an underlying spherical form.[14]

There may be an intriguing link between astronomy and these filigree techniques in medieval Islamic beads. Islamic craftsmen mastered filigree beadmaking just as mathematicians and Moorish navigators were recording that astrological patterns in the sky had correlations in the contours of the land and channels of the seas. Their findings were mapped with intricate linear constructions. These patterns, which were often drawn on globes, may well have served as prototypes for the first Islamic filigree beads.[15]

Not many gold beads remain from the early and medieval periods of Islam. Items of openwork filigree are very fragile, and jewelry made of precious metals was often melted down later into more fashionable shapes. Furthermore, there were probably never great quantities of filigree beads. Islam used gold sparingly, since the Koran calls for moderation in adornment, as in other things.

However, silver jewelry, including silver beads, was considered less ostentatious than gold and was worn in abundance throughout the Islamic world. In Tunisia, for example, silver was considered a symbol of truth and purity, while gold was associated with vice. Arabic euphemisms express the financial importance of jewelry, noting that "metals are for hard times," and "jewelry is for adornment and investment."[16]

In early nomadic and seminomadic Islamic cultures, craftspeople were often despised because their work did not contribute directly to the livelihood of the tribe. Silversmiths and goldsmiths were therefore often outsiders; frequently, they were Christians, Sabittes, or Jews rather than Muslims. The Jewish smiths of Sana in Yemen were famed throughout the Arab world for their craftsmanship.[17] Most of the Jewish Yemenite community emigrated in the 1950s, and their silversmithing traditions are now practiced in Israel.

Dating Islamic stone beads is often difficult. One reason for this is that Islam prohibits the burial of worldly goods. Even when this law was ignored, the stone beads found in burials are generally spherical or barrel-shaped forms, which were produced prolifically over the centuries and are not easily datable. There are exceptions, including the amulet-case (Bead Chart 526) and faceted beads, which can occasionally be dated by quality, material, and technical complexity. For reasons of finance and fashion, the majority of Islamic gold and silver beads have been melted down over the centuries. The relatively few surviving metal beads are dated primarily by their manufacturing techniques, since design patterns have changed little through time. Beaded necklaces were also regularly restrung and recombined from generation to generation, further eliminating historical clues.

Thanks to the profusion of glass vessels and objects created during the revival of glassmaking under Islamic rule, glass beads are less difficult to date. Most of the Islamic beads preserved from the seventh to the fourteenth centuries are made of glass, and have distinctive geometric, combed, feathered, festooned, and folded patterns with stylistic and technical parallels in Islamic glassware of the period. Also, it may soon be possible to assign Islamic glass beads accurate dates, as well as manufacturing locations, by studying the color of glass. Archaeological finds are not only revealing that patterns of distinctive colors changed over time, but that most glassmaking centers seemed to specialize in certain colors.[18] That specialization probably reflects not only the vagaries of taste, but also the availability of minerals and coloring agents which were obtained through trade.

Mongol conquests of western Asia in the fourteenth century ended major glass manufacturing in the region, a tradition that had lasted more than thirty-five hundred years. When Tamerlane captured Damascus in 1401, many craftsmen were removed to Samarkand. This included beadmakers from Tyre, where glass beads had been continuously produced since Phoenician times.

Although isolated glassmaking continued in regions of Egypt, Iran, Syria, Jordan, and Turkey, activity now centered on the West. By the fifteenth century, Venice had become the bead-producing capital of the world.

OPPOSITE, RIGHT: 90. Nineteenth-century necklace from Oman made of Austro-Hungarian Maria Theresa silver dollars (thalers) and silver beads. Oman was a prosperous international commercial center renowned over the centuries for its silver-work. From the mid-1700s until the 1930s, the chief source of silver for Omani artisans was the thaler, which had a consistently high silver content. The quality of silver was important because jewelry was bought both for adornment and investment.

The form of this necklace is traditional: thalers are linked by silver beads to a decorated medallion. The geometric and floral patterns are characteristically Islamic. Original pieces of this quality are rare, as silver was often melted down to make new, more fashionable jewelry.[IV] Central medallion: diameter, 9.8 cm. Private collection

The Age of European Expansion

From the Renaissance until the Industrial Revolution, beads occupied a minor place in European adornment. Lavish jewelry, reflecting the abundance of precious stones and metal flowing into Europe from colonies in the Americas and the East, dominated courtly and aristocratic fashion. Although beads were not greatly coveted by Europeans after the Renaissance, European glassmakers nevertheless mass-produced huge quantities of beads which were carried by explorers and traders to non-European peoples around the globe. Selling for great profits in the foreign markets, beads were an important component in the newly developed global trading networks. By the nineteenth century, new materials and manufacturing techniques enabled most Europeans to own jewelry, and as social mores discouraged ostentatious displays of precious jewels, beads once again came into style and were worn by all classes of people.

Shortly before 1500, technical improvements in navigation gave Europeans the ability and confidence to sail great distances. In rapid succession, bold captains ventured into previously unknown seas: Columbus landed in the Americas in 1492; Vasco da Gama reached India in 1498; and by 1519 Magellan had sailed around the tip of South America. Europe was now linked by sea to most of the earth's shores.

Prior to 1500, the Islamic world, India, and China had far wealthier and more sophisticated civilizations than Europe. Yet, within three hundred and fifty years, the balance was reversed. By 1850, Europeans controlled the oceans, had established colonies in Africa, Asia, and the Americas, and were running organized, immensely profitable worldwide commercial transactions. The expansion of European civilization was preceded by a period of significant change within Europe itself. In western Europe, during the late 1300s, there were secular challenges to church doctrine. Intellectual cu-

91. One hundred and twenty decorated wound-glass beads, most of which are from the nineteenth century. Beads of this type were made in vast quantities: distinct varieties number in the thousands. Illustrated here are a few of the less common types found in West Africa in recent years.[1]

From the late fifteenth to the twentieth century, explorers and traders carried European glass beads throughout the world. The beads were enormously popular in Africa and North America in particular. The result of this seemingly inexhaustible demand led to a proliferation of bead types, designs, and manufacturing techniques. Sizes ranged from micro (less than 1 millimeter) to macro

riosity focused on understanding and exploring the natural world. Through transla-
tions of Islamic works on medicine, mathematics, and astronomy, Westerners discovered
that the Muslims possessed sophisticated scientific knowledge far surpassing what was
available in Latin.[1] By the mid-fifteenth century a resurgence of interest in the classical
arts and sciences, known as the Renaissance, started in Italy. More than a thousand
years had elapsed since the decline of the Roman Empire, but Italians now looked to
their magnificent past for philosophical and artistic inspiration. Latin and Greek clas-
sics opened up a vision of life unencumbered by church doctrine, in which individual
expression was of central concern. With the intensified interest in ancient Greek and
Roman culture, aesthetic standards embodied in their writings, sculpture, and architecture became ideal norms. In painting and sculpture, systems of perspective, effects
of color, and realistic treatments of nature and the human form—expressed, for example, in the works of Michelangelo and Leonardo da Vinci—were investigated.[2] The
Renaissance spread throughout the Continent, profoundly affecting every aspect of
European life, including adornment. In contrast to medieval proscriptions, the wearing
of jewelry was embraced as an important component of dress.

By the mid-fifteenth century, necklines of women's clothing began to fall, and for
a brief period during the early Italian Renaissance jewelry ceased to convey status and
rank, serving instead simply to enhance female beauty. The new fashion was inspired
by the aesthetics of classical art and the study of human anatomy. In the late fifteenth
century, Sandro Botticelli portrayed Simonetta Vespucci with pearls entwined in her
flowing hair. Portraits by Piero della Francesca, for example, show simple bead necklaces of coral, garnets, and pearls setting off the sitter's slender neck or emphasizing
the soft beauty of the breast.[3] This short interlude of harmony between body, dress, and
ornament was soon replaced, however, by more aggressive jewelry styles that relegated
beads to a minor place in European adornment until the nineteenth century.

Jewelry of the late Renaissance and baroque periods (c. 1550–1750) reflected the
plentiful supplies of precious stones and metals that began to pour into Europe from
the Americas and the East (particularly India), a result of the new overseas colonies.
The fashion was to display wealth and power. Introduced by the Spanish court, whose
territories in the New World provided an abundance of gold, pearls, and emeralds, lavish, autocratic standards in dress and jewelry soon spread to other European courts
profiting from colonial resources.

The restraint shown in the early Renaissance disappeared. Court adornment typically included heavy gold chains, enameled and jeweled pendants, rings on every finger,
and precious stones and pearls sewn into clothing. The treasures of Europe's royal families epitomized this display of riches: the crown jewels of a country, a significant concentration of treasure, were not only symbols of status but were even pledged as surety
against loans and frequently used to underwrite the payroll for armies and govern-
ments. A heavy, ninety-eight-ounce gold chain worn by Henry VIII, for example,
served a dual purpose. Beyond its regal appearance, each link represented a unit of
currency; in times of fiscal emergency, the links could be removed and used for pay-
ments.[4] Thus, the weight and intrinsic value of these particular metals and gems were
of prime political importance.

As a result of the access to great supplies of precious stones—emeralds from
South America, colored gems from the East, diamonds from India and eventually Brazil—the cutting and polishing of stones was admired as a new science. Soft, rounded
cabochon forms were almost entirely replaced by the sharper geometric style of the lapidary.[5] By the baroque period, jewelry was designed primarily to display stones, par-

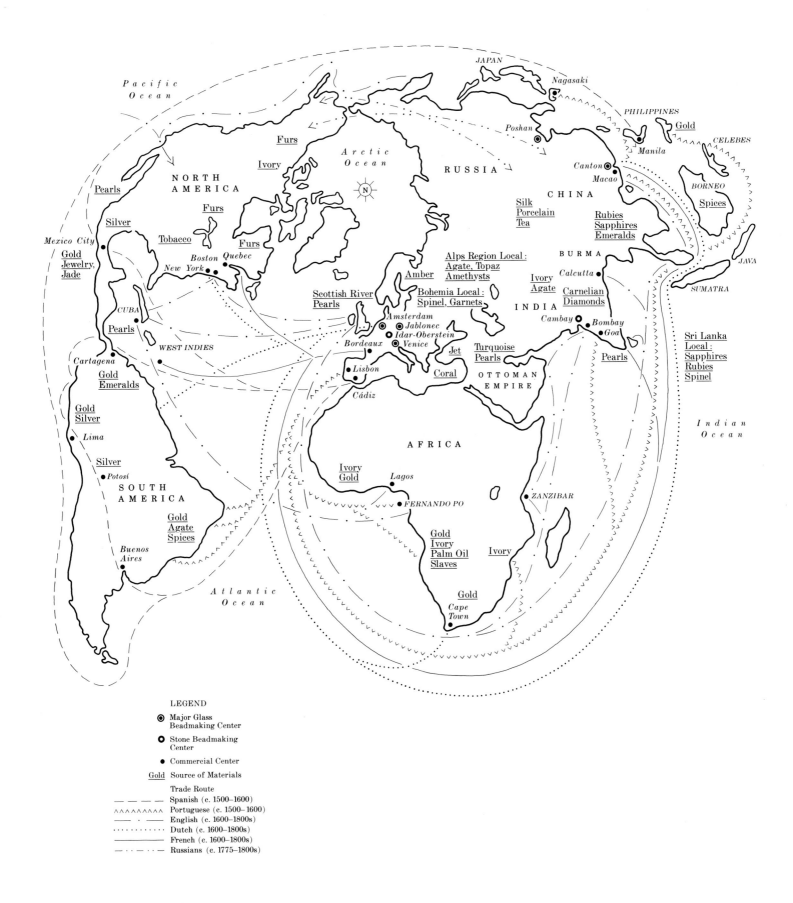

The Age of European Expansion:
1500 to 1850 A.D.

*Pacific
Ocean*

Furs

Ivory

*Arctic
Ocean*

RUSSIA

JAPAN

Nagasaki

Poshan

PHILIPPINES

Gold

Manila

CELEBES

NORTH
AMERICA

Pearls

Silver

Mexico City

Gold
Jewelry,
Jade

Furs

Tobacco

Boston *Quebec*

New York

Furs

Canton

Macao

CHINA

Silk
Porcelain
Tea

Rubies
Sapphires
Emeralds

BORNEO

Spices

BURMA

Amber

Alps Region Local:
Agate, Topaz
Amethysts

Scottish River
Pearls

Bohemia Local:
Spinel, Garnets

Calcutta

Ivory
Agate

Carnelian
Diamonds

JAVA

SUMATRA

INDIA

CUBA

Pearls

WEST INDIES

Amsterdam

Jablonec

Idar-Oberstein

Bordeaux

Venice

Jet

Turquoise
Pearls

Cambay

Bombay

Goa

Pearls

Sri Lanka
Local:
Sapphires
Rubies
Spinel

Cartagena

Gold
Emeralds

Lisbon

Coral

OTTOMAN
EMPIRE

Cádiz

*Indian
Ocean*

Gold
Silver

Lima

Silver

Potosí

SOUTH
AMERICA

AFRICA

Ivory
Gold

Lagos

ZANZIBAR

Gold
Agate
Spices

*Buenos
Aires*

FERNANDO PO

Gold
Ivory
Palm Oil
Slaves

Ivory

*Atlantic
Ocean*

Gold

*Cape
Town*

LEGEND

◉ Major Glass
  Beadmaking Center

◍ Stone Beadmaking
  Center

● Commercial Center

<u>Gold</u> Source of Materials

Trade Route

— — — — Spanish (c. 1500–1600)

ΛΛΛΛΛΛΛ Portuguese (c. 1500–1600)

— · — · — English (c. 1600–1800s)

· · · · · · · · Dutch (c. 1600–1800s)

———— French (c. 1600–1800s)

— ·· — ·· — Russians (c. 1775–1800s)

ticularly faceted diamonds, to their best advantage.

There were, nonetheless, some beads worthy of being worn by the elite. Queen Isabella, who ruled Spain with King Ferdinand from 1474 to 1516, and whose jewels backed Columbus's voyages to the New World, ordered her merchants to bring her beads. Inventory records kept for Isabella include bead necklaces of twenty-two-karat gold, amber, coral, jasper, and crystalline (possibly glass) beads, as well as jet beads shaped like crosses. Pearls were also gathered for her in enormous quantities: an inventory of 1499 notes she had strings with more than two hundred pearls on them.[6]

Moorish jewelry of the fifteenth and sixteenth centuries included thinly pierced gold beads from the province of Almería and hollow, enameled gold beads that contained scent.[7] In Venice, fine filigree came back into fashion toward the end of the sixteenth century. The best example of this is known from a necklace of beads in the Museo Poldi-Pezzoli in Milan. Each bead is constructed of fine openwork gold filigree decorated with stylized flowers in green and blue enamel. Faceted amber beads were sometimes capped with gold filigree.[8]

From the late sixteenth to the early eighteenth century elaborate pearl necklaces and bracelets accompanied extravagant displays of pearls embroidered onto clothing. The pearls were obtained from the Persian Gulf, the East Indies, and freshwater mountain streams in Saxony, Bohemia, and Bavaria. After 1675, when demand outstripped supply, Parisian craftsmen perfected imitation pearls (which had first been made in the 1400s). They lined the interiors of hollow glass beads with a nacreous solution of ground-up blackfish scales (found in the Seine), which was stabilized with wax.[9]

A new phase of jewelry design began with the Industrial Revolution, which was under way in England by the mid-eighteenth century and in full swing throughout the Continent by the nineteenth century. The emergence of a large middle class changed demands and customs. New materials and manufacturing techniques brought great quantities of fine jewelry within the reach of a mass audience. In earlier times, faience and glass beads had essentially fulfilled the same purpose, working with the available technology of their eras.

Before the nineteenth century, precious ornaments directly reflected the social rank of the wearer. This relationship was altered by the Industrial Revolution as well as by political events. The French Revolution and the revolutions of 1848 were generally followed by periods of austerity in reaction to court excesses: these were not times of luxury or display. As a result, the aristocracy altered their tastes. Beads of coral, amber, rock crystal, and glass were worn not only by the middle class, but also by the nobility for daytime jewelry. Cut-steel beads and cast-iron jewelry were substituted for precious stones and metal. The recessions that reigned over Europe after the Napoleonic Wars contributed to the rapid development of cast-iron jewelry after 1815. Cast-iron jewelry was already known in Paris by the time of the French Revolution, and there was a saying "I gave gold for iron." Garnet beads, made by town craftsmen and traded at marketplaces, were popular with rural people.[10]

Parures (sets) of Mediterranean coral and English jet beads were worn by wealthy European women during the 1830s.[11] After 1827, jet was used as "mourning" jewelry, a practice that continued throughout the century after Prince Albert's death in 1861 led his widow, Queen Victoria, to keep mourning almost constantly fashionable in England.[12] Mourning jewelry reached morbid depths when human hair from the deceased was woven into beaded necklaces.[13]

Nineteenth-century design was eclectic. The evolving mass-production techniques of the industrial age produced considerable concern that fine craftsmanship would disappear; thus, a demand developed for the styles of the past. Stimulated by archaeolog-

92. *An 1850s beaded bag from France. (The metal frame closure was added c. 1920.) Tiny glass "seed" beads (one-half millimeter to one millimeter long) crocheted with silk thread form the floral pattern. Although most European glass beads were exported, small, round seed and tubular "bugle" beads were used for embroidering clothing and accessories, a custom fashionable since the Renaissance. Length (top of frame to bottom of fringe), 28 cm. Private collection*

ical explorations in Egypt, Greece, Italy, Africa, and western Asia (most notably, German classicist Heinrich Schliemann's wonderful gold finds at Troy), jewelers revived the techniques and styles of ancient adornment. The excavations uncovered examples of English Celtic and Etruscan and Greek gold filigree beads that served as excellent prototypes for new jewelry styles.

Two of the most famous neoclassical goldsmiths, Italians Fortunato Pio Castellani in Rome and Carlo Joseph Giuliano in England, rarely set stones but often included beads in their work. The prevailing interest in antiquities meant jewelers returned to polished rather than faceted stones, which they chose from a select range of carnelian, onyx, and lapis lazuli and interspersed with granulated gold beads.[14] Castellani had an important collection of ancient bead necklaces that he studied in great detail. Some of these pieces, which are now owned by the British Museum, obviously had direct influence on his work (plate 45).

It was only with the introduction of the Art Nouveau style at the end of the nineteenth century that imitations of ancient jewelry styles ceased, and a contemporary, modern aesthetic developed that affected beads as well as all forms of adornment.

The Glass Bead Industry

The most important chapter in the story of beads from the Renaissance to the twentieth century belongs to the European glass bead industry. During this period, most explorers, traders, and missionaries carried glass beads with them as gifts or objects of barter. Their activities created considerable markets, and the result was an enormous increase in the volume of bead production, accompanied by a proliferation of bead varieties as well as continual improvements and refinements in manufacturing techniques.[15]

When Europeans set sail, their hosts accepted beads for a variety of reasons. Indonesians and Filipinos coveted stone and glass beads, which they had obtained from Indian, Chinese, and Middle Eastern traders for centuries. In the New World, however, glass was completely unknown and was treasured as a rare substance when it was introduced by the Europeans. The introduction of tiny, colorful glass "seed" beads was frequently welcomed as a replacement for more labor-intensive adornment techniques. Woodland and Great Lakes tribes in North America, for example, greatly expanded the range of decorative forms and colors that could be produced on clothing and other objects, using glass seed beads rather than traditional porcupine quills.

For Europeans, whose aim was to maintain maximum profits with a minimum commitment of manpower and resources, glass beads, exchanged for American furs or African ivory, gold, and slaves, yielded enormous margins—1,000 percent was the return on investment, according to a report in 1632—and thus became a central part of international trade patterns.[16] Beads, of course, were only a part of a complex trading cycle: rum, cloth, guns, and beads were sent from Europe to Africa; slaves from Africa were taken to the New World; and sugar, tobacco, and silver and gold bullion from the New World went to Europe.[17]

An important dimension of the European commercial expansion was the ability to integrate their efforts with preexisting trade networks. As a lively bead trade had existed in most of the world for millennia, European traders frequently used the same routes, where their further success depended on identifying local bead tastes and responding with appropriate goods. The prosperity enjoyed by major glass factories in Venice, Holland, and Bohemia and Moravia (present-day Czechoslovakia) was often a result of providing specifically shaped beads in desired colors and patterns. Since tastes varied widely between countries as well as neighboring villages, the variety and quantity of beads produced was enormous.

Beads traveled circuitous routes, and unraveling the workings of the bead trade is quite complex. Carnelian beads excavated from slaves' graves in Barbados were probably from India and accompanied tribesmen from Africa. Other stone beads found in Louisiana (dated 1731–63), Florida, Tennessee, Mississippi, and Venezuela may well have been sold in the New World by the Spanish, who obtained them from English, French, Dutch, or Portuguese traders.[18]

The glass bead trade was equally complicated. It is often difficult to know whether a bead was made in Venice or Holland, the date of its manufacture, or the exact route by which it arrived at a particular site. Not only did Venetians set up glass bead workshops in Holland, France, and Bohemia and Moravia (thus dispersing Venetian techniques and styles), but many middlemen carried beads throughout the trading cycles. Nevertheless, as a result of intensive archaeological and historical research during the past decade that has focused on the glass bead trade, accurate data and chronologies are emerging.[19]

Venetian Glass Beadmaking

The earliest and most renowned European glass beadmaking centers were in Venice, Holland, and Bohemia and Moravia. Although glass factories existed in Italy, France, Switzerland, Spain, Belgium, England, Germany, and the Baltic, Venetian glassmakers dominated the world market in volume, quality, and diversity until the twentieth century.[20]

Venice's rise to glassmaking supremacy corresponded with the decline of the western Asian industries. After Tamerlane's Mongol armies overran Damascus, Tyre, Aleppo, and Sidon in 1401, glass beadmaking practices that had lasted over three thousand years were effectively ended, and quality glass was no longer produced in the region. The Venetians filled this void, successfully inheriting the role of glass beadmaker for the Western world and subsequently taking over markets in Africa and Southeast Asia that had been supplied by India for centuries.

While it is not possible to trace a continuous tradition of glassmaking from Rome to Renaissance Venice, there is much evidence to suggest that the exceptionally strong reemergence and growth of the industry during the Middle Ages was made possible by Venice's cultural and maritime ties with Byzantium and the eastern Mediterranean. It is also believed that after the Ottomans sacked Sidon and Tyre and then captured Constantinople in 1453, glassmakers from these ancient centers went to Venice.

The beginnings of Venetian glass manufacture are not clear, but the discovery of glassmaking furnaces, vessel fragments, and mosaic cubes, dating from A.D. 600 to 650, on the island of Torcello in the Venetian lagoon implies glass production occurred in the vicinity from an early point in Venice's history.[21] Venice itself was founded by the Lombards in A.D. 568.

Although glassmaking is recorded at Venetian monasteries in 882, the foundations of their great glass industry were established primarily from 1200 to 1400.[22] In 1292, all glass factories were relocated from Venice to the island of Murano, a fifteen-minute boat ride across the lagoon, to protect Venice from the risk of fires (always a possibility from the constantly burning furnaces) and to keep glassmaking procedures secret.

The production and export of beads were always important to the Venetian glass industry, even though beadmaking can be traced only to the early 1300s. At that time, Venetian galleys carried beads to the Black Sea, Flanders, and England.[23] It is known, however, that in 1279 German peddlers in Venice were restricted to buying ten lires' worth of glass rods (which were presumably for making beads); by 1280, Venice had established a glass trade with the eastern parts of the old Roman Empire; and Venetian glass was shipped to Rhodes by 1345.[24]

PLATES 93–96 *Glass beads used in the Africa trade. This important collection of glass trade beads was acquired by the British Museum in 1865 from Moses Lewin Levin, a London bead merchant whose import-export business operated from 1830 to 1913. Accurately dated manufacturer's sample cards or catalogues, such as these examples, are extremely useful for documenting what was being produced and sold at a specific time and place.*

Most of these beads appear to be Venetian, although in 1898 the Levin Company was listed as an importer of Venetian, Bohemian, and German beads. While it is recorded that the beads were used for barter in Africa, many were also traded into North America.[11] Collection of the British Museum at the Museum of Mankind, London

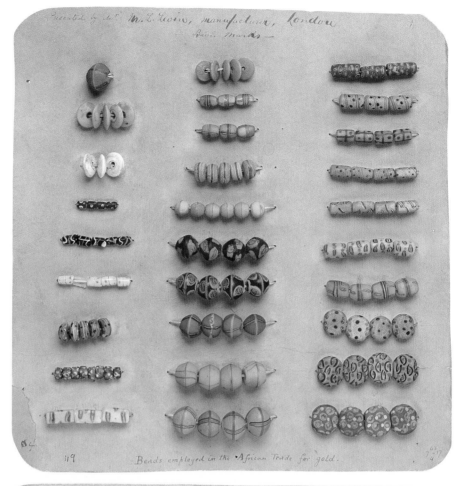

108

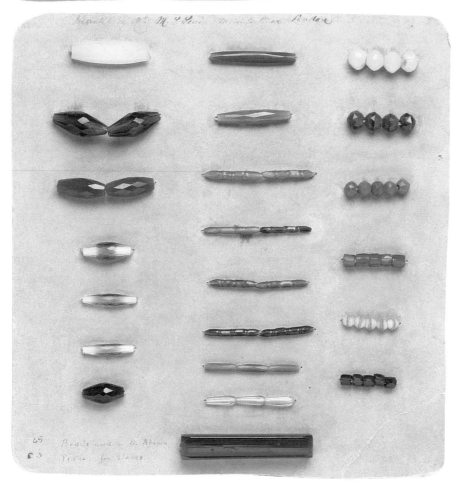

OPPOSITE, TOP: 93. *Beads traded in Africa for gold. Top left bead: diameter, 1.69 cm.*

OPPOSITE, BOTTOM: 94. *Beads traded in Africa for ivory. Top left bead: diameter, 1.48 cm.*

TOP: 95. *Beads traded in Africa for palm oil. Top left bead: length, 3.2 cm.*

BOTTOM: 96. *Beads traded in Africa for slaves. Top left bead: length, 5.2 cm.*

Although Venice could offer its glass industry enormous advantages over its competitors—it had a sophisticated network of commercial relationships and a powerful mercantile trading fleet with links to the Black Sea, the Mediterranean, and northwestern Europe—the authorities feared competition. To establish and maintain their monopoly, laws were enacted in 1490 that placed the glassmakers' guild under the direct jurisdiction of the Council of Ten—the highest governing body in the Venetian Republic. For the next fifty years, Murano glassmakers were forbidden, upon penalty of death, to divulge glassmaking secrets or to leave and set up competitive establishments elsewhere.[25]

After the move to Murano, beadmaking greatly increased in volume due to important changes in glass beadmaking techniques. Furthermore, Venetian glassmakers of the period were strongly influenced by highly complex ancient Egyptian and Roman glass artifacts which they were inspired to reproduce. By about 1490, the process of drawing hollow cane beads had been reinvented and introduced to Murano. Replacing the slower winding method, drawn canes permitted the mass-production of beads in a range of sizes.[26]

Glass beads are classified by their technique of manufacture: wound, drawn, wound-on-drawn, molded, mold-pressed, and blown. Different beadmaking centers generally emphasized the use of certain techniques. For this reason, it is helpful to understand how a bead was made when trying to assign its origin and its date.

Wound glass, a labor-intensive process, involves the winding of molten glass around a metallic rod or wire, similar to the way thread is wound around a spool. By forming molten material in this manner, there is no need to drill or perforate the bead as a separate step. In the manufacture of drawn-glass beads, however, drawn canes with a central hole are produced as a raw material from which great numbers of nearly identical beads can be created in a short time. In contrast to wound-glass beads, which are individually made and therefore expensive, drawn beads are made in great numbers and are relatively cheap. At the same time, the process allows for a great diversity of pattern, color, and finished shapes.

Murano and Venetian beads typically were made by drawn or wound techniques. Although a great deal of secrecy has always surrounded the drawn-glass beadmaking operations at Murano, descriptions written in 1834 and 1919 apparently represent procedures unchanged for centuries. Fifteen separate steps—from the initial fusing of raw materials to the packing of the beads for shipment—were rigorously followed. One of the most interesting stages was the stretching of the glass into hollow tubes. A hollow globe of molten glass was attached to two metal plates with rods. Two men, each holding one of the rods, ran quickly in opposite directions, drawing out a tube of glass at least three hundred feet long. The original bubble of air remained as an orifice or tunnel running the entire length of the tube. The tube was then cut into canes, the canes were made into beads, and the beads were finished by reheating techniques (tumbling and constricting) or by lapidary methods (grinding).[27]

Depending on stylistic variations, the glass globe could be composed of several differently colored layers, for example, or twisted during the drawing process to create a spiral of colors. Drawn-cane bead types varied from small monochrome seed beads (typically used for embroidery) to striped beads, Nueva Cádiz, and *cornaline d'Aleppo* (Bead Chart 40, 44, 45, and 48).

By 1592, beadmaking was permitted again in Venice, and lamp-wound beads became an important Venetian industry. Unlike the drawn-glass techniques, which required large furnaces, extremely hot fires, and an industrial organization, wound beads—made by winding molten glass over oil lamps—were produced in small cottage industries. Essentially a handcrafted art, lamp-wound beads were first made about 1615 in a seemingly endless variety of designs, including floral sprays, combed beads, eye beads, and mosaic glass (Bead Chart 55, 71, and 74). These were not secret processes, and they are continued today in Venice.[28]

It is estimated that there were more than one hundred thousand varieties of bead types and designs produced in Venice and Murano.[29] Particularly important types for commercial trade were glass seed and chevron beads (plate 101). Chevron (also called "star" or "rosetta") beads were sophisticated beads made from an early date with a complex manufacturing sequence that included compounding layers of materials and molding, drawing, dividing, and hand-finishing the beads.

The Venetians also reinvented mosaic glass beads using drawn techniques of compound and composite canes, similar to ancient Roman methods. They simplified the production of intricate designs and patterns by inventing molding techniques. Although these methods were known by the late 1400s, they were not widely used until the 1800s, when cottage industries producing lamp-wound beads flourished.[30]

By 1817, new processes introduced into the beadmaking industry included machinery to make perfectly round beads and the development of an extremely tiny microbead, frequently less than one millimeter in diameter. As their minuscule holes made them nearly impossible to thread, they quickly went out of circulation.[31]

An indication of the volume of Venice's bead production can be seen in the number of glassworks that were established. Between 1500 and 1525 there were 24 glass factories in Murano; by 1606, 251 bead firms were recorded in Venice alone. In 1764, forty-four thousand pounds of beads were produced weekly at 22 Venetian manufacturers —numerous smaller houses appear to have merged into several larger ones. After the Republic of Venice fell to Napoleon in 1797, the industry suffered a setback as many workmen were taken to France. The number of establishments on Murano decreased to 12 by 1836. When Venice recovered from the Napoleonic Wars, however, large quantities of beads were produced once again. Venetian shipments to the United States alone during the 1880s amounted to six million pounds of beads yearly.[32]

By the eighteenth century, Venice had a near-monopoly on the glass bead market. It was not possible, however, to maintain this position indefinitely. Local industries and markets had existed within Europe—in Germany, the Baltic, Bohemia, and Moravia— since the early Middle Ages, frequently supplying glass beads for rosaries. With help from renegade Venetians, the Bohemians, Moravians, and Dutch developed their own thriving bead industries.

Bohemian and Moravian Beadmaking

Glass beads are known to have been made in Bohemia and Moravia (today, provinces of Czechoslovakia) as early as the tenth century. In comparison to Venice, the region was at a marketing disadvantage, located far from populous European districts. Yet, vast northern hardwood (beech and oak) forests provided adequate supplies of fuel for glassmaking furnaces and ash for alkali (materials in short supply in Venice), compensating for the cost of transporting beads great distances.[33]

By the seventeenth century the Bohemians and Moravians had learned Venetian beadmaking secrets. By the end of the century, they were sufficiently organized to trade their beads abroad, in particular to the Baltic, Russia, Scandinavia, Holland, France, England, Spain, and the Ottoman Empire. After the mid-eighteenth century, their beads were found in all parts of the world.[34]

While there are often similarities between Venetian and Bohemian beads (the Bo-

111

100. *A 1903 catalogue
from the Shell Novelty
Company in New York
City shows the impor-
tance of European-
made beads in Ameri-
can fashions of the
early twentieth cen-
tury. The bunch of
10,000 beads shown in
the lower right hand
corner cost twenty-five
cents; the "Apache"
beadwork loom (upper
right) was priced at
sixty cents. For two
dollars, one could pur-
chase a complete bead-
ing outfit, including
the loom, 25 needles,
5 packages of assorted
beads, a spool of
thread, and 24 original
Indian designs.*

aggressive marketing. All operations, including cutting, coloring, drilling, and trading of the agates were tightly controlled by the same families for generations.[45]

Idar-Oberstein beads had elegant, smooth geometric forms, precisely drilled holes, and finished details, such as slightly larger holes at the end, so that threads holding the beads would not be chafed. It is of considerable interest to note that until 1966, when supersonic drills were finally used, all perforations were made with bow drills. Other than the extremely long, olive-shaped agates, which were drilled from two sides, all Idar-Oberstein beads are drilled through from one side (plate 98).[46]

The hues of the beads were particularly notable and had much to do with their popularity. The beads were artificially colored: nondescript gray agates were changed through a variety of techniques into stones of intense black, brown and white, red or-ange, and blue and green. The stronger colors were apparently desirable in many parts of Africa, as tribesmen believed that the stronger the color, the more protective powers were passed on to the wearer. Red, the color of blood, symbolized life. Hence, the wear-ing of dark red carnelian was believed to strengthen the owner's vitality. Apparently, it was not important if the color was natural or artificial.[47]

Flexibility to make a wide variety of shapes in a number of patterns and colors and the ability of the German merchants to identify the needs of specific African mar-kets contributed greatly to sales volumes. Idar-Oberstein beads significantly under-mined the Indian agate and carnelian industry, which had been supplying stone beads to Africa for centuries.

Beadmaking in France, England, and Spain

Although Roman glassmaking traditions contin-ued in France during the early Middle Ages, there is no obvious proof that bead manufactur-ing continued up to the Renaissance. The paternos-ters, however, had their own guild to make rosaries, dating from 1593. By 1750, glass beads were made in many cities, including Nevers, Dangu, Aubermesnil, and Villers. It is probable that beads of French manu-facture were traded to the Americas and Africa.[48]

There is no evidence that England ever produced glass beads for export during her reign as a colonial power. Beads brought to the Americas, India, and Africa by Eng-lish merchants were apparently obtained from Europe and, by the 1800s, from China.[49]

Spanish traders brought a variety of beads to the New World in the early sixteenth and seventeenth centuries. Beads distributed in the earlier days of their trade included Nueva Cádiz varieties, faceted chevrons, eye beads, and compound beads (some with three layers of color). There were also monochrome beads in a variety of sizes, ranging from seed beads in yellow, green, and blue to larger, predominantly blue spheres. By the mid-1600s, most of the complex, more ornate beads had disappeared.[50] Spherical tur-quoise blue beads (the "padre" bead; Bead Chart 1023) continued as one of the most popular types.[51] While the Spanish are reported to have made glass beads, all evidence suggests they were primarily carriers and traders of Venetian products.

The rise of the Venetian, Dutch, and Bohemian and Moravian bead industries and their domination of the world's bead market for over three hundred years had partic-ularly profound consequences for India. German stone and European glass bead pro-duction seriously undercut Indian bead manufacturers, who had been trading with Africa and Southeast Asia since before the Christian Era.

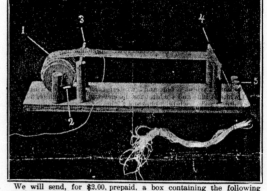

Chevron Beads

Perhaps no other bead has been as popular as the chevron. First invented in about 1500 by the Venetians, they continue to be produced up to the present time.[V] Throughout the seventeenth century, the Dutch also manufactured chevrons after Venetian glassmakers escaped from their tightly controlled industry.[VI] For almost five hundred years, these beads have been produced in the many millions and in several hundred varieties. The examples here are from a special group collected in West Africa—the greatest repository of antique European trade beads—from 1968 to 1985.

Chevrons are a specialized cane or drawn-glass bead. They are formed by forcing or blowing a single- or multiple-layered gather of glass into a tapered mold with corrugated sides, thus producing points on its outer surface.[VII] This pleated gather is subsequently encased with additional glass layers of various colors, which may again be molded to produce further outer layers with points. Finally, stripes may be applied to the surface. Still viscid, this multilayered, hollow gather is then quickly drawn into a cane (hence the terms "drawn" or "cane") of at least six feet, cooled, and finally sectioned into beads. These sections are often reheated or ground to produce a more finished product in various new shapes. The illustrations here include chevrons with from two to eight layers and a variety of points; twelve was the most common.

Figures 1–3 and 5 of plate 101 are examples of the first chevrons produced by the Venetians from 1500 to perhaps as late as the early 1600s.[VIII] All of these beads have seven layers, with the first and third layers (core to surface) a transparent or translucent light green (fig. 9). Although the outer layer is typically a translucent cobalt blue, figure 3 demonstrates black and green were used as well. Molded layers with twelve points are the most common.

Figure 4 is a rare star bead traded into the Spanish New World (especially Peru) in the early 1500s.[IX] Who manufactured it is unknown, although the Venetians are considered the most likely contenders. (This bead, in fact, was found in Africa.)

Heat-rounded chevrons of the type illustrated in figures 6–8 and 10 were apparently produced by the Dutch during the late 1590s and over the next hundred years. Figure 9 also seems to fit best into this group. However, all of these beads may be Venetian.

Little is known about chevron production in Venice during the 1700s, and it appears relatively few were produced. Figure 11 may be an example from this period.[X] In the 1800s, the Venetians again produced chevrons in large numbers with a great variety of colors, shapes, sizes, layers, and points. The vast majority have four or six layers, in red, white, and blue. Some of the more unusual examples from this period are represented in figures 9–26.

The red chevron (fig. 21) is an exception and was not found in West Africa. It is probably Venetian, from the early 1900s, and is one of several matched chevrons from a graduated string recently discovered in the United States.[XI]

Africa

The story of African beads—perhaps more than the beads of any other part of the world—is also the story of the many contrasting life-styles that have developed in Africa. Beadmaking has been influenced by environmental factors, the availability and distribution of raw materials, and exposure to Islamic and European culture and technology during the past fourteen hundred years.

To understand the beads of Africa it is crucial to appreciate the influence of geography on African societies. The continent is home to several distinct environments: deserts, tropical rain forests, woodlands, savannas, and fertile river valleys. Natural resources are distributed unevenly within these regions, and the structure of different economic, political, and religious systems reflects variations in the natural setting. Adornment, as an expression of peoples' values and their social and economic organizations, mirrors the wide-ranging contrasts that are the essence of this continent.

When power was concentrated in a ruler who controlled valuable resources—marketable commodities like gold and ivory, for example—he generally encouraged the development of arts and crafts, both to express his power visually and to have offerings to give to the gods out of gratitude for his privileged position. Beaded objects also served to distinguish rulers from ordinary people. Thus, the ornate beadwork produced for the Yoruba king, or *oba*, and his royal court by specialized craftsmen is much more complex than that produced by the pastoral East African Turkana and Samburu for themselves (plates 115 and 137). Nevertheless, for the latter, beads are an essential component of everyday dress, worn to signify their age grade, marital status, and station in society.

Beads are an integral part of a multilayered communication system in all Afri-

102. *Merchants selling glass beads at Bida, Nigeria. All field photographs in this chapter were taken between 1976 and 1986, unless otherwise dated. All of the objects, with noted exceptions, were made between the mid-twentieth century and the present.*

119

OPPOSITE: 103. *A Zulu shaman's necklace from South Africa made of twigs, tortoiseshell, seeds, snake vertebrae, teeth, glass beads, and leather and glass beaded amulets. It is a striking example of the African capacity to combine a variety of objects into an item of adornment. Length, 132 cm. Collection Ivory Freidus*

ABOVE: 104. *A necklace of ostrich eggshell disk beads made by the Turkana tribe of Kenya. Length, 66 cm. Collection Jill and Roger Caras, New York*

LEFT: 105. *A snake vertebrae and cowrie shell necklace, known as a "gift from God" and worn by an elder from the Dinka tribe of Sudan.*[1]

OVERLEAF, TOP LEFT: 106. *A necklace of elongated granite beads made by the Dogon of Mali. Beads of hard stone have not been worked extensively in Africa, except in a few regions such as Mali and Nigeria. The round pottery beads are a contemporary creation of the Baoule people of the Ivory Coast. Center granite bead: length, 1.6 cm. Collection Craft Caravan, New York*

121

can societies. Adornment, particularly with beads, communicates cultural values in a symbolic language that expresses rank, religion, politics, and artistic attitudes. Beads are central to the lives of all Africans—from hunting-and-gathering peoples of the southern Kalahari Desert to wealthy Nigerian and Ghanaian villagers—and their ability to reflect their cultural heritage is still more pronounced in Africa than in any other part of the world.

Bead Materials An enormous range of beads and raw materials for beads has been available to Africans for centuries. Throughout the continent, there has always been widespread use of organic materials for adornment—including seeds, nuts, shells, bones, tusks, and teeth. The earliest known African beads are disk-shaped forms made of ostrich eggshells recovered from Upper Paleolithic (10,000 B.C.) sites in Libya and slightly later Neolithic sites in the Sudan. Today, ostrich eggshell is still used for some beadmaking in East Africa, and large quantities of beads are made from this durable and accessible material in the Kalahari Desert by the !Kung San.[1] Cowrie shells, valued for their durability and their shape

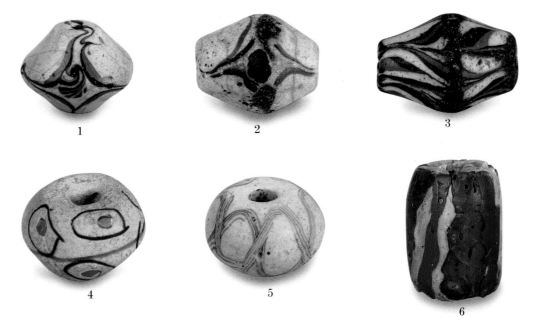

Bodom Beads

Bodom *of a certain age and design are greatly treasured today in Ghana and are thought to have magical or medicinal powers. All* bodom *are predominantly yellow and often have a black or dark gray inner core. Visible signs of use, such as the erosion and chipping of the outer surface and the exposure of a dark inner core (figs. 1–3), add significantly to their value.[II] The date for the advent of powder-glass techniques in Africa—and therefore the appearance of* bodom—*is not certain, although it is possible they appeared in the sixteenth century.[III]*

112. *This baked clay mold was used by the Krobo of Ghana to make powder-glass beads around 1930. A stick was set in the center of each bead's mold to form a hole. The beadmaker then placed horizontal layers of variously colored glass powders made from pulverized glass scrap into the mold. The mold was subsequently placed in a furnace and heated until the glass particles congealed into a granular mass without actually melting. Examples of the resulting beads appear in the lower half of the illustration. British Museum, London*

(symbolizing female fertility), also have an ancient history in Africa. Over ten thousand years ago, cowries were used as burial offerings; more recently, they have been considered legal tender.[2]

The manufacture of stone beads in sub-Saharan Africa was limited to a few localities. A variety of cylindrical and double-drilled stone beads were made by the Nok culture of Nigeria in the first millennium B.C.[3] A Nok terra-cotta male figurine wearing necklaces of what appear to be stone beads has been discovered. The tradition persisted, evidenced by bead-laden bronze king figures of the Ife culture that date to the fourteenth century A.D.[4] Beads recently recovered from ancient sites at Djenne in Mali also reveal that some stone was worked there at least by medieval times.

During the fifteenth century, stone beadmaking developed in the kingdom of Benin (in present-day Nigeria) with the encouragement of Oba Eware the Great. Benin craftsmen became experts at carving stone (often agate) beads coveted by the royal court. Beads were considered so important in old Benin that a member of the house of Iwebo (the keepers of the royal wardrobe) was sent by the *oba* to invest a worthy subject with beads. No titled chief was allowed audience with the *oba* unless he wore his necklaces, and if he lost them, he could be punished by death.[5] The beaded regalia of the *oba* became increasingly elaborate until, by the seventeenth century, entire costumes of coral beads, including skirts, shirts, crowns, and staffs, became the official royal dress (plates 132 and 133). (Coral had been introduced by the Portuguese in the early 1500s.)

A stone beadmaking industry is also known to have existed at Ilorin in Nigeria. Nodules of agate, carnelian, red jasper, and even old stone beads were brought to Ilorin by Arab and Sudanic traders. They were then worked or reworked by local craftsmen into beads. Most agate and carnelian beads found throughout Africa today, however, are either of Indian origin or are copies designed to imitate Indian beads that were made in the nineteenth and twentieth centuries by German manufacturers at Idar-Oberstein. Today, the Dogon of Mali continue to make large granite beads (plate 106).

The history of metal beads in Africa is somewhat obscure. It is known that most African societies have tended to develop beads based on indigenous materials, including locally available metals. Africans have used iron for tools and weapons since at least 300 B.C., but only more recently for adornment. Tin beads, however, in the shape of cowries, have been reported from a Nok site dating to the first millennium B.C.[6] In Kenya, where locally made iron was plentiful, large faceted iron beads have been manufactured by the Turkana for generations (plate 119). Today, Kenyan craftsmen make faceted aluminum beads from cast-bar stock.[7] Major deposits of silver are found in Ethiopia, and Ethiopian silversmiths are among the finest in Africa. For centuries, they have hammered or cast beads into a variety of shapes, often using the silver from melted-down coins.

European explorers and traders arriving in West Africa in the early fifteenth century noted an abundance of gold jewelry, including beaded necklaces and bracelets. Many West African gold beads described by Europeans were made by the Asante using a "lost-wax" casting process. This process, known in West Africa since the ninth century, is thought to have been introduced from the north via trans-Saharan traders.[8] It has been acknowledged for millennia that Africa was well endowed with gold. Sudanese mines supplied Old Kingdom Egyptian jewelers, and by the New Kingdom era gold was brought from sources farther south. Throughout the Middle Ages, Islamic Asia and much of Christian Europe depended on African gold.

By the fifteenth century, European observations of West African gold jewelry inspired explorers to search for the sources of the metal and other precious commodities,

113. *Young girls of Kenya's Pokot tribe wearing wooden beads they made. When the girls reach marrying age, these will be replaced by imported glass seed beads.*[IV]

OVERLEAF: 114. *Turkana girl with many layers of necklaces, representing her wealth.*

The Turkana are nomadic pastoralists living in a harsh environment, yet they create superb beadwork from leather, metals, wood, glass, and shells.

Turkana are well known for their ostrich eggshell beads, although today the collecting of ostrich eggshells is strictly controlled. If the Turkana men manage to avoid the mother ostrich and the game warden, they bring the eggs to their women, who chip the tough shell into rough shapes using stones or their teeth. Holes are then drilled in the center, and the edges are smoothed on a stone. Ostrich eggshell beads have been made this way in East Africa since at least 7000 B.C.[V]

including ivory and spices. Over the next several hundred years, sub-Saharan Africa was embroiled in a struggle between the European powers for control of its people, land, and riches. Beads—particularly ones of European glass—played an important role in this story.

Indeed, glass beads are the most common feature of African adornment and were imported into the continent from before the Christian Era. At least small amounts of Egyptian Ptolemaic (304–30 B.C.) and Roman-style eye beads found their way south across the Sahara, where they appear at Djenne in sites dating from 300 B.C. to A.D. 200.[9]

However, most archaeologically recovered beads were manufactured in India. Small, opaque glass beads found along the East and South African coasts were produced in India as early as 200 B.C., and have been found in African sites dating to about A.D. 200, suggesting that strong trade relations existed between the two continents.

The history of glass manufacturing south of the Sahara is still unclear. Although some of the world's earliest known glass beads come from Egypt (faience, considered the forerunner of glass, was invented either in Mesopotamia or Egypt about 3400 B.C., and wound-glass beads appear in Egypt between 2181 and 2133 B.C.), the influence of Egyptian glassmaking on the cultures of sub-Saharan Africa appears minimal. Glass beads were traded south from Egypt, but the beadmaking technology does not seem to have accompanied them. One of the earliest sources of indigenous glass beads is thought to be Mapungubwe in South Africa, where beads were made from A.D. 600 to 1200.

ABOVE RIGHT: **115.** *A Turkana married woman's dance apron. The motifs along the bottom of the skirt are similar to those pictured in plate 118. Length, 81 cm. Collection Jill and Roger Caras, New York*

ABOVE LEFT: **116.** *Two unmarried Turkana adolescents wear the* arrac, *a triangular goatskin apron decorated with a border of ostrich eggshell beads. These skirts gradually lengthen as the girls reach marrying age.*

BOTTOM LEFT: **117.** *All Turkana children wear strings of beads.*

BOTTOM RIGHT: **118.** *A married woman wearing a long skirt sewn with ostrich eggshell beads. The young children wear simple strands of beads.*

127

Africa: *Bead Materials and Distribution Patterns, Prehistory to the Present*

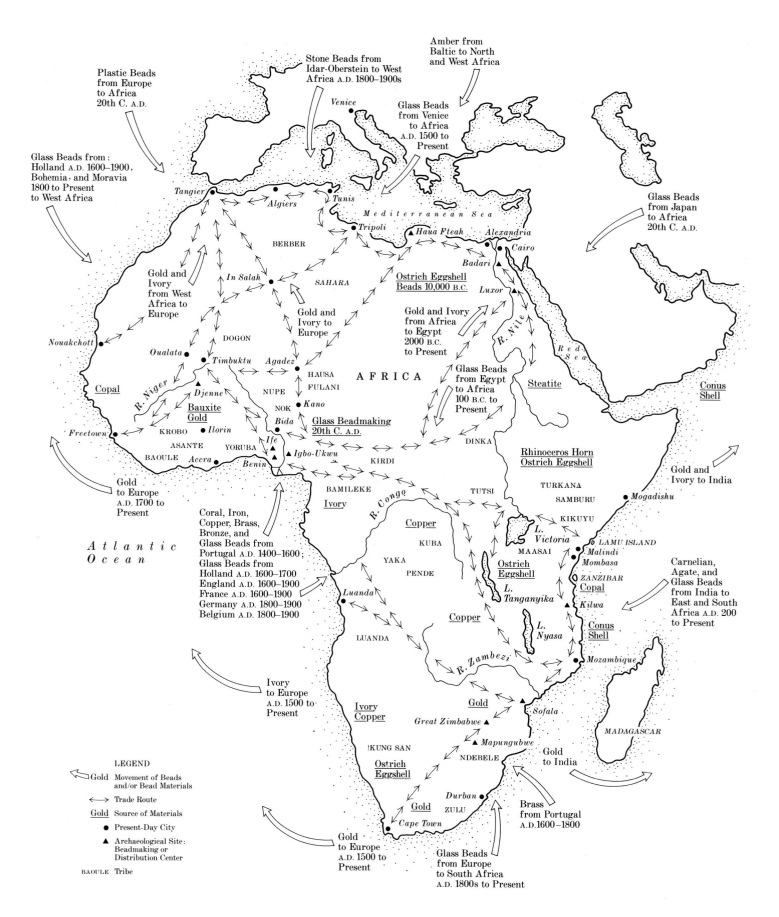

Plastic Beads from Europe to Africa 20th C. A.D.

Stone Beads from Idar-Oberstein to West Africa A.D. 1800–1900s

Amber from Baltic to North and West Africa

Glass Beads from Venice to Africa A.D. 1500 to Present

Glass Beads from: Holland A.D. 1600–1900, Bohemia, and Moravia 1800 to Present to West Africa

Glass Beads from Japan to Africa 20th C. A.D.

Venice

Tangier

Algiers

Tunis

Mediterranean Sea

Tripoli

▲ *Haua Fteah*

Alexandria

Cairo

BERBER

Gold and Ivory from West Africa to Europe

In Salah

SAHARA

Gold and Ivory to Europe

Ostrich Eggshell Beads 10,000 B.C.

Badari ▲

Luxor ▲

Gold and Ivory from Africa to Egypt 2000 B.C. to Present

R. Nile

Red Sea

Nouakchott

Copal

Oualata

R. Niger

Timbuktu

Agadez

HAUSA FULANI

A F R I C A

Glass Beads from Egypt to Africa 100 B.C. to Present

Steatite

Conus Shell

DOGON

▲ *Djenne*

Bauxite Gold

NUPE

NOK

Kano

Bida

Glass Beadmaking 20th C. A.D.

Freetown

KROBO ● *Ilorin*

Ife

● *Igbo-Ukwu*

KIRDI

DINKA

Rhinoceros Horn Ostrich Eggshell

Gold and Ivory to India

ASANTE

BAOULE *Accra*

YORUBA

Benin

BAMILEKE

Ivory

R. Congo

TUTSI

TURKANA

SAMBURU

● *Mogadishu*

Gold to Europe A.D. 1700 to Present

Coral, Iron, Copper, Brass, Bronze, and Glass Beads from Portugal A.D. 1400–1600; Glass Beads from Holland A.D. 1600–1700 England A.D. 1600–1900 France A.D. 1600–1900 Germany A.D. 1800–1900 Belgium A.D. 1800–1900

Copper

KUBA

YAKA

PENDE

KIKUYU

L. Victoria

LAMU ISLAND

Malindi

MOMBASA

Mombasa

Atlantic Ocean

● *Luanda*

MAASAI

Ostrich Eggshell

L. Tanganyika

ZANZIBAR

Copal

▲ *Kilwa*

Carnelian, Agate, and Glass Beads from India to East and South Africa A.D. 200 to Present

Ivory to Europe A.D. 1500 to Present

LUANDA

Copper

L. Nyasa

Conus Shell

R. Zambezi

● *Mozambique*

Ivory Copper

Gold

▲ *Sofala*

Great Zimbabwe ▲

MADAGASCAR

!KUNG SAN

▲ *Mapungubwe*

NDEBELE

Gold to India

Ostrich Eggshell

Durban

Brass from Portugal A.D.1600–1800

Gold

ZULU

Cape Town

Gold to Europe A.D. 1500 to Present

Glass Beads from Europe to South Africa A.D. 1800s to Present

LEGEND

⇦ Gold — Movement of Beads and/or Bead Materials

⟷ — Trade Route

Gold — Source of Materials

● — Present-Day City

▲ — Archaeological Site: Beadmaking or Distribution Center

BAOULE — Tribe

Scholars, however, are uncertain as to whether early African glass beads were made from the basic constituents, or whether glassmakers used pulverized bottles, glass ingots, or imported glass beads as their raw materials.[10]

By the ninth century, more than 165,000 stone and glass beads were used in ceremonies at Igbo-Ukwu to adorn bronze sculptures and staffs. The large quantity of these beads indicates their importance to the local population. Among the stone beads were carnelians from India. Most of the glass beads are of blue and yellow drawn-glass, probably of Indian manufacture, although some may have originated in the Islamic world. Several hundred years later, glass beads were made at Ife in western Yorubaland from imported glass. One crucible held nearly two thousand blue glass beads, known as *segi* or *popi*, widely used at the time.[11]

Since the sixteenth century, glass beadmaking in sub-Saharan Africa has been concentrated in today's Niger, Nigeria, and Ghana. This tradition remains intact, and today the Bida of Nigeria and the Krobo of Ghana are two of the most important African glass manufacturers. There are pockets of glassmaking elsewhere on the continent, including the Mauritanian towns of Kiffa and Oualata, where craftswomen have developed exquisite polychrome glass beads (plate 108). Beads from imported glass scrap continue to be made in both West Africa and Mauritania using two basic techniques: traditional winding and drawing, and using ground powder glass. Powder-glass beadmaking is almost unique to Africa, where it has become a sophisticated art form (plate 109).[12]

Empires, Kingdoms, and Trade

Beads were favored trade items with Indian, Middle Eastern, and European merchants. Shipments of beads began arriving in Africa by at least the fourth century A.D. While a few Arab traders penetrated the interior of Africa using established trans-Saharan trade routes, most Indians and Europeans were confined to coastal trading posts until the middle of the nineteenth century. From these commercial outposts, foreigners dealt with African middlemen who moved beads inland along the trade networks. It is not surprising that the early trading centers—including Kilwa, Zanzibar, Sofala, Djenne, and Timbuktu—today have archaeological sites rich in imported stone and glass beads.

Trade became a focal point for organizing human affairs: empires grew out of markets. The control of raw materials and their exchange for finished products led to an accumulation of wealth in favored areas, sometimes laying the foundations for the emergence of indigenous African states. During the seventh century A.D., Muslim Arabs conquered Mediterranean Africa and began to exchange brass, cloth, stone, glass beads, and Baltic amber for West African gold, ivory, and slaves. From A.D. 900 to 1500, they created important trade relationships aided by the development of Islamic empires within North and West Africa. Two of the most powerful states were Ghana, which prevailed from the eighth to the eleventh century, and Mali, a huge empire during the twelfth and thirteenth centuries that stretched from the Atlantic to the great bend of the Niger River. The empire of Mali was eclipsed by that of Songhai, centered in the flourishing cities of Gao and Timbuktu. Archaeological finds suggest that beads were a significant part of these empires' trade and their people's adornment.

To the south of the Sahara, Sudanic merchants traded among peoples who lived at the edge of the tropical forests that border the low-lying Guinea coast from Sierra Leone to Nigeria. Trade with the gold-producing region of West Africa was extremely active. By 1500, partly as a result of commercial contacts with the north, the foundations were laid for the development of the great forest states, notably the Benin and

119. *Turkana belt of copper and iron beads, c. 1960. With the exception of the Turkana, East African tribes ignore metalwork. These beads, made and worn by married women, indicate the clan to which their husbands belong. Iron beads indicate that the wearer's husband belongs to the Stone clan; a predominance of copper would symbolize his membership in the Leopard clan. The belt is worn every day. n.s. National Museums of Kenya, Nairobi*

OVERLEAF: 120. *Men's beaded corsets are among the most fascinating articles of adornment. This photograph shows Dinka cowherders of southern Sudan with beaded corsets fitted tightly to their bodies. The colors of the corset indicate the wearer's age group: red and white are for ages fifteen to twenty-five; pink and purple for twenty-five to thirty; and yellow for those past thirty.*[VI]

TOP LEFT: 121. *A young, unmarried Samburu girl dancing.*

Beads communicate social status for both Samburu women and men. A Samburu warrior describes a beautiful girl as follows: "She will have many beads right up to her chin; this is what makes her beautiful."[VII] *A beautiful girl has many admirers, who make gifts of beads, which both define and reinforce her beauty. By age sixteen, a girl will often have a substantial collection of necklaces, indicating her great desirability and thereby helping to secure a proposal of marriage.*

TOP RIGHT: 122. *Married Samburu woman. The beaded necklaces worn by the woman were obtained by the author while visiting a Samburu village in 1983. Although this woman sold the necklace to obtain money to educate her children, it was painful for her to part with it. Such necklaces are symbols of prestige, representing years of gifts.*

BOTTOM LEFT: 123. *Married Samburu woman with a giraffe-hair and red glass bead necklace. These necklaces are worn at dances and ceremonies and are coated with a mixture of animal fat and red ocher. They are believed to enhance the wearer's fertility.*

BOTTOM RIGHT: 124. *A Samburu warrior displaying beads, bracelets, and an elaborate ocher hairstyle. Bachelor warriors devote much time to decorating themselves to attract young women. "Young men accent and highlight their well-muscled, shining bodies with narrow bands, circlets, and bandoliers of beads around the neck, chest, waist, arms, and legs. Such effects give warriors their distinctive and proud appearance." VIII Beads are worn by men in most African pastoral societies, although the number of beads they use decreases once they become elders of the tribe.*

Akan kingdoms. At the same time, the first Europeans, mostly Portuguese sailors, reached these coastal kingdoms, thereby establishing their own direct source of African ivory and gold and connecting West Africa to European markets.

Along the east coast of Africa, a string of Muslim city-states, notably Mogadishu and Kilwa on the mainland and the island of Zanzibar, emerged as part of an Indian Ocean trading complex. Especially important to this network was the gold of Zimbabwe, which was shipped from the port of Sofala. In 1498, Vasco da Gama sailed from Portugal around the southern tip of Africa and visited some of these East African ports on his way to India. His journey marks the beginning of European intrusion into the highly lucrative Muslim trading preserve. It is known that Vasco da Gama bartered with beads in the town of Mozambique.[13]

Peoples on the West African coast began to trade with Europe in the late fifteenth century. First were the Portuguese, followed over the next four hundred years by the Dutch, English, French, Belgians, and Germans. They brought millions of Venetian, Dutch, and Bohemian glass beads to Africa. Exactly what happened to most of these beads is unclear. Over the years a variety of uses other than ornamentation has been suggested. Richard Burton, the explorer who searched for the source of the Nile, had his own theory about the ultimate fate of large quantities of imported beads:

It is difficult to divine what becomes of these ornaments: for centuries ton after ton has been imported into the country. They are by no means perishable substances and the people, like Indians, carry their wealth upon their persons. Yet not a third of the population was observed to wear any considerable quantity; possibly the excessive demand in the lands outlying direct intercourse with the coast tends to disperse them throughout the vast terra incognita of the central African basin.[14]

A consideration of the uses of beads may shed light on the mystery of their apparent disappearance. Henry Morton Stanley, in his book *How I Found Livingstone*, related that when he arrived at the northern stream of the Rugufu River, he distinctly heard the sound of "distant thunder in the west." His interpreters explained:

It is the great mountain on the other side of the Tanganyika, full of deep holes, into which the water rolls; and when there is a wind on the Tanganyika there is a sound like thunder. Many boats have been lost there, and it is a custom with Arabs and natives alike to throw cloth and especially white beads, to appease the God of the lake. Those who throw beads generally get past without trouble, but those who do not...are drowned.[15]

The beds of lakes, rivers, streams, and coastal waters may well be the resting places of some of those tons of lost beads to which Burton referred. Every year, thousands of beads of every vintage are washed up on the beaches of East Africa and its islands. Some of these without doubt are from shipwrecks, but others must surely be the offerings made by Arabs and Africans through the centuries.[16]

The importation of beads had important consequences for African history. Glass beads were bartered by Africans for incense, ivory, tortoiseshell, rhinoceros horn, palm and coconut oils, timber, pig iron, and gold. The same tightly structured trade networks that for centuries moved gold and ivory from the interior to West African ports, bringing beads back on the return trips, later served the slave trade. Between the 1500s and 1867, slavers shipped perhaps fifteen million Africans to the Americas, routinely exchanging European-made glass beads for their human cargo. One of the many records of this exchange came from a German priest visiting South Africa in 1653. "East of the Cape," he wrote, "nearly halfway to Mozambique, much gold, slaves, and other commodities were to be had at cheap rates for soft goods and glass beads of all sorts."[17]

132

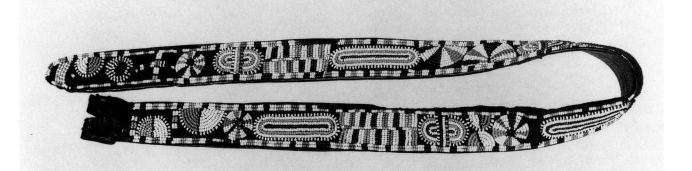

ABOVE: **125.** *Circumcised men of the Kikuyu tribe in Kenya wear this type of glass and leather beaded belt until they become elders; thereafter, they wear them only on special occasions. The beadwork pattern on this belt, made about 1969, is called* Kenyatta. *Width, 4.9 cm. National Museums of Kenya, Nairobi*

LEFT: **126.** *The late Mzee Jomo Kenyatta wearing the* Kenyatta *style of beaded belt for which he was named. (Photograph undated.) National Museums of Kenya, Nairobi*

133

TOP: 127. *On the left is a beaded collar to which is attached a small patterned panel, known as a "love letter." Zulu girls convey to their suitors, and wives to their husbands, feelings of courtship, love, hope, yearning, and sadness through the choice of colors and patterns woven into these flat beadwork panels. Blue may represent gossip, thought, or sky; red can symbolize "eyes red with weeping" from "seeking one's lover in vain," or can symbolize blood or fire; yellow can be for riches or poverty; white always means love and purity.*

Juxtaposed colors take on special meanings: a pink and white panel might say: "You are poor...but I love you." Such messages are part of the private dialogue in a couple's relationship and are rarely understood by outsiders.[IX]

On the right is a beadwork bag similar to those worn by young unmarried Zulu men in the early twentieth century, the time when Zulu men began wearing beads. Collar: length, 36 cm. Collection Tambaran Gallery, New York

RIGHT: 128. *An* umutsha, *a late nineteenth- or early twentieth-century Zulu belt made of several beaded ropes sewn together. It was worn by both young men and unmarried women. This is an example of a beadwork technique that developed at a time when beads became available in great quantities. Length, 80 cm. Collection Tambaran Gallery, New York*

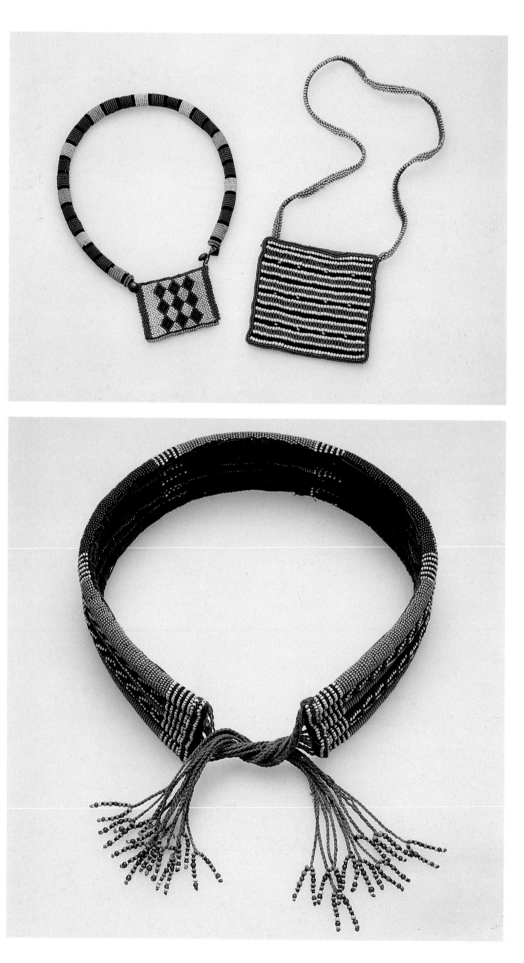

LEFT: **129.** *This mapoto, a beaded apron worn by married Ndebele women, was made of glass beads sewn on beaten goatskin. It is at least fifty years old. Architectural symbols of houses appear on the top panel, with abstract designs resembling aerial views of the kraal (homestead) below it. Ndebele beadwork designs frequently mirror the tribe's painted murals. Width, 45.72 cm. Private collection*

BOTTOM: **130.** *The mural art of Ndebele villages is strongly tied to their beadwork tradition. Both murals and beadwork use geometric patterns and incorporate elements from everyday surroundings, such as telephone poles, airplanes, and electric lightbulbs. The murals dissolve during the rainy season and are repainted annually, while the more permanent beadwork allows for the historical study of Ndebele symbols that have disappeared from the walls.*

131. *The* nyoga, *a long, beaded train, is an important part of the Ndebele bridal outfit. Nyogas have different widths and can be up to eight feet long. Attached to a blanket, the* nyoga *hangs from the wearer's shoulders and trails on the ground like a snake as she dances. Nyoga means "snake tail" and may be a fertility symbol. This example of a fine, early twentieth-century* nyoga *has a central abstract motif of woven red, green, and black beads set in a field of white beads.*[X] *Length, 176 cm. Collection Colette and Jean-Pierre Ghysels, Brussels*

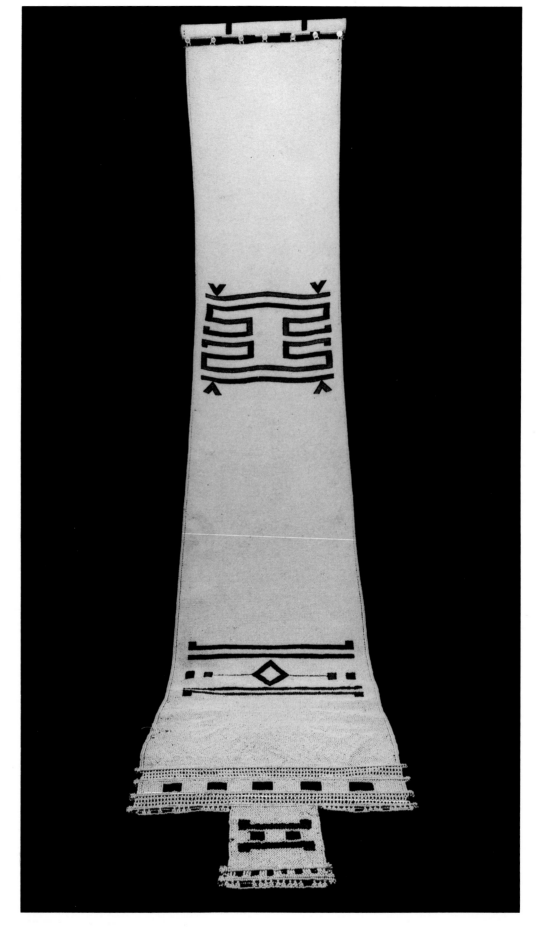

The Many Uses of Beads in African Societies

Beads became essential elements of personal adornment in almost every African society; but how they were (and still are) obtained and used depended on the group's social, political, and economic structure and on its role in the trade system.[18] For example, the Turkana, Samburu, and Dinka are subsistence-level herders occupying the arid grasslands and deserts of Kenya and the Sudan. Because they are constantly seeking fresh supplies of food and water for their livestock, bulky material possessions are impractical. Artistic expression therefore focuses on ornamenting the body rather than the homestead. In these tribes, both men and women wear beads as an essential part of everyday and ceremonial dress that communicates their ethnic affiliation, age grade, marital status, and wealth. The societies are organized according to age sets, a series of clearly defined levels through which each member of the group passes: childhood, warriorhood, and old age for men; childhood, womanhood, and marriage for women. Passage from one age set to the next is signaled by changes in clothing and adornment, including beads whose styles, colors, and assemblages beautify their wearers and communicate important information about them (plates 113–125).

Until this century, artisans in East Africa made beads of local, organic materials, such as shell, roots, seeds, and bone, strung with palm fibers or giraffe hair. When foreign trade invited contact with the Europeans, glass beads frequently replaced those made locally.

ABOVE LEFT: 132. *A sixteenth-century Benin bronze casting of the queen mother's head, showing a coral beaded headdress and coral bead collar. The beaded headdress covers the unusual hairstyle, called "chicken's beak." The casting was done by the lost-wax process. n.s. British Museum, London*

ABOVE RIGHT: 133. *A coral beaded cap, similar to the one shown on the bronze casting in plate 132, and a coral flywhisk. Both belonged to a sixteenth-century oba. n.s. British Museum, London*

Africa 1987

MOROCCO

TUNISIA

ALGERIA

LIBYA

EGYPT

SADR

MALĪ

MAURITANIA

R. Niger

NIGER

CHAD

R. Nile

SUDAN

SENEGAL

GAMBIA

GUINEA-BISSAU

GUINEA

BURKINA
FASO

DJIBOUTI

SIERRA LEONE

IVORY
COAST

BENIN

TOGO

NIGERIA

CENTRAL
AFRICAN REPUBLIC

ETHIOPIA

LIBERIA

GHANA

CAMEROON

SOMALIA

EQUATORIAL GUINEA

R. Congo

UGANDA

KENYA

GABON

RWANDA

L. Victoria

CONGO

ZAIRE

BURUNDI

CABINDA

L. Tanganyika

TANZANIA

ANGOLA

ZAMBIA

L. Nyasa

MALAWI

R. Zambezi

ZIMBABWE

MADAGASCAR

NAMIBIA

MOZAMBIQUE

BOTSWANA

SWAZILAND

LESOTHO

SOUTH
AFRICA

LEGEND

– – – International
Boundaries

especially that of cattle which is mixed with milk for food."[25]

The forms and colors of beads that people sought changed constantly and varied from region to region. It was not unusual for European traders to arrive in port with large quantities of a bead greatly coveted in the last transaction, only to discover that these particular beads were no longer desired. Certain beads, however, were quite popular for long periods of time. *Cornaline d'Aleppo* was popular in different forms. The cornerless, hexagonal dark blue glass beads were known to the Ndebele as "ambassador beads," because they were worn by shamans who "went into the Matopo Hills to ask advice from the great god of the Matabele." The complex millefiore and wound blue glass annular beads were worn by the chiefs who met David Livingstone, the British missionary, at Victoria Falls in 1855 (Bead Chart 50, 53, and 112).[26]

Special mention should be made of the predominantly blue "aggrey" bead, in use on the west coast of Africa before the European traders arrived. For five hundred years, scholars have disagreed on the source and appearance of this mysterious bead, described as "blue coral" and "produced by thunder" or "created by a supernatural power." According to local legend, the aggrey bead comes from the rivers and the earth.

It is now generally agreed that the aggrey was a blue glass bead. Blue glass beads called *akori* and later aggrey were recorded in Benin as early as 1568. It is believed by one specialist that the aggrey bead was made of silicate slag produced on the Guinea Coast by smelting iron from local ores. As the slag was deposited in rivers, the bead's legendary source is frequently connected with water. The bead's blue or green color may simply reflect mineral impurities in the glass. As people were—and are still—often buried with their treasured possessions, it is not surprising that many aggrey beads have been found in the ground, perhaps after a rainstorm has eroded a local cemetery.[27]

The Unity of African Beads

Although each African culture has evolved distinctive patterns of bead use, several unifying themes apply throughout the continent. Basic to the animism that pervades life in sub-Saharan Africa is the spiritual energy a fine bead necklace or beadwork piece imparts. Although both Islam and Christianity are practiced in Africa, they have been shaped to accommodate animistic beliefs in inanimate objects that, whether created by nature or man, have spiritual force. This is why African artifacts often have such a strong aesthetic presence, even if they are not necessarily technically sophisticated. It is also why we often respond strongly to an African necklace, independently of any knowledge about its origins, use, or imparted meaning.

African beadwork is meant to be noticed. As Angela Fisher has written in *Africa Adorned*, beads say, "Look at me!" They range from the layers of colorful necklaces worn in Kenya to a minimal beaded *cache-sexe* in Cameroon (plates 114 and 143). In Africa, as elsewhere, "One can find superior taste demonstrated through either restraint or abundance. A minimal costume may carry for some group the same prestige as an accumulative one does for another."[28] To draw further attention, the beads are often accompanied by sound effects: the rattling of cowrie shells, for example.

African beads are commonly part of an assemblage, a mixture of materials—twigs, shells, glass, and bones—put on a necklace or article of jewelry in a seemingly haphazard way, so that the object may not appear to have been designed. A marvelous example is the Zulu necklace shown in plate 103.

The concept of assemblage also extends to the layered necklaces worn by the Turkana, Samburu, and Berber women (plates 114 and 149). Multiple necklaces worn by

OVERLEAF, TOP LEFT: 145. *A silk-tasseled amber necklace typically worn by Berber women of Ouarzazate. The red felt spacers protect each bead. Length, 85 cm. Collection Ivory Freidus*

OVERLEAF, TOP RIGHT: 146. *Traditional necklace from the Draa Valley, southern Morocco. The egg-shaped central bead (taguemout) of enameled silver, made by Jewish silversmiths from the town of Kabylia, symbolizes fertility. Center bead: diameter, 5.08 cm. Collection Ivory Freidus*

OVERLEAF, BOTTOM LEFT: 147. *Necklace worn by dancers of the guedra, the ritual love dance performed by Moorish women for men. The beads are twisted around the wrist or worn around the neck. The wooden beads are inlaid with silver wire. On the tassel are glass and carnelian beads. This object is from Goulimine on the southern Moroccan-Mauritanian border. Length (including the tassel), 52 cm. Collection Colette and Jean-Pierre Ghysels, Brussels*

OVERLEAF, BOTTOM RIGHT: 148. *A necklace of filigree silver and heart-shaped, scented beads called* shah. *Made by Tunisian women according to an old Egyptian method, a* shah *contains ambergris, rose petals, saffron, cloves, nutmeg, and musk. The extraordinarily sensuous fragrance is accentuated by body heat and is said to last a lifetime.[XV] Length, 96.5 cm. Collection Ivory Freidus*

149

an individual draw attention and create an "altered and expanded image with the head held proudly high as if lifted by the mass of beads."[29] In much of sub-Saharan Africa, it is important to recognize not only the internal complexity of the individual beaded necklace, but also how an assemblage of necklaces creates an ensemble.

Finally, African adornment has been and is essentially a community art. The forms taken by beaded necklaces, bracelets, hats, and aprons are usually determined by a set of commonly held standards. For the most part, artist and wearer are not expressing their private feelings or inspiration. Rather, personal touches are executed within generally accepted limitations, so that beaded adornment, like all African art, unifies the community by conveying and reinforcing common understandings.

Beads were, and still are, used in Africa to create objects representing spiritual values basic to the survival of the community. These objects play a major role in rituals insuring continuity of the group: birth, circumcision, marriage, warriorhood, kingship, death. Susan Vogel's discussion of African art in *For Spirits and Kings* can be extrapolated to include the significance of much of African beaded adornment: "In societies without writing, art objects can acquire extraordinary importance as visual records....On a deeper level, works of art are endowed with complex meaning and serve as repositories of traditional knowledge. They are dense concentrations of ancestral wisdom that must be preserved and transmitted to succeeding generations."[30]

ABOVE LEFT: 149. *Berber woman from the Draa Valley with typically colorful, asymmetrical necklaces of amber, copal, coral, amazonite, shell, silver, and glass beads. The Berbers have treasured amber for centuries in the belief that it will cure a variety of illnesses.*

ABOVE RIGHT: 150. *Berber women of Ouarzazate in festival dress, wearing chains and beaded necklaces.*

The Far East: China, Korea, and Japan

T he use of jewelry in the Far Eastern civilizations of China, Korea, and Japan contrasts sharply with its role in Western culture and most tribal societies. Necklaces—a seemingly ubiquitous article of adornment elsewhere—were not typically worn in the Far East. Instead jewelry took the form of belt hooks and buckles, plaques, hairpins, bracelets, and other less prominent accessories. Beads often played both functional and decorative roles as attachments to headdresses, hats, and *inro* (small, ornamented containers).

Although beads were not common attire in the Far East, they were consistently manufactured for limited domestic use and for export. Quantities of beads made of precious or semiprecious materials and glass have been uncovered in the ancient tombs of royal or elite households. In antiquity, glass beads were highly valued treasures and were often combined with jade beads and gilded bronze elements, such as belt hooks. Glass beads were also made for export at various times in both China and Japan.[1] Jade beads were revered in China, Korea, and Japan: the character for "jade" and "bead" (玉) is the same in each of the three languages.

Far Eastern beads often demonstrate exquisite craftsmanship. Chinese eye beads dating from the fourth to the first century B.C. (plates 154 and 330) and Japanese ivory and metal *ojime* (slide fasteners for a personal carrying case) from the eighteenth and nineteenth centuries A.D. (plates 170–90) are among the most complex and beautiful beads ever made.

The atypical use of beads in Far Eastern societies has its origins in ancient cultural history. Archaeological evidence indicates that China, Korea, and Japan began their development as separate prehistoric entities. By the second century B.C., China had established the colony of Lo-lang in northern Korea, and a century later Japan was in

151. *An example of Japanese* ojime, *carved in the form of a clinging baby boy by the renowned nineteenth-century* netsuke *carver Ono Ryomin. Length, 1.9 cm. Collection Midori Gallery, Coconut Grove, Florida*

153

close contact with China and Korea.[2] Chinese exports, including raw materials, finished beads, craftsmen, and even a philosophy of adornment, soon flowed into Korea and from there to Japan.

By the sixth century, China was the major presence in the Far East, exerting influence over her neighbors in everything from political and religious systems to precepts for the forms and uses of jewelry. Chinese writing, governmental organization, technology, and art were the models for the region. Her influence ebbed and flowed in relation to the fluctuating fortunes of her power and trade.[3] At the same time, Korea and Japan developed independent and distinctive cultures, transforming China's cultural tenets into unique local expressions.

China, followed by Korea and Japan, was among the first societies to become literate. To be literate certified a man as civilized. Such a man did not find it crucial to appeal to a single supreme deity to define, stabilize, and insure his place in the world. (He might, however, consult a variety of ancestral and natural spirits.) Jewelry, therefore, was not worn to influence spirits. Almost without exception, beads seem to have been valued in the Far East more as status symbols than as protective amulets. Moreover, the use of such status symbols was rigorously controlled by civil law and by the precepts and taboos of the indigenous religions of Confucianism, Taoism, and Shintoism. Confucianism, the key to Chinese thought, was extremely influential in the development of Korean and Japanese philosophies (particularly among the ruling classes). It is a system of ethics rather than a religion of magic and superstition and is not given to the production of art, much less to ornament. (Aside from Buddhist prayer beads, the few examples of beads with ritual significance in the Far East are known primarily from earlier, pre-Confucianist times.) Chinese Taoism also advocates naturalness, contemplation, and the disavowal of worldly goods, and Japanese Shintoism stresses respect for the elements of nature—rocks, trees, waterfalls, and plants. Furthermore, Confucianism is based on social responsibility, respect for age and authority, and faith in a patriarchal government founded upon moral virtues. These codes kept a rigid class system intact: displays of wealth, particularly the wearing of jewelry, were reserved strictly for the elite.

Buddhism entered the Far East about the first century A.D. and was adapted to the traditional religious philosophies of each country. Differences in Chinese, Korean, and Japanese Buddhist prayer beads demonstrate the integration of Buddhism into indigenous beliefs. Interestingly, it was when Buddhism was at its height (about A.D. 400–900) that beads as items of adornment made their strongest impression on Far Eastern cultures, demonstrating the influence of this religion on all levels of society. By contrast, Confucianism was the religion of the intelligentsia, whose adherence to rationalism and strict social ethics did not allow for beads in ritual practices.

Unfortunately, most of the available information on ancient beads is gleaned from discoveries at royal and wealthy tombs, so that we know little of the possibly perishable adornment of ordinary citizens. It may be that the growth of trade by land and sea, which also helped to spread Buddhism, injected cosmopolitan attitudes about jewelry into Far Eastern society and gave greater access to beads and luxury materials to all classes of people.

Far Eastern history, however, is punctuated by periods of trade and cultural exchange followed by years of self-imposed cultural isolation. Active contact with India and Iran, for example, frequently coincided with important periods of bead development and use in Far Eastern societies. The spectacular beaded crowns, necklaces, and girdles of Korea's fifth- and sixth-century royal tombs, and the beautiful glass beads produced during the Nara period (A.D. 645–794) in Japan are examples of the impor-

154

The Far East — China, Korea, Japan:
Distribution of Beads and Bead Materials,
Prehistory to the Present

RUSSIA

Carnelian
Onyx, Agate
White Jade
Glass Beads
c. 500 B.C. to
A.D. 200

Japan Local:
Jade, Silver
Steatite, Gold
Agate, Crystal
Wood, Lacquer
Narwhal Ivory
Porcelain, Copper
Horn, Tortoiseshell
Glass Beads

Fossil Ivory from Siberia
Glass Beads from Manchuria
to China and Japan
A.D. 1600–1800s

MONGOLIA

Glass Beads from
China to Russia
18th C. A.D.

Amber (Baltic),
Coral (Mediterranean),
Turquoise (Iran),
and Ivory (India)
to Korea and Japan via
China A.D. 1600–1900

Beads of
Ostrich Eggshell and
Fossil Dinosaur Eggshell
12,000 B.C.

Glass Beads
from China
to Japan and
Korea

GOBI DESERT

HOKKAIDO

Agate, Carnelian,
c. 200 B.C.–A.D. 200

Cultured Pearls
20th C.A.D.

Jade (Khotan),
Coral (Mediterranean),
Glass Beads (Roman Empire),
Lapis Lazuli (Badakhshan),
Turquoise (Persia), and
Amber (Baltic) to
China, Korea, and Japan
via Silk Routes
c. 200 B.C. to
A.D. 1000

Beijing (Peking) ●

Zhou-kou-dian ▲
Stone Beads
16,000 B.C.

Anyang ▲   Poshan ●

HONSHU

Lolang ▲
Kongju ▲

Seoul ●

KOREA
Gold, Silver
Copal, Jet
Jade

JAPAN

Tokyo (Edo) ●

▲Turubong Cave

Kyoto ●

Silver
Glass Beads
c. 800 B.C.

Kyongju ▲

Osaka ●

Jade

Luoyang ▲   Jade Beads
c. 1500–1000 B.C.

Shoso-in ▲

Cultured Pearls,
Coral, and Glass Beads
from Japan to West
20th C. A.D.

Glass Eye Beads
c. 481–221 B.C.

Turquoise

Nagasaki ●

Kamikuroiwa ▲

KYUSHU   SHIKOKU

Silk, Porcelain, Lacquer,
and Silver to Western World
via Silk Routes c. 200 B.C.
to A.D. 1000

CHINA

Hangzhou ●

Mother-of-Pearl,
Tortoiseshell, Glass Beads,
and Carved Amber
to Africa via India
Glass Beads to North America
from China A.D. 1700
to 1900s

Silver
and Gold from
Japan to Holland
A.D. 1600–1800

Pacific
Ocean

Agate and
Etched Carnelian
from India to
China 206 B.C.
to A.D. 220

Gold   R. Yangtze   Changsha ▲

Silver
Copper

Silver
Copper   Jade

Copper

BURMA

Tortoiseshell,
Silver, Porcelain,
Gold, and Glass Beads
from China to Borneo
and Philippines
A.D. 1100–1400

Jade-Working,
Glass Beads

Guangzhou
(Canton) ●

Rubies, Emeralds,
Sapphires, Jadeite,
Topaz, Amethysts,
and Amber from
Burma to China
18th C. A.D.

Silver

Hebei ●   Macao ▲

TAIWAN

Ivory and
Aloes Wood
to China

Glass Beads
from China to West
A.D. 1700–1900s

Aloes Wood

LEGEND

HAINAN

THAILAND

Coral, Amber,
Pearls, Crystal,
Glass, and Diamonds
to China via Persians
6th C. A.D.

PHILIPPINES

⇦ Movement of
Beads and/or
Bead Materials

Gold Source of Materials

● Present-Day City

▲ Archaeological
Site: Beadmaking
and Distribution
Center

Rhino Horn,
Ivory (Africa),
Coral (Mediterranean),
Glass Beads (Holland,
Venice, and Bohemia) to
Nagasaki A.D.
1600–1800s

⟷ Silk Route

--- International
Boundaries

∿∿∿ Great Wall of
China A.D. 220

Coral, Diamonds,
Crystal, Carnelian,
Gold, Silver, Pearls,
Sapphires, Cat's Eye,
Tortoiseshell, Glass,
and Rhino Horn to
China via Chinese
12th C. A.D.

Rubies, Emeralds,
Garnets, Carnelian,
Coral, Sapphire, Balas,
Pearls, Cat's Eye, and
Quartz to China
via Arabs
14th C. A.D.

ABOVE: **152.** *Probably owned by an aristocrat, this carved and polished barrel-shaped bead of pale green nephrite was fashioned during the middle of the Eastern Zhou period, c. 500 B.C. By this time, jade craftsmanship had reached a high level of technical skill. The back-to-back spirals, derived from bronze designs, are typical Eastern Zhou motifs. Length, 4.1 cm. Royal Ontario Museum, Toronto*

RIGHT: **153.** *A bronze tomb figure of a kneeling attendant from the fifth or fourth century B.C., accompanied by a contemporary (or slightly later) miniature bead version of the same bronze bearer made of turquoise faience and perforated lengthwise. Comparable figures were also carved in jade. Bead: length, 1.85 cm. Royal Ontario Museum, Toronto*

OPPOSITE: **154.** *This remarkable group of seven Chinese eye beads from the "Warring States" period (481–221 B.C.) are some of the most technically complex glass beads ever created. Possibly influenced by Phoenician and Roman beads imported into China at*

tance of beads during times of cultural interchange. Indeed, many Korean and Japanese tombs have yielded a variety of imported beads.

Conversely, beads do not appear to have been generally available or important in most isolationist periods. The reasons for isolation were complex and varied in each country throughout the centuries. Frequently, isolationism was brought about by rulers attempting to avoid alliances between competing leaders (or enemies) in their own countries and outside powers. During the seventeenth century, when neo-Confucianism spread throughout the Far East, isolationism was a policy to save the country from European colonialism and the influence of Christian missionaries.

During times of isolation, which were often accompanied by a return to the tenets of strict Confucianism, cultural separation led to a decline in the use and manufacture of beads. In these periods, particularly from the seventeenth to the nineteenth century, isolationism was reinforced by sumptuary laws that mandated the styles of clothing, jewelry, and possessions appropriate to each social class. Since beads, which symbolized wealth and status, were restricted even among the elite, the importing, making, and wearing of them in quantity ceased to be an important practice. (An exception was the Japanese *ojime*.) The clothes of the elite, moreover, were often richly patterned and heavily embroidered, providing a substitute for jewelry. Nevertheless, glass beadmaking for export existed as a cottage industry in nineteenth-century China and Japan, when their ports were closed to foreign goods; and glass beads were frequently used for *ojime* in Japan.

China Some of the earliest ornaments in the world are Chinese. These include beads of stone, animal teeth, marine shells, and fish bone that have been recovered from the Upper Cave of Zhou-kou-dian, south of Beijing, dating to 16,000 B.C..[4] The stone beads were drilled and painted with red hematite powder—perhaps the first decorated artifacts in Chinese history.[5]

In the Gobi Desert, archaeologists have found beads, 12,000 years old, fashioned of ostrich and dinosaur eggshell. By the sixth millennium B.C., strings of cowrie shells existed, although it is not known if, as in Bronze Age China, these were used as adornment or currency (or both).[6]

Jade beads (Bead Chart 800) attributed to Anyang craftsmen of the Shang dynasty (thirteenth to eleventh century B.C.) have been discovered in association with China's earliest known wheel-made pottery, silk-weaving, and bronze-casting. It is surprising that no bronze beads are known, since Shang bronze-casting was well developed, and metal beads were frequently part of metallurgical industries in other areas. The Chinese, unlike peoples of other cultures, do not seem to have had a fondness for gold either.

Possibly the earliest Chinese glass beads—small, pale green forms imitating jade—have been found in ninth- and eighth-century B.C. tombs of the Western Zhou dynasty. Historically, the Chinese preferred to use bronze, lacquer, ceramic, and stone; glass was only a substitute for jade and precious stones. Nevertheless, by the fifth century B.C. they made remarkable glass beads, using lapidary (grinding), metallurgical (casting and molding), and ceramic methods (glazing and sandcore)—techniques not generally associated with glassmaking.

The last three centuries of the Zhou dynasty, known as the "Warring States" period (481–221 B.C.), were marked by artistic inventiveness in many areas. Artisans concentrated on secular objects for personal pleasure and adornment, including the famous Chinese eye beads (plates 154 and 330). First reported from princely tombs near Luoyang (Henan Province), and now excavated from other late Zhou burials as well, these

158

masterpieces of the beadmaker's art employ layered glass to create protruding eye-like motifs, often in complex geometric patterns. While it is possible that these beads were inspired by contemporary western Asian or Phoenician prototypes, their manufacture and chemical composition (lead-barium glass, rather than the soda-lime glass known in the West) strongly suggest they were made in China. Why such remarkable glass beadmaking flourished in China for several hundred years, only to disappear suddenly in the early Han period, remains an important unanswered question.[7]

Jadework also reached high levels of artistry during the later Zhou dynasty. Some of the finest jade jewelry and beads have been recovered from the Luoyang and other Warring States period tombs (plate 152). Faience and pottery beads from late Zhou times were made by ceramic techniques. They feature white, gray, or red cores overlaid with a glazed or slipped decoration that frequently is derived from the design of the glass eye beads (plates 155 and 159).[8]

The Qin dynasty (221–206 B.C.) unified China under a central government, and under the succeeding Han house (206 B.C.–A.D. 220) the country was exposed to contact with the West. Beads from different countries appear in China, while Chinese-made glass beads are now found in both Korea and Japan.[9]

To halt foreign intrusion, China extended her power in central Asia during the second century B.C., gaining control of the caravan routes that cross the Asian deserts. The most famous of these were the silk routes, a series of routes over which Chinese silks and pottery were transported as far west as Rome, while horses, jade, and melon and eye beads—common to ancient western Asia and the Mediterranean—appeared in China. Baltic and Burmese amber were also imported into China at this time.[10]

In Han dynasty times, China also established relations with the Kushan dynasty in Afghanistan and northern India, and built outposts along the silk routes in central Asia that served as commercial centers. Agate and carnelian beads (including etched carnelians) excavated from western Han tombs in Hebei Province in north China are similar to beads of the same date from India, Persia, and Afghanistan.[11] At this time also, Buddhism was introduced to China by the people of Kashmir and by sects along the silk routes. For centuries thereafter, Buddhist missionaries and Asian traders traveled the same routes, both transporting beads.

During the seventh and eighth centuries, emperors of the Tang dynasty (A.D. 618–907) presided over one of the greatest periods in Chinese civilization. China, along with Korea and Japan, was receptive to foreign contact; Buddhism flourished, as did artistic achievement. Unfortunately, only a limited number of Tang beads are extant, although a stunning gold and pearl necklace was excavated recently from a Sui dynasty noble's burial, and five gold beads, beautifully decorated with granulation and attributed to the Tang dynasty, are displayed at the British Museum.[12]

After An Lu-shan's rebellion of 755, the central government in China was weakened considerably. As a result, links with central Asia were disrupted, and subsequently overland trade with the West declined. As Tang rule faltered, a period of isolation set in, marked by intense nationalism: import controls were tightened, foreigners banned, and the "alien" Buddhists were persecuted.[13]

During the Tang, "Five Dynasties" (618–960), and Song (960–1279) periods, evidence of glass beadmaking is primarily available from literary references. The few known Tang glass beads are chemically similar to those made in the West; the lead glass of the earlier Zhou period was no longer used exclusively.[14]

The Song period, despite the self-imposed isolation of China, saw new levels of trade and cultural achievement. With the old land routes to central Asia and the West no longer under its control, China turned to the sea, slowly developing maritime trade

TOP: 155. *Faience beads, c. 400–100 B.C. Top bead: diameter, 1.3 cm. Royal Ontario Museum, Toronto*

MIDDLE ROW, LEFT: 156. *A bead of reddish brown opaque glass, possibly imitating carnelian, c. 400–100 B.C. Length, 2.6 cm. Royal Ontario Museum, Toronto*

MIDDLE ROW, RIGHT: 157. *Glass beads, c. 500 B.C., strongly resembling Phoenician and Egyptian eye beads of the period. Although the revolving, asymmetrical eyes are said to be Chinese, they may also have been Egyptian imports into China. Upper left bead: diameter, 1.4 cm. Royal Ontario Museum, Toronto*

BOTTOM LEFT: 158. *A hexagonal bead of transparent green glass. The Chinese often substituted glass for jade and other precious stones, working the glass by lapidary methods. The hexagonal faceting on this bead was achieved by grinding; thereafter, the form was drilled and polished. This bead was probably excavated at Changsha, Hunan Province, and dates to the late Zhou dynasty, fifth to third century B.C. Length, 8.1 cm. Corning Museum of Glass, Corning, New York*

BOTTOM RIGHT: 159. *A glazed pottery bead, possibly an ancient copy of a glass original, c. 400–100 B.C. n.s. Royal Ontario Museum, Toronto*

160

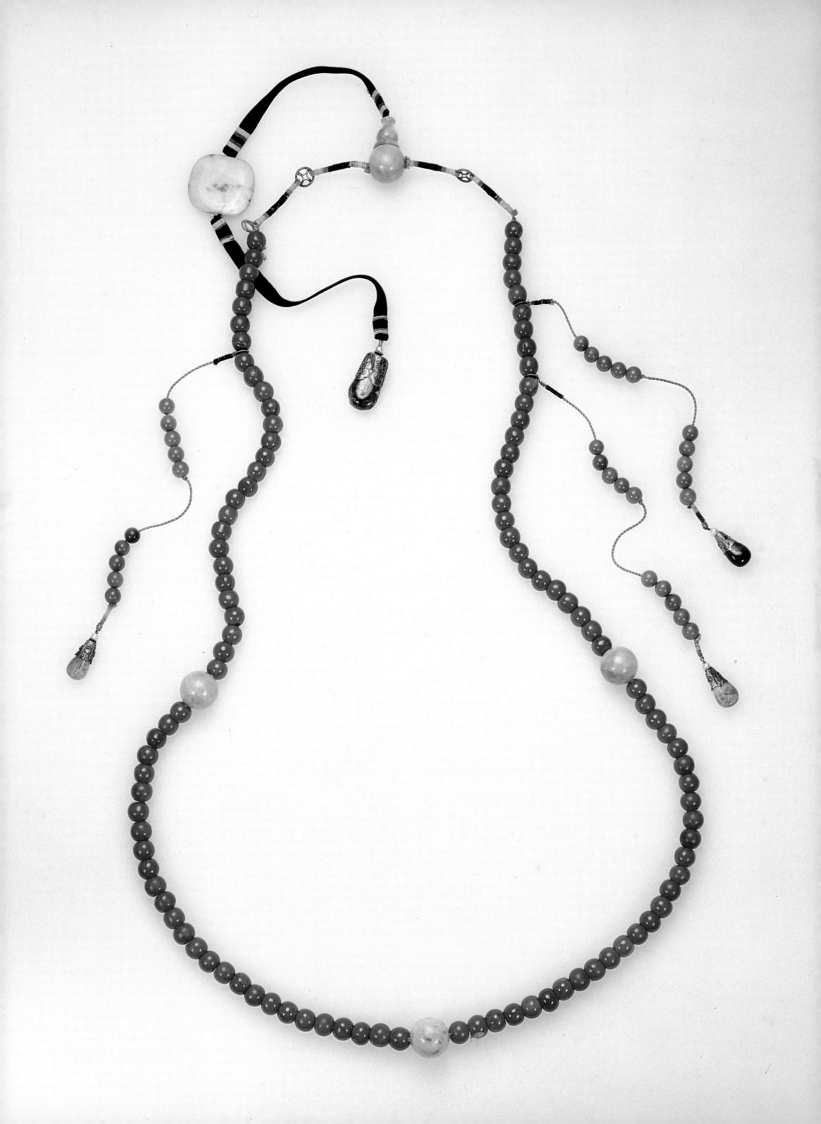

PREVIOUS PAGE: 160. *Official court beads or "Mandarin chain" worn by the emperor and the nobility during the period of Manchurian rule in China (1644–1912). Although the form of the chains was influenced by Tibetan Buddhist rosaries, they were used in China primarily as status symbols rather than prayer aids. This necklace is composed of 108 red Peking glass beads, four jade spacers ("Buddha heads"), a flat jade plaque, counter beads, and tourmaline dewdrop pendants. The bead-covered silk cord and terminal dewdrop pendant attached to the jade plaque was draped on the wearer's back, acting as a counterweight to the necklace. Mandarin officials fingered their beads, handling them like worry beads. They also used them as abacuses for business calculations. Length, 41.3 cm. Collection Ivory Freidus*

ABOVE LEFT: 161. *Jade* kogok *from Korea, date unknown. Length, 5 cm. Collection Albert Summerfield, Seattle*

ABOVE RIGHT: 162. Magatama *("sacred jewel") of blue glass from the Nara period (A.D. 645–794). Shaped by grinding, this bead has been bore-drilled from one side. Length, 2.9 cm. Corning Museum of Glass, Corning, New York*

relations with Southeast Asia, India, and the countries of the Persian Gulf. By the Yuan dynasty (1279–1368), trade with central Asia, Sri Lanka, and Russia resumed. The Venetian traveler Marco Polo, visiting China at this time, commented on the number of foreign ships and traders, predominantly Indians, in Chinese ports.[15]

Documentary sources for the Song and Yuan periods note that glass beads, presumably from China, were being exported with porcelain, gold, silver, tin, and silk.[16] Furthermore, many Chinese artisans settled in the foreign communities with which they traded, particularly Southeast Asia and India. By the seventeenth century, Chinese glass beadmakers living in Java were exporting their products to Borneo.[17] During the Qing (Manchu) dynasty (1644–1912), trade in porcelain, lacquerware, tea, and silver continued from a limited number of ports. Chinese craftsmanship was renowned for its elaboration and technical proficiency and enjoyed immense popularity in the West during the late seventeenth and eighteenth centuries.

Quantities of glass beads were manufactured during Qing rule. Most of these were sold to Russians and the Ainu of Hokkaido, Japan, during the eighteenth century, and to Indians, East Africans, and Americans in the nineteenth century. During the 1790s, Russians were so anxious to buy Chinese glass beads that they eliminated all import duties along their border.[18]

As Chinese beads were distributed through a variety of trade networks and through many transactions, knowledge of the origin of particular beads has often been lost. Chinese glass beads sent to Bombay in the mid-nineteenth century were resold to Africans for ivory.[19] Glass beads carried by Europeans during the early days of trade among Indians in the American Southwest and Northwest may frequently have been of Chinese origin, including the well-known "padre" and "pony" beads (Bead Chart 1023).[20] Clearer historical evidence and richer archaeological data on Chinese glass beads may help answer questions about a number of Asian bead types, including examples from Taiwan and Indonesia.

Trade with the West expanded in the 1840s, and within ten years China became a large-scale exporter of beads. These beads were the product of cottage industries lo- cated in several centers, notably in Canton in the south and Poshan in northeastern China. The beads commonly referred to as "Peking glass" were probably made in Poshan (Bead Chart 822–32). Glass beads continue to be made in China even today, frequently involving techniques reported over a hundred years ago.[21]

Chinese Court Beads

In 1644, the Manchu captured Beijing and established the Qing dynasty (1644–1912). Beads of precious and semipre- cious stones and glass were produced for necklaces called "court beads" or "Mandarin chains" by foreign observers. Worn by the Manchurian emperors and their court, these distinctive necklaces (plate 160) resembled Tibetan Buddhist prayer beads (plate 70) but differed from those of Tibet in both form and content. The Chinese beads expressed status and were permitted to be worn only by peo- ple of high rank. Sumptuary laws of the period established a complex set of rules de- termining acceptable materials for the beads, as well as identifying those who were allowed to wear them.[22]

Important symbolism was imbedded in the overall form as well as the separate components or "accessories" of the necklaces. Like their Tibetan prototypes, they had 108 principal beads. Four large additional beads, called "Buddha heads," set off four groups of 27 beads each. This division also expressed multiples of three, a sacred num- ber associated with Yang and heaven in old Chinese philosophy.[23]

It was during certain yearly rites, such as the annual sacrifices to heaven and earth conducted by the emperor in Beijing, that sumptuary laws regarding the wear- ing of court beads became quite important. The extensive regulations were followed by all court members and extended to high-ranking military officers and to civil ser- vants.[24] Although most aristocratic Chinese women refused to wear Manchurian dress

TOP RIGHT: 167. *Edo period glass beads. Left to right:* gangidama, *or "zigzag bead." Diameter, 1.8 cm;* kuchinashidama, *which derives its name from the seed of the gardenia* (kuchinashi), *whose form it resembles. In the West it is known as a melon bead;* sujidama, *or "line bead," possibly of Venetian origin or at least made in the Venetian style;* sarasadama, *a delicately patterned nineteenth-century bead that derives its name from imported Indian cottons;* marudama, *or "round bead," found in Japan but possibly made in China;* tombodama, *a "complex glass bead";* tombodama, *possibly of Venetian origin. Corning Museum of Glass, Corning, New York*

The Edo period beads shown on this page were probably ojime, *as their perforations are large enough to accommodate a double cord.*[II]

MIDDLE RIGHT: 168. *Glass beads made in Osaka during the 1970s by the late master beadmaker Kyoyo Asao (1918–1985). The beads incorporate traditional manufacturing techniques, including those used in the Nara and Edo periods. Far right bead: length, 2.1 cm. Corning Museum of Glass, Corning, New York*

BOTTOM RIGHT: 169. *A masterpiece of glass beadmaking produced in 1984 by Kyoyo Asao. Length, 2.4 cm. Collection Lease Waldron, Lexington, Massachusetts*

and court beads because they represented the hated foreign rulers, the bead materials of certain court women, such as the emperor's concubines, were exactly prescribed.

All the materials of the court beads mentioned in the Chinese dynastic laws—pearls, coral, honey amber, lapis lazuli, and turquoise—were imported, often from great distances. Understandably, they were highly treasured. Coral came from Italy or the Persian Gulf, amber from Burma and the Baltic area, turquoise from Persia, and lapis lazuli from Afghanistan. All of the jade, frequently used for the Buddha's-head spacer beads, came from Burma or the Khotan region of central Asia (Chinese Turk-menistan). Noblemen of lower rank and their wives wore glass beads. Fine glass was highly valued and sometimes was used to imitate precious stones. Ivory beads were also worn, including some with intricate cutout patterns. Elephant ivory came from India or Africa, walrus ivory from the North Pacific, and fossil mammoth ivory from Si-beria. Beads of rare woods, such as fragrant aloes wood, came from southern China. Aloes wood and rosewood were used for incense, and sometimes a small amount of am-bergris (sperm-whale secretion used for perfumes) was added to the incense and com-pressed into beads. When the beads were held, the warmth of the hand released their fragrance.

Few original Mandarin necklaces still exist. With the fall of the Qing dynasty in 1912, the Chinese were eager to break up the necklaces and sell off the various parts. The chains were a reminder of alien rulers, and the foreign costumes and jewelry were best forgotten.

Jade Beads The Chinese have venerated and worn jade for over five thousand years. The character for "king" (王) may have symbolized a string of jade beads. The character *pao*, signifying "precious," originally was the outline of a house enclosing symbols for cowrie shells and jade beads.[25] The Chinese were so fond of jade that those who could afford to carried small pieces with them at all times. When handled, jade supposedly passed some of its subtle virtue on to its owner; Chinese poets called it the "concentrated essence of love."[26]

For centuries, the riverbeds of the Khotan region of central Asia were the chief source of ancient jade (nephrite), although some jade may have also come from the re-gion of Lake Baikal in Siberia. Throughout their history, the Chinese prized nephrite rather than jadeite (the two minerals are both called "jade").[27] However, when a source of brilliant emerald-green jadeite ("imperial jade") was discovered in Burma during the eighteenth century, it was highly coveted, and it is from this jadeite that the most expensive jade beads and jewelry are made.

Despite its hardness, jade can be worked with only a bamboo drill if the right abrasives are used. Jade cannot be cut by steel, but only by stones harder than itself. By the late Shang times (Anyang period, 1300–1045 B.C.), the surfaces of flat jade beads, or plaques and pendants, were incised with complex designs. It has been suggested that bronze drill points were used along with abrasives made of crushed quartz.[28]

Korea The geographic proximity of China and Korea has led casual observers to believe that there must have been close interaction between them, when in fact history shows their border frequently acted as both a physical and cultural bar-rier. This is probably the result of a combination of the rugged border topography and the Koreans' deeply rooted resistance to foreign control. Nevertheless, their adornment does reflect some outside stimuli.

Elements of culture were introduced early to Korea by nomadic peoples from dis-tant northern Asia. It is not surprising, therefore, that ancient Korean art incorporates shamanistic symbolism associated with cultures from Siberia, Manchuria, and the Asian steppes. China was also a major source of influences, which were reinterpreted in uniquely Korean ways. These sources of ideas also played a role in the development of Korean beads.

Perforated bone beads from deer toes from Turubong Cave No. 2 near Seoul date to 18,000 B.C., while jade beads are known from Neolithic sites (5000–2000 B.C.). The best-known Korean bead, the *kogok*, was developed during the first millennium B.C. (plate 161).[29]

Called *kogok* in Korea and *magatama* in Japan, the crescent- or comma-shaped bead is found exclusively in Korea and Japan, each country claiming to have produced the earliest examples. In both countries, it is a sacred symbol: Korea combines a blue and red *kogok*-shaped figure, the yin-yang symbol, in its national emblem, while in Japan, the *magatama* is combined with the sword and mirror as one of the three emblems of royalty.[30]

Kogok beads are made of jade, lapis lazuli, carnelian, and glass. They were used on crowns and other jewelry in Korea's Old Silla dynasty (57 B.C.–A.D. 668). *Magatama* found in graves of the Japanese Yayoi and Kofun (Old Tomb period; 250 B.C.–A.D. 552) were molded in glass and carved from jade, carnelian, and other semiprecious stones.[31] Both *kogok* and *magatama* are directly related to the beginnings of glass production in each country. The earliest evidence of glass manufacturing in Japan is a Yayoi period mold used to cast *magatama*.[32] In Korea, a glass industry was established during the Three Kingdoms period (57 B.C.–A.D. 668) for the sole purpose of making *kogok*.[33]

Over the course of the "Three Kingdoms" period the Chinese were ousted from their colonies and three Korean states were formed—Paekche, Koguryo, and Silla. Royal tombs excavated in Paekche and Silla disclose quantities of both imported and locally made beads. Skilled goldsmiths produced dazzling crowns, girdles, and necklaces decorated with beads of gold, jade, and glass. Especially notable were the gold crowns of Silla, with jade and glass *kogok*. Paekche tombs in Kongju (A.D. 526–529) contained beads of gold, silver, jade, glass, and many other materials. Most of these beads were sewn onto clothing, and many were of the small drawn-glass variety in monochrome blue, violet, green, yellow, and orange. Several gold-in-glass beads, similar to those made in the Mediterranean region, were also found.[34]

A great variety of beads was discovered at the royal tombs at Kyongju in Silla, including faceted quartz crystal forms and a glass mosaic face bead from the fourth or fifth century A.D.[35] Although there are differences, this "face bead" may be related to other fourth-century face beads found in Scandinavia and attributed to Roman glassmakers working under Emperor Constantine during the last days of the empire.[36] Most glass beads found in the Silla tombs were imported, with India, the Roman Empire, and China being possible sources. The *kogok* used in the crowns are the only known beads of this period made of Korean glass. Jade beads (both nephrite and jadeite) in the tombs probably came from sources in Turkmenistan, Korea, and Japan, while amber found there may actually be copal from native Korean pine trees. The jet, pearls, gold, and silver all came from Korea.[37]

Most of Korea's imported beads and materials came over the silk routes into China from the Middle East, central Asia, India, and the West. This pattern of Korean trade conducted via China with the outside world continued for centuries.

The Yi dynasty (A.D. 1392–1910) was the last to rule Korea before its annexation by Japan in 1910. Yi rulers banned Buddhism and molded the nation's social and spiritual life according to neo-Confucianist principles derived from China's Ming dynasty.

ABOVE: **171.** *This* ojime *was made by Somin, a master metallurgist in the nineteenth century. It depicts a* shojo *carved in solid gold emerging from a sake jar. The eyeball, iris, and pupil are inlaid with iron and silver.* Shojo *are mythical creatures living by the sea, who love to drink sake, sing, and dance. These joyous creatures are a symbol of universal happiness. Length, 2.3 cm. (Reproduced actual size.) Collection Dave and Sandy Swedlow, Los Angeles*

RIGHT: **172.** Ojime *in plate 171 enlarged eight times.*

173. *Lacquer, made from the sap of the lacquer tree, can be layered on a wooden bead. Here, red, black, and silver lacquer on ivory creates a dramatic portrayal of a hunting falcon encircling the* ojime *as it swoops to catch a dragonfly. Diameter, 1.6 cm. Private collection*

174. *A lacquer* ojime *made of at least 19 yellow, black, and red layers of lacquer. Carved in relief, it depicts symbols of Japan's aesthetic life, including tea ceremony implements, musical instruments, and a basket of fruit called "citron Buddha's fingers" or "Buddha's hand." Diameter, 1.65 cm. Collection Dr. Ralph Maercks, Miami*

173

174

175

176

177

178

179

180

181

175. *A rare coral ojime beautifully carved into a seated monkey. Length, 2 cm. Private collection*

176. *A stained ivory version of "Hear no evil, speak no evil, see no evil." Length, 1.4 cm. Private collection*

177. *An ojime of stained stag antler carved as a monkey climbing the inro cord. Length, 2.5 cm. Private collection*

178. *An ojime showing a wood-gatherer pouring himself a bowl of sake. An example of "married" metalwork (the joining of different metals; in this case, gold, silver, and copper). Length, 1.82 cm. Collection Dr. Ralph Maercks, Miami*

179. *A teakettle with a paulownia tree, emblem of the imperial family. Length, 0.4 cm. Collection Dave and Sandy Swedlow, Los Angeles*

180. *A "married" metalwork ojime of an open strip of bamboo with a finely detailed wasp inside. Length, 2 cm. Private collection*

181. *An engraved ivory ojime of bamboo and a sparrow. Length, 1.45 cm. Collection Ann Meselson, Los Angeles*

Ojime Creating ojime *(slide fasteners) challenged the artisan to work within severe restrictions of space and form.* Ojime *had to be diminutive but sturdy, with a smooth, round shapes. Sharp projections could easily break off or catch on the kimono. Thus,* ojime *had to be finished on all sides, with the cord holes positioned to maintain the harmony of the overall design.*

During the eighteenth and nineteenth centuries, new classes of wealthy merchants commissioned ojime *of extreme fragility and intricacy. Four types of "artistic"* ojime *can be recognized: three-dimensional, miniature sculptural forms resembling* netsuke *(plate 184); engraved* ojime *(plate 181); cameo-style or high-relief carving across a solid surface, including deeply cut, openwork pieces (plate 185); and beads with lacquered and inlaid surfaces (plate 173).*

Sculptural ojime *presented a major design problem: how to carve an artistic opening in a small object while maintaining a precise tension in the double cord. Two solutions were found: running a straight perforation through the carved body or creating a form, such as a monkey, mystic, coiled snake, or child, that would appear to be climbing up the cords (plate 151).*

The other three forms of ojime *use the same technique to accommodate a double cord: a straight perforation through the center. Beads with a wide perforation (typically 4.5 to 5 millimeters in diameter) are distinguishable as* ojime.

One hallmark of the best Japanese design is restraint. This quality is seen in the positioning of a simple coral ojime *between an elaborate* inro *and* netsuke *in many Edo period ensembles. These early* ojime *were simple spheres that created space between the decorated* inro *and* netsuke. *By the late Edo period and throughout the Meiji period, however, the plain, globular forms were eclipsed by beautifully sculpted, complex designs that can be appreciated as individual sculptures in their own right. Most of the* ojime *shown in plates 170–190 are from these later periods.*

BOTTOM: **186.** *Animals. (1) spotted ivory Japanese pug; Length, 1.4 cm. Collection Dave and Sandy Swedlow, Los Angeles; (2) coiled bronze snake. Length, 1.3 cm. Collection Judith Feinberg, Miami; (3) bat, symbol of prosperity, happiness, and good luck, made of bronze with inlaid gold eyes. Length, 2.1 cm. Collection Dave and Sandy Swedlow, Los Angeles. Bottom row, left to right: (4) nest of rats made in ivory. Diameter, 1.5 cm. Private collection; (5) an exceptionally realistic white rat, reclining with its tail wrapped around its body. The eyes have been drilled completely through the ivory head and inlaid in transparent horn, giving them a lifelike appearance. Diameter, 2.2 cm. Collection Midori Gallery, Coconut Grove, Florida; (6) hare among horsetail plants (equiseta), an allusion to the moon hare, the Japanese equivalent of the West's man-in-the-moon. Length, 2.25 cm. Private collection*

187. *Legends. (1) Yoshisada, a fourteenth-century hero, exemplified the samurai code of honor. When he was finally defeated at the battle of Fujishima, his head was publicly displayed in Kyoto. Length, 2 cm. Collection Judith Feinberg, Miami; (2) an ivory ojime depicting the falconer's story. As the holder rotates the ojime, in this case three times, a story unfolds in the round. The first view shows a daimyo inspecting his fiefdom with his prize falcon on his arm. As the ojime is turned, his retriever appears; with another turn, a villager is seen running across a bridge to receive him.[IV] Diameter, 1.75 cm. Collection Midori Gallery,*

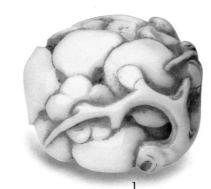

1

2

3

4

5

Flowers

1

2

3

4

5

6

Animals

1

2

3

4

5

6

7

8

Legends

Coconut Grove, Florida; (3) a dragon in swirling clouds, the only mythological creature among the twelve zodiac animals. Length, 2.1 cm. Collection Midori Gallery, Coconut Grove, Florida. Bottom row, left to right: (4) an ivory zodiac, represented by twelve creatures in cyclical order: rat, ox, tiger, hare or rabbit, dragon, snake, horse, sheep or goat, monkey, cock, dog, and pig. It was popular to wear an ojime depicting the creature of the owner's year of birth. Length, 2.1 cm. Collection Midori Gallery, Coconut Grove; Florida; (5) a badger of stained ivory. Beloved in Japanese folklore as a trickster. Length, 1.9 cm. Private collection; (6) an ivory tengu emerging from its egg. This mythical creature has an eagle's beak, wings, and claws, with a humanoid body. Length, 1.85 cm. Private collection; (7) an ivory Daruma. As the founder of Zen Buddhism, Daruma sat meditating for nine years and his legs atrophied, thus he is always depicted legless. Daruma is an adored Japanese subject. Height, 1.6 cm. Private collection;

1

2

3

4

Tales of the Sea

This meant a return to sumptuary laws and a limited use of beads.[38] Strings of beads were allowed to tie down hats but were not to be worn as necklaces. Men's topknots and ponytails were held in place by long barrel-shaped beads, while women wore beads sewn onto headdresses and attached to a tasseled ornamental knot (*maedup*) or a pendant (*norigae*).[39] The elite used beads of amber, jade, coral, turquoise, and carnelian for these purposes, while glass served those of lower rank.[40]

In the eighteenth and nineteenth centuries, Koreans wore "perfume beads" made of aromatic spices and gums. Blue, white, green, or red in color, they were strung on white horsehair, and often dangled from fans.[41]

Today, Koreans cut semiprecious stones (amethyst, quartz, carnelian, crystal, and agate) into beads and export pearls from Cheju Island. Glass beads are made by lampwinding techniques learned from the Japanese in the 1920s. There is also a special type of necklace bead made by hand from a mixture of flour and glue.[42]

Japan

Over the centuries, the Japanese have been the recipients of cultural influences from China, Korea, and the West. Rather than being overwhelmed and transformed by foreign influences, however, they have selectively integrated new ideas into their distinctive culture.

The Japanese are known for the intimate rather than the heroic in design. Surrounded by water, resources, including space, are scarce in Japan, so economy has always been practiced in all things, including design. This is best expressed in the art of miniaturization—the economizing of everything material, cultural, and natural. The concept of artistic microcosms—self-contained worlds within a confined space—was developed by the Japanese and employed in activities from gardening and flower arrangement to personal adornment. No item was too small or unimportant to be designed as a totality in which function and aesthetics were integrated.

The earliest Japanese beads were made from perforated shells, bones, and stones found in Initial Jomon sites (dating about 10,000 B.C.) on Shikoku, Hokkaido, and Honshu.[43] By Middle Jomon times (3600–2500 B.C.) adornment was abundant and made in a variety of stone, including jade.[44] The Yayoi period (200 B.C.–A.D. 200) witnessed development of the potter's wheel, metal forging and casting, and the first glass beads. Unlike the Chinese, the Japanese valued glass beads as "jewels," leaving a profusion of them in sites dating from almost every period of their history.

After 50 B.C., Yayoi people were in regular contact with China via Korea. It is believed that most early Japanese glass beads—small, round, translucent forms in limited shades of green and blue—were made either from imported glass ingots or from Chinese glass objects that had been melted down.[45] From the Yayoi period until at least the eighteenth century, China and Japan traded glass beads and shared bead technology. An important bead style that manifests Korean-Japanese relationships found in Yayoi tombs was *magatama*, comma-shaped beads closely resembling the Korean *kogok*, made in both stone and glass (plates 161–2).

The Old Tomb period (A.D. 250–552) is marked by the appearance of large, conspicuous burial mounds containing tombs in which beads were the most numerous artifact. It is believed that the hundreds of thousands of beads found throughout the country and dating to this period held spiritual significance. Bead shapes of the Old Tomb period were spherical (plates 163–5), cylindrical, and faceted, and materials included glass, quartz, green jasper, agate, jadeite, and steatite. *Tombodama*, complex multicolored glass beads, appeared for the first time, as did opaque, reddish glass beads similar to the *mutisalah* found in India, East Africa, and Southeast Asia.[46] Clay figures (*haniwa*) wearing glass bead necklaces, bracelets, and anklets have been excavated from Old Tomb period sites. Gold, silver, and bronze crowns, horse trappings, and earrings were also ornamented with glass beads.

An influx of Chinese and Korean craftsmen occurred during this period, and most Japanese glass beads were made by Chinese immigrants or by Japanese glassmakers working under the guidance of foreign craftsmen.[47] There were also many imported Chinese glass beads, yet no examples of China's remarkable Han eye beads have ever been found in Japan.

Japanese beadmaking was primarily a part-time cottage industry, with glass probably made at a central place and distributed as rods to individual artisans working at home and using clay cooking stoves. Glass beads from this period were formed by winding and cut-tube methods, although some were molded or even shaped by lapidary (grinding) techniques.[48]

Buddhism entered Japan at the beginning of the Asuka period (A.D. 552–645), a time when the Chinese and Koreans deeply influenced the Japanese. Glass beads continued to have spiritual significance, serving in Buddhist rituals. At this time, beads were strung in complex arrangements using a variety of bead styles.[49]

During the Nara period (A.D. 645–794), new ideas, including those associated with Buddhism, were introduced to Japan from Byzantium, Syria, Persia, India, and central Asia through active trade along the silk routes. Nara beads show the impact of this trade. Japanese craftsmen were stimulated by the many imported objects made in Sasanian Persia (A.D. 226–651), a country famed at this time for its beautiful glass and agate beads. Japan and Sasanian Persia were in direct contact, and the Persians appear to have had an important influence on the newly refined designs and techniques characteristic of Nara beads.

Most beads known from the period are preserved, not as mortuary goods, but in the *Shoso-in*, the imperial treasure-house, a unique monument to the Emperor Shomu, who was buried with all his possessions in A.D. 765. These beads are of superb technical quality and of great variety in shape and raw materials.[50] The large number of glass beads stored in the *Shoso-in* is particularly striking: approximately 75,000 beads in 250 strings of 100 to 300 beads each.

By the Nara period, the spiritual role of beads gave way to largely decorative functions. Beads were used primarily to decorate furniture, sword handles and sheaths, clothing, and crowns. One headdress was described as inset with twenty-six thousand beads of pearls, rock crystal, coral, jade, and multicolored glass.[51]

The great age of Nara-period beadmaking lasted less than a century in all, and it was followed by a steady decline in glass beadmaking over the next eight hundred years—although glass beads were still used for sacred purposes, including adornment of portable Shinto shrines, in Buddhist rosaries, and the decoration of Buddhist images. There are records of stone beads during the Heian period (897–1185), and these are described as cut from "cold agates," jaspers, and crystal.[52]

The sheaths of Heian swords were wrapped in beads, and at the shrine of the Sun Goddess at Ise a listing of sacred treasures in 1037–39 included a sword "wrapped with three hundred beads."[53] In 1869, while excavating for a sacred enclosure north of the shrine, three swords of exquisite craftsmanship were uncovered, one with a string of three hundred beads of precious stones wrapped around the sheath.

Extensive trade with China characterized the Muromachi period (1392–1573), and imports flooded the country. Portuguese and Spanish merchants began visiting the island of Kyushu in southern Japan, accompanied by missionaries. On the west coast,

Nagasaki was opened to the Portuguese in 1570. Although Europeans presumably introduced their beads, most surviving examples from this period are Chinese.[54] During the Momoyama period (1573–1615), Chinese and possibly Venetian beads were imported into Japan. While some foreign stimulation of Momoyama beadmakers is apparent, it was not until the succeeding Edo period that Japanese beadmaking began to flourish.

The Edo period (1615–1867) brought an end to several centuries of civil war as Japan was unified under the Tokugawa shogunate. The arts, including beadmaking, thrived. New designs and techniques from abroad helped to inspire an outpouring of locally made glass and other beads. In fact, it was during this period that most Japanese glass beads were made. Frequently, it is unclear whether an Edo bead is a Venetian import or made by a Japanese or Chinese craftsman imitating foreign styles. Although Japanese artisans were stimulated by seventeenth- and eighteenth-century European glass beads, most learned from Chinese beadmakers residing in Nagasaki or indirectly from European books. By the nineteenth century, when European beads were readily available, Japanese glassmakers had essentially developed their own craft.[55]

Like China, Japan remained for the most part closed to the West until the nineteenth century, except for limited entry of Dutch and Chinese ships at the port of Nagasaki. Nonetheless, quantities of Bohemian, Dutch, and Venetian glass beads were brought in by Dutch traders, and Chinese glass beads were either imported or the products of Chinese glass beadmakers established in the Nagasaki area.

During the years of isolation, when trade was restricted to Nagasaki, merchants in this area not only circulated goods between Japan and Europe but also obtained products from Southeast Asian countries. Dutch traders gave prized glass beads to Japanese provincial lords and important government officials, thus providing Japanese beadmakers with examples of a wide range of glass bead technologies in use at the time in other nations. During this period, most beads, including those made of gold, silver, iron, copper, ivory, coral, glass, crystal, and wood, served as *ojime*, slide fasteners, used to hold *inro*, personal carrying cases, in place. *Ojime* became status symbols and the focus of enormous creative attention.

Ojime The Japanese say, "Nothing is beautiful that is not also useful, and nothing is useful that is not also beautiful." *Ojime* were no exception: they were meant to be worn not as ornaments but as fasteners for small cases in which an individual carried items of everyday necessity on his person. The traditional Japanese costume, the kimono, has no pockets; while women kept small articles in their sleeves, men carried personal possessions such as medicine, seals, tobacco, and coins in containers suspended by cords from the *obi*, a wide sash binding the kimono at the waist.

These containers ranged from simple leather pouches to elaborately lacquered wooden *inro*. The *inro* were divided into compartments held in place by two cords that joined at the top where they passed through a bead, called an *ojime*. The cords were finally attached at their far end to a *netsuke*, a counterweight placed under the *obi* to insure that the *inro* would not slip out (plate 170).

The elevation of the *inro*, *netsuke*, and *ojime* ensemble into an art form reflects social, political, and economic circumstances in Tokugawa Japan, which was strictly divided into social classes: nobility, samurai, merchant, farmer, or artisan. Edicts prescribed the appropriate dress for each class, forbidding jewelry to all, including the nobility. In the early days, farmers, merchants, and artisans carried pouches; gentlemen wore *inro*. With peace and stability, merchants prospered, becoming patrons of the arts. *Inro* ensembles were their means of discreetly displaying wealth and taste. Probably considered insignificant, *inro* were not restricted by sumptuary laws.

Chronicles indicate that by A.D. 700 the Japanese wore pouches containing flints to make fire, but there is no record of beads being used in this context. The earliest reference to *ojime* dates from the beginning of the seventeenth century: "There is the fashionable, pleasure-loving young priest of today....A flat silk sash patterned with gold dust, is wrapped around his waist....Suspended from his sash are a yellow dyed *kinchaku* [coin purse], and an *inro* of *maki-e* [gold sprinkled over lacquer]....The cord for these is secured by an *otome* [cord cinch] with bull's eye design."[56]

Early *ojime* in no way resembled the beautifully sculpted beads collected today. They were simple devices of stone, coral, bone, and other materials thought to have magical or curative powers. Jade promoted longevity; the disintegration of coral warned of poison; stag antler assured virility.

By the late eighteenth century, *inro* became less functional but were used instead to display status. The *Shikigusa*, a work published in 1777, relates: "These days, even common people wear *inro* suspended from the sash, but do not use them for carrying medicine. They just like the exotic effect such articles have. These objects have become nothing more than ornaments to show off to other people."[57]

By the early nineteenth century, matched sets of increasingly elaborate *inro, netsuke*, and *ojime* were commissioned and collected, and the subject matter of the three parts was carefully coordinated.[58] The *ojime* as an art object reached its zenith between the late eighteenth century and the reign of Emperor Meiji (1868–1912), the period following reestablishment of contact with the West.

Most artistic *ojime* are of ivory, although they were made of many organic materials found in Japan, including horn, bone, wood, seeds, and tortoiseshell. Ivory was imported from India and Africa or obtained from arctic dolphins. Indigenous woods included cypress, cherry, ebony, boxwood, persimmon, camellia, and yew. *Ojime* were also made of native gold, silver, and copper—copper-tin and copper-silver being frequently used alloys. Glass *ojime* were frequently worn by the less affluent classes.[59]

Most *ojime* artists came from two closely related disciplines: *netsuke* carving and metallurgy. The *ojime* was a natural extension of the *netsuke* artist's craft of carving miniature works of art. Metallurgists created *ojime* using the same detailed metalwork techniques they formerly employed in making elaborate accessories for prestigious samurai swords.[60]

Ojime captured the full spectrum of Japanese life: history, religion, flora, fauna, people, and daily events. Hardly a subject was omitted, and the rounded *ojime* form lent itself to depicting narratives, too (plate 187, 2–4).[61] As Japan was opened to trade after 1854, Western dress began to replace the kimono and its accessories. By the turn of the century, the Japanese industrial revolution was in full swing, and few *netsuke, ojime*, and *inro* were made. Today, *netsuke* and *ojime* are again being created for decorative purposes.

Following Admiral Perry's arrival in 1853, traffic in glass beads expanded as part of a general increase in Japanese export manufacturing. By the 1870s, Japanese beadmakers were traveling to Austria, Italy, and India to learn modern manufacturing techniques. Today, mass-production of glass beads thrives alongside the work of a few accomplished beadmakers, such as the late Kyoyo Asao, who revived old techniques to produce his masterpieces. But it is with pearls that the Japanese have made their greatest impact on twentieth-century adornment. By 1913, Mikimoto had perfected the cultivation of pearls, making it possible for almost anyone to own them. The Japanese continue to excel in pearl farming and control the industry worldwide.

OPPOSITE: **197.** *Eighteenth-century Mogul enameled gold necklace with pearls and emerald beads. Once precious stones were pierced, they lost some of their intrinsic value, thus such necklaces conveyed their owners' great wealth. The necklaces of gems and metals created by jewelers of the Mogul court are among the most elaborate ever made, yet their designs are unusually well integrated and not overwhelmed by details. Length, 42.5 cm. Collection Tambaran Gallery, New York*

LEFT: **198.** *Sapphire beads in shades of blue, yellow, and pink. These contemporary Indian beads were faceted and pierced by craftsmen on a dirt floor with a bow drill, a method practiced since Mogul days. The shapes of the pure yellow sapphires are similar to motifs in very early Mogul jewelry. The carefully matched and graded stones of the five-strand necklace weigh 530 carats. Necklace: length, 67.5 cm. Collection Dr. Stephen Paul Adler/Collector's Edition, New York*

The Beads of Nagaland

Nagaland, a tribal territory that gained statehood within India in 1977, is located in a rugged, mountainous region bordering southwest Burma. The nearly eighteen hundred Naga tribes are of Mongolian descent and many remained isolated until the twentieth century, partly due to their remote location and partly because of their reputation as headhunters. Beaded jewelry was an important part of Naga attire.

The traditional Naga people were farmers who lived in villages. The tribes shared an animistic religion. Like many events in Naga life, agricultural seasons were marked by ceremonies to drive away evil spirits and to insure the harvest. Because the Naga lived in a world they perceived as threatened by malevolent spirits, they believed only those with personal power could survive. This power is concentrated in the head; by taking a man's head, the hunter could possess the victim's power and enhance his own prestige in the community.[IV]

Their isolation notwithstanding, all Naga jewelry is made from traded objects: shells from the Bay of Bengal, carnelian and brass bells from India, and glass beads from India and occasionally from Venice. How the Naga obtained their beads in the past is not clear. Some beads from Venice and many varieties of glass beads made in India were traded to Nagaland, with certain tribes, such as the Angami, probably controlling much of the trade. Carnelian beads from India and imported shells represented wealth.

A people without notable painting and sculpture traditions, the Naga created exceptionally beautiful beaded jewelry, which was endowed with social symbolism. The Naga wore very little clothing, so that beaded jewelry (and tattooing) represented most of their adornment: the degree of ornateness indicated the wearer's exact rank. Their beads were frequently worn during festivals and ceremonies to celebrate plantings, harvests, and successful headhunting.[V]

After a victorious raid, beaded necklaces, passed down through the family and stored in baskets at home, were taken out. The heads seized in the raid were distributed, and the dancers adorned themselves with as many as ten necklaces each and danced all night. The necklaces were then stored, awaiting the next ceremony. Certain necklaces were never worn by day.[VI]

As the Naga culture disintegrates today through increasing contact with the modern world, and beads and shells are no longer traded, jewelry-making has almost disappeared. With traditions eroding and adornment no longer functioning in a ritual context, the craft has lost its meaning. Beaded family heirlooms are now traded for items considered useful—penicillin, down parkas, and transistor radios. The necklaces illustrated in plates 199–205 probably date to the early 1900s.

199. *An Angami Naga warrior wearing a necklace of the type shown in plate 201. This is an early twentieth-century photograph. Courtesy of the Smithsonian Institution, Washington* D.C.

OVERLEAF, TOP LEFT:
200. *The necklace of a successful Naga headhunter. Such assemblies of brass heads and spirals, tiger teeth, and glass trade beads were worn only by men who had actually taken heads. The brass heads (comparable to a shrunken-head trophy) symbolize the number of kills credited to the owner. The marigold yellow beads from India were highly prized. Row of brass heads: length, 22.5 cm. Collection Mimi Lipton and Hansjörg Mayer, London*

OVERLEAF, BOTTOM:
201. *An Angami necklace from southern Nagaland composed of rare, imported items, including shells, blue and yellow glass, and faceted carnelian beads from India. Bone spacers separate the strands. The two shells symbolize two horns; these may have religious significance, since horns represent fertility. Cut sections of conch shell are characteristic of Angami jewelry. They are worn on the shoulders and back, resembling the huge stone monoliths that surround this tribe's religious buildings. Back shell: length, 14 cm. Private collection*

RIGHT: 204. *A Naga sash worn over the shoulder and across the chest, made from strands of Indian glass beads, large shell disks, and dyed goat-hair tassels. The dyed goat hair symbolizes the flames that have ravaged enemy villages. Length, 132 cm. Collection Tambaran Gallery, New York*

OPPOSITE: 205. *A necklace made to be worn by an important man of the Konyak tribe, with orange, marigold yellow, brown, and white glass trade beads, shell beads, brass bells, and incised conch shell sections. The fastenings are crocheted grass or palm fibers. More than any other Naga tribe, the Konyak have withstood modernization, retaining the jewelry and customs of the past. They are considered the best craftsmen among the Naga. Necklace length (from top bone divider to center of necklace), 60 cm. Typical orange bead: length, 1.3 cm. Collection Tambaran Gallery, New York*

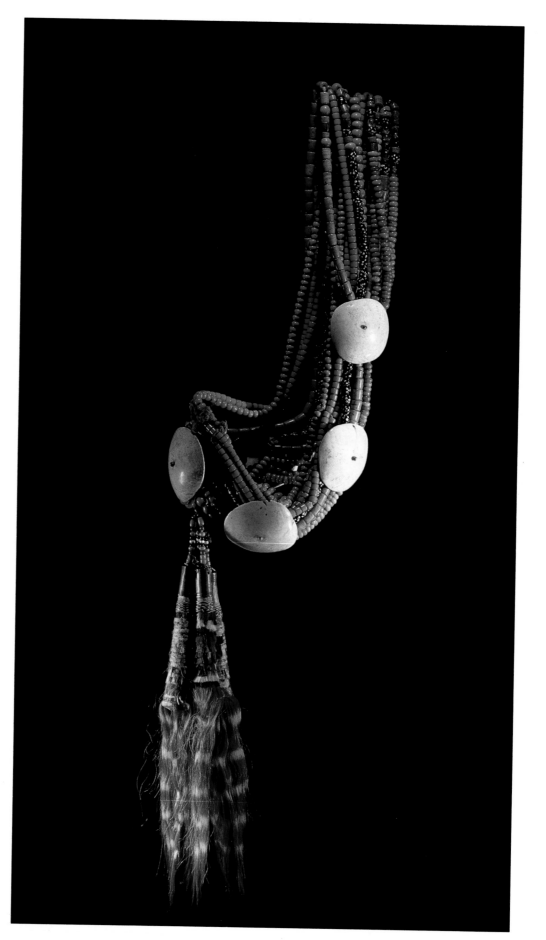

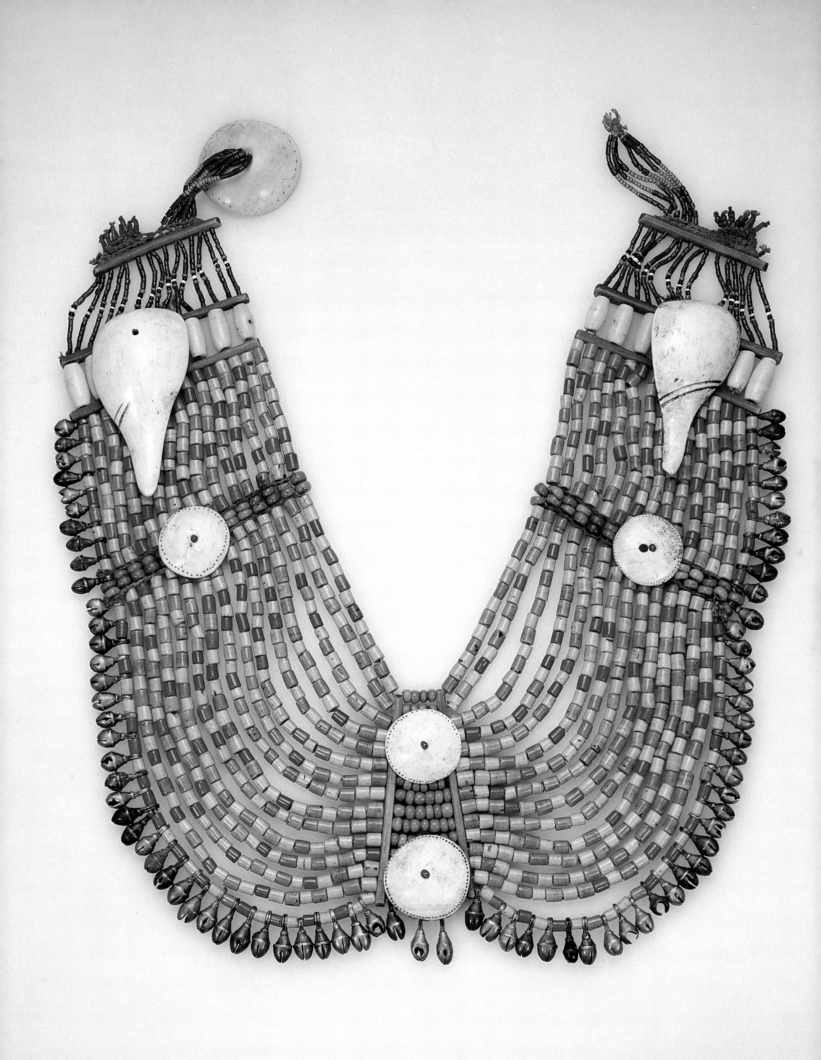

The Mogul Period

Under the Moguls, the Muslim rulers of northern India from the early sixteenth to the eighteenth century, jewelry became very sophisticated. The Mogul dynasty was founded by Babur (1485–1530), great-grandson of both Tamerlane and Genghis Khan. Babur overran Agra and Delhi, and he eventually captured all of northern India. Under strong central rule and free from most internal warfare, the new empire's trade and creativity flourished. Great wealth was concentrated in the hands of the Mogul rulers and their courts, and they desired elaborate personal ornamentation. Exquisite craftsmanship, with lavish displays of precious metals and stones, were hallmarks of imperial Mogul jewelry. Persian jewelers, known for their fine detailing, were invited to establish workshops in India, and they evolved an Indo-Persian style that even today remains unique.[33]

The Moguls epitomized the idea that "the glory of a prince is made more tangible by his buildings, his library, and his jewels."[34] With this motto, they presided over one of the great creative ages of Indian civilization, patronizing painters, architects, and jewelers. The Mogul emperors used their economic power to subsidize mining operations for rare minerals, then encouraged artisans to create new forms of jewelry utilizing these materials. Beadmaking with precious stones flourished. Even the most valuable stones—emeralds, rubies, and sapphires—were made into beads, despite the risk of diminishing their value by piercing them (plate 197).

The size of gems was considered all-important, and it was unthinkable for an artisan to cut a stone to one-third its original size simply to add brilliance.[35] Mogul beads made of precious stones were usually cabochon-cut, accentuating color rather than light (making faceted jewelry seem excessively flamboyant by comparison). This may also explain why using gemstones as beads is rare; only a few examples from Rome, Byzantium, and China are known outside of India.

The Moguls were not shy about displaying their jewels and the vast quantities of pearls they obtained from the Persian Gulf. In 1658, the Frenchman François Bernier observed that even the orthodox and puritanical Emperor Aurangzeb was bedizened on state occasions, wearing a "necklace of immense pearls suspended from his neck which reached his stomach in the same manner as many of the Gentiles wear their beads," an apparent reference to the European manner of wearing rosaries.[36]

The clothes and jewels of Mogul women also reflected the status of their men. Manucci, the Venetian physician at the court of Aurangzeb, noted: "Generally, they [the women] had four or five rows of pearls hanging from their necks, in a chain coming down to the lower part of their stomach. Upon the middle of the head was a bunch of pearls which hung down the center of the forehead with a valuable ornament of costly stones formed into shapes of the sun, the moon or stars, or, at times, even of flowers.... They girded their waists with gold belts set with precious stones and even the strings with which they tied their trousers had pearls at the ends. On their legs they wore metal ornaments or strings of costly pearls while the shoulders were covered with necklaces like scarves."[37] As Mogul power declined toward the end of the eighteenth century, much of their jewelry was broken up for sale as separate items or taken to other countries. Today, only a fraction of the Mogul court jewelry remains intact in India.

Experimentation with new designs and fine craftsmanship was essentially reserved for the rich in Mogul India. By contrast, jewelry for ordinary people tended to remain simple and traditional. In times of economic crisis, it was often melted down and the stones sold; so it was important that there be no loss in the intrinsic value of the metal and stone, making ordinary jewelry more valued for its material than its workmanship.

The Decline of Indian Beadmaking

While the Moguls of northern India were rewarding themselves with the riches of the continent, the rest of India and her beadmaking industries were in decline. Venice and the German city of Idar-Oberstein established themselves as beadmaking centers by the fifteenth century and began to encroach upon India's market. As Europeans colonized the globe, India's role as a major exporting bead producer was steadily destroyed.

Initially, both Venice and Idar-Oberstein copied the popular and successful Indian beads. The German center concentrated on agates, while the Venetian glassmakers, using drawn-glass techniques, began manufacturing the small seed beads that Indians had been supplying to international markets for centuries.[38] At least one early Venetian imitation can be identified: the long, opaque red-over-green tubes (and later a red-on-white version) of *cornaline d'Aleppo* that copied a fifteenth-century Indian bead.[39]

The Indian bead industry also declined because new industrial techniques enabled the Europeans to produce large quantities of beads in uniform sizes, shapes, and colors—qualities not easily achieved with Indian manufacturing techniques. Furthermore, the New World market, with its immense demand for glass beads, which had not been previously available to Indian beadmakers and traders, greatly strengthened the European bead industry. By 1805, the British government formulated economic policies obliging Indians to buy European goods, and by the end of the nineteenth century India herself was importing vast quantities of beads.[40]

Craftsmen, Tools, and Techniques

Beadmaking in India has always been considered a full-time, specialized craft. For centuries, it was divided among experts in a specific raw material: gold-, silver-, and coppersmiths, as well as specialists in faience, steatite, shell, ivory, and pottery, worked in the industry. Other specialized contributors included the refiner, enameler, precious-stone merchant, cutter, polisher, and even the stringer.[41] Crafts and trades tended to be hereditary and based largely on the caste system. However, the making of carnelian and agate beads at Cambay, an important traditional center of the Indian stone bead industry, has been controlled since the country's independence by those with enough money to buy stones and finance the operation.[42] Cambay stone beads have a limited range of shapes (they come in spheres, cones, bicones, faceted bicones, long rectangulars) and are created with the same primitive tools and techniques that have been employed for centuries.[43] The rough bead forms are smoothed by finer chipping, then ground smooth, drilled, and polished. Today, grinding and polishing are done mechanically. The faceting of beads, a common practice in India by the third century B.C., is used to enhance the brilliance and luster of the stone, while hiding minor defects. Cambay carnelians are often heat-treated to alter chemically the stone's iron compound, thereby accentuating its orange color.[44]

Indian Beadmaking Today

The Indian beadmaking industry remains strong. The mining of agate in Ratanpur and stone beadmaking in Cambay are important industries, while glass beadmaking has grown stronger since India gained independence in 1947 (Bead Chart 635–48). There are four major glass beadmaking centers today: Firozabad produces glass for India's beadmakers; Purdalpur is known for copies of Venetian millefiore beads; Papanaidupet is recognized for a unique drawn-glass technique; and Banaras makes glass beads in the Czech style.[45] Even rubies, emeralds, and sapphires, pierced and strung as beads, enjoy renewed popularity.

Central Asia

Central Asia is a hybrid of peoples and cultures. It includes the area from Siberia in the north to Iran, Afghanistan, Pakistan, and northern India in the south; from the Caspian Sea in the west to Mongolia in the northeast and China in the east. Today's northern Afghanistan, Soviet Central Asia (Turkmenistan, Uzbekistan, and Kazakhstan), and the Himalayan lands of Tibet, Nepal, Ladakh, Sikkim, and Bhutan are all part of this historic region.

Glancing at its location and geography, one would not expect central Asia to have been a major hub of cultural interaction. On the contrary, one might well imagine its great land mass, lack of access to the sea, and forbidding terrain of precipitous mountain ranges and formidable steppes—open, semiarid grassland stretching from eastern Europe to the heart of Asia—would have made its peoples isolated and their societies impenetrable. Yet, through the ages, central Asia has been one of the world's great melting pots.

Passing between the great civilizations of the Mediterranean and western Asia to the west and India and China to the east, overland trade routes crisscrossed central Asia, interconnecting the nomadic pastoralists and sedentary agriculturalists of the high, outlying plateaus. Local buyers and sellers converged at centers along the routes, in oases or river valleys. In time, these centers became towns and cities, closely linked to the growth of internal and international trade. With the merchants came new concepts—visibly expressed in their religious, political, and social customs and in their adornment—that were absorbed into the local practices of central Asia's societies. Refugees from Burma, India, and possibly China, facing religious and political persecution at home, found the Himalayans to be especially tolerant of their diverse beliefs. Indeed, the strongest cultural transfusions were injected by Indian and Chinese trav-

206. *Prayer beads held by a Buddhist monk in Nepal, 1983. All photographs of people in this chapter were taken from 1983 to 1986, unless otherwise noted.*

elers, particularly those who frequented the eastern parts of central Asia and the Himalayas. Afghanistan and Turkmenistan, on the other hand, were influenced more by the cultures of northern Iran and the Mediterranean. Each ethnic group therefore developed distinct characteristics.

Despite their geographic remoteness and their receptiveness to various foreign ideas, the peoples of central Asia shared common historic and economic circumstances that frequently led to strong cultural similarities. Jewelry is an excellent indicator of these likenesses. The inhabitants of Turkmenistan, Mongolia, and the Himalayas, for example, wear turquoise beads because they share ancient beliefs about the material's amuletic properties. In a region where the networks of cultural interaction are immensely complex, beads, bartered for centuries, not surprisingly reflect the history.

For millennia, almost every person in this part of Asia has worn substantial quantities of beads and always prominently displayed them. Whether as objects of wealth and social status or as talismans, beads were and are part of the daily spiritual and secular life of the people. Beads were usually imported. In finished form or as raw materials, they have always been a major component of central Asian trade. Italian coral, Burmese and Baltic amber, Chinese turquoise and silver, and precious gems from India have passed through the region. The elaborate trade routes—involving nomadic herdsmen, local merchants, and international brokers—that carried goods from Asia and to the West also served to distribute beads to people along the way.

Adornment is one manifestation of the divisions in wealth and circumstances between the pastoral nomads, village agriculturalists, and city dwellers. Each group wore jewelry that was appropriate to its social standing and development. There are frequently greater similarities between beads worn by nomads from Turkmenistan, Nepal, and Mongolia than between the Nepalese nomads and Nepalese urban dwellers, or even between different social classes in Nepalese cities. This is partly because the wealthy could create elaborate ensembles of foreign imports that were not readily affordable to others. Yet, despite differences in materials, jewelry from central Asia has a common purpose: to endow the owner with the bead's or jewel's spiritual and protective properties. Given this unifying premise—a continuation of ancient shamanistic beliefs overlaid with Buddhist, Hindu, or Islamic tenets—each ethnic and economic group has chosen distinctive ways to articulate its adornment.

Trade Routes   Dating to the days of the Roman Empire, the silk routes were the most famous of Asia's trading channels. By the second century B.C., demand for Chinese silk in the Mediterranean greatly increased the importance of the active East-West routes, even though some journeys were nine thousand miles long, took as much as a year to complete, and were often dangerous. The overland routes were divided into regional segments, each requiring merchants to know different languages and to have elaborate social connections and means of protection. Rarely did a trader who began a journey in China see the Mediterranean, although Indian and Chinese traders may have traveled between their respective countries.[1] The fame of the Venetian Marco Polo, who traveled the silk routes into China during the thirteenth century, is due not only to the uniqueness and length of his odyssey, but also to the fact that he lived to tell about it.[2]

A dazzling array of finished beads and bead raw materials, including silver, coral, amber, glass, and lapis lazuli, was transported eastward along the silk routes, while caravans originating in China arrived at the emporiums of Samarkand, Balkh, Kabul, and Antioch laden with silk, porcelain, lacquer, and vermilion. The international bead trade helped link the extreme ends of the ancient world from the earliest days of the

Central Asia: *Distribution of Beads and Bead Materials, 3rd Millennium B.C. to 20th Century A.D.*

Bohemian and Venetian Glass Beads to Central Asia 20th C. A.D.

Amber from Baltic to Central Asia

Rome

Glass Beads and Coral from Europe and Egypt to China via Silk Routes 100 B.C.–A.D. 1000

Sarmatian Glass Beadmakers to England 100 B.C.–A.D. 260

SIBERIA

Beads of: White Jade (Nephrite) and Imported Carnelian, Onyx Agate, Glass 500 B.C. to A.D. 200

Coral

▲ *Ust-Labinskaya* Scarabs Glass Beads 100 B.C. to A.D. 100

▲ *Sara* Western Glass Beads 5th C. B.C.

MONGOLIA

▲ *Melitopo* Western Glass Beads 4th C. B.C.

SARMATIA

R. Euphrates

KAZAKHSTAN

Pazyryk ▲

▲ *Minusinsk* Bronze Beads c. 750 B.C.

Copper Tin

TURKMENISTAN

Beads of: Cowries, Carnelian Glass, Turquoise 500–400 B.C.

Turquoise from Iran and China Coral from Mediterranean to Mongolia A.D. 500 to Present

Antioch

Lapis Lazuli to Egypt

EGYPT

R. Tigris

▲ *Kokcha*

UZBEKISTAN

Lulan

Egyptian Glass Beads A.D. 200–300

Djeitun ▲

Zaman-Baba ▲

Samarkand ●

Kashgar ●

Beijing (Peking)

SUMER

Anau ▲

Ur ▲

Tepe Hissar ▲

Altin-depe ▲

IRAN

Balkh ● *Muminabad* ▲

TAKLA MAKAN

Dunhuang ●

CHINA

Turquoise

Herat ● Lapis Lazuli

Khotan ●

Turquoise Silver

ARABIA

Pearls

AFGHANISTAN

Mundigak ▲

Kabul ●

LADAKH

dZi Beads Gold

QINGHAI

Xian (Changan) ●

Lahore ●

Jade

Agate, Spinel Peridot

PAKISTAN

R. Indus

T I B E T

SICHUAN

Silk, Porcelain, Lacquer, and Silver from China to West via Silk Routes 100 B.C.–A.D. 1000

Gold Garnets

Lhasa ●

SIKKIM

Turquoise Silver

NEPAL BHUTAN

Carnelian, Agate

R. Narmada

BURMA

Coral from Mediterranean to Central Asia A.D. 1100 to 1900

INDIA

Shells

Emeralds Sapphires White Jade (Nephrite) Amber and Rubies to Central Asia A.D. 700 to Present

Bay of Bengal

Indian Ocean

Pearls

MALDIVE ISLANDS

Cowries

LEGEND

⠀⠀⠀ Great Wall of China

⟷ Silk Route

← – – Trade Route

● Present-Day City

▲ Archaeological Site: Beadmaking and/or Distribution Center

⟸ Gold Movement of Beads and/or Bead Materials

Gold Source or Archaeological Concentration of Materials

SARMATIA Region

⌒ Mountains

207. *A Tibetan amber bead capped with silver and inlaid with turquoise. The embellishment of surfaces is seen frequently in Himalayan adornment. The larger the bead, the greater its talismanic and status value. Diameter, 9.5 cm. Collection Mimi Lipton, London*

OPPOSITE: 208. *Necklace worn by the great-great-grandmother of Lama Kinga Rinpoche. A note from the lama (a monk or holy man) translated from Tibetan reads: "We don't know how old the actual ambers are, but we do know that this necklace has been with our* labrang *("family") for more than one hundred years. The design of the vase-shaped dZi beads is prehistoric."[1]*

This necklace includes coral, amber, lapis lazuli, and dZi beads, including two round dZi with very rare "lotus" patterns and two less precious dZi on the upper part of the necklace with designs resembling the "horse tooth" pattern. The satin ribbon has the wax seal of the lama. Center amber bead: length, 9 cm. Collection Ivory Freidus

silk routes. Egyptian and Roman glass beads have been excavated in the Warring States period (481–221 B.C.) and Han dynasty (206 B.C.–A.D. 220) tombs.[3] Under the Kushan dynasty, which controlled territories from northern India to central Asia during the second century A.D., there was intensive trade between India and the eastern provinces of the Roman Empire. This is seen in the discovery at Kara Bulak, near Ferghana in Turkmenistan, of beads made of carnelian, agate, lapis lazuli, rock crystal, faience, gold-in-glass, and millefiore glass. They were all imported from India, Afghanistan, and the Roman Mediterranean world and can be dated, for the most part, to between the first and the second centuries A.D.[4]

With the end of the Kushan period in the fourth century, the main silk routes came under the control of nomadic Turkish tribes who arrived in central Asia as part of the great movement of populations during the Migrations Period. Under tribal rule, the silk routes were extended into the Himalayan kingdoms of Tibet and Nepal, while international trade flourished between Byzantium, Sasanian Persia, India, Samarkand, and the Far East. Beads from the West are found in China, Korea, and Japan through the eighth century. However, following the establishment of more economic sea routes by the tenth century and periods of Chinese isolationism, East-West trade via the silk routes greatly diminished.

Buddhism and Beads

From A.D. 100 to 700, the expansion of trade routes through central Asia was accompanied by the introduction of Hinduism and the spread of Buddhism. Although Islam eventually dominated western central Asia, and Hinduism and Christianity developed some followers, Buddhism made the greatest impact on the region as a whole.

Central Asian Buddhism, rooted in Tibet, was a blend of orthodox Buddhist teachings adapted to indigenous folk practices. The belief system had a profound influence on adornment. Living in rugged and sometimes treacherous country, Tibetans attributed numerous misfortunes to evil spirits that resided in the environment, their animal herds, and even in their own bodies. By wearing talismans in the form of prayer boxes or beads, they believed dangerous spirits could be appeased or suppressed. Jewelry was therefore an important part of people's daily dress, and in most Himalayan countries even the humblest citizens owned a few amuletic turquoise beads.[5]

Turquoise and coral, both thought to have significant protective powers, were applied to religious images and used in many ritual objects. Most sculptures of Buddhist and Hindu gods in central Asia display beads and are often inlaid with semiprecious stones.[6] The beads are archetypal and mirror the colors of primal substances: red (coral) represents blood, fire, and light; blue (turquoise) is for water, sky, and air; yellow (amber) is for earth. By wearing beads made from these precious or semiprecious stones, people affirmed their connections to the spiritual realm. By serving as a daily reminder, jewels put people in touch with spirits and deities. Jewels were offered to be set into statues as an act of devotion and also as a way to impart the powers of these stones to the image itself. This gave the image further talismanic power that in turn could help the worshiper.

Tibet Despite its awesome physical barriers, Tibet was a closed country for only limited periods. Tibetan records from before the seventh century A.D. are rare, but there is evidence that relations existed between tribes of the central Tibetan valleys and both the Chinese and Greco-Roman civilizations. Ties with India were also important and eventually led to the adoption of Buddhism in the eighth century. The Mongolians on several occasions played important roles in Tibetan political affairs, and they adopted Tibetan Buddhism toward the end of the sixteenth century. European Christian missionaries were also active in Tibet during the seventeenth and eighteenth centuries. China, Tibet's great neighbor, saw her influence wax and wane, but relations between the two countries extend from prehistory to the present.[7] Formal ties were established during the Tang dynasty (A.D. 618–907).

Until it was absorbed into China in 1959, Tibet was a Buddhist theocracy ruled jointly by a powerful hierarchy of lamas (monks) and lay nobility that recognized the Dalai Lama as their spiritual and temporal leader. It was by far the most influential country in the eastern regions of central Asia, with Ladakh, Bhutan, Sikkim, Nepal, Mongolia, and the Chinese provinces of Qinghai and Sichuan functioning to varying degrees as cultural outposts of Tibet.[8]

Jewelry in these countries shared important similarities with the jewelry of Tibet. All personal adornment had religious significance, and rosaries were used widely for both counting prayers and making numerical calculations. "Court beads" worn in China by the ruling Manchurian nobles and high officials during the Qing dynasty (A.D. 1644–1912) were in fact elaborate Tibetan rosaries.[9]

Since Tibet's subsistence needs, except for tea, were met from within the country, most trade in the region involved importing luxury goods, including beads and bead materials.[10] Tibetan jewelry is often monumental in scale, to express the rank of the owner, and sturdy enough to withstand life on the road. It is characterized by decorative surface designs, bold handling of precious and semiprecious stones, and the liberal use of turquoise, coral, and amber beads. Tibetan beads are simple and well proportioned. There is an exuberance of color in the jewelry, which almost acts as an antidote

209. *A gilded copper representation of the Buddha, richly ornamented with turquoise and coral beads. Central Asian religious statues are frequently adorned with semiprecious stones, which have their own spiritual powers, thereby enhancing the spiritual power of the image itself. Height, 47.7 cm. Collection the Newark Museum, New Jersey.*

OVERLEAF: 210. *This necklace from Ladakh combines an extremely unusual variety of beads, including silver-disked amber inlaid with turquoise, coral, agates, pearls, wood, and silver. The four silver-capped, cream-colored beads are of an unidentified material, probably stone or stained bone. Two phum ("lesser dZi") beads are near the top of the necklace, and there is one imitation phum. The center dZi is of a type identified as "variety A." Its ends are unetched natural agate.*

Among the appliances hanging from the chain is an ear cleaner. The safety chains dangling from the bottom fasten the necklace to the wearer's robe. Length, 106 cm. Collection Ivory Freidus

with it became a specialty of Newari craftsmen. Although gold beads are used in specific types of necklaces, the most popular bead materials are still the familiar Himalayan combination of imported turquoise, coral, and amber, in addition to shell, bone, and glass. Customers ask for widely recognized designs for their made-to-order jewelry, often supplying craftsmen with the stones and metals to be used.[21]

A distinctive beaded necklace unique to Nepal is the *tilari*, composed of multiple strands of red glass beads joined by a cylinder formed from seven gold or silver beads. Worn by most Nepalese women, the *tilari*, combined with vermilion powder applied to the hair, indicates the wearer is married. A Nepalese man gives a *tilari* to his bride on their wedding day, and the wearing of a *tilari* expresses a wife's wish for her husband's longevity.[22]

Western Central Asia: Ancient Turkmenistan and Afghanistan

Archaeologists have worked in the western lands since the nineteenth century and have been able to create a chronology for many bead forms. Turkmenistan and Afghanistan are famous for beautiful stone beads, many of which were traded south to Mesopotamia, Iran, and the Mediterranean as early as the third millennium B.C.

The first beads documented in Turkmenistan and Afghanistan are from the Neolithic site of Djeitun in Turkmenistan, the earliest agricultural community in central Asia. Beads excavated at Djeitun, dating to 5000 B.C., include crudely shaped disks, plaques, and tubes of bone, marine shell, stone (including turquoise), and clay. There were also zoomorphic pendants.[23]

By the late fifth millennium B.C., southern Turkmenistan was a prosperous region of agricultural oases and developed towns. Brightly colored pottery and quantities of

212

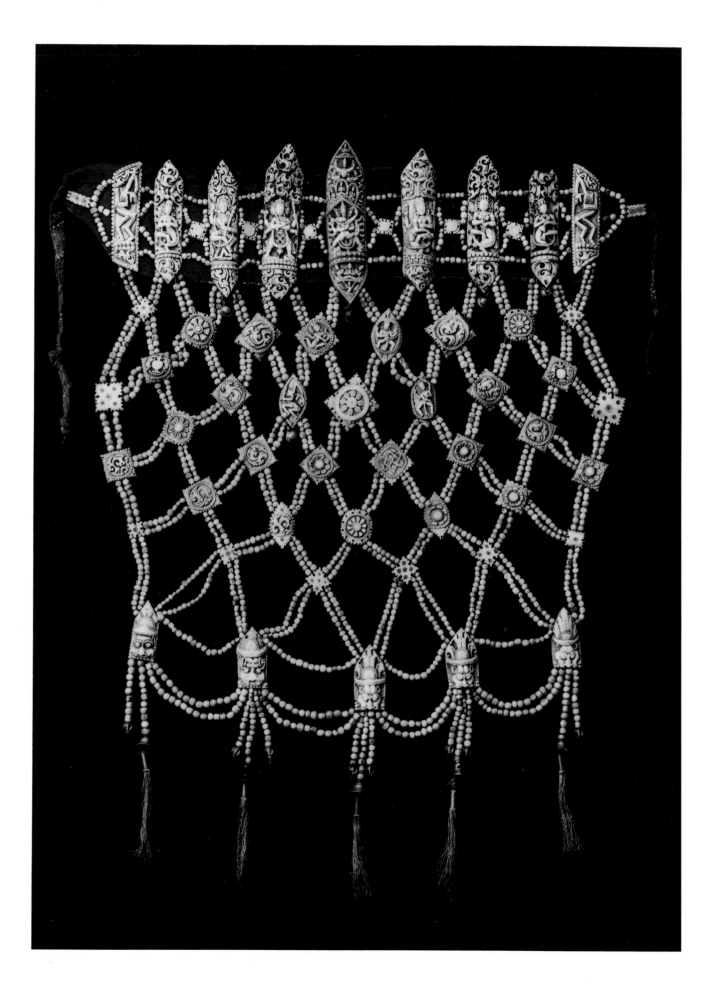

beads, many of which resemble contemporaneous forms in northern Iran, were made. In fact, archaeological evidence suggests that most people in southern Turkmenistan and northeastern Iran belonged at this time to a single culture with local variations. By 4000 B.C., beads of carnelian and other semiprecious stones began to appear in Turkmenistan.[24]

The Anau and Namazga cultures used beads by the fourth millennium. Turquoise beads, in particular, are known from every phase of the Anau culture, including cylindrical, barrel, annular, disk, and bean-shaped forms. Children's bodies were often buried with turquoise and other beads under the earthen floors of dwellings.[25]

By 3000 to 2500 B.C., many beads in western regions of central Asia were made of white alabaster (gypsum) with incised geometric designs, but others were made of turquoise, azurite, quartz, agate, or chalcedony. During this period, the peoples of southern Turkmenistan carried on active trade relations with the communities of Sialk and Hissar in northern Iran and were probably in contact with Sumerian Mesopotamia via the trade routes that carried lapis lazuli from Afghanistan.[26]

Between 2300 and 1800 B.C., graves of elite people in southern Turkmenistan included clay and stone seals and quantities of well-made semiprecious stone beads. A woman's grave at Altin-depe, dating to about 2100 B.C., contained one hundred agate, carnelian, and lapis lazuli beads, some capped with gold.[27]

This richness in grave goods marks the beginning of urban life in central Asia and accompanies higher levels of agricultural productivity, monumental architecture (resembling the ziggurats of southern Mesopotamia), and specialized craftsmanship. The increase in cultural sophistication paralleled and was obviously brought about by a significant expansion in trade with Iran, the Indus Valley, and Mesopotamia.[28]

Archaeological sites in Afghanistan have recently yielded quantities of exquisitely made stone beads, many of which appear to have been traded to the great civilizations of western Asia and India. Many etched carnelian beads, for example, have been found in Afghanistan, Mesopotamia, and the Indus Valley. A remarkably sophisticated culture developed in Afghanistan by 3000 B.C., due in part to wealth attained through the export of mineral resources. By the fourth millennium, the finest deep blue lapis lazuli was quarried in the Badakhshan region of northeastern Afghanistan. Trade routes from many directions intersected in eastern and northern Afghanistan and formed the lapis routes, which not only carried lapis lazuli to Egypt, the Near East, and the Indus Valley, but also brought finished beads of agate and rock crystal to the Mediterranean region.[29]

Remarkably beautiful beads of identical shapes, craftsmanship, and materials (lapis lazuli, carnelian, agate, gold, and silver) occur in aristocratic burials at the royal tombs of Ur, dating between 2500 and 1800 B.C., and in contemporaneous sites in Turkmenistan and Afghanistan. Since these beads (particularly the distinctive agates) occur in the greatest quantity in Afghanistan, and the finest examples are frequently excavated there, this country appears to be their place of origin.[30]

Both the quality and quantity of beads appear to have declined in southern Turkmenistan and Afghanistan by 1600 B.C., perhaps the result of the collapse of the Sumerian and Indus Valley civilizations. The decline of these first important societies of central Asia may also be associated with the emigration of Bronze Age tribes from the northern Mongolian steppes to western Asia in the mid-second millennium B.C.[31]

As trade with the western Asian states ended, the primary stimulus for making beads disappeared. Continued contact with northern Iran is suggested, however, by large, biconical steatite beads decorated with incised concentric circles from first-millennium sites in Turkmenistan that appear in identical forms in Iran.[32]

215. A beautiful apron of beads made from human bones. Such aprons were worn by Tibetan tantric priests during ceremonies to drive away evil spirits. The use of human bones for ritual objects symbolizes the transient nature of earthly life.[111] Length, 72 cm. Collection Mimi Lipton, London

ABOVE: 216. *A collection of dZi beads.*[IV]
Left to right: (first two beads) asymmetrical pattern of white lines on natural background; asymmetrical pattern of white lines on blackened background; two blackened beads with applied white stripes; two beads with applied stripes and shapes characteristic of Indus Valley beads; blackened bead with applied white stripes; two-eyed dZi; six-eyed dZi showing circles ("eyes") and stylized eye and zone patterns; round dZi with tiger stripes; two-eyed dZi (top) and "Earth Door, Sky Door" pattern; unusual phum dZi with a W in a cartouche. Far left bead: length, 3.7 cm. Collection David Ebbinghouse, Bloomington, Indiana

RIGHT: 217. *Top to bottom: rare, "pure" nine-eyed dZi, considered the most precious type; dZi with stripes but no eyes; unusually shaped dZi, recalling bead forms of ancient Mesopotamia and Iran;[V] natural agate bead. Second from top bead: length, 11.5 cm. Collection Ivory Freidus*

dZi Beads

The unique dZi bead, a black-and-white (or dark brown) bead of etched or treated agate, is revered in Tibet. To Tibetans and other Himalayan peoples, the dZi is a "precious jewel of supernatural origin" with great power to protect its wearer from disaster.[VI]

There is little precise information available on dZi beads. They are found primarily in Tibet, but also in neighboring Bhutan, Ladakh, and Sikkim. Shepherds and farmers pick them up in the grasslands or while cultivating fields. Because dZi are found in the earth, Tibetans cannot conceive of them as man-made. Since knowledge of the bead is derived from oral traditions, few beads have provoked more controversy concerning their source, method of manufacture, and even precise definition.

Mythical stories are usually told to explain the origin of dZi. In ancient times, it is said dZi adorned the gods, who discarded them when they became blemished, thus explaining why they are seldom found in perfect condition. Another story is that dZi were originally insects that moved around like worms and became petrified.[VII] One Tibetan gave the following version: "There is a legend of a man on a horse who saw the bead move. If you don't cover it with dust, it will disappear. The man threw dust over the bead and caught it, and it petrified. But dZi beads do not remain with unlucky people. The same man traded the bead for so many yak. The point is, the bead was not meant to be with him—the animals were."[VIII] Other Tibetan tales concern unfortunates who sell a valuable dZi, only to become ill or die soon after.[IX] Tibetans are loath to sell prized dZi even for the highest prices.

In some ways dZi resemble etched carnelian beads traded between Mesopotamia, Afghanistan, and the Indus Valley during the third millennium B.C. (Bead Chart 600). Indian and Iranian craftsmen continued making these beads into the first millennium A.D. Although the techniques for making dZi beads may be derived from ancient Indian craftsmen, the beads themselves are never found there. Because dZi are found only in the Himalayas, it appears certain that they were made locally.[X]

The actual etching of the dZi agate is accomplished by several methods, and scholars have classified all etched beads, including dZi, into several major types and subdivisions based upon their technique of manufacture.[XI]

The exact origins and dates of dZi remain elusive. Because Tibetan religious beliefs have long prevented archaeological excavations, no beads have been recovered in Tibet under controlled research circumstances. Chinese texts, however, mention dZi beads as early as the seventh century A.D. Legend suggests the beads (or the technical knowledge for making them) came to Tibet in very ancient times from Iran or the "Empire of the Arabs," where the Bon faith, Tibet's pre-Buddhist religion, possibly originated as well.[XII] The antiquity of dZi beads has been suggested as a major reason for their great value throughout the Himalayan region.

"Pure" dZi beads (in the traditional Tibetan system for evaluating dZi) are regarded as the most valuable and desirable variety. To qualify as pure, a bead must be genuine etched agate and lie within a certain range of styles. It should also have a sharply delineated pattern, symmetrical shape, strong color, glossy surface, and no flaws. The nine-eyed dZi illustrated in plate 217 (top) is a pure dZi with the most highly desired pattern. Etched agate beads not considered pure are called chung dZi, or "less important dZi." [XIII]

OPPOSITE, TOP: 218. *Khampa women in eastern Tibet wearing typical coral and turquoise necklaces.*

OPPOSITE, BOTTOM LEFT: 219. *Sherpa woman wearing Nepalese gold earrings, a necklace made of Indian silver coins, simulated red coral and amber beads (made of glass and plastic or resin), and a Buddhist rosary of beads cut from conch shell. The silver beads dangling to her side help her keep count of thousands of mantras (sacred chants or prayers).*

OPPOSITE, BOTTOM CENTER: 220. *Tibetan woman wearing an aristocratic jewelry ensemble. A small gold charm box is suspended from her necklace of coral and turquoise beads with a matched pair of two-eyed dZi beads near its apex. On her throat, she wears three more two-eyed dZi strung with multiple strands of pearls.*

OPPOSITE, BOTTOM RIGHT: 221. *A wandering merchant, or* saddhu, *in Nepal, identifiable by his necklace of* rudraksha *seeds spaced with red coral (or glass simulations), which symbolize the red eyes of the Hindu god Siva, the deity of Yogis. He also wears glass simulations of black onyx and turquoise beads.*

LEFT: 222. *Mongolian tribal headdress. Throughout central Asia, the most spectacular part of a woman's ensemble was often her massive headdress, which varied in style from region to region and served to* identify kinship groups or tribes. It was both an emblem of rank and a family's portable bank of coins, silver, and semiprecious and precious stones. Much wealth was concentrated in such showy adornment, particularly among the women of nomadic groups.

In this very beautiful tribal headdress, the silver headband is inlaid with coral and turquoise and draped with coral, turquoise, and malachite beads. As in Tibet and Nepal, the combination of coral and turquoise occurs repeatedly throughout Mongolia. Length, 61 cm. Collection Ivory Freidus

RIGHT: 223. A Nepalese woman wearing a necklace of turquoise, coral, and granulated silver beads with a center dZi bead. All Himalayan peoples love to collect and display their beads. They are worn daily to exorcise evil spirits while laboring in the fields, marketing, or attending a special gathering. Festivals are occasions to wear everything one owns. Many Nepalese wear the popular combination of turquoise, coral, and amber beads. When these are unaffordable, copal, glass, and plastic beads are substituted.

The Steppes

Life on the steppes depended on mobility and taking advantage of scattered, seasonal pastures. As early as 3000 B.C., the horse, ass, and camel were domesticated and had adapted to the semidesert conditions.[33] With the development of horseback riding by 1400 B.C., nomadic pastoralism as a way of life spread rapidly through the area.[34]

Ranging widely in search of grazing lands, the nomads frequently came into conflict with their settled neighbors, and from time to time they threatened the established civilizations in China, the Near East, and Europe: the Great Wall of China remains a powerful symbol of the efforts to defeat this threat. Many nomads were excellent merchants, and their traveling life-style encouraged the spread of ideas and culture. Stone, glass, and metal beads were distributed between Mongolia, China, Siberia, central Asia, and Europe through their extensive trade networks.

Adornment for both themselves and their animals was of prime importance to the peoples of the steppes, among whom were Scythians, Sarmatians, Mongols, and Turks. Burials from several regions illustrate their material wealth.[35] In the Altai Mountains, southwest of Minusinsk in Siberia, some of the richest graves have been found in valley pastures used by tribes during the summer months. The Altai were an important source of copper and tin ores. Bronze metallurgy was well established there by 1500 B.C., and people of the seminomadic Altai Karasuk culture wore quantities of distinctive bronze beads and pendants.[36]

Between 600 B.C. and A.D. 100, wide-ranging trade in beads and metals was conducted throughout the steppes. Glass beads, for example, from La Tène in Celtic Europe, arrived in China via the northern steppes by 500 B.C.[37] In the Altai region, evidence of the wealth attained through trading metal ores is seen in the size and richness of treasures in their tombs. Six of the largest tombs, excavated near Pazyryk, belonged to chieftains of an eastern nomadic tribe related to the Scythians. Dating between 500 and 400 B.C., the tombs, though looted of most gold artifacts, still contained beads of bone, Persian turquoise, and Indian cowrie shells, glass, and carnelian. Women's leather boots were elaborately decorated with embroidery, and glass beads were sewn to their soles.[38]

At Sara, Western-style glass beads were found from the fifth century B.C., while at Ust-Labinskaya, glass beads (probably Western-made) and Egyptian scarabs are reported in sites dating between 100 B.C. and A.D. 100. At the same time, the Sarmatians, at the western edge of the steppes, made distinctive glass beads, some of which found their way to Britain.[39] Coptic glass beads from Egypt, dated between A.D. 200 and 300, were excavated at the Lulan and Niya sites in the Takla Makan basin.[40] About A.D. 1402, glass beads were made in Samarkand, the result of Tamerlane's occupation of Syria and the subsequent arrival of many glassmakers in Samarkand.[41]

Mongolian populations of the eastern steppes wore large numbers of turquoise and coral beads, introduced by their contacts with Tibetan and Turkish tribes. Noble Mongolian women displayed elaborate headdresses of gold and gilded silver, incorporating strands of coral and turquoise beads (plate 222). Most Mongolian jewelry was obtained from Tibet, either through trade or pilgrimages. China supplied Mongolia directly with turquoise beads, and greenish blue stones were the preferred color.[42]

Along the Amur River, at the eastern edge of the steppes, beads were made of local white jade, while glass, Indian agate, carnelian, and onyx were imported (via China) from the first millennium B.C. to A.D. 100.

Contemporary Beads Today, jewelry worn by the nomadic and village women of the western regions of central Asia often resembles the adornment of their ancient steppes ancestors. In Afghanistan, bridal necklaces with multiple strands of coral and silver amulets, interspersed with intricate melon-shaped silver beads, are family heirlooms.[43] Turkmenistan brides display elaborate headdresses of repoussé silver, chains, and carnelian beads. Carnelian and silver jewelry worn by Turkmenistan women frequently constitutes a substantial part of the family wealth. In hard times, jewelry can always be sold for at least the value of the precious metals and stones. Kirgiz and Uzbek women fashion their own beads of coral, silver, and shell, and string multicolored neck collars of glass beads.[44] Stone beads still have talismanic value. Amber is tied around a baby's neck to prevent skin diseases, while coral and carnelian are said to protect sight, and blue stones (lapis lazuli and turquoise) or blue glass diverts the evil eye.[45]

Southeast Asia and the South Pacific

Southeast Asia is a mosaic of large and small land masses scattered over an enormous area of the South Pacific. Throughout history most of the region has been accessible to seaborne traders. Beads have been an important element in the region's trade for thousands of years.

Mainland Southeast Asia is a tropical subcontinent with rugged, forested highlands intersected by rivers. The fractured landscape has fostered cultural diversity: highland forest tribes, cut off by mountain ranges, have lived in isolation for centuries: people of the plains and river valleys, on the other hand, have maintained contact with the coast and participated in regional trade systems. Some of the lowland cultures evolved into sophisticated states whose cultures were influenced either by China or by India (depending upon their proximity). This interchange was reflected in the name "Indochina," which now refers to Laos, Cambodia, and Vietnam but prior to World War II referred to the entire region.

An array of Southeast Asian islands, including Taiwan, Indonesia, and the Philippines, lie at the crossroads of sea routes linking India, China, western Asia, and Europe. Throughout this vast area, merchant seamen forged cultural links, carrying artistic styles from island to island and to the mainland. Their routes were determined by ocean currents and two monsoons (southwest from June through September, northeast from late October through late March). In this way, the peoples of Taiwan, Indonesia, and the Philippines were significantly influenced by the cultures of India, China, and the Southeast Asian mainland.

Southeast Asian beads are as varied and fascinating as any in the world. As necklaces, beaded textiles, or even as individual objects, they were immensely important to all the region's peoples. Among the earliest beads found in Southeast Asia were those

224. *Hats are worn everywhere in Sarawak. One of the most elaborate is this* sa'ong *of the Kenyan Dayak group. It is embellished with appliqué designs in cloth and beadwork, and used by a woman as a sunshade on ceremonial occasions. Diameter, 51.4 cm. Collection Ivory Freidus*

225. *Gold melon beads, believed to be from the Angkor period, c. A.D. 900–1200 (the classical age of Khmer art). These beads reflect artistic influences from India prevalent in Southeast Asia at the time. Typical bead; diameter, 0.79 cm. Collection Kronos*

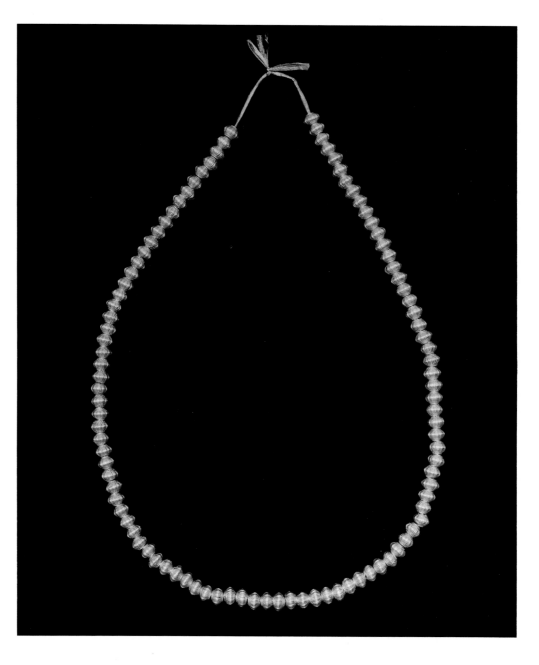

excavated from Neolithic caves (2500–1000 B.C.) at Sarawak in Borneo. Included in the find were necklaces of clay beads alternated with bored shell and animal teeth.[1] Archaeological evidence also indicates that beads were traded into Southeast Asia long before the arrival of Europeans. The "Indian red," or *mutisalah*, beads, made in south India, were sold in Sumatra by at least the first century B.C. (plate 228). Early sites also contain beads of agate, carnelian, crystal, and amethyst, stones found in substantial deposits in India and Sri Lanka. The beads themselves are made in a range of shapes and by various manufacturing techniques that closely resemble Indian styles. Early glass beads made in Southeast Asia were probably manufactured from glass scrap imported from the Middle East or the Mediterranean. "Roman-style" glass beads, particularly eye beads, may have been imported after the fall of the Roman Empire but before the twelfth century, and certainly before Europeans arrived in Southeast Asia (plate 232).[2]

Jewelry had a number of functions in the lives of premodern Southeast Asian is-

LEFT: 226. *Bronze beads from Burma, possibly modeled to resemble seedpods, may have been derived from motifs used by Chinese craftsmen in the Shang dynasty (1523–1027 B.C.). Collection Colette and Jean-Pierre Ghysels, Brussels*

ABOVE: 227. *Detail of bronze beads shown in plate 225. Typical bead: diameter, 0.9 cm.*

land people, serving as personal adornment, protective amulets, and political badges of rank, as well as dowries, ceremonial exchange goods, and sacred altar objects for summoning spirits from the supernatural world. In Indonesia, Malaysia, Sarawak, and the northern Philippines, many layers of social and religious iconography were incorporated into jewelry, which was kept as ancestral treasure and family heirlooms symbolic of their owner's place in the world.[3] Through various designs and colors, jewelry publicly displayed important ideas in the local systems of politics, kinship, and myth. The significant role individual beads (as contrasted with assemblages) had in certain Southeast Asian cultures is striking. On the islands, beads have been used singly in an array of cultural practices, ranging from celebrations of marriage to sanctifying new houses to insuring favorable harvests. Beaded textiles were also accorded high value, although generally not by the same groups.

Beads were important symbols in village life. They were used to strengthen political alliances and to protect warriors from natural and supernatural threats.[4] Today,

ABOVE: 228. *Mutisalah beads. The famed "Indian reds" are found throughout mainland and island Southeast Asia in archaeological sites of the pre-European era.*

An opaque red glass bead, the mutisalah *is quite identifiable despite the fact that it comes in a great variety of shapes. Scholars agree that the* mutisalahs' *original home was South India, where they are found in large numbers (primarily in Indian megalithic sites dating to about 200 B.C.). The beads were made at a number of locales until at least the sixteenth century.* Mutisalah *are still highly prized in Timor, where in 1965 a twelve-inch-long string equaled the price of a water buffalo.[1] Typical bead: diameter, 1.5 cm. Corning Museum of Glass, Corning, New York*

RIGHT: 229. *Rear view of a headdress of a woman from the Akha tribe of Thailand. It was worn in ceremonies as well as in daily field work. The helmet shape identifies its wearer as a member of the Mawn Po clan. The hat is heavily encrusted with silver buttons, coins, and beads. Numerous strands of red glass beads are attached to the sides, falling nearly to the wearer's waist.[11] Length (from top of helmet to bottom of long bead strand), 61.6 cm. Collection Ivory Freidus*

TOP: 230. *Dayak sword, called* mandau *or pararejo, with strings of multicolored glass beads and a hornbill skull hanging from the wooden scabbard. Collected in Java in 1902. Sword: length, 72 cm. Private collection*

BOTTOM LEFT: 231. *Detail of tiny glass beads attached to Dayak sword scabbard illustrated in plate 230. Typical bead: length, 1 cm.*

BOTTOM RIGHT: 232. *Glass beads from a Kalimantan necklace. The striped beads are from Venice. The other beads are of unknown origin, although they are quite similar to ancient Roman and western Asian types. Top left bead: diameter 1.2 cm. J. Camp Gallery, New York*

227

Southeast Asia and the South Pacific:
Distribution of Beads and Bead Materials,
7500 B.C. to A.D. 1800

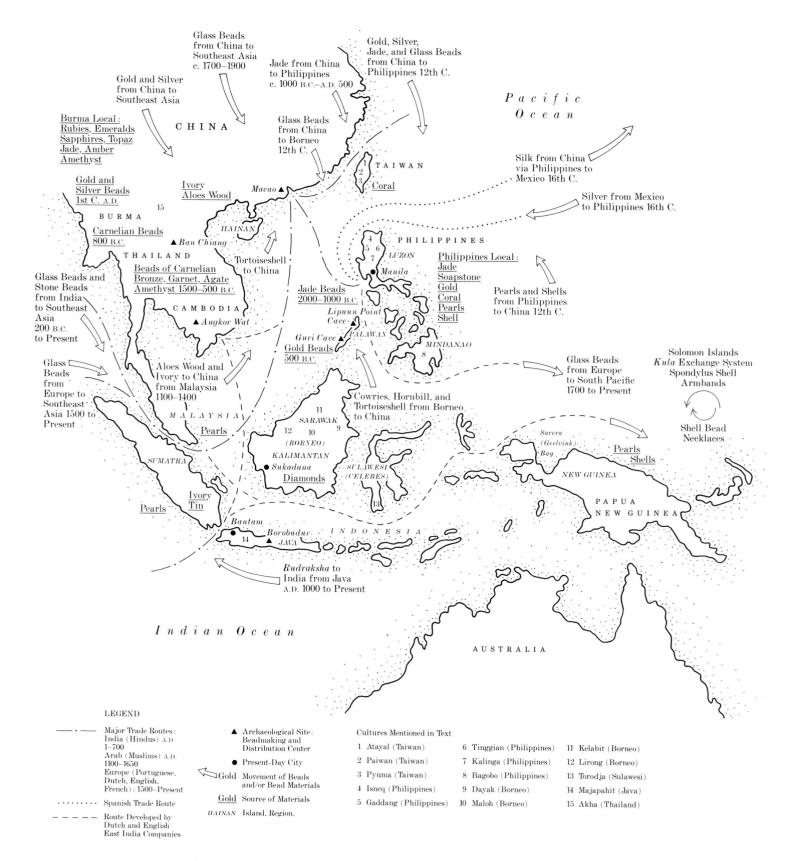

Glass Beads
from China to
Southeast Asia
c. 1700–1900

Gold, Silver,
Jade, and Glass Beads
from China to
Philippines 12th C.

Jade from China
to Philippines
c. 1000 B.C.–A.D. 500

Gold and Silver
from China to
Southeast Asia

*Pacific
Ocean*

Burma Local:
Rubies, Emeralds
Sapphies, Topaz
Jade, Amber
Amethyst

C H I N A

Glass Beads
from China
to Borneo
12th C.

Silk from China
via Philippines to
Mexico 16th C.

Gold and
Silver Beads
1st C. A.D.

Ivory
Aloes Wood

Macao ▲

1
2
3

T A I W A N

Coral

Silver from Mexico
to Philippines 16th C.

15

B U R M A

HAINAN

▲ *Ban Chiang*

PHILIPPINES

4

Carnelian Beads
800 B.C.

Tortoiseshell
to China

5 6
7 *LUZON*

Philippines Local:
Jade
Soapstone
Gold
Coral
Pearls
Shell

T H A I L A N D

• *Manila*

Beads of Carnelian
Bronze, Garnet, Agate
Amethyst 1500–500 B.C.

Jade Beads
2000–1000 B.C.

Pearls and Shells
from Philippines
to China 12th C.

Glass Beads and
Stone Beads
from India
to Southeast
Asia
200 B.C.
to Present

C A M B O D I A

▲ *Angkor Wat*

*Lipuun Point
Cave* ▲

MINDANAO

8

Guri Cave ▲
Gold Beads
500 B.C.

PALAWAN

Solomon Islands
Kula Exchange System
Spondylus Shell
Armbands

Glass
Beads
from
Europe to
Southeast
Asia 1500 to
Present

Aloes Wood and
Ivory to China
from Malaysia
1100–1400

Glass Beads
from Europe
to South Pacific
1700 to Present

Shell Bead
Necklaces

Cowries, Hornbill, and
Tortoiseshell from Borneo
to China

11

M A L A Y S I A

SARAWAK

*Sarera
(Geelvink)
Bay*

Pearls

12 10 9

Pearls
Shells

(BORNEO)

SUMATRA

KALIMANTAN

NEW GUINEA

• *Sukadana*
Diamonds

*SULAWESI
(CELEBES)*

Ivory
Tin

13

P A P U A
N E W G U I N E A

Pearls

• *Bantam*

14

Borobudur ▲
JAVA

I N D O N E S I A

Rudraksha to
India from Java
A.D. 1000 to Present

I n d i a n   O c e a n

A U S T R A L I A

LEGEND

—— · —— Major Trade Routes:
India (Hindus) A.D.
1–700
Arab (Muslims) A.D.
1100–1650
Europe (Portuguese,
Dutch, English,
French): 1500–Present

· · · · · · · Spanish Trade Route

— — — Route Developed by
Dutch and English
East India Companies

▲ Archaeological Site:
Beadmaking and
Distribution Center

● Present-Day City

⇦ Gold Movement of Beads
and/or Bead Materials

Gold Source of Materials

HAINAN Island, Region,

Cultures Mentioned in Text

1 Atayal (Taiwan)
2 Paiwan (Taiwan)
3 Pyuma (Taiwan)
4 Isneq (Philippines)
5 Gaddang (Philippines)

6 Tinggian (Philippines)
7 Kalinga (Philippines)
8 Bagobo (Philippines)
9 Dayak (Borneo)
10 Maloh (Borneo)

11 Kelabit (Borneo)
12 Lirong (Borneo)
13 Torodja (Sulawesi)
14 Majapahit (Java)
15 Akha (Thailand)

228

island tribal people continue to possess a detailed knowledge of each bead they own. A rare, ancient bead has a reputation similar to that of a precious stone or a fine antique in other parts of the world. The history of each bead, its name and age, is understood. In Sarawak, older women can easily identify sixty or more different types of scarce, ancient beads.[5]

Various Southeast Asian island cultures valued one bead over another. The Kalinga of the Philippines treasured agates, while some groups in Borneo and Taiwan preferred ancient polychrome glass beads. *Mutisalah* beads were admired everywhere. In the tropical climate of much of Southeast Asia, organic materials, such as seeds or wood, quickly rot; durable stone and glass beads were considered sources of strength and longevity. Among the Maloh tribes in central Kalimantan in Borneo, there were important myths about hazardous journeys embarked on by brave heroes in search of particularly valuable beads. These same people tied beads to the wrists of couples at marriage, and when a new communal dwelling was built, they placed beads in the holes dug for the structure's main posts.[6] The Kelabit of Borneo called the *mutisalah* bead *bau'u si' ada* ("head of the ghost"), affixing two of them to the end of a sharpened stake that was placed in the ground near a rice field to insure a bountiful harvest.[7]

Thailand, on the Southeast Asian mainland, lay far from the Chinese and Indian sea routes and thus remained culturally self-contained. Nonetheless, an enormous variety of beads continues to be excavated from the region's burial sites, indicating the importance of beads to the ancient Thai cultures. Archaeologists have found bronze beads dated between 1500 and 500 B.C., made during the Bronze Age.[8] Stone beads, including carnelian, agate, garnet, and amethyst, were fashionable from very early times until at least the eleventh century A.D. Of particular interest are long, tubular stone beads referred to as "magic beads," which have a long history throughout the area (dating back to about 3400 B.C.) and eventually were copied in glass.[9] While some of the beads were probably imported from India (with which Thailand was then closely associated), others were locally made. Although the extensive looting of archaeological sites has destroyed much information, evidence strongly indicates local stone bead manufacturing existed from a very early date. Etched agate and carnelian beads with patterns far more common in Thailand than India suggest that Thailand may have been another production center for these beads. Clay cylinders with deeply incised designs, rather similar to western Asian seals, were found at the site of Ban Chiang and may have been worn as beads.[10]

Glass beads from Ban Chiang, associated with pottery and iron tools, date to about 300 B.C. Predominantly of opaque orange red (although one burial also contained a few translucent blue and yellow samples), the beads are probably of Indian manufacture. However, there is speculation that Thai or Indian craftsmen living in Thailand may have produced some of these beads. Glass beadmaking, under Indian influence, definitely appears to have been under way in parts of Thailand by at least the tenth century A.D., especially along its western coast.[11]

Gold and silver beads from central Thailand date to the first centuries A.D., the period of Indian influence in Southeast Asia. Necklaces of beautifully crafted gold beads in various shapes, including melon and cornerless cube, are associated with Thailand's Mon or Dvaravati period (A.D. 500–1000) as well as the classical age of Khmer art (A.D. 900–1200) in Cambodia, when Indian influence stretched across the sea.[12] Carnelian beads from Vietnam, dating to about 800 B.C., resemble those found in the Philippines. In both instances this may reflect early trade, probably through middlemen, with India.[13]

OVERLEAF, TOP: 233. *A woven beadwork skirt from the Maloh tribe in Kalimantan. The beads have been woven into solid panels, although the Maloh may not have actually practiced the weaving of cloth. The ceremonial costume of the Maloh consists of a highly decorated short skirt, jacket, and headcloth.*

Maloh beaded skirts and jackets are decorated with motifs only they can identify. The geometric shapes represent familiar objects from the Maloh natural world translated into designs that were derived from Islamic motifs. In this skirt, the geometric forms represent the "tree of life," a symbol of rebirth popular in Indonesian art. An important motif illustrated here is the squatting human figure, kaletau, *which probably represents a guardian or ancestor spirit.*

Beaded costumes are reserved for ceremonial occasions when the residents of the communal longhouse gather to celebrate marriages, funerals, and successful harvests. The Maloh believe that displaying their finest beaded textiles helps produce a bountiful harvest.[III] Height, 51.9 cm. Private collection

OVERLEAF, BOTTOM: 234. *A Dayak beadwork baby carrier* (ba), *which holds the infant during the first months of life. Shells, beads, and the teeth of bears, crocodiles, and pigs— animals with protective spirits—are often suspended from the wooden carrier to make a rattling sound, which frightens away evil spirits. An even num-*

232

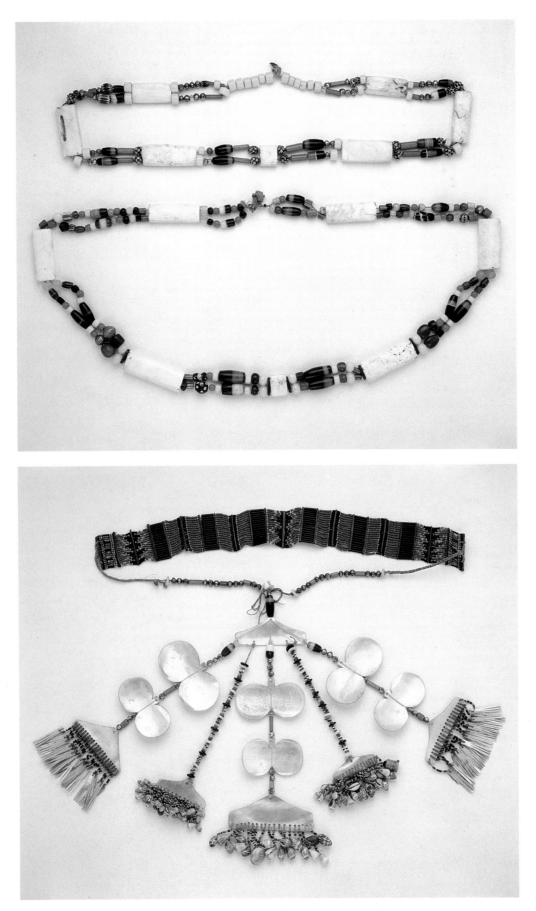

Indonesia Indonesia, the largest island complex in the world, stretches from the Malaysian peninsula to New Guinea. It includes Sumatra, Borneo, Java, and Sulawesi (formerly Celebes), as well as western New Guinea (West Irian) and thirteen thousand smaller islands. This extensive island chain has been exposed to the almost continuous influences of China, India, and Islam since prehistoric times, yet strong indigenous cultures also developed. Not surprisingly, Indonesia is a complex mixture of peoples, who have produced a rich and varied art.

The archipelago's great natural wealth in spices attracted traders from the mainland Asian powers. Most of the arts of Indonesia show the influence of the Chinese and Bronze Age Dong Son culture (700 B.C.–A.D. 100) of mainland Southeast Asia. Indian traders, acting as middlemen between the Far East and the Mediterranean, entered Indonesia about 300 B.C., while trade with China actually began about 400 B.C. Great Hindu and Buddhist empires thrived in Java, Sumatra, and Bali between the second and fifteenth centuries A.D.[14] By A.D. 100, small colonies of Indian traders were established along the trade routes. They introduced their philosophy, law, literature, and beads to the islands.

The island cultures of Java and Bali were particularly influenced by India and founded Indian-style court cultures. Their art, while inspired by Indian design concepts, has its own distinctive character. The Indianization of Javanese and Balinese cultures is reflected in bas-reliefs and freestanding carvings of male and female deities, which, by at least A.D. 800, are adorned with quantities of beads.

At the site of Borobudur in central Java stands a mountainous Buddhist temple, constructed during the eighth and ninth centuries and composed of a series of terraces that represent levels of existence, ranging from earthly life at the bottom to spiritual enlightenment at the top. Sculptures of people, beautifully dressed in beaded jewelry and sitting under trees hung with fruitlike strings of gems and beads, populate the lower levels. The upper terraces contain simple, unadorned, and indistinguishable Buddhas, examples of the rewards accorded the virtuous. The whole complex is designed to link purity with simplicity. At the same time, the human figures on the lower levels show beads are part of a life of sensuality and joy.[15] This is in contrast to their use in Tibet and Nepal, for example, where Buddhist and Hindu religious images wear jewelry and beads to reflect the talismanic properties of adornment.

Islamic influence began to reach Indonesia by A.D. 1200, and today 90 percent of the people are Muslim. Portuguese, English, and Dutch traders first arrived in the 1500s, with the Dutch East India Company forming the basis of the Indonesian colony. The area was not entirely free from European control until 1949, when Indonesia's independence was recognized.

Stone and glass beads were introduced to Indonesia by Indian and Chinese traders. In fact, Indonesian stone beads are identical to those manufactured at Arikamedu in India several centuries before the Christian Era, demonstrating the regions shared both finished beads as well as local craftsmen's interpretations of Indian styles. The earliest glass beads found in Indonesia are monochrome (predominantly yellow, blue, or green hues) and were made by drawn or wound techniques. Opaque red *mutisalah* beads existed in every region of mainland and island Southeast Asia, suggesting *mutisalah* beads were from a common manufacturing tradition but were a broadly shared cultural phenomenon.[16] Pre-sixteenth-century European polychrome glass beads are extremely rare. Those that have been identified are generally eye, chevron, and zone beads (plate 232). Ancient polychrome beads are highly prized by the Dayak of Borneo, the mountain tribes of the Philippines, and the Paiwan of Taiwan. In early twentieth-century Borneo, a slave could still be bought for a single polychrome bead.[17]

240. *A necklace of 325 perfectly interlocked gold disk beads, excavated from a late pre-Hispanic site (c. A.D. 1500) in the Philippines. Length, 40.6 cm. J. Camp Gallery, New York*

TOP AND MIDDLE:
241–42. Matching Bagobo jacket and trousers with exquisite ornamentation of glass and shell beads. A fine example of the technique of embroidering and appliquéing beads to textiles (in contrast to weaving solid panels, see plate 233). Jacket: length, 44.5 cm.; trousers: length, 64.2 cm. Received at the Smithsonian Institution from E. H. and S. S. Metcalfe in 1915. National Museum of Natural History, Smithsonian Institution, Washington, D.C.

BOTTOM: *243. Basketry, both as a craft and an art form, has a long history in the Philippines. This purse or basket was made with a twined weave, then covered with native-made cloth and a heavy beadwork panel.*

The series of connective diamonds in the central panel of this basket are typical, except that the pattern is created with multicolored glass seed beads and not with the traditional rattan.[VI] This is a Bagobo basket, collected in the Philippines in 1927. Height, 15.2 cm. National Museum of Natural History, Smithsonian Institution, Washington, D.C.

OPPOSITE: *244. Back side of a kimono embroidered with shell beadwork from the Atayal tribe, northern Taiwan. The tiny shell disk beads were strung and then sewn onto the garment. Most Taiwanese clothes were made by sewing rectangular pieces of cloth together; neck openings and tailoring are rare.[VII] Typical shell disk bead: diameter, 0.25 cm. Collection J. Camp Gallery, New York*

236

Middle and South America

Ever since their Asiatic ancestors crossed the Bering Strait into what is to-day Alaska, at least fifteen thousand and perhaps as many as thirty-five thousand years ago, American Indians have been developing and adapting their cultures to the myriad environments of North, Middle, and South America. By the time the Spanish arrived almost five hundred years ago, a wide range of Indian cultures of varying complexity existed between the Arctic Sea and the Strait of Magellan. Most of the Americas was occupied by various forms of village-farming societies, but there were also simple hunting-and-gathering societies, which stood in stark contrast to the great civilizations of the Maya, Aztec, and Inca. Despite the cultural sophistication of the notable Middle and South American civilizations, they lacked important technological assets, including gunpowder, and they were highly vulnerable to European diseases, which prevented them from warding off the Spanish conquest of the New World. From 1519 to 1533, the conquistadors defeated both the Aztec and Inca empires and profoundly changed the customs of their people. Prehistoric Middle and South American peoples had produced a variety of beautiful beads, but the most valued were those of jade and gold. Important symbolic reinforcements of the status structure, beads were significant features of Indian societies, and their manufacture and distribution was carefully controlled. With the breakdown of Indian civilizations and the elimination of the elite, jade and gold beads disappeared.

Beads appear early in the history of Middle and South American cultures. Snail shell beads from southern Mexico date to 7500 B.C., and a stone discoidal bead from the Mexican Valley of Tehuacán dates to about 3000 B.C.[1] Beadmaking in Middle America developed as farming societies were established and ceremonialism and increasingly complex social and political relationships evolved as part of village life. Much of the

250. *Maya pottery fig-urine from the Island of Jaina, Campeche, dating to about A.D. 800. Note the necklace of large jade beads and the jade ear flares. Height, 17.2 cm. University Museum, University of Pennsylvania, Philadelphia*

evidence for the Middle American beadmaking tradition is found in archaeological sites. Beads appear in substantial numbers beginning with the Pre-Classic period (1500 B.C.) and continuing through the late Post-Classic civilizations of the Mixtec and Toltec up to A.D. 1500. These beads (and their counterparts in South America) are well preserved, for they were buried prior to the arrival of the Spanish. Bead evidence after 1519 is scanty because the products of major jewelry-making cultures like the Aztec and Inca were largely destroyed by the Spanish during or soon after the conquest.

Until the Spanish arrived, beadmaking was a flourishing industry, particularly among the more complex Middle and South American societies. From the emergence of the Olmec civilization in the thirteenth century B.C. to the collapse of the Aztec and Inca empires twenty-seven centuries later, native craftsmen wrought exquisite gold and jade bead necklaces throughout Middle and South America. Located on the Gulf Coast (present-day Veracruz and Tabasco), the Olmecs (1250 to 400 B.C.) created the first great civilization in Middle America. They produced beautiful beads, particularly of jade, that used motifs similar to the articulation of their stone sculpture (plate 253). Mayan (A.D. 1–900) craftsmen of southern Mexico and Guatemala also made elaborate beads. Ceramic figurines, painted scenes on pottery, and limestone carvings show Mayan gods and rulers wearing large beads (the latters' crown jewels). Carved Mayan beads often incorporated motifs identical to those seen on buildings, pottery, sculpture, and paintings (plates 254–6). In Peru, the Chavin civilization (1200–300 B.C.) produced elaborate stone sculpture, monumental architecture, and new techniques for textile manufacturing, as well as beads made from hammered sheet gold (plate 257).

As cultures grew more complex throughout Middle and South America, the need to identify rank and social position increased. In the early civilizations of Mexico, Guatemala, and Peru, elaborately carved stone (especially jade) and fabricated or cast gold beads became hallmarks of elite status. Their size, quantity, quality of design and workmanship, made them effective devices for communicating social distinctions. The unusually large size of Middle American Mayan jade beads, for example, reflects their role as repositories of wealth and symbols of status. Quantities of scarce (although locally available) materials, like jade, were concentrated in the hands of the elite, who retained these valuable substances in the form of oversize beads. Farther south, however, cultures such as the Peruvian Chimu in the Andes Mountains did not have jade, and they lived a considerable distance from the sources of most other coveted materials such as turquoise, spondylus shell, and malachite. Consequently, their beads tended to be smaller in scale, made from a wider range of raw materials, and used in more intricately designed assemblages. At the same time, since the Chimu were near sources of gold, their gold beads tended to be oversize.[2]

Jade Beads In Middle America, jade beads were made primarily by the Olmecs, the Maya, and the peoples of Costa Rica between 100 B.C. and A.D. 600. South of Costa Rica, beadmakers used other hard stones. This may reflect the proximity of the Mexican, Guatemalan, and Costa Rican groups to jade sources. Jade beads first appear in Pre-Classic Olmec tombs about 1000 B.C. made of a distinctive blue green stone (plate 253). It was during the Classic period (A.D. 1–900) that apple green jade, probably found in the Guatemalan highlands, began to appear in Mayan and Teotihuacán bead offerings. In the Post-Classic period, the supply of jade seems to have diminished, and later Mixtec and Aztec offerings often disclose less brilliantly colored jade. As a result, earlier Olmec and Mayan jade beads and pendants were sometimes reworked.[3]

Jade was very rare in Europe before the Spanish conquest of the New World in

the sixteenth century. Although preoccupied with the search for gold, the Spaniards did notice that the Indians held this beautiful green stone in high esteem. To the Aztecs, green, symbolizing water and vegetation, was an ideal color. The Aztec Emperor Montezuma, presenting the Spanish explorer Hernán Cortés with a gift of jade for Charles V, told the astonished Spaniard that "a fine piece of jade was worth two loads of gold."[4] Shortly thereafter, jade beads saved the life of the conquistador Bernal Diaz del Castillo. When the Spanish explorers were forced to flee from the Aztec capital, Tenochtitlán, Castillo traded his captured booty of gold and silver for a few jade beads, which did not weigh him down when he swam to safety and later were exchanged for food.[5]

RIGHT: 252. *Two alliga-
tor effigy beads from
Costa Rica's Atlantic
Watershed region dat-
ing between A.D. 1 and
500. The combination
of human and alligator
forms had symbolic
importance in prehisto-
ric Costa Rica. These
beads are unusual in
that they have been
carved and perforated
to hang vertically.*[1]
*Left bead: height, 15
cm. Instituto Nacional
de Seguros, San José,
Costa Rica*

OPPOSITE, TOP LEFT:
253. *A superb Olmec
crescent-shaped jade
pectoral bead from the
first millennium B.C.*

*The Olmec were
skilled stone carvers.
Their jade carvings
exhibit the monumen-
tality of their stone
sculpture.*

*The incised design
represents a stylized
crocodile deity in pro-
file. It was probably cut
into the stone with a
cactus spine using
pumice abrasive. Red
cinnabar fills the inci-
sions. The soft, glossy
finish was achieved by
polishing with sand
and water, a technique
requiring great
persistence.*

*The use of cinnabar
with burial objects con-
sidered precious (gold,
silver, and jade) was
widespread throughout
Middle and South
America. The custom
was also common in
China during the first
millennium B.C., a
point frequently men-
tioned as evidence of
ancient trans-Pacific
contact. Length, 19 cm.
Private Collection*

TOP RIGHT: 254. *The
mat motif incised on
this jade bead and
inlaid with red cinna-
bar has a long and
important history in
Mayan art. A mat was
the Mayan equivalent
of the royal throne.
Only rulers had the*

Mayan Jade Beads

Like the Olmecs and the Aztecs later, the Maya considered jade more precious than gold. Mayan nobility wore quantities of jade beads, and jade objects frequently accompanied elite individuals to the grave. All Mayan jade was imported, primarily from the region that today is Guatemala.

Although Mayan craftsmen were capable of creating precise and complex forms, their beads are rarely geometrically perfect, a fact that reflects both the stone's scarcity and its hardness. In order to lose minimal amounts of the precious material, a stone's irregularities and surface blemishes were incorporated into the finished design.

The Mayans preferred apple-colored and emerald green jade to the gray and blue green shades favored by the Olmecs. When carving jade, Mayans attempted to work around the green layers of the stone, further contributing to the uneven shape of the finished bead. Jade does not flake like flint or obsidian, and it must be ground and polished, another reason why the finished object conforms to the stone's natural shape. The acceptance of these irregularities is additional evidence of the scarcity and high value placed on this stone.[II]

Mayan beads were generally treated as single objects, whether in adornment or as mediums of exchange. With the exception of an elaborate burial at Tikal, Guatemala, where a large collar of graduated jade beads was found on a skeleton, most perfectly matched sets of beads only occur as representations on carvings, pottery, and stelae. In reality, various sizes of tubular and spherical beads were combined in an irregular order.[III]

right to sit on the mat and use its symbol.[IV] This bead dates to the first century A.D. and is from Izapa on the Mexico-Guatemala border. Length, 12.7 cm. Collection Edward Merrin Gallery, New York

BOTTOM LEFT: 255. A Mayan jade bead, A.D. 200–500, carved from a water-worn pebble that has been slightly modified, perforated, and polished. The surface of many beads are water-worn, indicating that jade pebbles from river gravels were the source of the raw material. The exact location of jade-yielding alluvial gravels was a carefully guarded secret.[V] Diameter, 3.8 cm. Collection Edward Merrin Gallery, New York

BOTTOM RIGHT: 256. Mayan jade beads dating from A.D. 300 to

The Codex Mendoza, an Aztec document containing ideographic writing and dating to the Post-Classic time, describes the use of jade beads as tribute, trade items, and currency. The codex also helps us to understand how raw jade was located and mined.[6] The term *jade* describes two distinct minerals, jadeite and nephrite, which vary greatly in quality and color. Ancient Middle American cultures generally worked with jadeite, while nephrite was used in early Chinese carvings and beads.[7] The term *jade* comes from the Spanish *piedra de ijada*, which means "loinstone." By the year 1600, the Spaniards, apparently influenced by Indian folk medicine, believed that wearing jade would cure kidney ailments.[8]

Jade is harder than steel; therefore carving it without metal tools was a masterful achievement. Because of its mineralogical structure, jade cannot be chipped like flint, but has to be worked by slow grinding and polishing. Techniques for shaping jade probably developed from those used earlier on other stones, once the potential of stone and bamboo abrasives was recognized. While pre-Hispanic jadeite beads are often quite large, their drilling and cutting may not have been as time-consuming as we imagine. It is possible, using ancient methods, to saw through one inch of jade in four hours.[9]

Gold Beads Gold was available to pre-Hispanic Middle and South Americans in metallic nuggets largely found in riverbeds. Because the metal is scarce, readily identifiable, preservable, and not easily altered, it is an ideal repository of value. Its softness also makes it an excellent medium for creating valued jewelry.

In ancient America, both gold and silver were sacred materials closely connected with the sun god. Aztecs called gold "excrement of the gods," and silver, "white gold." Inca legend declares gold to be the "sweat of the sun," and silver, "the tears of the moon."[10] Gold is the one metal made into beaded objects in all three regions of pre-Hispanic Middle and South America, and in each region a distinctive style emerged. The earliest known gold artifacts, thin, hammered sheets of the metal, are associated with the Chavin culture of coastal Peru and date to 500 B.C. (plate 257). Even in later times, when goldsmiths of the Peruvian Chimu and Inca cultures employed more complex casting techniques, there was still a preference for working in sheet gold. A second region in which gold was worked extended from Colombia through Panama and into Costa Rica. Gold ornaments from this area in the form of small sculptures were generally cast rather than hammered.[11] Goldworking also appears in Mexico with the Mixtecs of Oaxaca (A.D. 720–1580) during the Post-Classic period (A.D. 900 and after). The Mixtecs' delicate gold beads, often combined in necklaces with multicolored stone beads, contrasted sharply with the Peruvian use of sheet gold.[12]

Pre-Hispanic Middle and South American goldsmiths were remarkably skillful. At the Panamanian site of Coclé, several strands of beads were found, each nine feet long and containing approximately twelve hundred identical cast-gold beads. These beads have thin gold exteriors cast over inner cores that have disintegrated with time. Although Middle and South American beads are generally characterized by their large size, necklaces of miniature gold beads, each only one-sixteenth of an inch long, have been discovered, dating between A.D. 500 and the Spanish conquest.[13]

Lacking iron tools, the Indians created gold beads and intricate gold jewelry and sculpture with stone hammers and chisels, obsidian and copper knives, bone drills, and copper tubes. By the sixteenth century, some of the Indian craftsmanship rivaled that of ancient Egypt or Greece. Montezuma's craftsmen, for example, used gold and precious stones to produce lifelike effigies of all the animals found in the Aztec empire.

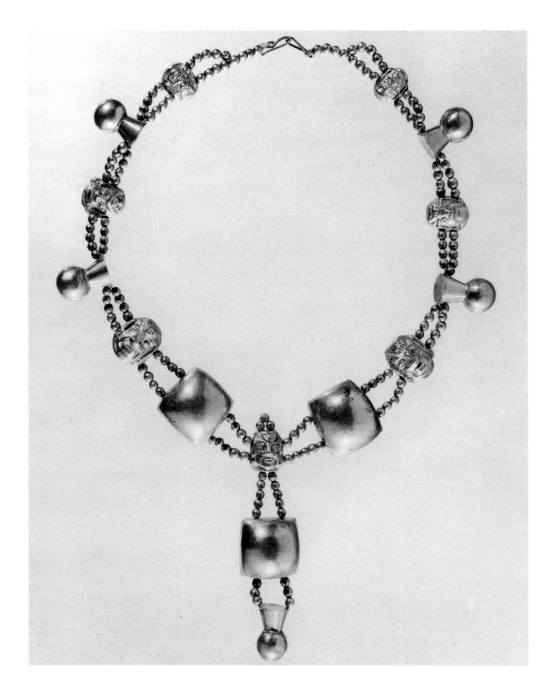

relationship to textiles. Chimu craftsmen developed the technique for joining two pieces of metal together by observing similar techniques in the textiles of the earlier Parcas, Nazca, and Mochica cultures.[VII] Photograph courtesy of the Taft Museum, Cincinnati

LEFT: 258. Two rows of small gold beads joined by mask-shaped and cushion-shaped beads. Found in a Chimu grave (A.D. 1000–1470) at Eten Chiclayo in northern Peru. Necklace: length, 35.6 cm. British Museum, London

When Spanish goldsmiths examined Aztec pieces sent home by Cortés, they were unable to understand how they had been made. Although sixteenth-century European documents are filled with descriptions of extraordinary indigenous New World gold jewelry, nearly every piece collected by the Spaniards was melted down. Only a few Aztec artifacts survived. Nothing remains of the Inca treasure.

Mixtec and Tairona Beads

While the Olmecs and Maya treasured jade, the Mixtecs prized turquoise, which they associated with the color of the sky and sea. It has been suggested that turquoise may have replaced a decreasing supply of jade.[14] The Mixtecs excelled in making delicate polychrome necklaces by combining beads of gold, amber, jade, amethyst, shell, pearls, and turquoise. They also produced fine necklaces of rock crystal.

TOP: 259. *Beads made of hollow gold balls by Chimu craftsmen. Two identical hemispheres were created by tapping a gold sheet into a deep die or by shaping the beads over a domed wooden form. The two halves were then affixed with an organic glue; there is no evidence of soldering.*[VIII] *Bottom necklace, largest center bead: diameter, 5 cm. Collections of Andre Emmerich Gallery and Edward Merrin Gallery, New York*

BOTTOM: 260. *A gold breastplate with a bold relief mask in the center, excavated in the Calima region of Colombia. This kidney-shaped pectoral, formed from a hammered sheet of gold, has repoussé patterns along its rim, adding both decoration and strength to the edge. Five strands of gold beads, some cast and some made of rolled strip, are attached to the breastplate. When the wearer of this armor moved, the metal flashed in the sun and the beads rattled—a dramatic accompaniment to any costume.*

The Upper Calima Valley is famous for its rich grave sites. Because this piece comes from uncontrolled excavations, its age and cultural context are uncertain. It is dated between A.D. 500 and 1500. Pectoral: length, 35.5 cm. British Museum, London

252

TOP: 261. *Like most early stone beads, the cone-shaped perforations in this Chavin quartz crystal bead (c. 1000 B.C.) are broad at the mouth but contract to a much smaller diameter at the center, where the drill holes meet. Diameter, 5 cm. Collection Suzanne Donnelly Jenkins, New York*

ABOVE: 262. *A typical Tairona flared-tubular bead. The bead was formed by a craftsman who utilized the subtle banding of the quartz or carnelian stone to its best design advantage. Length, 8.1 cm. Private collection. Courtesy Andre Emmerich Gallery, New York*

LEFT: 263. *The beads and amulets in this Tairona necklace from*

253

Some of the most exceptional beads excavated in ancient Middle America were found in a royal or aristocratic Mixtec burial in Tomb 7 at the Oaxacan site of Monte Albán, dating to the end of the fifteenth or early sixteenth century. Included were necklaces of jet, jade, pearl, amber, coral, shell, and rock crystal beads. One spectacular necklace consisted of thirty-nine gold beads cast as replicas of jaguar molar teeth, with a long bell suspended from each tooth. Another necklace was made of gold beads cast as miniature turtle shells (plate 271). Most Mixtec bead necklaces have a row of gold bells.[15]

Well-crafted stone beads of carnelian and rock crystal were made between A.D. 800 and 1500 by the Tairona (which means "goldworker"), who lived along the Caribbean coast and neighboring foothills of the Sierra Nevada de Santa Marta of northern Colombia. Through this region passed the trade routes linking Middle America with the Andes. The Tairona produced quantities of finely made gold, stone, and shell beads (plates 262–263).[16]

Beads and Pre-Hispanic Trade

The Olmecs were responsible for creating a trading system that extended over much of Middle America. Jade was an important commodity in their commerce. Eventually, complex trading networks were established all across Middle and South America, involving the exchange of agricultural products for scarce mineral and marine resources. Many items of jewelry, especially beads, were traded through this network and have been excavated hundreds of miles from their place of manufacture or the sources of their raw materials. For example, turquoise and sodalite used in bead-making were exported from Bolivia to neighboring southern regions.[17] Farther north, most of the turquoise used for beads and inlay work by Middle Americans was obtained from sources in present-day Arizona and New Mexico.

Middle and South American cultures are particularly noted for their exquisitely carved beads from jade, rock crystal, onyx, carnelian, and other semiprecious stones. Elaborate jade and serpentine beads, some with likenesses of animal or human deities, are unique to Middle American pre-Hispanic sites.[18] Since Middle and South American beads were largely elite commodities, it is not surprising that they are generally of large size and made of scarce materials—jade, gold, and rock crystal—whose sources were frequently controlled by individuals of rank. Costa Rica is particularly famous for unusually long tubular beads, including a jade bead dating between A.D. 300 and 700 that is twenty-four inches long—the longest perforated object known.[19]

Glass Beads

Although glass trade beads were never as important in Middle and South America as they were in North America, they were still treasured by the indigenous cultures. Historical accounts and several archaeological excavations document the introduction of glass beads into the Caribbean, Mexico, and South America by the early Spanish explorers, including Columbus, Cortés, and Francisco Pizarro. Many of these beads were gifts, others served as important trade items during the sixteenth century.[20]

It also appears that since glass was unknown to the Indian populations, the Spanish were not adverse to treating glass beads as if they were made of precious stones. In 1518, Diaz del Castillo entered the Río de Tabasco in Mexico, where he encountered canoes full of Indian warriors, who did not welcome the party until "we showed them strings of green beads and small mirrors and blue cut-glass beads, and as soon as they saw them they assumed a more friendly manner, for they thought they were [jadeite] which they valued greatly."[21] He also recorded other episodes in which glass beads were exchanged with the Aztecs for gold and precious stones. When Cortés entered the Aztec city of Tenochtitlán, Montezuma awaited him "under a canopy of brilliant green feath-

Middle and South America: *Distribution of Beads and Bead Materials, 1500 B.C. to A.D. 1600*

Turquoise from
Southwestern U.S.
A.D. 800–1500

Copper to
Southwestern U.S.
A.D. 800–1500

Silver
from Mexico
to Europe
16th C.

Glass Beads
from Europe
via Spanish
16th C.

MEXICO

TOLTEC

Silver
Copal

Jade
Cinnabar
Obsidian

Gold
Jewelry

▲ *Teotihuacán*

▲ *Tenochtitlán*

AZTEC   ● *Veracruz*

Tehuacán Valley
Monte Albán

▲ *Jaina*

MAYA

Maya Beads
A.D. 1–900
Jade
Stone
Shells

Glass Beads
from Europe
via Spanish
16th C.

Silver
to Philippines
16th C.

San Pedro Quiátoni ●
MIXTEC

Quartz
Copper
Stone
Shells
Silver
Gold

OLMEC

Yaxchilán
▲ Jade

GUATEMALA

Quiriguá
Izapa
▲

HONDURAS

Serpentine
Obsidian

Caribbean
Sea

Mixtec Beads
A.D. 1500
Gold
Jade
Amber
Amethyst
Shells
Pearls
Turquoise
Rock Crystal
Copper
Obsidian
Coral
Jet

Olmec Beads
1500–400 B.C.
Jade
Stone

Pearls from
Margarita
Island
and Cabagua
(Nueva Cádiz)
to Europe
16th C.

COSTA RICA

Jade Beads
100 B.C.–A.D. 600

Jade

Amber
Gold

Gold
to Europe
16th C.

Carnelian
Quartz
Shells
Gold

Pearls

Nueva Cádiz
Beads

TAIRONA

Coclé
▲

SINU

Gold

Stone Beads, Gold Beads
A.D. 800-1500

VENEZUELA

PANAMA

Pearls

MUISCA

Emeralds

Gold

COLOMBIA

Pacific
Ocean

Gold
to Europe
16th C.

Turquoise Beads
Lapis Lazuli Beads
1200 B.C.

Gold

MANTEÑO

Salango
▲ ECUADOR

● *Guayaquil*

PUNÁ ISLAND

Pottery
Beads

Beads of :
Black Coral
Gold, Silver
Quartz, Jasper
Steatite, Turquoise
Sodalite, Pottery
Spondylus Shells
Platinum

Mochica Beads
A.D. 300–800
Gold, Turquoise, Shells

▲ *Moche*

▲ *Eten Chiclayo*
▲ *Chan Chan*

CHAVIN

Silver
Stone

CHIMU

Nueva Cádiz
Beads

Chimu Beads
A.D. 1100–1300
Silver
Gold
Copper
Emeralds
Turquoise
Rock Crystal
Amethyst
Amber
Jade
Pearls
Shells
Jet

PERU

Gold
to Europe
16th C.

NAZCA

Gold

INCA

Machu Picchu
▲
Gold Jewelry

Turquoise
Sodalite

ICA

Spondylus
Shells

NAZCA

BOLIVIA

Lapis Lazuli

LEGEND

Gold   Movement of Beads
        and/or Bead Materials

Gold   Source of Materials

●   Present-Day City

▲   Archaeological Site:
        Beadmaking and/or
        Distribution Center

- - - - Present-Day International
        Boundaries

OLMEC   Culture

Silver
to Europe
16th C.

INCA

▲ *Potosí*
Silver
16th C.

CHILE

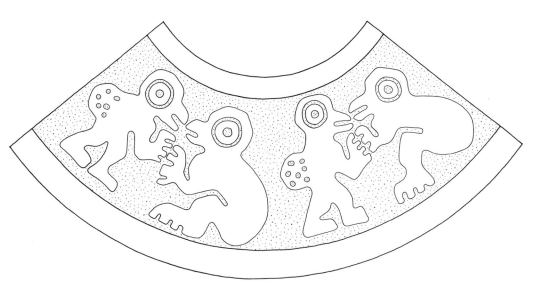

ers, bordered with gold and silver embroidery and hung with pearls. He was richly attired—even his sandals were of gold trimmed with precious stones. Cortés, dismounting from his horse, himself an impressive figure with his steel armour and red beard, presented the gift he had brought, a necklace of glass beads strung on a gold cord scented with musk. With great ceremony, the necklace was placed around Montezuma's neck. A reciprocal gift to Cortés was a necklace of hand-wrought gold crabs set with shells."[22]

The majority of glass beads distributed in southeastern North America and in Middle and South America during the sixteenth century were monochrome drawn-cane beads (Bead Chart 38). Also documented are faceted, multilayered chevron beads and striped beads, similar to those manufactured by the Dutch. Of particular interest is the Nueva Cádiz bead, named for an archaeological site on an island off the coast of Venezuela occupied by the Spanish from 1498 to 1545 (Bead Chart 1133 a–g).

The Nueva Cádiz, generally a long, tube-drawn bead with a square cross section and three-layer construction, is closely related to the chevron bead in its manufacturing technique. A major difference is that Nueva Cádiz beads were sometimes "twisted" and generally consisted of three layers of glass—chevron beads from the same period have seven layers—and their distribution was primarily limited to the Spanish New World, particularly Peru, between the late 1400s and 1560. Small quantities of Nueva Cádiz beads have been found in Africa, but they do not appear to be contemporaneous with New World examples.[23]

The Nueva Cádiz bead is a very sophisticated bead, the product of advanced glass-making technology. There is no important tradition of Spanish beadmaking, and since its distribution was so limited, Venice has been discounted as a source. Germany, France, and Holland have all been suggested as possible manufacturers, but at this point the question of its source remains unanswered.[24] Nueva Cádiz beads disappeared after 1560, perhaps as a result of the Spaniards' newly achieved control of trade and goods production in the New World. The beads recovered from the Nueva Cádiz site, for example, were undoubtedly part of the pearl trade centered in Cabagua and Margarita Island. When the pearl beds were depleted, these expensive beads were replaced by cheaper, less complex styles.[25]

Glass beads traded into Middle and South America following the initial period of Spanish settlement include many of the well-known Venetian polychrome and eye beads. The popularity of red *cornaline d'Aleppo* beads (Bead Chart 50) in Guatemala, even

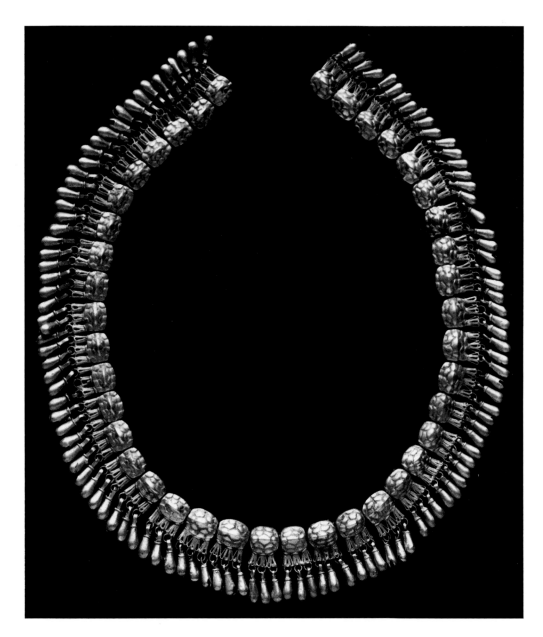

ABOVE: 270. *Pottery bead (or spindle whorl) from Ecuador, found by a collector on an embankment near a stream north of Guayaquil. Possibly Manteño culture, A.D. 500–1500. Length, 1.5 cm. Collection Phyllis and Peter Mroczkowski, New York*

LEFT: 271. *A Mixtec gold necklace with turtle effigy beads and bells. Dating to the late fifteenth or the early sixteenth century, the beads were found at Oaxaca, Mexico. Length, 50.2 cm. Museum of the American Indian, Heye Foundation, New York*

today, has been attributed to their similarity to coral, a highly valued material introduced by the Spaniards.[26] In San Pedro Quiátoni, a small town in Oaxaca, heirloom necklaces include unusual pendant beads formed of glass rods, looped at one end and averaging about two and a half inches in length (Bead Chart 1135). Of unknown origin, these beads were probably made in Europe and date between the sixteenth and eighteenth century.

Jewelry and beads created in Middle and South America since the European conquest exhibit varying degrees of influence from both the prehistoric and Spanish cultures. The craftsmen of Mexico, for example, where mineral wealth was such an integral part of the country's history, continue to produce large quantities of beads from silver, gold, and semiprecious stones, including amethyst, garnet, opal, crystal, and onyx. Jewelry designs frequently incorporate ancient Mayan, Aztec, or Mixtec motifs, or use gold-filigree techniques derived from eighteenth-century Spanish styles. This blend of native and Spanish heritage, using ancient and contemporary techniques, is characteristic of jewelry throughout Latin America.

259

North America

For thousands of years prior to European colonization, Indian civilizations made the North American continent their home. Anthropologists place the more than three hundred North American Indian tribes into broad cultural groups, organized by geographic areas: Woodland (southeastern and northeastern), Great Lakes, Plains, Intermontane, Southwest, California, Northwest Coast, and Subarctic. The linking of cultural characteristics with environments developed as an aid to interpreting the diverse life-styles and material cultures of a wide range of tribes.

North American Indian languages appear to have no word for art; artistic expression was fully integrated into many aspects of life and not treated as a separate activity. Objects were crafted to serve a host of functions, both secular and sacred. The extent of their complexity and that of the overall artifact assemblage depended on the life-style of the group and the resources available to them.

Although each group of Indians produced objects specific to their customs and beliefs, all North American Indians seem to have shared an appreciation for beads. At least eight thousand years before Europeans crossed the Atlantic, Indians were making, wearing, and trading beads of shell, pearl, bone, teeth, stone, and fossil crinoid stems.[1]

Imported glass beads, first introduced to North American native populations by Christopher Columbus in 1492, had a significant economic and aesthetic impact on Indian material culture. The earliest glass beads were gifts from explorers and missionaries, but in the sixteenth century the small seed beads became an important medium of exchange in the expanding North American fur trade. The availability of these small beads, along with the introduction of trade cloth and thin steel needles, led to the decline of age-old decorative techniques, including quillwork, and the rise of beadwork as

272. *Typical Southwestern jewelry assembly of turquoise, coral, bone, shell, and silver beads. Southwestern tribes valued shell beads over those of glass. Shells symbolize water to a people for whom rainfall is crucial to survival. Among the southwestern Indians, turquoise and silver jewelry became an important repository of wealth.*[1]

These necklaces were probably made between 1920 and 1950, but the disk and tabular beads are ancient forms. Center turquoise tabular bead, second necklace from top: length, 3.5 cm. Bottom two necklaces: collection Ivory Freidus

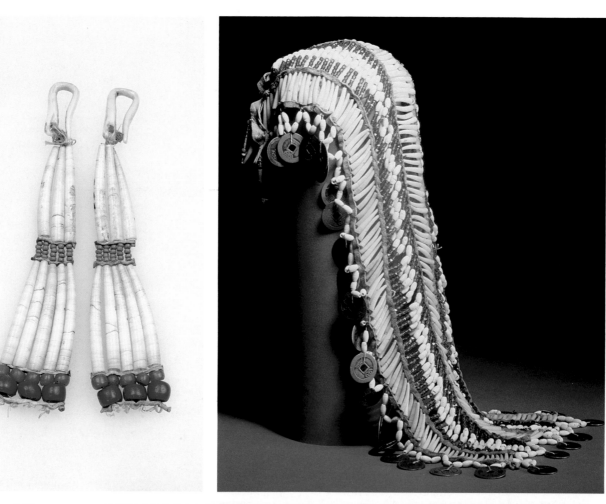

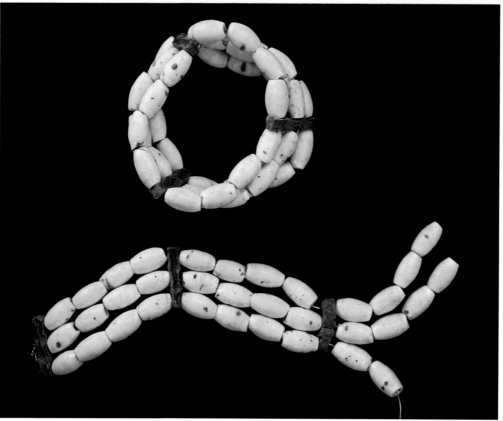

TOP LEFT: 275. *Earrings of* Dentalium pretiosum *shells and glass trade beads, worn by an Inuit girl. They were collected at Hershell Island. Dentalium shell had both monetary and decorative value. The shell was distributed through intertribal barter from the Pacific to the Arctic. Length, 6.7 cm. McCord Museum, McGill University, Montreal*

TOP RIGHT: 276. *A Yakima bridal headdress. The bride's wealth is reflected in the use of highly valued dentalium shells. The Chinese coins and imported blue glass beads came into the Northwest with the trans-Pacific fur trade during the mid-nineteenth century.[11] Length, 32 cm. Denver Art Museum*

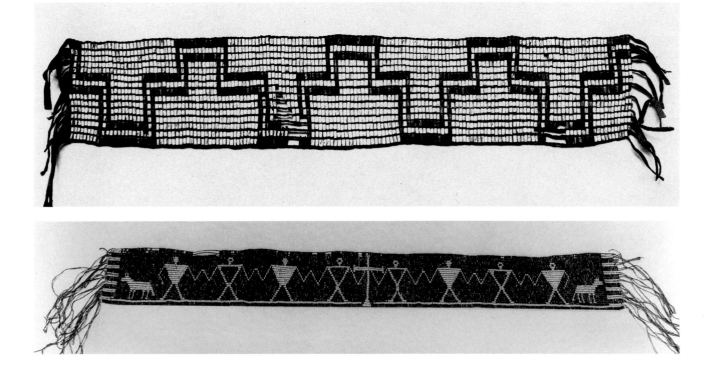

originating on the California coast, was excavated from a Nevada site dating to 6000 B.C.[6]

The best-known shell bead was wampum: small, cylindrical, centrally drilled white and purple beads made primarily of the quahog clamshell. Strung on leather thongs or woven into belts with sinew thread, wampum was sometimes worn as decoration but developed far greater significance as currency and was used for objects commemorating major political and ceremonial events.

Averaging a quarter of an inch in length and an eighth of an inch in diameter, the white beads were made from the columnella of univalves, periwinkles, or conchs, while white and purple beads came from the Atlantic Ocean clamshell. Although the introduction of European steel tools facilitated the manufacture of large quantities of wampum, the bead appears to have already occupied an important place in pre-European East Coast Indian life. In 1497, Jacques Cartier, a French explorer, encountered shell beads he called "esurgny" near present-day Montreal. "The thing most precious that they have in all the world, they call it esurgny; it is as white as any snow: they take [the shells] in the [St. Lawrence River]....Of them they make beads and wear them about their necks as we do gold, accounting it the most precious thing in the world." Esurgny was possibly wampum. After Cartier, wampum is not mentioned for over a hundred years. Later, the Dutch recognized its economic, social, and political importance to the Indians and introduced the concept to English settlers in 1628.[7]

North American Indians had no written languages, therefore messages were transmitted through symbolic designs. Woven wampum belts developed as a device for recording important events. Signaling peaceful, warlike, or other intentions between tribes (or between tribes and the colonists), the belts were manufactured using beads of one color, with symbolic designs in another color. White represented peace, promise, and good intentions, whereas purple conveyed hostility, sadness, or death. A white belt might therefore express an alliance or peace; a purple one announced war.

Although no Indian culture developed a universally recognized series of hiero-

century wampum belt, which is 27 rows wide and has nearly 10,000 beads, certifies the conversion of an Indian tribe or village to Christianity. The white beads symbolize the pascal lamb, Christian cross, and the white man, while the darker ones represent the Indian. Length, 153.7 cm. McCord Museum, McGill University, Montreal

LEFT: 282. A lithograph published in 1825 depicting Nicholas Vincent Tsawanhonei, chief of the Huron, holding the wampum belt commemorating the Treaty of Montreal, an agreement reached between the French and Huron allies and the English. It was recorded in wampum in 1701. McCord Museum, McGill University, Montreal

ABOVE: 283. The Wampum belt commemorating the Treaty of Montreal depicted in plate 282. Length, 89.9 cm. McCord Museum, McGill University, Montreal

NICHOLAS VINCENT TSAWANHONHI,

PRINCIPAL CHRISTIAN CHIEF AND CAPTAIN OF THE HURON INDIANS ESTABLISHED AT LA JEUNE LORETTE, NEAR QUEBEC, HABITED IN THE COSTUME OF HIS COUNTRY, AS WHEN PRESENTED TO HIS MAJESTY GEORGE IV, ON THE 7TH OF APRIL, 1825, WITH THREE OTHER CHIEFS OF HIS NATION, BY GENERALS BROCK AND CARPENTER. THE CHIEF BEARS IN HIS HAND THE WAMPUM OR COLLAR ON WHICH IS MARKED THE TOMAHAWK GIVEN BY HIS LATE MAJESTY. GEORGE III. THE GOLD MEDAL ON HIS NECK WAS THE GIFT OF HIS MAJESTY ON THIS PRESENTATION

They were accompanied and introduced into England on the 14th Dec.r 1824 by Mr W Cooper, who though an Englishman they state to be a Chief of their Nation and better known to them as Chief Tourhaanché

ABOVE: 284. *Detail of a quilled bridle cover. Quillwork, a decorative technique created by North American Indians, became the prototype for much native woven and embroidered beadwork. Denver Art Museum*

RIGHT: 285. *A Cheyenne pipebag, c. 1880, that combines beadwork with quilling. Small glass seed beads are used here to reproduce drawings of men's war exploits. The subject matter is unusual. Beadwork was made by Plains women, who typically created abstract geometric designs, leaving it to the men to paint naturalistic forms.*

In most tribes, tobacco was cultivated and smoked by men only. The tobacco plant had a sacred character and was invariably used on solemn occasions, accompanied by prayers. This finely beaded bag depicts the "awe and respect with which the ceremonial pipe and tobacco were treated. When not in ceremonial use, the pipe bowl and stem were taken apart and stored separately in the bag; only when they were united did the pipe actually become charged with supernatural power."[V] *Length, 99 cm. Denver Art Museum*

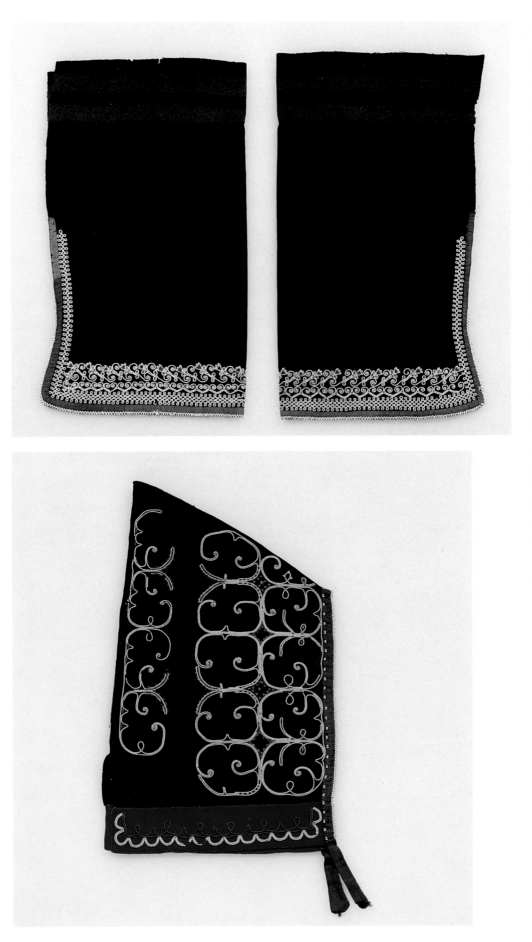

TOP: *286. Iroquois (Mohawk) womens' half-leggings of fine blue trade cloth with white, yellow, red, and green beadwork. The beadwork design is adapted from ribbon-work appliqué, a European style taught to young Huron and Iroquois girls in French mission schools. Made in 1894. Length, 42.5 cm. McCord Museum, McGill University, Montreal*

BOTTOM: *287. Micmac female headdress of blue black trade cloth, with double-curve design and rows of scallops, created in fine seed beads and sewn with moose hair. These floral patterns, typical of prevailing French neoclassical taste, merged neatly with curvilinear forms used by Woodland Indians for centuries. Bilaterally symmetrical patterns, such as this double curve, may originally have been made by Indian women literally biting patterns into folded sheets of birchbark. Length, 39.3 cm. McCord Museum, McGill University, Montreal*

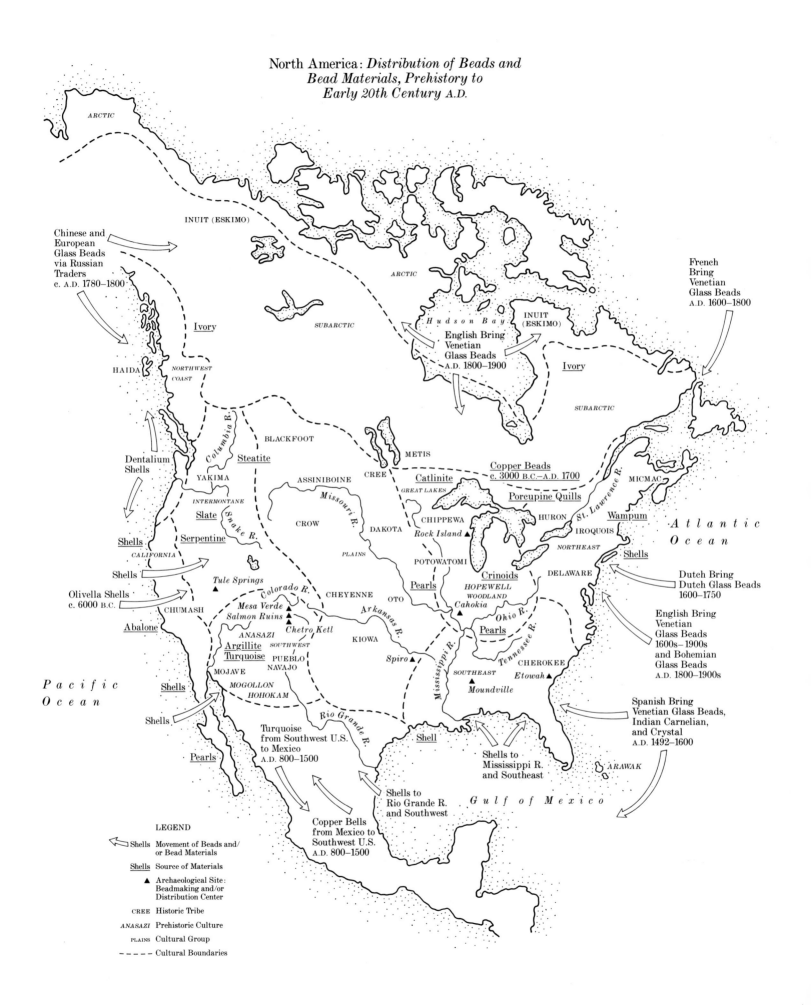

North America: *Distribution of Beads and*
Bead Materials, Prehistory to
Early 20th Century A.D.

ARCTIC

INUIT (ESKIMO)

ARCTIC

Chinese and
European
Glass Beads
via Russian
Traders
c. A.D. 1780–1800

French
Bring
Venetian
Glass Beads
A.D. 1600–1800

Hudson Bay

INUIT
(ESKIMO)

English Bring
Venetian
Glass Beads
A.D. 1800–1900

Ivory

SUBARCTIC

Ivory

SUBARCTIC

HAIDA

*NORTHWEST
COAST*

Dentalium
Shells

Steatite

BLACKFOOT

METIS

Copper Beads
c. 3000 B.C.–A.D. 1700

MICMAC

YAKIMA

CREE

Catlinite

GREAT LAKES

Porcupine Quills

St. Lawrence R.

Columbia R.

ASSINIBOINE

Missouri R.

*A t l a n t i c
O c e a n*

INTERMONTANE

Slate

CROW

DAKOTA

CHIPPEWA

Rock Island ▲

HURON

IROQUOIS

Wampum

Serpentine

Snake R.

PLAINS

POTOWATOMI

NORTHEAST

Shells

CALIFORNIA

Crinoids

DELAWARE

Shells

Shells

Tule Springs ▲

Colorado R.

CHEYENNE

OTO

Pearls

HOPEWELL

WOODLAND

Cahokia ▲

Dutch Bring
Dutch Glass Beads
1600–1750

Olivella Shells
c. 6000 B.C.

CHUMASH

Mesa Verde ▲
Salmon Ruins ▲

Chetro Ketl ▲

Arkansas R.

Ohio R.

Pearls

English Bring
Venetian
Glass Beads
1600s–1900s
and Bohemian
Glass Beads
A.D. 1800–1900s

Abalone

ANASAZI

SOUTHWEST

KIOWA

Spiro ▲

Tennessee R.

CHEROKEE

Etowah ▲

Argillite
Turquoise

PUEBLO

MOJAVE

NAVAJO

Mississippi R.

SOUTHEAST

Moundville ▲

Spanish Bring
Venetian Glass Beads,
Indian Carnelian,
and Crystal
A.D. 1492–1600

*P a c i f i c
O c e a n*

MOGOLLON

HOHOKAM

Shells

Rio Grande R.

Shells

Shells

Shell

Pearls

Turquoise
from Southwest U.S.
to Mexico
A.D. 800–1500

Shells to
Rio Grande R.
and Southwest

Shells to
Mississippi R.
and Southeast

G u l f   o f   M e x i c o

ARAWAK

LEGEND

⇦ Shells Movement of Beads and/
or Bead Materials

Copper Bells
from Mexico to
Southwest U.S.
A.D. 800–1500

Shells Source of Materials

▲ Archaeological Site:
Beadmaking and/or
Distribution Center

CREE Historic Tribe

ANASAZI Prehistoric Culture

PLAINS Cultural Group

- - - - Cultural Boundaries

glyphics, the wampum patterns were known by most tribes. A few images were almost immediately recognizable: a hatchet design woven into a belt meant war, while figures of two or more people holding hands meant peace and friendship. The width and length of the belt corresponded to the importance of the event.[8]

A simple square weave was used to make wampum belts. The warp threads consisted either of leather or fiber cords, while the weft elements were made of vegetal fibers or sinew threads (fig. 7). The first officially recorded wampum belts were made by the Pennsylvania Susquehannock Indians in the 1620s.[9] Twenty years later, wampum belts were reported among the Iroquois, who eventually dominated their manufacture and trade among Indian groups. European colonists employed wampum in transactions with the Indians and among themselves. All thirteen original colonies used wampum as currency. Massachusetts made it legal tender in November 1637. New York was still fixing the exchange rate in 1701.[10]

The use of wampum spread throughout North America in the seventeenth and eighteenth centuries. It is found in Rock Island, Wisconsin, about 1675–1700, and as far south as the mouth of the Mississippi River by 1762. Lewis and Clark gave it to the Sioux and Arikara on the Missouri River.[11] Eventually, the demand for the bead exceeded the capacity of East Coast Indians to provide it. As a result, European colonists in New York and New Jersey started manufacturing wampum in the 1740s for use in the Indian trade. A wampum factory established in the mid-eighteenth century by John Campbell of Passaic, New Jersey, was operated by his descendants until 1917. In addition to the manufacture of wampum, some tubular glass beads seem to have been made to imitate wampum as well.

The Glass Bead Trade

Most of the beads introduced to the New World by Europeans were made of glass, a material unknown to the native cultures.[12] The first documented glass bead in North America was excavated from the site of Vinland, the short-lived Viking colony situated in what is now Newfoundland and abandoned about 1347. This clear, spherical bead may have been part of a rosary worn by a Viking woman. The Vikings traded extensively with northeastern Indian groups, so it is not certain whether the first glass bead was a personal ornament or imported for trade.[13]

Prehistoric North Americans' appreciation for beads helped the Spanish explore and colonize the New World. One of Christopher Columbus's first acts upon reaching the Bahamas in 1492 was to offer glass beads to the Arawak Indians. His October 12 log entry is the earliest record of glass beads in America:

> A large crowd of natives gathered there....In order to win the friendship and affection of that people and because I was convinced that their conversion to our Holy Faith would be better promoted through love than through force, I placed some of them with red caps and have some strings of beads which they placed around their necks, and with other trifles of insignificant worth that delighted them and by which we have got a wonderful hold on their affections.[14]

Using glass beads to win Indian friendship was a prevalent custom in the days when England, France, Sweden, Holland, and Spain all vied for control of North American territories. The practice lasted through the American Revolution, when gift-giving gradually gave way to trading beads for fur.

Through the fur trade, glass beads had a significant effect on North American Indian life. Early explorers found the American continent teeming with wildlife and

TOP LEFT: 288. *The beadwork designs on this early twentieth-century Inuit woman's parka (amautik) reflect two important eras of Eskimo history. The tiered geometric designs and triangular forms recall patterns of skin tattooing, a traditional ritual practiced by Inuit women. The use of glass beads and the decorative floral motifs show the influence of trade with foreign whalers.[VI] Length, 124 cm. McCord Museum, McGill University, Montreal*

TOP RIGHT: 289. *An Inuit dance apron (probably early twentieth century). Length, 51 cm. Collection Tambaran Gallery, New York*

FIG. 2. Appliqué Quill-work: *quills are folded between two rows of stitches.*

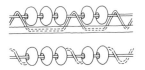

FIG. 3. Appliqué Bead-work: *overlay or spot stitch.*

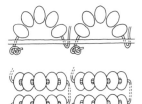

FIG. 4. Appliqué Bead-work: *"lazy" stitch.*

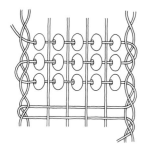

FIG. 5. Woven Bead-work: *single-thread weft and warp.*

soon established a system in which horses, guns, alcohol, and other items were exchanged for the fur pelts so coveted in Europe. When glass beads were introduced as a trade item, they were widely sought after by Indians for their colors and ease of use. They often replaced Indian-made beads of bone, shell, copper, and stone.

Beads were important to the early fur trade because they were compact and easily transportable. One beaver skin was worth a six-foot string of small blue beads in Sault Sainte Marie in 1860, or one "bunch" of seed beads at Fort McPherson in the Canadian Northwest. The red bead known as *cornaline d'Aleppo,* or "Hudson Bay beads" to traders in the north, carried an exchange value of six beads to one beaver skin.[15]

Lewis and Clark found the so-called Russian (a smooth or faceted blue glass) bead to be especially valued by the Indians on the Columbia River in the Pacific Northwest (Bead Chart 112). They noted that:

In the evening seven Indians of the Clot Sop nation came over in a canoe; they brought with them two sea-otter skins for which they asked blue beads and such high prices that [we] were unable to purchase them without reducing our small stock of merchandise. Merely to try the Indian who had one of these skins, I offered him my watch, handkerchief, a bunch of red beads, and a dollar of the American coin, all of which he refused and demanded '*ti-a-co-mo-shack*' which is chief's beads and the most common blue beads, but few of which we have at this time.[16]

Catholic missionaries in North America regularly gave beads as gifts to potential Indian converts. Writing from the Illinois country in 1694, Father Gravier noted that: "It is true that the hope of getting a red bead—which is a fruit the size of a small bean, which has been sent to us from Martinique or other Islands (Oh, that I had a bushel of them!)...incites the children to answer well; but they must answer very well for several days to obtain either the rosary, the red bead, or the cross."[17]

The first glass beads traded in quantity were for necklaces that were, for the most part, available in white, blue, and black. These colors were cheaper to produce than red or yellow beads, thus providing a greater margin of profit to the trader. Indians may also have requested beads in white, blue, and black because they suggested the white and purple shades so treasured in shell wampum. Blue beads were particularly popular in the Plains, possibly because that color was rare in Indian dye sources.[18] In the western Great Lakes region about 1675, the French introduced smaller "pony beads," thus named because they were transported by traders on ponies. Beginning about 1840, colorful, tiny seed beads, usually two millimeters or less in diameter, were traded in bulk, the result of the standardization of manufacturing techniques in Venice and Bohemia, which made it possible to produce beads of uniform size, shape, and color.

Polychrome glass beads were particularly prized by Plains tribes and were used as offerings to the spirits. These complex glass beads, of Venetian or occasionally Bohemian manufacture, were not as widely distributed as glass seed beads. Probably due to their greater cost, polychrome glass beads are found sparingly in archaeological sites throughout most of the continent.

There is much confusion over how glass beads were introduced to Arctic peoples. It is likely that "Russian" or "Siberian" beads were not made in Russia, but were carried by Russian traders to the west coast of North America, subsequently moving eastward via intertribal trade. These beads may have been acquired by the Russians in China (where they had been imported from Europe) and brought to the Northwest coast as part of the fur trade. Alternatively, the beads were made in Venice or Bohemia, shipped to Hong Kong by English trading companies, and traded to Russians who brought them to the Northwest coast; or they may have come directly from Europe, brought by English merchants to the Hudson Bay Company posts in Canada.[19]

There is, incidentally, no evidence for the legend that tells of the Dutchman Peter Minuit purchasing Manhattan for twenty-four dollars worth of glass beads. This colorful story was first mentioned by historian Martha J. Lamb in 1877 and subsequently repeated in numerous books as well as a famous painting by Alfred Frederick.[20]

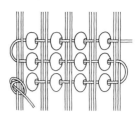

FIG. 6. Woven Bead-work: *single-thread weft and double warp.*

The Impact of Imported Glass Seed Beads

American Indians used beads in two basic ways: stringing and beadwork. Beadwork involved appliqué (embroidery) on a piece of animal skin or cloth, or the creation of a fabric of beads by weaving them on a loom. With the introduction of seed beads, the ways of decorating clothing and objects changed dramatically. Whereas large beads were strung and pony beads used sparingly to outline areas and edges, glass seed beads, aided by the availability of thin steel needles, covered entire surfaces.

Traditional decorative methods were influenced significantly by the introduction of seed beads. Large necklace and pony beads did not supplant the indigenous practice of quilling and painting. However, with the appearance of quantities of inexpensive seed beads, women began to sew, embroider, and weave beadwork equal in quality to the finest quillwork and paintings.

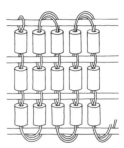

FIG. 7. Woven Bead-work: *cylindrical shell beads on double weft and single-warp threads. This was the technique generally used for making wampum belts.*

Quillwork was a unique American Indian technique. Each region had its own styles, colors, and sewing methods; it was developed to perfection by tribes of the Pacific Northwest, Great Lakes, and eastern Plains before the first European beads entered the New World. Whitish porcupine quills were softened in water, flattened, colored with vegetable dyes, and fastened to skins in patterns resembling embroidery (fig. 2).

Appliquéd glass beadwork developed from this earlier quillwork. Indian women, who had previously decorated objects by the time-consuming technique of quilling, quickly realized that many familiar patterns could be executed more easily in beads when cloth fabrics replaced buckskin. By 1800, quillwork appears to have been generally abandoned, although in a few areas, it continued long after beads were available.

Woven beadwork produced in the Woodlands, Great Lakes, and eastern Plains was significantly influenced by quilling. At first sight, the ribbed surface of quillwork can be mistaken for small cylindrical beads strung on the weft, the thread carried by the shuttle. A variety of weaving techniques, usually based on the square weave, was used for making beaded wampum belts, sashes, and bags.

In glass beadwork appliqué, two basic stitches are encountered: the "overlaid" or "spot" stitch (also called "couching") and the "lazy" stitch (figs. 3 and 4). The sewing technique of the overlaid stitch is like that of quillwork: several beads on a sinew thread are attached to buckskin or cloth by another sinew thread sewn across it. This stitch is ideal for the floral and other curvilinear patterns favored by the Woodland Indians.

The "lazy" stitch was primarily used by Plains tribes for geometric patterns not requiring the intricacy of the overlaid stitch. It consisted of rows of beads sewn only at the ends, creating the ridged or scalloped effect distinct to the central and western Plains. Lazy stitch—nicknamed for the ease with which it could be used to cover large areas—was an ideal technique for geometric and abstract forms characteristic of Plains art. It is also a perfect example of the type of beadwork that derived from designs previously done in quillwork.[21]

OVERLEAF: 293. *A Cherokee shoulder bag. The ammunition pouch carried by eighteenth-century British soldiers became the prototype for the shoulder bags worn as part of men's dress clothing among tribes in the southeastern U.S.*

Although the bilateral figures on the lower left strap resemble prehistoric Southeastern symbols engraved on shell and stone disks, the designs on this pouch were probably invented by the beadmaker.[VII]. Pouch: width, 20.3 cm. Denver Art Museum

294

295

296

297

294–97. *The beadwork designs on these four bandolier bags, dating to about 1875, illustrate the influence of the environment on the aesthetics of Indian groups in four geographic areas—the Woodlands, Great Lakes, and eastern and western Plains. In the eastern Woodlands, abundant plant life and soft, dappled light led to the use of curvilinear, flowing forms with naturalistic leaf and floral patterns (top left). For the western Plains tribes, the use of geometric, angular patterns mirrors the stark, strong forms so prevalent in dry grassland landscapes (top right). The elaborate geometric patterning of the eastern Plains, on this Dakota (Sioux) bag (bottom left), which is said to have been owned by Sitting Bull, shows the influence of Caucasian rug designs on Plains Indian beadwork. Included in the household furnishings of settlers moving West, Oriental rugs became a source of new designs, which the Dakota incorporated into their beadwork. These patterns became identified as "Indian design" when taken East with the Buffalo Bill shows. There were more simplified geometric patterns made by Indians of the western Plains (bottom right).* VIII *Plate 297: length, 26.7 cm. McCord Museum, McGill University, Montreal*

Beadwork of the Plains Tribes

Indian cultures developed in ways that reflect their natural environment. Thus, the Haida of the Pacific Northwest, who lived in immense spruce and redwood forests, were prolific woodcarvers; the Pueblo people, whose lives were organized by mythology and rituals tied to maize agriculture, symbolized this ideology in much of their pottery; and the Plains people adorned their abundant supply of animal hides with paint, quills, and eventually beads. Frederick Dockstader explains in *Indian Art in America*: "Their work revolved and grew out of the natural resources provided by their Creator. In turning these resources into artistic objects, they returned the compliment."[22]

The people of the Plains, a vast grassland stretching from the Great Lakes to the Rocky Mountains, depended almost entirely on the buffalo for food, clothing, shelter, and most of their raw materials. Their nomadic existence, intimately tied to the seasonal movements of the buffalo herds, precluded many material possessions. Consequently they wore small, easily transportable objects that served several functions. A beaded bag of soft leather could be worn, hung in the tent as decoration, and rolled up for removal to a new campsite at a more promising hunting ground.

Although personal possessions were few, Plains Indians fashioned garments from animal skins and elaborately decorated them with beadwork. Each tribe employed its own distinctive designs and techniques. The care devoted to adornment reflected their views of the spiritual world. Respect for the buffalo was paramount, for this animal

OPPOSITE: 298. *A Dakota (Sioux) woman with a beaded dentalium shell shirt and long dentalium shell and leather earrings—typical adornment for Plains women in the latter half of the nineteenth century. Photograph taken c. 1886. Smithsonian Office of Anthropology, Bureau of American Ethnology Collection*

299. *Blackfoot Indians in full beaded regalia, Calgary, Alberta. Photograph taken about 1920. Notman Photographic Archives, McCord Museum, McGill University, Montreal*

279

ABOVE: 300. *Beadwork blanket strip used to cover the seams of the buffalo robe of an Assiniboin Indian. Similar objects are held by two Blackfoot men (far right) in plate 299. Rondel: diameter, 24.5 cm. McCord Museum, McGill University, Montreal*

RIGHT: 301. *Blackfoot loop necklace from the Canadian Plains. This is a man's necklace of brass and colored glass trade beads strung on rawhide. Length: 63.5 cm. McCord Museum, McGill University, Montreal*

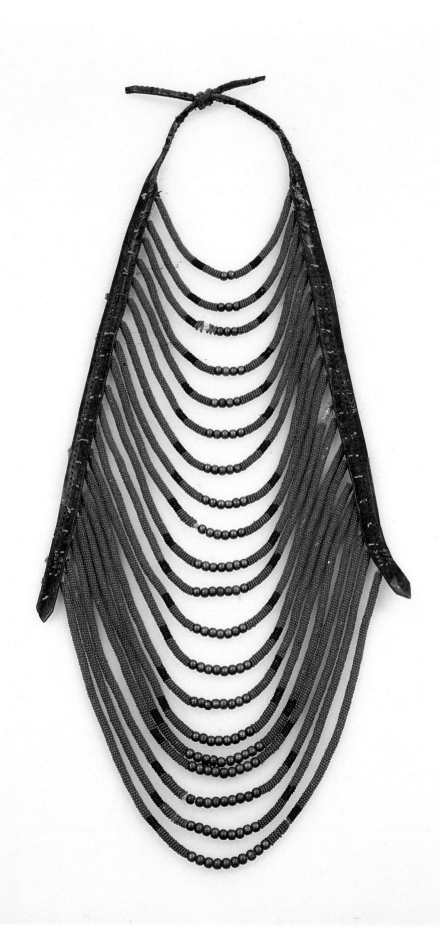

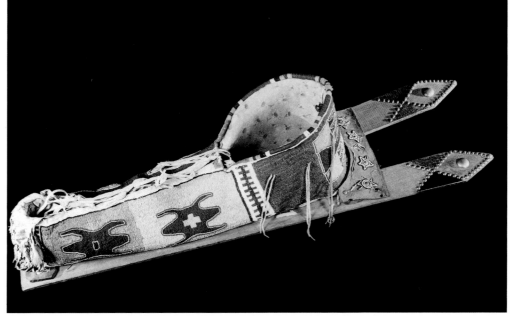

TOP: 302. *Dakota (Sioux) girl's dress, made of buckskin covered with solid beadwork sewn in "lazy" stitching (see Fig. 3), c. 1880–85. This technique is effective for decorating large areas with the strong, geometric designs characteristic of western Plains art. The light blue background is a typically Dakotan motif. Length, 28.5 cm. McCord Museum, McGill University, Montreal*

BOTTOM: 303. *Many American Indian women went to great lengths to provide secure carrying cases for infants. This can be seen in the elaborate care taken to decorate the cradleboard for the child of Kiowa Chief I-See-O. Reinforced with a protective rawhide lining and supported on a wooden frame, the cradleboard could be carried on the mother's back or leaned against a tree or rock. The pointed stakes in the frame of this Plains tribe cradleboard shielded the baby in case of a fall from a horse.[IX] Length, 112 cm. Smithsonian Institution, Washington, D.C.*

TOP: 304. *The red ochre backing identifies these as the moccasins of a shaman. The circle is a recurring (Blackfoot) Plains motif; it has neither beginning nor end and symbolizes the sun, the moon, the calendar year, and life itself.*[X] *Length, 26.7 cm. McCord Museum, McGill University, Montreal*

BOTTOM: 305. *A buckskin "dream vision" shirt with decoration oriented to the wearer ("self-directed"). It is painted, beaded, quilled, and adorned with strands of human hair. The symbols stand for two red hands. Length (across shoulders), 160 cm. Acquired by the Smithsonian Institution in 1899 from Crow Indians in Montana. Smithsonian Institution, Washington, D.C.*

OPPOSITE: 306. *A Midewinin song "reminder" panel. The Midewinin, or Grand Medicine Society, of the Great Lakes region was an institution that cured the sick and functioned on behalf of the tribe's welfare. Since ceremonies were lengthy, there were memory aids to help recall the correct sequence of prayer and song. Members carried cloth plaques like this one to help them remember the magic songs. Length, 31.8 cm. Denver Art Museum*

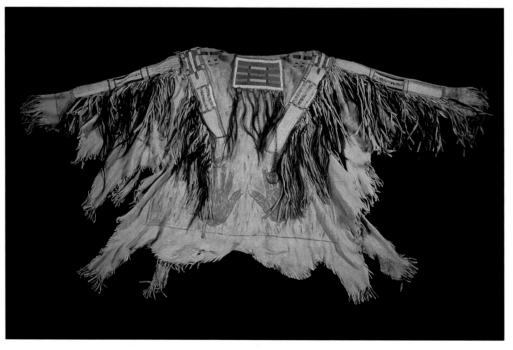

alone supplied all the basic needs of the community. The relationship was refined:

> The skins of game were more than just practical, everyday material for clothing and shelter for they contained some of the spiritual power of the animals from which they had been taken. In life the skin had given the animal its form. Wearing it, or resting in its shelter, symbolized and reinforced the constant and powerful spiritual bond between game and the people whose survival depended on the continued generosity of animals in surrendering their lives. Beautifying a dressed skin not only benefited its human owner but also did honor to the spirit of the animal. Art was part of the customary, indeed obligatory, propitiation of the slain animal to obtain its good will and prevent its wrath and revenge.[23]

Plains Indians believed the world was filled with power that resided in objects, animals, or even people. To obtain this power and to establish a communication with his spiritual guardians, the Indian kept a solitary vigil. This visionary experience often produced "vision art"—highly personal, original creations. It was felt that knowledge obtained in this manner would diminish in sacred power if shared with other people. During these meditations, various devices were used to direct and concentrate thought. "A comparison with the use of mantras in Buddhistic meditation is justified insofar as many Indians refer to their spiritual guardians as 'soul-spirit.' It resides in themselves. Self-directed decorations are Native American mantras."[24]

The Plains people decorated themselves, their homes, and their possessions; above all, they ornamented and honored their horses. Horses, introduced in the Southwest by the early Spanish explorers, gave the Plains Indians much greater mobility. With the horse, buffalo hunting shifted from drive-and-ambush techniques to collective hunting, resulting in a dramatic increase in the number of buffalo killed.

The Crow of the upper Missouri River were among the richest and most beautifully adorned Plains tribes. Charles Larpenteur, who traded with the Crow in 1833, described the visible results of their abstinence: "As they do not drink, their trade was all in substantial goods, which kept them well dressed, and extremely rich in horses; so it really was a beautiful sight to see that tribe on the move."[25] Crow beadworkers lavished care and skill on paraphernalia that was visible when the camp was on the march; special emphasis was given to the accoutrements of the horses.

Much of the Plains Indians' decoration was created specifically to be viewed in motion. The Indian craftsman had the "movement of the body, the graceful motion of the horse, and the wafting of the Plains breeze in mind when he developed the corona of feathers, the elaborate fringe, and the many pendants of cloth, leather and beadwork."[26]

Beadworkers took pride in their ability to do fine work. If a man wished to compete with a neighbor who owned a pair of fully beaded moccasins, he could have his wife bead his moccasins on the soles as well as on the tops. (However, moccasins beaded on the soles, known as "spirit moccasins," were designed primarily for burials.) A competitive woman might bead her dress all the way to the bottom edge instead of restricting her beads to the yoke.

Intertribal trade and gift-giving often involved objects of beadwork, resulting in the frequent merging and reinterpretation of styles. For example, the floral motifs of the northeastern Woodland were transformed into stylized floral patterns of the Great Lakes (plates 294–97). As tribes moved west in search of game and fur in the nineteenth century, artisans of different tribes were in contact more often.

Exposure to European styles directly affected Indian creativity. Along the colonial frontier, Indians observed the floral motifs on furniture and clothing of the

307. *The Metis of southern Canada are people of mixed Indian and European ancestry who built a distinct intermediate culture. This mid-nineteenth century costume combines native and foreign elements. The coat is an exact copy of a Prince Albert jacket, although it is made of leather and decorated with Indian porcupine quill embroidery. The half-leggings have typical Metis beaded floral patterns. Denver Art Museum*

ABOVE: 308. *Blackfoot ceremonial "medicine pipe". Pipes of this kind, with long, elaborate stems, were used for formal smoking at important meetings, including religious ceremonies to summon divine help in various undertakings. This pipe is decorated with an unusually large number of beads. Length, 95.2 cm. Plates 308–9: McCord Museum, McGill University, Montreal*

RIGHT: 309. *Blackfoot stone and leather war clubs of various types were used in hand-to-hand combat. This aggressive, beaded image was intended to be seen by the enemy in the last flash of his life. Length, 50.8 cm.*

286

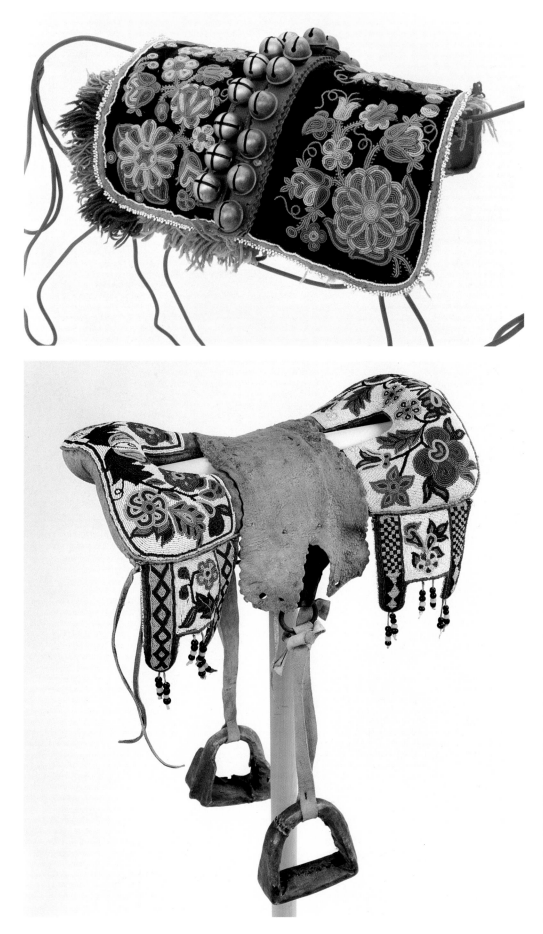

ABOVE: 310. *Cheyenne saddle blanket from the 1840s decorated in typical western Plains beadwork. The availability of large "pony" beads led to the design of bold, geometric patterns. Length, 178 cm. Denver Art Museum*

TOP LEFT: 311. *A late nineteenth-century Metis dog blanket and bell harness from the MacKenzie River basin. The Metis traded their craftwork throughout the northern and central Plains and into the Northwest Territories.*

The western Sioux referred to the Red River Metis in Minnesota as the "flower beadwork people," and throughout the Northwest many Indians confirm the Metis origin of their own floral designs.[XI] These artifacts reflect the Indians' encounter with European culture on the American frontier.[XII] McCord Museum, McGill University, Montreal

BOTTOM LEFT: 312. *A Cree ceremonial saddle from the early 1900s owned by Yellow Horse. The form of the saddle shows early Spanish influence, yet it has the Woodland style of floral decoration, which had spread to the Plains. Length, 48.2 cm. McCord Museum, McGill University, Montreal*

The Special Beads: Amber and Pearls

> In the sea of changeable winds, his
> merchants fished for pearls;
> In the sea where the North Star culminates,
> they fished for yellow amber.[1]

Over the centuries, the beauty, scarcity, and durability of several natural substances have captured people's attention, and certain ones of these, particularly amber and pearls, have become the subjects of an entire culture of adornment.

Amber Amber is the fossilized sap of extinct trees that lived in temperate and subtropical forests during the Eocene period, sixty million to forty million years ago.[2] Warm to the touch and light in weight, amber exists primarily in yellow and golden honey tones and in a variety of less common opaque and translucent colors, ranging from ruby red to iridescent greens and blues.

The most significant amber deposits are on or near the coasts of Sweden, Denmark, northern Germany, Poland, and the Soviet Union, buried under 100 to 130 feet of sand and marl in a layer of clay called "blue earth." Today, most of the world's amber comes from the blue earth stratum in the Samland district of Poland, but only about 15 percent of it is of gem quality and suitable for jewelry. Important deposits also occur in a bed that extends fifty miles into the Baltic Sea. Following heavy storms, amber is often retrieved on the beaches and in the shallow waters of the Baltic countries, and it can even be found as far away as the French and English coastlines.

Amber was probably the first gemlike material ever used for personal adornment. Beads and pendants of amber were found in Upper Paleolithic sites of Magdalenian

316. *A grouping of amber necklaces probably dating to the nineteenth century. From the outside: (1) Baltic amber (succinite); (2) Persian amber or copal; (3) a variety of Baltic amber, "Butter Amber"; (4) Romanian amber (Rumanite); (5) Sicilian amber (Simetite). Necklace, center bead: length, 4.4 cm. Private collection*

France and Spain, dating from 15,000 to 10,000 B.C. At Mezhirichi, overlooking the Dnieper River southeast of Kiev, Soviet archaeologists have uncovered amber from a hundred miles away, which was probably traded to the local residents in about 13,000 B.C.[3]

Baltic amber's golden color and pliable nature made it a favorite trade item beginning at least in Neolithic times. Tribes of the Baltic area, central Russia, western Norway, and Finland traded both the raw material and finished beads as early as 3000 B.C.[4] Amber is found in Neolithic and second-millennium B.C. Bronze Age graves in nearly every European country.

By the Bronze Age, Baltic amber was traded along north-south routes that followed major European rivers. One of the most important of these started in Jutland (Denmark), crossed central Germany via the Weser and Elbe valleys, followed the Moldau through Moravia and Austria, crossed the Alps by the Brenner Pass, and met the Po River and the north coast of the Adriatic Sea before descending to the Peloponnisos and traveling on to Crete by sea. A secondary land route followed the Danube and went to the Balkans, while a third began in Germany at Saxe-Thuringia and turned west into Brittany and the English kingdom of Wessex. About 600 B.C., another route followed the Netherlands coast to the Rhine, and then went down the Rhone and terminated at the Mediterranean port of Massilia (Marseilles).[5] Quantities of amber beads have been excavated from sites on all of these routes. (Heinrich Schliemann, for example, found four hundred Baltic amber beads at Mycenae.) Generally, amber was transported as raw material and then worked into beads and pendants by its recipients (see map, page 50).

The Baltic Bronze Age trade in tin and copper (used to manufacture a bronze alloy) evolved simultaneously with the transcontinental amber trade.[6] From about 1600 B.C., amber and tin were Baltic commodities traded to the south, both in exchange for finished bronze weapons and various tools of the more sophisticated Mediterranean cultures.

During the mid- to late second millennium B.C., with central Europeans serving as middlemen, Mycenaean, Phoenician, and Etruscan traders were the focus of a wide-ranging amber network. Striking similarities exist between amber bead necklaces found in Jutland, Wessex, Mycenae, and the Rhine Valley. At the same time, Baltic amber was traded from the Aegean into the eastern Mediterranean countries: a Mycenaean pot that contained Baltic amber beads was excavated at Ras Shamra in Syria.[7]

The earliest literary references to the uses of amber appear in Book XVIII of Homer's *Odyssey*. Written about 700 B.C., it is set in the period after the fall of Mycenae (1100–900 B.C.). Odysseus's wife, Penelope, receives from a suitor, Eurymachus, "an elaborate chain strung with beads of amber like golden sunshine."[8] Also, the narrator, Eumaeus, describes his experiences in Syria: "The Phoenicians...sent a messenger.... The crafty fellow came to my father's house hawking a golden collar beaded here and there with amber...the serving women in the hall and my lady mother were offering him bids for it and devouring it with their eyes."[9]

The word *electricity* comes from *elektron*, the Greek name for amber.[10] When rubbed, amber develops negative electrical static and can pick up small pieces of paper or lint. This phenomenon, observed by Plato and Aristotle during the fourth century B.C., probably increased the esteem and mystery of the gem in the eyes of ancient people.[11] Certainly, amber's electrical properties and golden color underlie the many curative properties ascribed to it over the millennia.

In ancient Greek mythology, amber was believed to be the solidified tears that were shed annually by the Heliades mourning the death of their brother. To the Greek statesman Nicias, it was the essence of sunrays "congealed in the sea and then cast upon the shore." One legend describes amber as the solidified urine of the lynx (one of its names is *lyncurius*).[12] It was even thought to be petrified dolphin or seal sperm.[13] These myths notwithstanding, both the Greeks and Romans knew that amber was tree resin, and it was described with remarkable accuracy by the Roman historian Pliny.

The Phoenicians, either ignorant of amber sources or shrewd merchants seeking to protect their sources, began a strategy of concealing the location of the raw gem from their rivals. The Etruscans, however, learned of the Baltic source and became amber importers, as did the Romans, who sent expeditions to the region during the second century A.D.[14]

Following the collapse of the Roman Empire, the amber trade declined, a casualty of the Teutonic migrations. By the late Middle Ages, however, Baltic amber was once again actively collected and traded, its traffic strictly controlled by German merchants' monopolies for the next several hundred years. From the 1300s to the 1800s, members of established central European guilds manufactured amber beads primarily for Catholic, Buddhist, and Muslim rosaries. Apprentices desiring to join guilds were required "to prove their proficiency by cutting a quarter of a pound of perfectly round, evenly drilled beads by eye, without the aid of a compass."[15]

Amber was also regarded with esteem in the East. The Persians, Turks, Arabs, and Chinese were especially fond of it. A remarkable eighteenth-century Chinese amber necklace was owned by Englishman Thomas Kinton in the twentieth century. Each bead was finely carved into the shape of a Mandarin's head, "every face having a different expression. Some were smiling, some grimacing, others wore a solemn look."[16]

In addition to the Baltic, important amber sources included Sicily, Romania, and Burma, where the amber-bearing trees were concentrated in prehistoric times. However, the quantity of the gem obtained from these regions was comparatively small. Baltic amber ranges from pale yellowish white to reddish brown to almost black, although tones of yellow are most common.[17] Sicilian amber is also yellow, but occurs in a rare ruby red hue as well as green, brown, blue, and purple; furthermore, it often has a luminescence, possibly due to its origins in volcanic soil near Mount Etna. Dark colors typify Romanian amber, including rose red, smoky gray, dark garnet, brownish red, and a greenish blue, green, and brownish green variety with agate like patterns (called "Amber of Piatra"; plate 316). Deep red, highly fluorescent Burmese amber is one of the rarest and most beautiful types known (plate 318).[18]

Variations in the color of amber are due to the presence of foreign matter encountered by the sap after it was secreted. Dark amber, for example, may result from the presence of wood ash or iron pyrites. Blue amber contains carbonate of lime, while several colors reflect the presence of sulfuric acid from decomposing humus.[19] As amber ages it darkens, often obtaining a dark patina. It may change from yellow to reddish brown in as little as one hundred years,[20] although there is speculation that some amber discovered in Greek tombs by archaeologists may be a dark red Sicilian variety. It is argued that much amber used in the classical world came from Sicily.[21] This has not been proved, however, since analysis discloses that most ancient amber has a yellow core and traces of succinic acid, which are features characteristic of the Baltic variety.[22]

Amber may be transparent or opaque. The resin is cloudy or clear due to the presence or absence of masses of minute air bubbles. As amber resin ran down the tree, it frequently engulfed insects, twigs, and leaves, and acted as an embalming agent. Millions of years later, these inclusions have supplied valuable information about the flora and fauna of the prehistoric amber forests.[23]

TOP: 317. *A bronze bracelet with a finely crafted biconical oblate amber bead. This typical piece of Hallstatt or early Celtic jewelry displays the ancient affection for amber. Fifth to fourth century B.C. Diameter, 7.1 cm. British Museum, London*

BOTTOM: 318. *A necklace purportedly of Burmese amber (Burmite) that was possibly cut in nineteenth-century Egypt. Largest bead: length, 5.7 cm. Collection Wolf Hunger, London*

OPPOSITE: 319. *Faceted Baltic amber (succinite) said to have belonged to a member of the Russian imperial court. The amber was cut in the Baltic at Königsberg. Center bead: length, 3.1 cm. Collection Wolf Hunger, London*

294

Substances frequently confused with amber include copal, ambroid, and Bakelite.[24] Copal, a natural resin, exists in a semifossilized state ("true copal") and as resin taken directly from living trees ("raw copal"). It is believed that in earlier times copal was used to make beads. However, most beads called copal are, in fact, amber or plastic.

True copal is found in large quantities on the island of Zanzibar, off the coast of Tanzania, where it is mined from shallow deposits during the rainy season, when the ground is soft. Raw copal is also collected in Zanzibar as gum from a tree resembling birch. Both are also found on the west coast of Africa and in New Zealand, Brazil, and Malaysia.[25] It has been suggested that true copal may be a million years old and is undergoing complex chemical changes that would lead eventually to the formation of true amber.[26] Ambroid, or "pressed amber," is formed by compressing small pieces of amber together. Although genuine amber, it lacks the subtle beauty of true amber.[27]

It has long been thought that Bakelite, a hard thermoset plastic invented in 1909 by Leo Hendrik Backelund, is the artificial material used to imitate amber, generally in jewelry of the 1920s and 1930s. In reality, most plastics resembling amber are varieties of cast-phenolic resins, distinguished by their intense color and translucence, whereas Bakelite is opaque and usually dark.[28]

Today, true amber and ambroid beads continue to be made in the Baltic states of the Soviet Union, primarily for export. Although available in various colors and shapes, most beads are tumble-polished and free-formed.

Pearls Like amber, pearls are an organic substance, the product of a living organism. Whereas amber is a multi-million-year-old fossilized plant resin, pearls are formed by glandular secretions of certain living oysters and mussels. Pearls are found in both sea and freshwater mollusks all over the world.

Pearls are nature's ultimate gift to the bead world. Perfected by natural processes, they differ from other gems in requiring no additional cutting and polishing to enhance their beauty. Pearls need only to be set or pierced and strung.

Over the centuries, fantastic theories were created to explain the origin of pearls. Chinese myths suggest they were conceived in the brains of dragons, while Indian writers placed their origins in clouds, elephants, boars, conchs, fish, serpents, bamboo, and oysters—albeit the latter was thought to be the most important source.[29]

That pearls occur in oysters was known by at least ancient Greek and Roman times. Until the sixteenth century, however, little was understood about the actual pearl-formation process. Fascinated by their luminescence and subdued beauty, various ancient poets wrote that pearls were the solidified tears of angels or water nymphs. The most popular explanation was that pearls were formed when drops of dew or rain fell into the open shells of oysters at breeding time. At certain seasons of the year, the oysters would rise to the surface of the ocean in the morning, open their shells, and, aided by the warmth of sunlight, become impregnated with dewdrops that in time were transformed into lustrous pearls. Without the right mixture of light and air, faulty pearls resulted. Pliny, the astute Roman scientific writer and historian, observed in his first-century A.D. *Historia naturalis* that the fruit of the shells were pearls, whose luster and size varied according to the quality and quantity of dew they received.[30]

Challenges to the dew-formation theory began in Renaissance Europe. By 1608, Pedro Teixeira of Portugal noted the similarity between pearls and the interior of the shells in which they were formed. Scientists confirmed this observation by discovering that irritating the soft body of a mollusk with a grain of sand or a piece of seaweed, for example, caused the mollusk to surround and absorb the foreign matter with a secretion. While all mollusks coat the intrusion, only those that line their shells with mother-of-pearl (nacre) produce pearls. The image of this lowly creature responding to a bodily intrusion by transforming it into a beautiful gem symbolic of all that is pure and beautiful has stimulated poets for centuries. As the Persian poet Hafez said: "Learn from yon orient shell to love thy foe / And store with pearls the wound that brings thee woe."

The iridescent pearly luster, called "orient," gives pearls their value as gems. This luster is an optical phenomenon caused by light refracting off the nacre, which is 90 percent calcium carbonate and 10 percent conchiolin, a gluelike protein that binds together the calcium carbonate crystals. Nacre is deposited on the surface of the pearl in overlapping platelets that cause waves of light to be reflected from different surface levels. The color of pearls varies with the nacre's thickness and with the color of the upper conchiolin layer, depending on water conditions and the type of mollusk. Different regions produce pearls of different tints.[31] The shape of the intrusive nucleus and its position within the mollusk result in pearls of various forms and sizes. The Romans believed that no two pearls were ever exactly alike, thus they named them *unio* ("unique").[32]

Pearls are widely discussed in historical and religious writings. The high esteem accorded them by the ancient Hebrews is illustrated in various references in the Talmud and in the Old Testament. (In the story of Abraham and Sarah, only Sarah's beauty is ranked above pearls.) Classic Indian Sanskrit literature (A.D. 1–100) also frequently refers to pearls. Arab writings often relate pearls to paradise: each person admitted to the celestial kingdom is provided with a tent of pearls and attended by beautiful maidens resembling "hidden pearls."[33]

Among the earliest surviving examples of pearl jewelry is a three-strand necklace of an Achaemenid princess of about 350 B.C., found at the site of Susa, the ancient royal Persian winter residence.[34] Another early pearl necklace fragment was found in a large hoard of jewelry at Pasargadae, probably hidden about 330 B.C. from Alexander the Great's advancing army (Bead Chart 319).

By Ptolemaic, Hellenistic, and Roman times, pearls had become an important part of adornment. Seneca, writing about A.D. 50, commented: "Pearls offer themselves to my view. Simply one for each ear? No! The lobes of our ladies have attained a special capacity for supporting a great number. Two pearls alongside of each other, with a third suspended above, now form a single earring. The crazy fools seem to think that their husbands are not sufficiently tormented unless they wear the value of an inheritance in each ear."[35] The dresses of Roman women were so laden with pearls, Pliny noted with irony, that the wealthy must "trample and walk over them." He further added that pearls adorned rich ladies not only in the daytime, but also at night, "so that in their sleep, they might be conscious of possessing beautiful gems."[36]

The Romans ranked pearls among the most precious of gems and paid exorbitant prices for ones of exceptional importance. Single pearls worth over a million dollars were recorded, such as the one presented by Julius Caesar to Brutus's mother, Servilia.[37] As Roman court behavior degenerated, so their use of pearls increased. It is said that the Emperor Caligula not only wore pearl-encrusted slippers, but after appointing his favorite horse, Incitatus, to the governing council, he also gave him a pearl necklace.[38]

Pearls continued to be esteemed after the establishment of Constantinople as the capital of the eastern Roman Empire. The famous mosaics at San Vitale in Ravenna depict Emperor Justinian in a pearl-encrusted helmet and Empress Theodora in a pearl tiara with numerous strings of pearls descending to her waist.[39]

During the Middle Ages, when jewelry was discouraged by the church, gems en-

riched European ecclesiastical art. In addition, from the ninth to the fourteenth century, medicine frequently employed remedies made of pulverized gems, including pearls. While small, inexpensive pearls were used for the most part, those who could afford them consumed larger ones.[40]

By the fourteenth century, pearls had become fashionable again throughout Europe. Both men's and women's clothing was pearl-embroidered at most important festive occasions.[41] Fifteenth-century women wore hairnets (called "frets") of gold threads adorned with pearls. A fret of pearls was considered a sufficient legacy for a duchess to leave her daughter.[42] By the late Renaissance and Baroque periods, paintings portray pearls sewn onto dresses, with multistrand pearl necklaces displaying power and wealth. A sixteenth-century English portrait of Queen Elizabeth I shows her massive assemblage of pearls and aptly symbolizes the materialism that was so much a part of the era of European expansion. (Elizabeth, in fact, loved pearls so much she did not hesitate to add hundreds of fake ones to her dress too.[43]) The importance of pearls in sixteenth- and seventeenth-century Europe is also expressed in the literature of the period. Pearls form a frequent metaphor in many Shakespearean plays. Antony proclaims his love for Cleopatra with an offer of jewelry: "I'll set thee in a shower of gold, and hail / Rich pearls upon thee." The extravagant use of pearls during the sixteenth and seventeenth centuries was in part due to a greatly expanded supply. New trade routes to the East had increased supplies from the Persian Gulf and Sri Lanka (Ceylon), the richest pearl fisheries in the world, while newly acquired territories in the Americas provided quantities of the gem from temperate coastal waters off Venezuela, Panama, and Mexico. These marine sources were supplemented by pearls from freshwater mussels available in mountain streams throughout Europe, particularly in Bohemia, Bavaria, Saxony, Russia, and Scotland.[44] River pearls had been abundant in Europe since ancient times. British river mussel pearls, described as basically of golden brown tones, were highly valued by the Britons and may have been part of the bounty Julius Caesar was seeking when he invaded Britain in 55 B.C.[45]

Even in antiquity, the princes of India and Persia were known to have had first choice of the finest pearls due to their proximity to the Persian Gulf and Sri Lanka, where pearl-producing saltwater oysters were found. Legendary pearl collections were accumulated by Indian royalty. Perhaps the most renowned belonged to one of the nineteenth-century Gaikwars of Baroda, in northwestern India. His treasures included a sash of one hundred rows of pearls with a pearl and emerald tassel that had an estimated value in 1908 of half a million dollars. He also had a carpet of solid pearls with a central panel of diamonds.[46]

Records indicate that both the Persian Gulf and Gulf of Mannar were fished for pearls in antiquity. Not only the Phoenicians, but the ancient Greeks, Romans, Arabs, and Chinese traded in Sri Lanka for pearls. Marco Polo visited and described this pearl industry in the late thirteenth century.[47] Most Chinese pearls were apparently from freshwater sources, and a pearl fishery at Hepu was first recorded in 111 B.C.[48]

The Russians wore quantities of pearl jewelry, which were not the exclusive property of the rich; indeed, freshwater pearls were widely available to the general populace. Jewish women of humble background in southern Russia, for example, owned black velvet caps embroidered with pearls. They wore their caps all day while working and placed them under their pillows at night. These highly valued caps were passed down to their children.[49]

With the colonization of the Americas, the focus of the pearl industry switched to the New World. The Spaniards noted the South American Indians' pearl ornaments and soon found the oyster beds. On his third and fourth voyages to America, Columbus

were paid so poorly that they inevitably became enslaved to their masters. Lowered by ropes often to depths of forty to fifty feet, many divers were killed, maimed by sharks, or blinded from the saline waters (plate 321).[60]

It was primarily through the efforts of Japan's Kokichi Mikimoto that a controlled approach to growing pearls was developed in 1913, and the hazardous methods of natural pearl fishing declined in importance. It is not surprising that it was in Japan, where nature is revered in its purest forms, that man and nature jointly created such perfection as the pearl.[61]

The only difference between natural and cultured pearls is that in natural pearls the foreign object (the nucleus around which the oyster secretes nacre) enters the mollusk accidentally, while in cultured pearls it is deliberately inserted by a technician. Thereafter, the mollusk takes over.

When Mikimoto introduced his cultured pearls in London in 1919, at prices considerably below those of natural pearls, dealers tried hard to discredit the gems as simulations or imitations. Mikimoto had to prove in courts of law around the world that his cultured pearls were genuine, identical to natural ones except that the nucleus had been inserted. Without X rays, even experts are not able to distinguish between cultured and natural pearls.

The culturing of pearls was actually known to the Chinese in the thirteenth century, and to the Swedish naturalist Carolus Linnaeus by the eighteenth. Several Japanese also had early successes, but it was Mikimoto who developed the techniques for creating round pearls and fought the battles in the pearl market to establish their legitimacy. Called the "pearl king," he was the main force behind contemporary Japan's billion-dollar pearl-farming industry.

Today most of the world's pearls are cultured, and about 70 percent of them come from Japan.[62] Pearls are produced in other regions, such as the South Pacific, frequently in close association with the Japanese. An exception are Burmese pearls, considered among the finest in the world. Burma farms and auctions off its own pearl crop. In the United States, a company that supplied the mussel-shell nuclei from the Mississippi to the Japanese for over thirty years has also started growing its own cultured pearls in Tennessee, Louisiana, and Texas. The first major harvest occurred in the spring of 1987.[63]

Pearls are organic and therefore tend to disintegrate if improperly worn or stored. Claude Arpels, founder of the jewelry firm Van Cleef and Arpels, has related an experience in India shortly after the country's independence in 1947:

> A chest of pearls from the estate of one of India's richest maharajahs was available to me. When the coffer was opened, it brimmed with pearls, like a prop from *The Arabian Nights*. Everyone imagined himself a millionaire until I touched them and my hand was white with powder. Pearls come from nature, the sea. Luster is said to be the life of a pearl. It was a bitter disappointment to us all when I announced "They're worthless." The cache had been in a vault for years, locked away from light, air, and moisture. They were dehydrated and dead as ancient bones.[64]

It is fitting that to prolong the life of pearls they must be kept in regular physical contact with their owners—an expression of the intimate ties between people and nature.

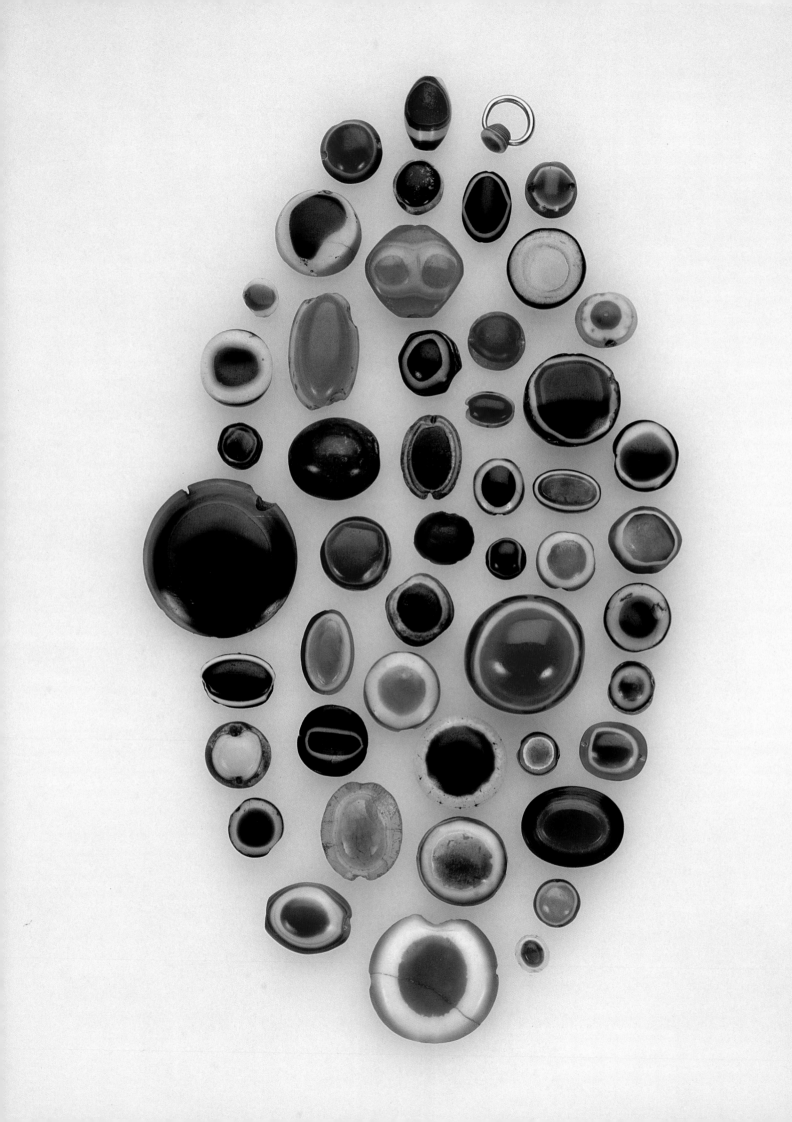

The Magical Eye Bead

T n many societies there is still a widely held belief that eye contact with a particular human, god, or malevolent force, such as an illness, can cause sudden harm to people and their property, or it can afflict them with evil emotions, like jealousy and hatred. Belief in the evil eye may have originated in Paleolithic times and can be seen in various manifestations throughout history.

Evil eye ideology is complex. Different cultures interpret its effects in different ways, and remedies and preventive measures vary from one culture to another. The power of the eye is generally regarded as harmful, yet the gaze of some gods (for example, Horus in dynastic Egypt) is considered beneficial. Eyes are often represented on amulets or painted onto buildings or tombs to counteract the evil eye. In parts of India and Africa, the cowrie shell is believed to represent the human eye and is therefore valued as protection against the evil eye. The protective eye can also take the form of beads. In many cultures, "eye beads" are worn to deflect the evil eye or to neutralize its effects.[1]

Belief in the evil eye may be linked to man's earliest ritual activities. For example, bear skulls from a Paleolithic cave in the Alps were found with the bears' limb bones inserted into their eye sockets, presumably by fearful hunters attempting to avoid revenge from the slain bears' spirits or vengeful eyes.[2]

Archaeological evidence strongly suggests that concepts linking eyes and protective magic to beads evolved in western Asia. By 3000 B.C., goddess figures displaying large, staring eyes, accentuated breasts, and prominent bead necklaces appeared at the site of Tell Brak in eastern Syria. Called "Eye Goddesses," they are interpreted as representations of an infant's early view of the world.[3] The protective, maternal eyes per-

326. In western Asia, eye beads were used since at least the third millennium B.C. as protective amulets to deflect the evil eye or neutralize its effects. This remarkable collection of onyx, chalcedony, and banded-agate beads were made for the most part between the third and first millennium B.C. Each has been cut and polished to look like an eye. Most of these beads were acquired in the Middle East as bakshesh, *gifts exchanged at the consummation of a business deal. Collection Derek Content, Houlton, Maine*

307

haps signify the main source of security and mother-infant communication. The breasts represent the provision of hunger-gratifying milk, and the neck beads symbolize the protective force of eye beads that keeps the infant safe at moments when the mother's eyes might be temporarily diverted.

The earliest written references to the evil eye occur on Sumerian clay tablets dating to the third millennium B.C.[4] Stone beads with incised eye designs and banded agates cut to produce an eye effect are known from Mesopotamian sites of the same period, as are etched carnelians with eye patterns. The latter also occur in mid- to late third-millennium B.C. sites in the Indus Valley and Afghanistan. Identical polyhedral beads with eyelike dots on each facet were recovered from Lothal and Kalibangan in the Indus Valley.[5] Agate eye beads of superb quality were also found in the royal Sumerian graves at Ur. Bead amulets called *udjat*—the eyes of Horus—were widely used in ancient Egypt from the Fifth to the Twelfth dynasties (2494–1786 B.C.). The enormous quantities of *udjat* found in Egyptian burials indicate they must have been of great importance.

While Jewish doctrine clearly disavows folk beliefs based on magic, the ancient Hebrews feared the evil eye and employed protective measures against it. During the third century B.C., Abba Arika, founder of the Rabbinic Academy at Sura, a city in Babylonia, claimed that ninety-nine out of one hundred human deaths were the work of the evil eye.[6] To protect buildings, particularly houses of worship, a symbol known as the "much-enduring eye" was painted on buildings. A third-century A.D. synagogue excavated at the Syrian town of Dura-Europos has such a painting on its ceiling. Christian churches were similarly safeguarded, as demonstrated by a mural in a sixth-century A.D. monastery at Bawit in Egypt.[7]

It is within the Islamic faith, however, that belief in the evil eye and the wearing of protective eye bead amulets have the strongest representation. In all periods of history, Arabs have had a profound fear of the evil eye, even to the point of calling it "the beautiful eye" to avoid its damaging effects.[8] Muslims say that "the evil eye empties the castles and fills the graves."[9] They believe that no one, rich or poor, is safe from its wrathful stare. To counter the evil eye, most Muslims wear some form of protective amulet from birth, including eye beads.[10]

The full manifestations of the evil eye beliefs are not clearly understood by anthropologists. In 1972, a symposium was held to discuss historical and contemporary concepts of the phenomenon and to examine cross-cultural relationships. Among the conclusions reached was the idea that belief in the evil eye originated in western Asia or India and spread from culture to culture through diffusion. Some expressions probably developed independently in the South Pacific and the Americas.[11] Interestingly, it seems that the concept of the evil eye appeared first with groups of shepherds who domesticated animals and competed for land and livelihood with settled farmers—circumstances typical of western Asia and the Mediterranean region beginning in Neolithic times. By contrast, less complex hunter-gatherer societies do not seem to have placed particular importance on the protective eye.[12]

The historical distribution of eye beads would appear to support this observation. The earliest and greatest quantities of eye beads appear in western Asia, India, and Egypt. By the middle of the first millennium B.C., they occur in Europe and in certain localities within China, presumably reflecting recent Western influences, although there was a close association between the words for "eye pupil" and "bead" in the Chinese language.[13]

Ancient eye beads recovered in Southeast Asia and in Africa were probably introduced during the spread of Islam, although they may date back to the days of Ro-

man traders. The Dayak of Borneo prized glass eye beads, thought to be of Mediterranean (Roman) origin, and believed that the older the bead the greater its protective powers against the evil eye.[14]

With the invention or introduction of glass into western Asia, Egypt, and Europe, one of the first objects created was the eye bead. This is not surprising, given the visual similarity between rounded, shining human eyes and most glass beads. Although there are some stylistic variations between glass eye beads, many similar forms were produced over long periods of time. To assign correct dates and places of manufacture to specific varieties of eye beads, it is necessary to identify the manufacturing techniques employed in each case.

In his 1916 study, still considered the most comprehensive work to date on the subject, Gustavus Eisen divides glass eye beads into three basic categories based on the techniques used to produce the eye. The processes often succeed one another within a culture. Eisen's categories are simple eye spots, stratified eyes, and mosaic eyes.[15]

Eye-spot beads were the earliest type made in most regions. They appear as glass drops or as rings impressed into the bead matrix in New Kingdom Egypt (Eighteenth and Nineteenth dynasties, 1567–1200 B.C.). The inlays did not always adhere well to the matrix, and many fell out. Stratified eyes were popular with the Egyptians, Phoenicians, and Chinese through at least the first millennium B.C. (plate 329, 8–17). The eyes were produced by a drop of glass placed on a matrix. The glass was pressed in while the matrix was still soft. Another drop was later placed on the first drop. By this layering technique the eye was built up. The bead was then ground into its final cone form with the outer edge of each layer exposed, giving the appearance of a series of rings. If the drops were properly sized when applied, no grinding was necessary. One way of recognizing this technique is that eyes made of transparent glass are thick and dark in their centers. In some instances, multilayered eyes were made separately, then pressed into the matrix. New Kingdom Egyptian glassmakers of the Eighteenth and

327. Gold and carnelian beads and a banded-agate eye bead from the royal Sumerian graves of Ur, in Mesopotamia, 2200–2000 B.C. This is one of the earliest examples of an eye bead recovered in an archaeological context. Length, 9 cm. British Museum, London

328. *A Phoenician-made necklace with glass eye beads and a central mask or head pendant, recovered from Grave 1 at Tharros, Sardinia, 600–300 B.C. Necklace: length, 31.5 cm. British Museum, London*[I]

OPPOSITE: 329. *Figs. 1–45. A cross-cultural grouping of stone, bone, and glass eye beads dating from the fourth millennium B.C. to the present. All beads are shown actual size. For further description, see note II.*

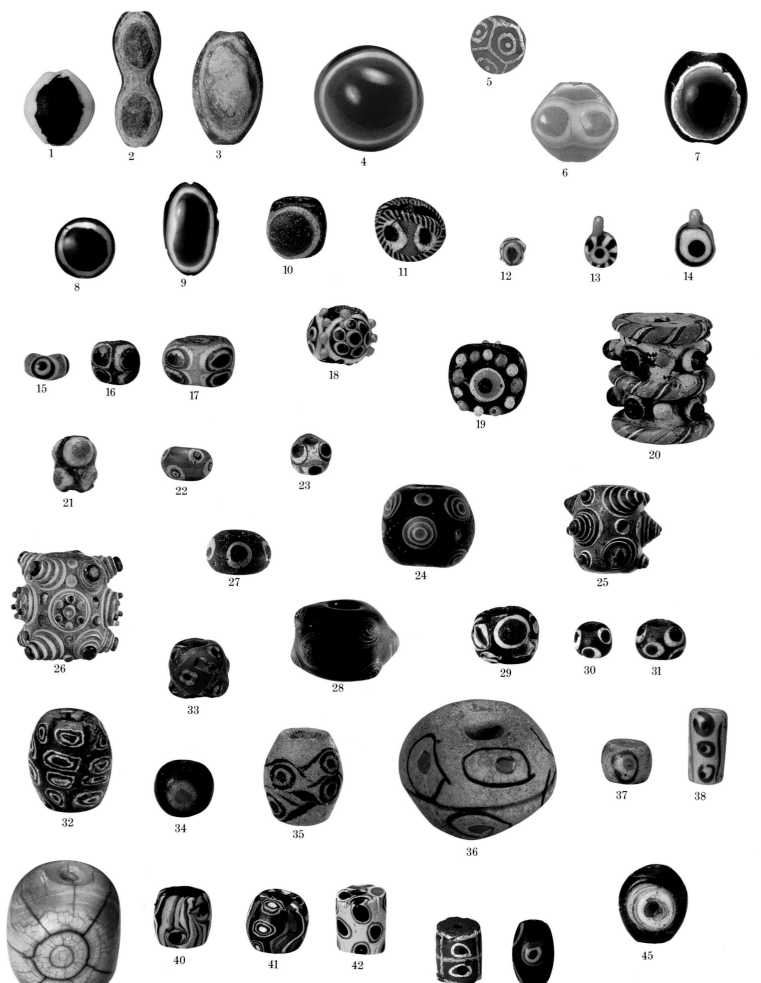

Nineteenth dynasties made distinctive and beautifully complex eye beads using a combination of stratified-eye and inlaid-coil techniques (plate 329, 11).

Mosaic rod eyes appeared by the fifth century B.C. but were not common until about 200 B.C. when they began replacing stratified eyes, a process completed by late Roman times. Mosaic rods were made from glass rods dipped in molten glass of alternating colors, a technique that produced compound glass. When cool, the multilayered rods were cut into sections or disks, each disk representing a ready-made eye with rings. These eyes were then attached to a core, or fused together, so that the eye pattern ran through the entire bead (plate 329, 32). In both the stratified and mosaic varieties, patterns ranged from simple spots to more intricate designs composed of multiple eyes surrounded by additional dots, rings, and bars.

Multilayered eye beads of remarkable complexity were made by the Chinese from 400 to 200 B.C. (plate 329, 24–26). In the latter half of the first millennium B.C., many types of glass eye beads were both imported into and manufactured within various centers in the Mediterranean, central Europe, and Russia. These included beads with raised spiral eyes, presumably produced in Celtic workshops between 200 and 1 B.C. (plate 329, 28). With the decline of the Celts and the collapse of the Roman Empire in the fifth century A.D., European glass beadmaking shifted to the Rhineland. Eye beads, however, do not seem to have been part of that region's production.[16]

The magic of eye beads still exists. In North Africa, a Bedouin will work for several days to obtain a fine stone eye bead. Caravan leaders refuse to begin a journey unless each man and animal has attached to them a blue bead or amulet as protection from the evil eye.[17] In Mauritania, mirrorlike glass beads are considered excellent protection against the evil eye because they reflect images.[18] In central Asia, favorite designs for *dZi* beads among Himalayan peoples are the eye patterns.

A preference for blue beads, particularly blue eye beads to avert evil spirits, appears to be of historical and cross-cultural significance.[19] The majority of ancient glass eye beads have a blue matrix with white, yellow, or blue eyes. Today, in Greece, donkeys, mules, and cows often have protective blue beads and tassels on their bridles or across their foreheads.[20] Blue beads of turquoise, glass, faience, or plastic are also frequently pinned to children's clothing in Yugoslavia, Turkey, and Greece.[21]

The gaze of the evil eye has always been thought particularly harmful to pregnant women and children, possibly since it threatens the very existence of the human population.[22] This is poignantly expressed in recent photographs and television images of starving Ethiopian children with strands of blue glass beads around their necks and wrists.

The history of eye beads reminds us once again that beads have always functioned in culture as more than adornment. Worn by people for over five thousand years, this particular class of beads, perhaps more than any other, reaches across a wide range of cultures and a great span of time. Interestingly enough, despite their pervasiveness, eye beads rarely appear to have been used to express wealth or status.

The Twentieth Century: Europe and North America

Twentieth-century beads from Europe and North America display a great diversity of materials and techniques and reflect widely varying life-styles. In previous eras, one type of jewelry often remained in use for prolonged spans of time. During this century, however, profound changes in technology, communications, and economic structures have altered every aspect of life. It is not surprising that the making and wearing of jewelry would be affected along with so much else. Perhaps the one theme linking these last eight and a half decades has been change, clearly operative in all forms of adornment, including beads. At the same time, however, necklaces of round beads made in traditional materials—stone, glass, metal, amber, and pearls—continue to have a timeless appeal.

The story of twentieth-century Western beads begins in Europe with examples of elegance and luxurious ostentation. The royal houses still in power provided the focus for most social life. Gemstones, particularly diamonds and pearls, were especially fashionable and were used in matching sets (parures) of earrings, necklaces, chokers, pins, bracelets, and hair ornaments. Clothing and jewelry were lavish but conservative, and they were generally adaptations of styles first designed in the eighteenth century, when large and resplendent jewels conveyed status and wealth. Across the Atlantic, American moneyed aristocrats, whose fortunes were amassed after the Industrial Revolution, were equally inclined to displays of elaborate jewelry. European trends were followed in America, and jewels were purchased from the great London and Paris firms, including Cartier and Bulgari, where work was produced with fine technical skill but limited artistic originality. In these decades, beads, except for pearls and occasionally jade, were not part of the adornment of the wealthy.

331. *A choker of fumed (iridescent) aqua-colored glass beads—a technique developed by Louis Comfort Tiffany to simulate ancient iridescent glass—combined with metallic-thread-wrapped wood beads, silk ribbon, brass beads, and an antique glass bead cluster. The curved tubular beads are drawn-glass canes; the ribbing was formed in a patterned mold. The weight of the glass is counterbalanced by the use of the lighter metal and cloth components, otherwise it would be too heavy to wear.[1]*

In collaboration with glass artisan Norman Courtney, designer Jane Nyhus handcrafted all the beads, 1986. Necklace: diameter, 17.7 cm. Jane Nyhus Designs, Seattle

332. *Working in Swit-*
zerland, a country
noted for its textile art-
ists, Verena Sieber-
Fuchs has developed a
unique approach to
crocheting with beads.
This group of black-
and-white necklaces
incorporates yarn and
glass beads, 1976. Neck-
lace: diameter, 30.3 cm.
Verena Sieber-Fuchs,
Zurich

Not everyone was satisfied with the prevailing conservative styles. By 1900, several groups of artists and designers, including the founders of the Arts and Crafts movement and Art Nouveau style, had profoundly altered tastes. Indeed, Art Nouveau jewelry, although a radical departure in design and philosophy from establishment aesthetics, was very popular with the elite. The great political revolutions of the eighteenth and nineteenth centuries had been followed by periods of austerity as a result of the populace's reaction to the past excesses of the ruling classes. In the latter half of the nineteenth century, however, there was a tendency to revive the styles of earlier eras. Stimulated primarily by hostility to the evolving industrial age and its machine-made, impersonal products, everything from home furnishings to jewelry was inspired by ancient or bygone examples. Archaeologically excavated Etruscan gold beads, for instance, were copied by the Italian jewelers Alessandro and Auguste Castellani. If individuality seemed to have been lost to mass production, a return to past, familiar styles offered psychological security, and appeared to guarantee fine handcraftsmanship by requiring the use of intricate details (such as Etruscan-style granulation).

At the same time, a few designers rejected historical mannerisms. They preferred to search for new forms more appropriate to modern society. Englishman William Morris (1834–1896) was among those interested in combining functional and aesthetic considerations in design. The English Arts and Crafts movement, led by Morris, not only attempted to revive handicraft traditions (in the belief that machines put artisans out

of work) but promoted socialism and stressed the moral obligation of integrating beauty with the accessories of daily life. Their efforts to elevate social standards by offering good design to a mass audience was a revolutionary phenomenon. In France, a similar philosophy emerged with a group that adhered to a style called *Art Nouveau*, the French name for certain new developments in architecture and the decorative arts. Unlike Morris, however, Art Nouveau craftsmen were not as antagonistic toward mechanization. Instead, they hoped to make the machine their servant in art. While this was not a time of prolific beadmaking, the attitudes that evolved were very conducive to the rise of the egalitarian bead as a fashionable item shortly thereafter.

One of the most successful manifestations of Art Nouveau was its jewelry, and its most outstanding practitioner and designer was a jeweler, René Jules Lalique (1860–1945). Lalique achieved fame in two separate areas: jewelry and glass, both of which included beads. Instrumental in ending the materialistic attitudes that had governed jewelers for centuries, Lalique believed the monetary value of materials was irrelevant. He chose substances not for their rarity, size, or value, but for their soft, subdued colors and textures. Lalique employed a mixture of precious and nonprecious materials in his work. He experimented with moonstones, chrysoprase, opals, ivory, bone, baroque pearls, molded glass, enameling, silver, and gold. His jewelry was valued for its imagination and craftsmanship rather than the intrinsic worth of its materials. Eventually, he chose to work entirely in glass. It was in the latter phase of his long career that he

ABOVE: 333. *A necklace of yarn crocheted with black glass seed beads, 1978. Outside necklace: diameter, 33.32 cm. Verena Sieber-Fuchs, Zurich*

OVERLEAF, TOP LEFT: 334. *These mold-pressed glass beads were produced in the 1920s by the famed Art Nouveau jeweler René Jules Lalique. The blue grape clusters and green ivy leaves, strung and knotted on silk, were motifs typical of the period's art. Typical ivy leaf bead: diameter, 3 cm. Collection Primavera Gallery, New York*

317

TOP RIGHT: 335. *An Art Deco beaded bag, 1930, in the pattern of an Oriental rug, woven on a loom with glass and cut-steel seed beads. Length, 27 cm. Collection Sylvia Pines/Uniquities, New York*

BOTTOM: 336. *A group of oversize wooden beads created by New York artist Mia Fonssagrives-Solow. The artist was inspired by Paleolithic and Neolithic beads. Standing white bead (far right), length, 25.5 cm. Artist's collection*

PREVIOUS PAGE: 337. *A contemporary necklace using one millimeter (or smaller) glass and faceted steel beads that date from the late nineteenth century. Each tiny bead is individually knotted, a method insuring the necklace has a high degree of flexibility and suppleness. Made by Austrian jeweler Jacqueline Lillie in 1982. Length, 47 cm. Collection Byzantium Gallery, New York*

RIGHT: 338. *Silver and gold metallic beads crocheted with silver wire to form a gossamer-like net beret, 1982. Diameter, 20 cm. Collection Verena Sieber-Fuchs, Zurich*

OPPOSITE: 339. *A necklace of beads constructed from a stack of variously colored formica Colorcore circles, 1984. Each bead is composed of twenty-two circles, stacked, glued, and drilled, while the outside striped layers are shaped by a power sander. The asymmetrical interiors result from cutting irregular segments out of some of the circles, so that when stacked the beads have a spatial, architectural quality. Strung on rubber-sheathed stainless steel wire, each perforation is covered with a metal cap. This is such a labor-intensive process, New York jeweler Robert Ebendorf can produce only one bead per day. Typical bead: diameter, 3.6 cm. Artist's collection.*

made exquisite mold-pressed glass beads (plate 334).

Americans, too, were influenced by the new European developments. The most important American Art Nouveau designer was Louis Comfort Tiffany (1848–1933). Although influenced by Lalique, Tiffany developed his own artistic style, which was particularly effective in glass. His important contributions included the invention of fumed glass, a technique developed to simulate ancient iridescent glass. This was achieved by spraying hot glass with a liquid coating that devitrifies the glass surface and produces a luminous rainbow effect.[1] While Tiffany created only a few (primarily gold) beads, his fumed-glass technique has been revived by contemporary glass beadmakers and is an important influence on their work.

The Arts and Crafts movement and Art Nouveau style were short-lived but have had long-term effects on craftsmen and jewelers. The merger of artist and craftsman, the responsible awareness of social issues, and the obligation to bring good design within the reach of ordinary people inspired future generations of artists and designers. The practice of combining materials according to their aesthetic value rather than material worth continues today among a large and talented group of jewelers and beadmakers.

The era of the Arts and Crafts movement and Art Nouveau style ended by 1914, and World War I virtually halted jewelry production for four years. In many countries, the imperial courts and their supporting nobility disappeared, and the clientele for jewelry shifted from wealthy segments of the population to the emerging middle class. A taste for luxury items again developed among the elite, but it was modified somewhat by the increasingly influential middle class, whose limited resources and restrained attitudes toward flamboyance established the standards of clothes and jewelry. Moreover, the outcome of the war profoundly altered the structure of society. The arrival of women at the workplace—they had been conscripted to fill the jobs of men in the ser-

TOP: **340.** *One-of-a-kind poured and carved plastic resin beads made by New York designer Cara Croninger in 1983. A pioneer in working this material into jewelry, Croninger has mastered transforming the liquid resin into imitations of almost any conceivable material, including amber, ivory, marble, crystal, emeralds, and granite.*

Although made of plastics, her jewelry's strong and attractive primitive qualities are the result of both her search for universal imagery as well as her ingenious production methods. Liquid resins with added pigments or dyes are poured into molds (frequently receptacles from the week's grocery supplies—orange juice bottles, sardine cans, and cookie tins). The material hardens into blocks in the molds, which are then sawed into cubes and carved into beads. Drilling, frequently the most hazardous phase as the beads can easily fracture (a problem experienced by beadmakers since at least the third millennium B.C.), is done with an electric drill before the bead is completed, enabling the design to be balanced around the perforation. Necklace: length, 70 cm. Private collection

RIGHT: **341.** *Robert Ebendorf created this necklace with beads made from Chinese newspaper. Two beads are covered with lacquer and 24-karat gold foil, separated by silver, copper, and ebony components. Typical bead: diameter, 5 cm. Victoria and Albert Museum, London*

322

342. *A necklace of fine silver eggs with enameled black rat snakes. The necklace took metalsmith David Freda three months to execute in 1983. A taxidermist and illustrator before becoming a jeweler, Freda lives in the Catskills. In the mountain range, he found a clutch of 23 hatched snake eggs. Feeling how light they were, he immediately thought to use them as beads and subsequently reproduced the forms in silver, heat-treating and polishing the material to give it an iridescent, pearl-like effect. He also captured and studied a live snake so as to portray its striations accurately. Typical bead diameter, 2.8 cm. Collection Estate of Barbara Rockefeller, New York*

vices—meant a different type of jewelry was required—adornment which could move freely on the body and would be equally appropriate at work and social events.[2]

Perhaps the most significant change in the jewelry industry after 1920 was the development of mass-produced costume or fashion jewelry. To meet the demands of the rapidly growing middle-class clientele, who requested low- to medium-priced jewelry (of which beads were a major component), both old and new materials and techniques were employed. Although shoddy and unimaginative work was produced, it was balanced by a wide range of well-made, exciting new designs. Whereas the jewelry industry had traditionally been extremely conservative (precious metals and stones were too expensive an acquisition for much experimentation), costume-jewelry makers could afford to take risks and use bold shapes and colors. Glass beads of great originality were made in Jablonec, in Czechoslovakia, for example. While some Czech glass beads imitated precious stones, including ruby, carnelian, and turquoise, many were highly artistic creations in their own right. In Japan, during the first quarter of the twentieth century, Kokichi Mikimoto (1858–1954) discovered methods for mass-producing cultured pearls that revolutionized the pearl industry. As a result, larger numbers of less wealthy women could afford to wear pearl jewelry, a luxury formerly reserved for the world's elite.

New materials—particularly plastic—were light in weight, inexpensive, and could be worked by relatively unskilled labor into a variety of shapes and designs. The thermoset plastics (Bakelite and phenolic resins) were used for making beads that imitated ivory, jet, and amber. Hard plastics, they could be cast and then cut and carved like gems. As each bead was made separately, it was possible to give each an individual design.[3] Beads of German silver (an alloy of copper, nickel, and zinc) became quite popular and were frequently used in the Indian jewelry of the American Southwest. It was, however, when fashion designers (such as Coco Chanel) draped necklaces of glass beads and artificial pearls around haute couture outfits that costume jewelry became truly acceptable.

In high design, the romantic and idealistic Art Nouveau jewelry, which utilized heavy glass and metals articulated with motifs from nature and stylized sinuous lines, was replaced by lighter weight materials and more abstract geometric forms. During the 1920s, the Art Deco style emerged, characterized by simple studied compositions of squares, circles, and triangles. Jewelry and beads produced during this period show the influence of Cubist painting as well as the clean and simple design standards of Germany's Bauhaus, the foremost academy of modern design and architecture in pre–World War II times. In Copenhagen, the metal jewelry and beads of designer Georg Jensen (1866–1935) in the 1920s and 1930s symbolized the pleasing, clear designs that today are described as modern.[4]

The period we designate "contemporary" began after World War II when a series of events strongly influenced the direction jewelry continues to take. Following the war, the rising affluence of the West continued to expand the large market for medium-priced jewelry. At the same time, the development of inexpensive commercial air transportation made international travel accessible to everyone. Trips to Asia, Africa, and South America exposed tourists to exotic ethnic groups and their colorful and appealing, handcrafted (frequently beaded) jewelry. Furthermore, due to the speed of travel and communications, it became possible to keep up with the latest ideas. As a result, contemporary jewelry and beads rarely exhibit national characteristics, and works of highly diverse cultures show a decided kinship in the use of forms, materials, concepts, and techniques. A massive international exchange of information truly has created a world jewelry community.

Contemporary jewelry can be classified into three branches: precious one-of-a-kind jewelry from traditional firms, including Cartier, Tiffany, and Bulgari; costume or fashion jewelry, usually of mass-produced, inexpensive materials; and artist-craftsman jewelry, frequently produced in small workshops, where innovative designs and combinations of materials are used.[5]

The great jewelry houses such as Cartier and Tiffany have enjoyed commercial success for decades. They have always adapted to the new demands of a changing clientele. When royal and aristocratic European patronage disappeared, it was replaced by a new elite of wealthy Americans and Middle Eastern potentates. There appears to be no lack of interest in owning large and resplendent jewelry.[6] Contemporary fine jewelry emphasizes precious materials. Items of jewelry are often considered investments, and except for pearls, gems are typically set rather than pierced for beads. While the craftsmanship is generally exquisite, traditional designs are the rule.

Costume jewelry, however, frequently incorporates beads. Trendy necklaces and bracelets, which are intended to last no longer than the dresses they adorn, express the very essence of our time. While often only a thin line divides fine costume from artist-

343. *A belt woven by an American Indian craftsman, using glass seed beads and incorporating motifs from the medieval tapestries at the Cloisters in New York City. 1984. Width, 6.2 cm. Collection Maureen Zarember, New York*

OVERLEAF, TOP LEFT:
344. *Entitled* Charm Beads, *this assemblage includes beads of gold and silver cloisonné, and champlève enamel on gold, silver, and copper. Although he works primarily in enamel, William Harper juxtaposes different materials, placing beads of gold and opulent enamels next to shells and animal vertebrae. He believes that these combinations inspire new perceptions about the qualities of materials, a philosophy shared by Art Nouveau jewelers. Harper's work also incorporates a rich variety of talismanic symbols, a result of his profound interest in tribal and ethnic art.[11]Necklace length, 51.6 cm. Collection Estate of Barbara Rockefeller, New York*

craftsman jewelry, the main difference is that costume jewelry is mass-produced by machines, while artist-craftsman work is handcrafted.

Contemporary artist-craftsmen are currently creating the most innovative and exciting beads, and it is their work that is the focus of the illustrations in this chapter. Most reject the notions of jewelry being investments or short-lived fashion. Value is related to the craftsmanship and the expression of ideas rather than the monetary worth of rare and precious materials. There is no limit to forms and materials used. Gold, silver, and other precious and semiprecious materials are frequently employed in combinations with wood, glass, bone, stainless steel, paper, brass, copper, acrylic, and fabric. A shared sensibility seems to be the reevaluation of how materials could and should be used.

It is interesting to note that most jewelry techniques and materials used today were known by Roman and possibly earlier times. With the exception of help from recent centrifugal-casting, vacuum-forming, drawplating, and electroplating techniques, almost every piece of jewelry made today could have been produced two thousand years ago. The technical and chemical knowledge is now greater, but the techniques were known. The few new bead materials used by craftspeople include plastics and metals connected with the aerospace industry, such as titanium, tantalum, and niobium (plate 346). There is also much experimentation with joining metal alloys of different compositions—"married metals" (Bead Chart 1306).

Divisions between craftsmen, jewelers, and beadmakers continue to disappear, a trend started in the early 1900s. Jewelry forms are now closely merged with garments, seen, for example, in the beadwork of Verena Sieber-Fuchs (plates 332 and 338). Glass is enjoying a resurgence in contemporary jewelry, and many necklaces and earrings now feature studio-made glass beads. Such beads are almost always made from drawn canes, as this method allows for a wide variety of designs, patterns, and colors.[7] At the same time, techniques for creating iridescent (fumed) glass, invented by Louis Comfort Tiffany at the turn of the century, have been rediscovered (plate 337).

Since the beginning of time, jewelry has never functioned on its own: it has always communicated all themes of human behavior. Beads continue to have personal connotations for the wearer, expressing personal tastes, status, and (directly or indirectly) political affiliation. During the 1960s, beads (popularly called "love beads") were worn by American and Western European men and women as an antiestablishment

statement. Dressed in colorful ethnic garb and beads, counterculture people were sending out visual as well as symbolic messages. By substituting the dress and adornment of Third World countries for business suits and military uniforms, they not only conveyed their rejection of American military policies in Vietnam, but showed yearnings for what were perceived to be the gentler, more humane life-styles of other societies. The "flower children" were advocating universal love and the communal family. Tribal and ethnic beads were an important part of their image.

A historical overview of beads from early people to our own age reveals the extraordinary breadth of human creativity. At the same time, it indicates the basic, almost primitive qualities that have been consistent factors throughout the centuries. The purposes for which people adorn themselves may vary, but the underlying aims are constant—be they amuletic, political, or sexual. For adornment, even in our changing and frenetic age, we continue to use and feel comfortable with forms that go back to prehistory—in particular, the simple bead.[8] Tastes change but the bead endures. Strung on necklaces, serial images encircle the body, giving us the same pleasure our Ice Age ancestors had. In one form or another, people are deeply attached to beads: they create a bridge of continuity between the past, the present, and the future. Although a necklace may be exotic and from a distant culture, one feels a sense of continuity, of unity despite diversity. And in wearing it, we connect ourselves to its makers, to their remote culture, and to the substances of the earth—stone, amber, shells, and metals. We experience the universe in a bead.

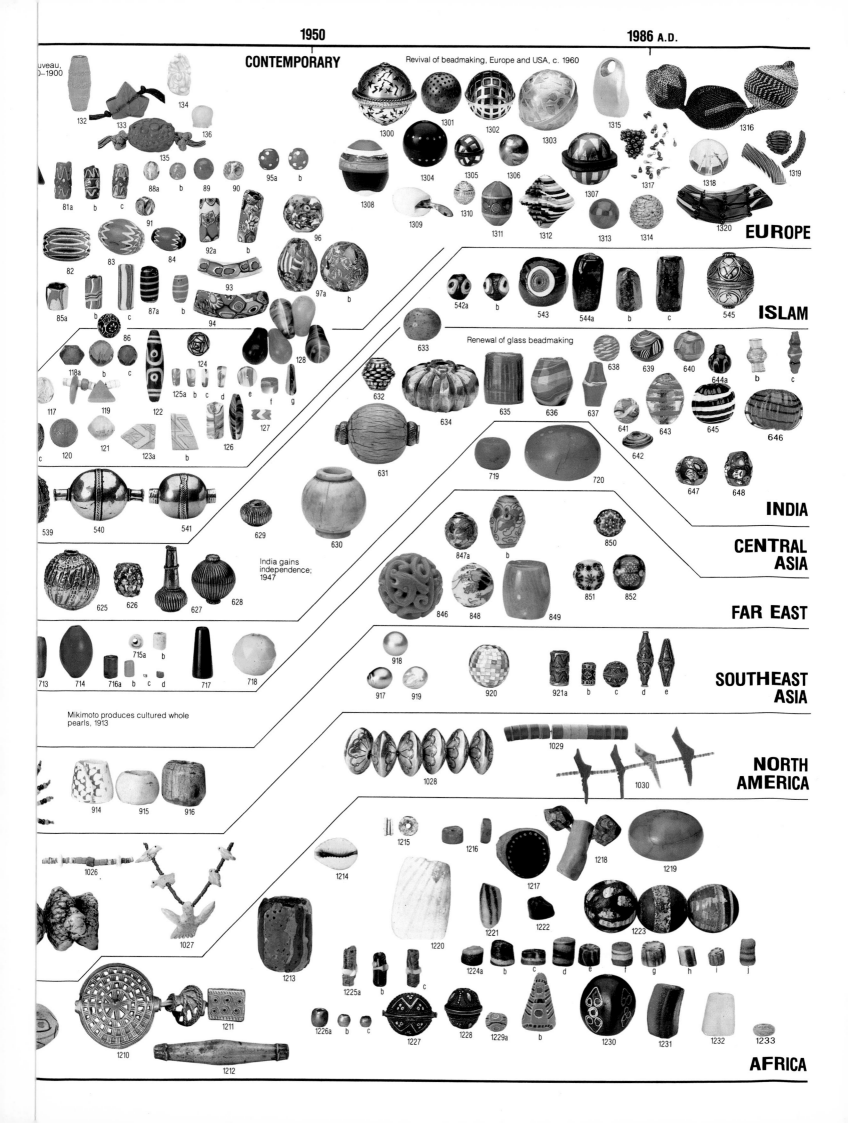

CONTEMPORARY

Revival of beadmaking, Europe and USA, c. 1960

uveau,
0–1900

132
133
134
135
136

81a b c
88a b 89 90
95a b

82 83 84
91
92a b
96

85a b c 87a b
93
94
97a b

86
118a b c
124
125a b c d e f g
128

117 119 122
123a b
126
127

120 121

539 540 541
629
630

625 626 627 628
631

India gains
independence;
1947

713 714 715a b
716a b c d
717 718

Mikimoto produces cultured whole
pearls, 1913

914 915 916

1026

1027

1210
1211
1212

1300 1301 1302 1303 1315 1316

1304 1305 1306 1307 1317 1318 1319

1308 1309 1310 1311 1312 1313 1314 1320

EUROPE

542a b 543 544a b c 545

ISLAM

Renewal of glass beadmaking

633 638 639 640 644a b c

632 641 643 645 646

634 635 636 637 642

631 647 648

719 720

INDIA

847a b 850

**CENTRAL
ASIA**

846 848 849 851 852

FAR EAST

918 917 919 920 921a b c d e

**SOUTHEAST
ASIA**

1028 1029

1030

**NORTH
AMERICA**

1214 1215 1216 1217 1218 1219

1220 1221 1222 1223

1213 1224a b c d e f g h i j

1225a b c

1226a b c 1227 1228 1229a b 1230 1231 1232 1233

AFRICA

Bead Chart Key

EUROPE

PREHISTORY TO THE RENAISSANCE (NOS. 1–37)

1. Fossil shell. East Gravettian culture, Upper Paleolithic period, Pavlov, Czechoslovakia, 28,000 B.C.
2. Ivory. Breast form, East Gravettian culture, Upper Paleolithic period, Dolni Vestonice, Czechoslovakia, 28,000 B.C.
3. Jet. Female torso form, Magdalenian culture, Upper Paleolithic period, Petersfels, East Germany, 13,000 B.C.
4. Bone. Horse's head, Magdalenian culture, Upper Paleolithic period, Espélugues, France, 10,000 B.C.
5. Bone. Horse's head, Magdalenian culture, Upper Paleolithic period, Le Portal, France, 10,000 B.C.
6. Amber. Feltwell Fen, Norfolk, England
7. Jet. Yorkshire, England
8. Segmented faience. Wessex culture grave, Wiltshire, England
9. Amber. Norfolk, England
10. Bronze. Kent, England
11. Bronze, amber, and glass. Hallstatt-type beads, Castaneda Misox, Grave 1, Switzerland
12. Wound glass with zigzag trail. Celtic, La Tène (?), France
13. Wound glass with four stratified eyes. England
14. Wound glass with trailed spiral. England
15. Twisted bicolor glass annular. England
16. Wound glass. England
17. Wound glass with trailed spiral upon vestigial horn. Celtic, England
18. Amber. Roman Period, British Isles
19. Faience. Melon form, Roman period, British Isles
20. Jet. Half-melon form, Roman period, British Isles
21. Wound glass with zigzag trail. Celtic/Roman period, British Isles
22. Wound-glass annulars. Roman period, British Isles
23. Faience. Roman period, British Isles
24. Wound-glass annular. Roman period, British Isles
25–29. Granulated and filigree gold. Denmark
30. Gold inlaid with garnet and lapis lazuli. Anglo-Saxon, England
31. Gold and garnet. Olbia, Russia
32. Wound glass with trailed and dragged design. Frankish, Rhine Valley
33. Glass. Viking, Eidem, Norway
    a–b. Wound glass with trailed decoration
    c–e. Mosaic glass
34–35. Wound glass with trailed decoration and mosaic glass inset. Viking, possibly made in eastern Europe
36. Wound glass with mosaic glass insets. Viking, possibly made in eastern Europe
37. Boxwood "paternoster" bead. Flemish (diameter, 5.7 cm.)

VENICE (NOS. 38–97)

38. Wound and drawn glass. "Seed," "pony," and tubular beads
39. Glass. Seven-layer faceted chevron
40. Glass. Seven-layer, twisted-stripe star bead
41. Wound glass. Corn kernel shape
42. Glass. Seven-layer chevron
43. Glass. Six-layer chevron
44a–b. Drawn glass. Brick red over dark green core
45a–c. Drawn glass. White stripes on light green core, "gooseberry" bead
46. Wound polychrome glass
47. Wound polychrome glass
48. Drawn-glass "seed" beads
49. Wound glass with polychrome dots. *Alta Verapaz* bead
50. Wound glass with yellow core. *Cornaline d'Aleppo* bead
51. Drawn(?) glass with polychrome decoration
52a–d. Wound glass with polychrome trailed and dragged decoration
53a–e. Wound-glass annulars
54a–d. Drawn glass with stripes. "Wafer" beads
55a–i. Mosaic *(millefiore)* glass
56a–b. Mosaic *(millefiore)* glass
57. Wound glass with compound trailed decoration
58a–b. Glass. Four-layer chevrons
59. Wound glass with compound trailed decoration
60. Wound glass with polychrome decoration
61a–d. Wound glass with polychrome decoration
62. Wound glass with compound trailed decoration
63. Wound compound glass with trailed and mosaic decoration
64. Wound glass with trailed decoration (imitating native African beads)
65a–e. Wound glass with polychrome and mosaic glass decoration
66. Wound glass with polychrome decoration
67. Wound glass with trailed and combed decoration (imitating folded mosaic beads)
68. Wound glass with polychrome decoration
69. Wound glass with polychrome decoration
70a–d. Wound compound glass with polychrome decoration
71a–b. Wound glass with dragged decoration. "Feather" beads
72. Wound glass with dragged trails
73a–c. Wound glass with polychrome decoration
74a–b. Wound glass with dragged decoration
75. Wound glass with polychrome spiral trail
76. Mosaic glass
77a–c. Mosaic glass
78a–b. Mosaic glass
79a–d. Drawn and compound, hot-pinched glass star bead
80. Drawn and compound, hot-pinched glass star bead
81a–c. Wound glass with raised polychrome decoration
82. Glass. Six-layer chevron
83. Glass. Six-layer chevron
84. Glass. Five-layer chevron
85a–c. Wound glass with polychrome decoration
86. Mosaic glass. Possibly made in Bohemia
87a–b. Wound glass with polychrome decoration
88a–b. Wound glass with foil inclusion
89. Drawn glass with internal aventurine layer
90. Wound glass with gold leaf and polychrome decoration
91. Wound glass with aventurine and dragged polychrome decoration
92a–b. Mosaic glass
93. Mosaic glass
94. Mosaic glass
95a–b. Wound compound glass with polychrome dots
96. Wound glass with "scrabble" glass. "End-of-the-day" beads
97a–b. "Scrabble" glass. "End-of-the-day" beads

THE NETHERLANDS (NOS. 98–111)

98a–c. Glass. Striped three-layer star beads, possibly made in Venice
99a–b. Wound glass
100a–c. Wound glass
101a–c. Wound glass
102a–f. Wound glass
103a–b. Glass. Striped five-layer star beads
104. Glass. Striped three-layer star bead
105a. Glass. Six-layer chevron
     b. Glass. Five-layer star bead
     c. Glass. Three-layer star bead
106. Wound glass. Pentagonal cylinder, "St. Eustace" bead
107a–c. Drawn glass
108a–c. Glass. Striped four-layer star beads
109. Glass. Five-layer chevron
110a–b. Wound compound glass with polychrome stripes
111. Wound glass with trailed decoration

BOHEMIA AND MORAVIA (NOS. 112–128)

112a–c. Drawn and faceted glass. "Russian" bead, possibly made in Venice
113. Wound opaline glass. Possibly made in Venice
114. Molded glass imitating faceted carnelian (length, 12 cm.)
115. Molded glass simulating ivory tooth
116a–c. Molded glass
117. Molded glass. Art Nouveau style
118a–c. Molded and faceted glass
119. Molded glass simulating turquoise. "Hubbell" beads, made for the southwestern United States trade
120. Molded glass
121. Molded glass. "Vaseline" or "mossi" bead
122. Plastic. Imitation *dZi* bead, made for Himalayan regions trade
123a–b. Molded and etched glass. Art Deco style
124. Molded glass with metallic coating
125a–b. Molded glass
126. Molded glass
127. Molded glass. "Chain" or "snake" beads

128. Molded glass

BALTIC

129. Amber
  a. Romania (Rumanite)
  b. Baltic (succinite)
  c. Baltic or Iran (succinite?)
  d. Baltic (succinite)
130. Faceted Baltic amber (succinite)

IDAR-OBERSTEIN

131a–o. Agate and carnelian

FRANCE

132–136. Pressed or molded glass. Art Nouveau style, made by René Jules Lalique

WESTERN ASIA

EARLY WESTERN ASIA (NOS. 200–219)

200. Shell. Natufian culture, Eynan, Israel, 10,000–8000 B.C.
201. *Nassus* shell. Natufian culture, Gilgal II, Israel, 9000–8000 B.C.
202. Dentalium shell. Natufian culture, Eynan, Israel, 10,000–8000 B.C.
203. Bone. Natufian culture, HaNahal Cave, Israel, 10,000–8000 B.C.
204. Stone. Natufian culture, HaNahal Cave, Israel, 10,000–8000 B.C.
205. Bone (breast forms) and dentalium shell. Natufian culture, El Wad, Israel, 10,000–8000 B.C.
206–208. Shell
209a–b. Shell
210. Shell
211a–b. Shell
212. Shell
213. Animal tooth
214. Shell
215a–b. Calcified coral
216. Calcified coral
217–219. Shell

MESOPOTAMIA (NOS. 220–246)

220a–b. Stone. Arpachiyah
221. Steatite with linear markings. Arpachiyah
222a–d. Early sealstones with linear markings. Arpachiyah
223. Stone
224. Stone
225a–b. Stone
226a–c. Stone eye beads
227a–c. Mother-of-pearl. Jemdet Nasr period
228a–c. Mother-of-pearl. Jemdet Nasr period
229. Stone
230. Stone
231. Shell
232a–b. Steatite cylinder seal with plaster impression. Uruk (Warka) (length, 6 cm.)
233. Etched lapis lazuli
234a–c. Lapis lazuli, carnelian and gold
235–236. Lapis lazuli and gold. Ur, Sumer (size unknown)
237a–c. Lapis lazuli, carnelian and gold. Ur, Sumer (size unknown)
238. Etched carnelian. Ur, Sumer (length, 1.65 cm.)
239. Gold filigree. Ur, Sumer (length, 3.31 cm.)
240. Gold melon form
241. Fluted gold
242. Agate eye bead
243. Banded agate
244. Gold-capped agate. Ur, Sumer (length, 4.5 cm.)
245. Gold. Flat-winged disk
246. Gold-capped agate. Uruk (Warka) (length, 6.04 cm.)

ANATOLIA (NOS. 247–261)

247–260. Steatite
261. Limestone

AFGHANISTAN (NOS. 262–278)

262. Stone. "Shaft-of-wheat" bead, possibly made in Iran or northern Syria
263a–f. Banded agates
264a–e. Banded agates
265. Banded agate
266. Banded agate eye bead
267. Banded agate
268. Carnelian. Possibly made in Tepe Marlik or Amlash, Iran
269. Gold coiled wire
270. Limestone
271. Lapis lazuli
272. Lapis lazuli. "Spoon" bead
273. Agate bead with concave face and flat back
274. Gold-winged disk. Possibly made in Iran or Troy, Anatolia
275. Gold-winged disk
276. Gold-capped jasper. Possibly made in Afghanistan, Anatolia, or Aegean
277. Etched carnelian
278. Gold, lapis lazuli, carnelian, turquoise, and feldspar

IRAN, SYRIA, AND IRAQ (NOS. 279–300)

279. Banded agate
280. Stone
281a–h. Lapis lazuli
282a–c. Alabaster
283a–f. Alabaster
284a–c. Obsidian
285. Stone
286. Stone
287. Jet
288. Alabaster(?)
289. Stone. Mari, Iran
290. Steatite and shell. Mari, Iran
291. Stone spacer
292. Alabaster
293. Jasper. Possibly made in Afghanistan
294. Gold spacer. Iran
295. Gold quadruple-spiral
296a–b. Gold spacers. Iran
297. Faience lion bead. Susa, Iran
298. Silver core covered with gold wire cloisons and inlaid with lapis lazuli and yellow stones. Tell Atchana (Alalakh), Iraq
299. Gold quadruple-spiral. Mari, Iran
300. Rock crystal scaraboid. North Syria, Iran, or Anatolia

IRAN (PERSIA): Pre-Achaemenid to Parthian Period (NOS. 301–322)

301a–c. Banded agates
302a–c. Amber
303. Banded agate
304. Banded agate. "Spool" bead, Iran or Afghanistan
305. Chalcedony
306. Glass with dragged trail decoration. Tepe Marlik, Iran
307a–d. Wound glass with zigzag trail. Possibly made in Amlash, Iran
308a–e. Granulated gold. Iran
309a–e. Bronze
310. Bronze
311a–b. Banded agate spacers
312a–b. Faience (?) Ziwiyeh, Iran
313. Blue chalcedony with gold. Achaemenid period
314. Banded mosaic glass. Possibly made in Iran
315. Banded agate. Possibly made as early as 1000 B.C., Iran or Afghanistan
316. Granulated gold
317a–b. Gold lotus blossom beads. Achaemenid period, Iran or possibly Egypt
318. Coral
319. Gold and pearl beads with a bell-shaped pendant from a hoard of jewelry hidden about 330 B.C., when Alexander's army was advancing eastward. Among the earliest surviving examples of pearls (diameter of largest pearl, 0.5 cm.)
320. Banded agate

321. Wound glass with mosaic glass inset. Gilan, Iran
322. Wound glass with stratified eyes. Persepolis, Iran

IRAN (PERSIA): Parthian/Roman Period (NOS. 323–347)

323–326. Banded agate
327. Banded mosaic glass
328. Gold and garnet. Sarmatian culture, Caspian Sea region
329–332. Faience. Iran
333a–c. Banded agates
334a–c. Mosaic banded and faceted glass
335. Banded agate
336. Banded mosaic glass
337. Banded agate
338. Banded agate
339. Banded mosaic glass
340. Banded mosaic glass
341a–f. Faience. Iran
342. Banded agate
343. Banded agate
344. Banded mosaic glass
345. Banded mosaic glass
346a–d. Banded agate
347a–d. Banded mosaic glass

ROMAN EMPIRE (NOS. 348–373)

348a–c. Banded agates
349a–c. Mosaic glass
350. Wound glass
351. Wound-glass melon form
352. Wound glass with pressed facets (cornerless cube)
353a–c. Wound glass with stratified eyes
354. Wound glass with floral and figural mosaic plaques. Possibly made in Egypt
355. Wound glass with mosaic glass insets. Possibly made in Egypt
356a–c. Wound glass
357. Emerald crystal beads on gold wire links
358. Emerald crystal bead
359. Carnelian cornerless cube
360. Garnet
361a. Carnelian
  b. Rock crystal
  c. Amethyst
  d. Carnelian
362a. Drawn and pressed glass tabular
  b–d. Wound and pressed glass tabulars
363. "Etched" carnelian. Parthian to Sasanian periods
364. Stone "altar" bead
365. Granulated silver
366. Mosaic glass with floral and checker plaques
367. Wound glass with marvered crumb decoration
368. Wound glass with inlaid eye spots
369. Wound glass with mosaic canes
370. Wound glass with marvered crumb decoration
371. Mosaic glass with eye spots
372a–c. Folded mosaic glass
373. Folded mosaic glass

MEDITERRANEAN

CRETE, CYPRUS, AND GREECE (NOS. 374–392)

374. Gold, lapis lazuli, and carnelian breast-shaped beads. Aegina Treasure, Minoan period, Aegina island
375. Gold duck bead. Palace of Knossos, Crete
376. Gold relief shell or flower bead. Mycenae
377–378. Gold. Mycenaean, Enkomi, Cyprus
379. Gold rosettes. Mycenae, Ialysos, Rhodes
380–382. Gold. Mycenaean, Enkomi, Cyprus
383. Mold-cast glass pendant beads. Mycenae
384. Gold. Mycenaean, Enkomi, Cyprus
385. Bronze wine jug bead. Potidaea, Macedonia (length, 3.8 cm.)

386. Bronze wine jug bead, Potidaea, Macedonia (length, 2.6 cm.)
387a–d. Gold. Ephesus, Turkey
    a. Length, 0.8 cm.
    b. Diameter, 0.6 cm.
    c. Diameter, 1.5 cm.
    d. Length, 0.9 cm.
388a–c. Gold. Ephesus, Turkey
    a. Length, 0.8 cm.
    b. Length, 0.9 cm.
    c. Length, 0.8 cm.
389a–b. Gold. Ephesus, Turkey
    a. Length, 1.2 cm.
    b. Length, 1 cm.
    c. Length, 1 cm.
390. Gold melon beads
391. Amethyst
392. Rock crystal

PHOENICIA AND ETRURIA (NOS. 393–402)

393. Granulated gold beads with wound-glass stratified eye beads and modeled-glass pendant bead. Pendant, Phoenician; beads, Etruscan (pendant: length, 3.1 cm.)
394. Granulated gold. Etruscan
395a–c. Wound glass with stratified eyes. Phoenician
396. Wound glass with composite stratified eyes and raised spots. Phoenician
397. Modeled grotesque face pendant bead. Phoenician, North Africa, or Syrian-Palestinian coast
398. Wound glass with modeled polychrome face and raised spots. Phoenician, Carthage, or Syrian-Palestinian coast
399–400. Modeled glass head pendant beads. Phoenician, possibly made in Carthage
401. Modeled glass ram's head pendant bead. Phoenician, Carthage or Syrian-Palestinian coast
402. Wound glass with spiral-wound coils and raised stratified eyes. Phoenician, Carthage, or Syrian-Palestinian coast

HELLENISTIC PERIOD (NOS. 403–410)

403. Granulated gold. Greece
404. Gold and garnet spool beads on gold wire links. Crete
405. Garnet spool beads on gold wire links. Probably made in eastern Greece
406. Granulated gold and green glass. Greece
407a–b. Folded and pressed heart-shaped glass. Rhodes
408. Embossed and filigree gold with garnet inlay. Olbia, Sardinia
409a–c. Sandwich gold-in-glass. Hellenistic or Roman periods
410. Gold Hercules-knot bead. Eastern Mediterranean, late Hellenistic to Graeco-Roman periods

EGYPT

PREDYNASTIC PERIOD TO ROMAN EGYPT (NOS. 411–481)

411a–d. Shells. Badarian period
412. Bone. Badarian period
413a–b. Ivory. Badarian period
414. Copper. Badarian period
415. Alabaster. Badarian period
416. Stone. Badarian period
417. Glazed steatite. Badarian period
418. Alabaster drop. Nagadah period
419. Stone. Nagadah period
420. Glazed faience. Nagadah period
421. Alabaster. Nagadah period
422. Agate. Early Dynastic period
423. Ivory. "Serekh" bead, Early Dynastic period
424. Glazed faience. Early Dynastic period
425. Cowrie shell. Badarian to Early Dynastic period

426. Copper and carnelian. Early Dynastic period
427. Steatite, lapis lazuli, garnet, and shell. Early Dynastic period
428. Green glazed steatite and shell beads with carnelian pendant. Early Dynastic period
429. Carnelian. Old Kingdom period
430. Stone, faience, and glazed "crumb" bead. Old Kingdom period, Fourth to Fifth Dynasty, Mostagadda
431a–b. Faience
432. Carnelian, stone, faience, and shell. Old Kingdom period
433. Electrum, gold, carnelian, and feldspar. Old Kingdom period, Fourth to Fifth Dynasty, Mostagadda
434. Carnelian and faience. Old Kingdom period
435. Faience. Old Kingdom period
436. Bead amulets of carnelian, turquoise, and amethyst. First Intermediate Period
437. Cigar-shaped faience. Middle Kingdom
438. Carnelian, gold, and feldspar acacia seed beads and gold cowrie shell effigy bead. Lahun, Twelfth Dynasty (size unknown)
439. Garnet. Middle Kingdom
440. Gold-capped carnelian. Middle Kingdom period
441. Gold-capped amethyst. Middle Kingdom period
442. Amethyst. Middle Kingdom period
443. Stone with gold. Middle Kingdom period
444. Amethyst and gold. Middle Kingdom period
445. Wedge-shaped faience spacer. New Kingdom period
446a–e. Faience. New Kingdom period
447. Faience spacer. New Kingdom period
448a–b. Folded and ground(?) glass. New Kingdom period, Eighteenth to Nineteenth Dynasty
449. Wound-glass heart amulet bead. New Kingdom period, Eighteenth to Nineteenth Dynasty
450. Wound-glass pomegranate. New Kingdom period, Eighteenth to Nineteenth Dynasty
451a–c. Faience. New Kingdom period, Eighteenth to Nineteenth Dynasty
452. Wound glass with impressed coils and stratified eyes. New Kingdom period, Eighteenth to Nineteenth Dynasty
453. Wound- and carved-glass heart amulet bead. New Kingdom period, Eighteenth to Nineteenth Dynasty
454. Faience lotus blossom. Amarna, New Kingdom period, Eighteenth to Nineteenth Dynasty
455. Wound pear-shaped or fig-shaped bead with zigzag trail. New Kingdom period, Eighteenth to Nineteenth Dynasty
456a–b. Faience. Amarna, New Kingdom period, Eighteenth to Nineteenth Dynasty
    a. Grape cluster
    b. Mandrake fruit
457. Carnelian lotus seed pod
458. Amethyst
459. Wound-glass double duck bead. New Kingdom period, Eighteenth to Nineteenth Dynasty
460. Faience frog. Amarna, New Kingdom period, Eighteenth Dynasty
461a–d. Faience. Amarna, New Kingdom period, Eighteenth Dynasty
    a. Petal
    b–c. Seed pods
    d. Daisy
462a–e. Wound glass with stratified eyes. New Kingdom period, Eighteenth to Nineteenth Dynasty
463. Faience spacer bead depicting figures of the god Horus as a child and as a warrior with prisoners (length, 4.5 cm.)
464. Faience disk beadwork

465. Wound glass with eye spots
466. Wound glass with raised eye spots
467. Wound glass with stratified eyes
468. Faience scarab. Ptolemaic period
469. Banded mosaic glass. Ptolemaic period
470. Banded mosaic glass. Ptolemaic period
471. Mosaic glass. Ptolemaic period
472–473. Mosaic glass with checkerboard pattern. Roman Egypt
474. Tabular glass with mosaic plaques. Roman Egypt
475. Figural mosaic glass. Roman Egypt
476. Mosaic glass. Roman Egypt
477. Floral mosaic glass square tabular. Roman Empire, Egypt, or Rome
478. Faceted mosaic glass. Roman Egypt
479. Wound glass with floral mosaic plaques. Roman Egypt
480. Mosaic glass tabular. Roman Egypt
481. Wound glass with polychrome crumb and mosaic decoration. Late Roman Egypt

BYZANTINE

(NOS. 482–486)

482. Amethyst
483. Emeralds, pearls, and sapphires with gold wire links. Piazza della Consolazione Treasure, Rome
484. Sapphire with gold chain
485. Gold filigree
486. Wound glass with dragged trails

ISLAM

(NOS. 487–545)

487. Folded mosaic glass
488. Molded glass amulet case form with marvered crumbs
489. Wound glass with dragged trails
490. Folded mosaic glass tabular with stratified layers
491. Mosaic glass melon-form collared bead
492. Wound-glass melon-form collared bead
493a–b. Folded mosaic glass dove beads
494–495. Wound glass with dragged trails
496. Folded mosaic glass
497. Wound-glass pendant bead with trails
498. Wound-glass pendant bead with dragged trails
499. Rock crystal amulet case pendant bead
500a–c. Folded mosaic glass tabular pendant beads
501–502. Wound glass with dragged trails
503. Wound(?) glass with dragged trails
504a–c. Wound glass with zigzag trails
505. Folded mosaic glass with equatorial band
506. Wound glass trailed with mosaic band
507. Wound glass with zigzag trails
508. Wound glass with dragged trails
509–510. Filigree and granulated gold. Syria
511. Wound and faceted (cut) glass. "Cornerless cube" bead
512. Faceted lapis lazuli. "Cornerless cube" bead
513. Wound glass with spiral trails
514–516. Wound-glass pendant bead with trails
517. Wound glass with dragged trails
518a–c. Glazed quartz
519. Wound glass with dragged indented trails
520. Lapis lazuli inlaid with turquoise
521. Faceted lapis lazuli without its inlay (probably gold)
522. Collared lapis lazuli inlaid with turquoise
523. Faceted carnelian
524. Rock crystal
525. Folded mosaic glass spacer bead

526. Rock crystal amulet case pendant bead
527. Wound glass with mosaic canes. Made in western Asia
528. Mosaic glass canes, no core. Made in western Asia
529. Wound-glass melon form
530. Glazed quartz *higas* ("clutched fist")
531. Glazed faience. Gorgan, Naispur, Iran
532. Hollow cassolette filigree gold bead of enamel cloisonné set with emeralds and rubies. Moorish Spain
533. Gold inlaid with emeralds, rubies, and/or garnets. Morocco
534a–c. Wound glass with dragged trails. (534 b and c possibly made in Venice)
535. Wound glass with dragged trails
536. Amber or copal. Iran
537. Granulated silver. Yemen
538–539. Silver. Yemen
540–541. Silver. Turkoman
542a–b. Wound glass with stratified eyes. Hebron, Jordan
543. Wound glass with stratified eyes. Goerce, Turkey
544a–c. Wound glass. Hebron, Turkey
545. Silver and bronze. Kazakh

INDIA

(NOS. 600–648)

600a–c. "Etched" carnelian. Indus Valley manufacture, c.2600–1600 B.C.
601a–c. Banded agate. Pakistan region
602a–b. "Etched" agate. Kushan period
603. Drawn glass. "Mutisalah" bead
604a–c. "Etched" carnelian. Kushan to Gandra periods, Pakistan region
605. Collared carnelian
606. Stratified mosaic glass. Possibly made in India, Pakistan, or Afghanistan
607. Folded and pinched mosaic glass. Possibly made in Afghanistan or Pakistan region
608. Wound glass with dragged trails. Northern Pakistan region
609. *Rudraksha* bead (*Eleaocarpus ganitrus* seed)
610. Folded mosaic glass. Possibly made in Afghanistan or Pakistan region
611a–b. Carnelian
612. Banded mosaic glass. Possibly made in Pakistan region
613a–d. Stone
614a–f. Drawn-glass "trade wind" beads. Possibly made in Brahmapuri, India
615. Stone
616a–d. Stone
617. Carnelian
618. Drawn-glass "seed" beads collected in Indonesia. Possibly made later in India or Venice
619a–e. Stone
620. Carnelian
621a–b. Carnelian
622. Emeralds. Mogul period
623–629. Silver
630. Ivory
631. Ivory and silver
632. Silver chain bead
633. Glazed ceramic. "Donkey" bead
634. Gold-plated silver melon form
635. Wound glass with powdered-glass decoration
636. Wound mosaic glass
637. Wound glass with trail
638. Wound glass with bicolor spiral trail
639. Wound glass with mosaic decoration
640. Wound glass with mosaic decoration
641. Compound wound glass with trails
642. Wound glass with spiral trail
643. Wound glass with spiral trail
644a–c. Wound glass with trails
645. Wound glass with spiral trail and pressed melon form

646. Wound glass with spiral trail and pressed melon form
647. Mosaic glass face bead. Probably made in India or Pakistan region
648. Mosaic glass face bead. Probably made in India or Pakistan region

CENTRAL ASIA

HIMALAYAN REGION (NOS. 700–720)

700. "Etched" agate. Date unknown
701. "Etched" agate. Nine-eyed *dZi* bead, Date unknown
702a–c. Opalized palm wood with artificial decoration. *Puntek* bead, Mizzoram, Burma
703a–h. Opalized palm wood with artificial decoration. *Puntek* bead, Mizzoram, Burma
704a–f. All beads shown at 25 percent of actual size
  a. Amber
  b. Turquoise
  c. Coral
  d. Gold-capped amber
  e. Coral with turquoise inlay
  f. Coral
705. Gold-capped amber inlaid with turquoise (diameter, 9.5 cm.)
706. Turquoise
707a–b. Shell
708. Carnelian
709. Carnelian
710. Rock crystal
711–714. Wound glass. Probably made in India
715a–b. Wound glass. Probably made in India
716a. Drawn glass. Probably made in India
  b. Wound glass. Probably made in India
  c. Drawn glass. Probably made in India
  d. Wound glass. Probably made in India
717. Pressed amber. Probably made in Europe
718. Faceted glass. Possibly made in India, China, or Bohemia
719. Molded glass. Probably made in Bohemia
720. Amber

FAR EAST

CHINA, KOREA, AND JAPAN (NOS. 800–852)

800. White jade (nephrite) with etched pattern of twisting snakes and traces of red pigment. Western Zhou period, reportedly from Anyang, Shang dynasty, China
801. Etched and cut jade (nephrite) with patterns of dragons in profile and traces of red powder. Late Western Zhou period, China
802. Incised jade (nephrite) with patterns of geometric motifs and eyes and traces of red pigment. Early Eastern Zhou period, China
803. Molded glass with ground hexagonal facets. Probably made in Changsha, Hunan province, Late Zhou period, China
804. Etched jade (nephrite) with patterns of spirals and eyes. Eastern Zhou period, China
805. Etched jade (nephrite) with patterns of diagonally incised, ropelike bands and curvilinear motifs. Eastern Zhou period, China
806. Ground jade (nephrite). Eastern Zhou period, China
807. Wound glass with stratified eyes. Eastern Zhou "Warring States" period, China
808. Wound glass with stratified eyes. Eastern Zhou "Warring States" period, China

809. Kneeling faience attendant. Eastern Zhou "Warring States" period, China
810. Wound glass with stratified and compound eyes. Eastern Zhou "Warring States" period, China
811. Wound glass with raised stratified eyes. Eastern Zhou "Warring States" period, China
812. Glazed pottery(?) with stratified eyes. Eastern Zhou "Warring States" period, China
813. Wound glass with stratified eyes. Eastern Zhou "Warring States" period, China
814. Wound glass with raised stratified and compound eyes. Eastern Zhou "Warring States" period, China
815. Wound glass with trails and raised eyes. Eastern Zhou "Warring States" period, China
816. Cut jade (nephrite). Han dynasty, China
817–818. Wound-glass *kodama* with red pigment. Tomb period, Japan
819. Wound-glass *marudama*. Tomb period, Japan
820. Jade *kogok*. Korea
821. Molded, ground, and drilled glass *magatama*. Japan
822a–c. Wound glass. Qing dynasty, China
823a–c. Wound glass. Qing dynasty, China
824. Wound glass with applied spots. Qing dynasty, China
825. Wound glass imitating jade. Qing dynasty, China
826a–b. Wound-glass melon forms. Qing dynasty, China. (826b possibly made in Venice)
827a–b. Wound glass. Qing dynasty, China
828a–c. Wound glass. Qing dynasty, China
829–832. Wound glass. Qing dynasty, China
833. Ivory *ojime* peony blossom. Edo period, Japan
834. Wound glass with applied spot. Edo period, Japan
835. Wound-glass *gangidama* with zigzag trails. Edo period, Japan
836. Glass *tombodama*. Edo period, Japan
837. Wound glass with mosaic and filigree glass *sarasadama*. Edo period, Japan
838. Stained ivory monkey *ojime*. Edo or Meiji period, Japan
839. Wound-glass melon form. Edo period, Japan
840. Wound glass with mosaic decoration, *sarasadama*. Edo period, Japan
841. Wound-glass *tombodama*. Edo period, Japan
842. Lacquer *ojime* with quail motif. Edo or Meiji period, Japan
843. Wound glass with encased goldfish. Meiji period, Japan
844. Ivory *ojime* with *shibayama* (inlay jewelwork) technique. Meiji period, Japan
845a–c. Wound glass. China
846. Carved coral. China
847a–b. Enameled cloisonné. China
848. Painted porcelain. China
849. Coral. China
850–852. Wound glass with mosaic inset. Artist: Kyoyu Asao

SOUTHEAST ASIA

(NOS. 900–921)

900a. Glass. Ban Chiang, Thailand
  b. Glass. Possibly Ban Chiang, Thailand
901. Drawn glass. "Mutisalah" bead
902. Gold. Jatinou, Java
903a–e. Constricted glass tubes. Possibly Majapahit culture (1293–1400 or earlier), Java
  a. Compound glass with dragged trails
  b–e. Applied mosaic decoration
904. Dentate gold disks. Pre-Hispanic period, Philippines

905a–b. Shell. South Pacific
906. Amber (Burmite). Burma
907. Coconut shell. South Pacific
908. Carnelian, agate, drawn glass, and chevron. Kalinga, Philippines (carnelian, agate, and drawn-glass beads made in India; chevron beads made in Europe)
909. Drawn glass. Of unknown origin, Borneo
910. Wound glass with stratified eyes. Of unknown origin, Borneo
911a–c. Wound glass. Of unknown origin, Borneo
   a. Double bead with compound stripes
   b. Mosaic trails
   c. Trails and spots
912. Wound glass with mosaic decoration. Of unknown origin, Borneo
913. Drawn-glass seed beads. Probably made in India, Philippines
914–915. Shell. Philippines
916. Ivory. Philippines
917. Baroque South Sea pearl
918. Round South Sea pearl
919. Baroque South Sea pearl
920. Shell mosaic. Philippines
921a–e. Granulated silver. Bali

NORTH AMERICA

(NOS. 1000–1030)

1000a–f. Rolled copper. Montgomery Co., Ohio
1001. Copper. Montgomery Co., Ohio
1002. Freshwater pearl. Dickison site, Peoria Co., Illinois
1003. Freshwater mussel shell. Dickison site, Peoria Co., Illinois
1004. Rolled copper bead. Wilson site, White Co., Illinois
1005. Copper. Wilson site, White Co., Illinois
1006. Freshwater pearls. Arkansas
1007. Turquoise. Pueblo Bonito, Chaco Canyon, Anasazi Pueblo I–III, New Mexico
1008. Turquoise frog beads. Salmon Ruin, New Mexico
1009. Turquoise. Pueblo Bonito, Chaco Canyon, Anasazi Pueblo II, New Mexico
1010. Turquoise. Pueblo Bonito, Chaco Canyon, Anasazi Pueblo II, New Mexico
1011. Turquoise duck. Pueblo Bonito, Chaco Canyon, Anasazi Pueblo II–III, New Mexico
1012. Turquoise. Chaco Canyon, Anasazi Pueblo III, New Mexico
1013. Bird bone. Ohio
1014. Shell. Arkansas
1015. Conch shell. Madisonvale, Ohio
1016. Columella shell
1017. Dentalium shell. Washington
1018a–f. Shell. Prehistoric Iroquois
1019a–c. Claystone
1020. Abalone shell. Northwest Pacific coast
1021. Black stone with shell inlay and asphaltum adhesive. Chumash culture, Santa Barbara coast, California
1022. Wampum, purple and white clamshell. Iroquois
1023. Wound glass. "Padre" bead, possibly made in China
1024. Turquoise disks and tabulars. Navajo culture, Southwest
1025. Turquoise nuggets. Navajo culture, Southwest
1026. Silver, shell, coral, and glass. Southwest
1027. Claystone with turquoise fetishes. Zuni Pueblo, Southwest
1028. Stamped silver. Navajo culture, Southwest
1029. Claystone, onyx, turquoise, and tortoiseshell *heishi*. Santo Domingo Pueblo, Southwest
1030. Shell *heishi* with turquoise fetishes. Santo Domingo Pueblo, Southwest

MIDDLE AND SOUTH AMERICA

(NOS. 1100–1135)

1100. Crystal with cinnabar. Chavin culture, Peru
1101. Jadeite. Olmec culture, Mexico
1102. Rock crystal. Chavin culture, Peru (diameter, 5 cm.)
1103. Etched jadeite pectoral bead with cinnabar. Olmec culture, Mexico
1104. Carved stone. Late Olmec culture, Guerrero, Mexico
1105. Jade alligator effigy bead. Costa Rica
1106. Jadeite. Maya culture
1107–1108. Carved jadeite. Maya culture
1109–1110. Jadeite with cinnabar. Maya culture
1111. Etched jadeite with cinnabar. Maya culture
1112. Carved jadeite parrot head bead. Maya culture
1113. Jadeite. Uxmal, Maya culture
1114. Sawn jadeite. Maya culture
1115a–d. Shell. Maya culture
1116–1119. Etched and carved pottery beads or spindle whorls. Manteño culture, Ecuador
1120a–c. Stone. Tairona culture, Colombia
1121. Carnelian. Tairona culture, Colombia
1122. Gold squash bead. Chimu culture, Peru
1123a–b. Gold. Chimu culture, Peru
1124–1125. Gold Janus head. Chimu culture, Peru
1126. Black stone bird bead. Chimu culture, Peru
1127–1128. Shell, black stone, carnelian, turquoise, rock crystal, green stone, jasper, and spondylus shell. Chimu culture, Peru
1129. Rock crystal, shell, and stone. Chimu culture, Peru
1130. Spondylus shell. Ica culture, Peru
1131–1132. Spondylus shell. Inca culture, Peru
1133a–g. Drawn, compound square cross section, straight or twisted glass (c and d are striped). "Nueva Cadiz" bead, Peru
1134a. Drawn, compound, striped, and twisted glass. Peru
   b. Drawn, square cross section, faceted chevron. Peru
   c. Drawn, faceted seven-layer chevron. Peru
   d. Drawn, reheated, and striped star bead. Peru
1135. Glass pendant. San Pedro Quiátoni, Oaxaca, Mexico

AFRICA

(NOS. 1200–1233)

1200a–c. Glass beads. Djenne, Mali
   a. Wound glass with glass insets
   b. Mosaic glass canes, no core
   c. Wound glass with mosaic glass canes
1201. Mosaic glass canes, no core. Djenne, Mali
1202. Mosaic glass canes, no core. Djenne, Mali
1203. Bronze. Mali
1204. Bronze. Mali
1205. Bronze. Lost-wax casting technique. Baoule culture
1206. Bronze. Lost-wax casting technique. Baoule culture
1207. Striped powder glass. *Bodom* bead, West Africa
1208. Swirled powder glass. *Bodom* bead, West Africa
1209. Spotted powder glass. *Bodom* bead, West Africa
1210. Gold, lost-wax casting technique. Asante culture
1211. Gold, lost-wax casting technique. Asante culture

1212. Brass. Ivory Coast
1213. Molded and striped powder glass. West Africa (length, 6.3 cm)
1214. Cowrie shell. Eastern Zaire to western Senegal
1215. Ostrich eggshell. East Africa
1216. Bauxite. East Africa
1217. Carved *Dhoum* palm nut. Kenya
1218. Plant roots. Kenya
1219. Plastic (phenol formaldehyde) simulating amber. Made in Europe
1220. Shell. "Hippo tooth" bead, Ivory Coast and Nigeria
1221. Striped powder glass. West Africa
1222. Wild seed. Kenya
1223. Pottery. Baoule culture, Ivory Coast, West Africa
1224a–j. Molded and striped powder glass. West Africa
1225a–c. Wound and trailed "Bida" glass. Bida, Nigeria
1226a–c. Silver. Ethiopia
1227. Silver. Mauritania
1228. Silver. Mauritania
1229a–b. Complex powder-glass bead and pendant. Mauritania
1230. Plastic bead with metal inlay
1231–1232. Recycled glass. West Africa
1233. Granulated gold. Mauritania

CONTEMPORARY EUROPE AND NORTH AMERICA

(NOS. 1300–1320)

1300. Pierced silver. Artist: Robert Ebendorf, New York
1301. Pierced and oxidized silver. Artist: Young-Ja Baek, New York and South Korea
1302. Brass bands applied to oxidized silver base. Artist: Young-Ja Baek, New York and South Korea
1303. Silver with 24-karat gold overlay. Artist: Robert Ebendorf, New York
1304. Oxidized silver with 24-karat gold appliqué heat soldered onto surface. Artist: Robert Ebendorf, New York
1305. Oxidized sterling silver with plaid overlay. Artist: Young-Ja Baek, New York and South Korea
1306. "Married" metals: copper, silver, and brass with reticulation. Artist: Nina Safdie, Montreal
1307. Acid-treated niobium and gold leaf with ebony wood spacer. Artist: Ivy Ross, New York
1308. Poured and carved resin. Artist: Cara Croninger, New York
1309. Silver and enamel snake's egg bead. Artist: David Freda, New York
1310. Granulated gold. Artist: Jean Reist Stark, Pennsylvania
1311. Inlaid wood and brass. Artist: Dr. Carl G. Becker, New York
1312. Layered Formica. Artist: Robert Ebendorf, New York
1313. Petrified wood. Artist: Neil Dwire, Tucson
1314. Petrified dinosaur bone. Artist: Neil Dwire, Tucson
1315. Painted wood. Artist: Mia Fonssagrives-Solow, New York (length, 15.2 cm.)
1316. Knotted antique glass "seed" beads. Artist: Jacqueline Lillie, Vienna
1317. Glass bead cluster. Artist: Jane Nyhus Designs, Seattle
1318. Drilled acrylic with injected color. Artist: Nina Safdie, Montreal
1319. Iridescent drawn and twisted glass. Artist: Jane Nyhus Designs, Seattle
1320. Fused and slumped glass with brass fittings. Artist: Jane Nyhus Designs, Seattle

Bead Shape Table: *Typical Bead Shapes Throughout the World*

The name for each bead shape is from Classification and Nomenclature of Beads and Pendants *by Horace C. Beck, which remains the classic bead shape reference guide. The shapes depicted on this chart are those most commonly found in stone and glass.*

 ANNULAR

 CYLINDER DISK

 CONVEX CONE DISK

 CYLINDER DISK WITH ONE CONCAVE END

 OBLATE

 SPHERICAL

 ELLIPSOID

 BARREL

CYLINDER

TUBE

 SQUARE CYLINDER

 CONVEX CONE

 LONG CONVEX CONE

 SHORT TRUNCATED CONVEX CONE

SHORT CONVEX BICONE

 TRUNCATED CONVEX BICONE

 PEAR-SHAPED

TRUNCATED PYRAMID

 CONE

 SQUARE TRUNCATED CONE

BICONE

TRUNCATED BICONE

CONCAVE CONE

CONCAVE BICONE

TRUNCATED CONCAVE BICONE

DOUBLE-CHAMBERED CYLINDER

 CYLINDER WITH TWO CONCAVE ENDS

 CONCAVE CYLINDER (SPOOL BEAD)

 ROUNDED CONVEX
RHOMBOID WITH
LENTICULAR CROSS
SECTION

 LENTICULAR

 CONVEX
RECTANGULAR
WITH LENTICULAR
CROSS SECTION

 ROUND TABULAR

 SQUARE TABULAR

DIAMOND-SHAPED
OR LOZENGE

TRIANGULAR PRISM

PLANO-CONVEX
ROUND

 SEMICIRCULAR

MELON

FLUTED

 CORNERLESS CUBE

 PENTAGONAL

 FACETED
HEXAGONAL
SPHERE

 FACETED
OCTAGONAL
CYLINDER

 FACETED
HEXAGONAL
BICONE

 FACETED
POLYGONAL BICONE

FACETED
OCTAGONAL
TRUNCATED BICONE

 MULTIFACETED
SPHERE

MULTIFACETED
BICONE

SPIRAL-FLUTED
BARREL

PANEL BEAD

COLLARED

SEGMENTED

TOGGLE

CROSS

RAYED

COG

 SPACER

 DROP PENDANT/
BEAD

 PYRAMID PENDANT/
BEAD

Bead Chart Glossary

Annular. Disk bead with a large diameter perforation.

Aventurine. (Italian for "by accident".) Clear or light-colored glass containing millions of metallic fragments (usually copper) or filings, which give the glass a golden sheen. Aventurine glass is used as the base material for beads and for decorative elements on beads. In addition, it is worked by lapidary techniques and is commonly called "goldstone."

Chevron. See Rosetta Bead.

Compound. In drawn and wound beads, "compound" means having two or more distinct layers of glass, one upon the other.

Constricted Glass Tubes. See Drawn Glass and Gold-Glass Beads.

Core-Formed Glass. See Wound Glass.

Cornaline d'Aleppo. (Literally, Aleppo [Syria] carnelians.) Compound beads of two layers, usually a reddish exterior over a white or yellow (sometimes pink) core. The beads may be either drawn or wound. It is assumed that the form originated to imitate banded carnelian onyx beads and stones popular in western Asia. The name is often incorrectly applied to other compound beads of similar manufacture.

Crumb Glass. A simple method of decorating glass beads is to roll the softened bead over multicolored small glass pieces, creating the effect of dots and blotches. There are several varieties. The dots may be spaced apart or close together, rounded or angular, or raised or flush with the surface of the bead. These varieties have individual names such as "scrabble" glass and "blotched" glass.

Dragged Trail. There are basically two forms of this technique—the "feather" pattern and the "festoon" pattern. In both instances the technique begins similarly. Glass of a contrasting color is trailed onto a base in parallel lines. Then a metal instrument is used to drag the trails in a perpendicular direction. The dragging process has also been called "combing." In festoon, all trails are dragged in one direction. In feather design, the dragging alternates up and down.

Drawn Glass. In the manufacture of glass beads, drawn canes with a central hole are produced as a raw material from which multitudes of nearly identical beads can be created in a short time. In contrast to wound-glass beads, which are individually made and therefore expensive, drawn beads are made in great numbers and are relatively cheap. At the same time, the process allows for a great diversity of pattern, color, and finished shapes. Drawn beads are finished by reheating techniques (tumbling and constricting) and by lapidary techniques (grinding).

dZi **Bead.** An artificially decorated stone bead of the greatest importance in the Himalayan region. Probably of great antiquity. (See "Etched" Agates.)

"End of the Day" Beads. See Crumb Glass. A popular name given to beads believed to have been assembled from scrap glass left on the factory floor at the end of the day. However, it is more probable that this was a standard production technique.

Equatorial. The middle girth of the bead perpendicular to the perforation, often called "the belt" or "the equator."

"Etched" Agates. The most popular name for a class of treated stone beads with artificial designs. They were first made c. 2500 B.C. in western Asia and appear to have a nearly unbroken chain of production into modern times.

Eye Beads. Beads of any material with circular or spotted decoration may be considered eye beads. They range from very simple to extremely complex crumb beads, mosaic glass beads, and natural and treated stone beads.

Faceted. See Lapidary Techniques.

Faience. Faience can be defined as the direct ancestor of glass, although it has also been perceived as a type of ceramic with a quartz body and glassy glaze. It is composed of partially fused quartz sand, usually with mineral colorants. It is widely believed to be the first artificial material. It was probably devised as a cheaper substitute for rare luxury materials, principally lapis lazuli and turquoise. The major centers of its manufacture were Egypt and western Asia.

Feather. See Dragged Trail.

Filigree. See Mosaic Glass.

Foil Inclusion. See Gold-Glass Beads.

Glass. There are many different types of glass with a variety of properties. Glass is composed of quartz sand, soda or potash, and lime. Understanding the constituent parts and the techniques used for manufacture helps identify the approximate time and place of manufacture.

The basic ingredient is silica, provided by small crystals of quartz sand. Soda or potash, an alkali, limits the melting point of the silica, while lime strengthens the glass as it cools. Without lime, glass is too brittle.

When raw crystalline materials are heated to about 1,200 degrees Celsius, their crystal structures collapse, causing small groups of atoms to assume the random structure of liquid. When cooled at the proper speed, the molecules become "frozen" in a glassy state.

Soda is obtained by burning seaweed. Potash is obtained from wood ash. Historically, character of glass varied with the location of the glass factory. Soda glass was usually produced in areas adjacent to the sea; potash glass in wooded areas.

Gold-Glass Beads. These are created from tubes or canes in which a core layer of clear glass is surrounded by a thin layer of gold foil, which itself is surrounded by a subsequent layer of clear glass. (Hence, they are also called "sandwich" glass.) They derive from late Egyptian and early Roman production. The precise method of manufacture of the beads from the tubes or canes is a matter of speculation and conflicting ideas. It is recognized, however, that the tubes in a heated condition are constricted to form the rounded ends of beads, the segments within segmented beads, and the ends of collared beads.

Formerly, it was assumed that the tubes of glass were drawn. This does not seem likely as the gold foil would not be as ductile as the glass. The processes used for construction are unknown. However, two variations seem likely: (1) The heated cane may be rolled over a sharp tool, and (2) a glassmaker's tool (like a caliper) is used to pinch

or constrict the softened cane to form the ends, segments, or collars.

Lamp Bead. The product of the cottage industries in Venice and Murano, where the beadmaker sat at a fueled lamp and created beads through the process of heating preformed rods of glass. These rods form the bead itself and any subsequent decoration. See Polychrome and Drawn Glass.

Lapidary Techniques. The lapidary or stone-cutter shapes his products with a variety of tools and techniques, several of which remain virtually unchanged since the earliest times; namely, flaking, grinding, cutting, and polishing. Lapidary skills have often been applied to the production of glass beads. This began in ancient times but includes more recent Chinese products too.

Married Metal Technique. The joining of different metals to each other by soldering to form one continuous surface.

Marvering. To shape and consolidate heated glass during its manufacture, it is rolled over a flat marble, stone, or cast-iron surface called a "marver," or "marvering" board.

Millefiore. See Mosaic Glass.

Mold-Cast Glass. One of the earliest methods of working with molten glass was to pour it into open forms. Upon cooling, the glass was released from the mold and finished by hand.

Molded Glass. In the manufacture of molded beads, a preformed cane is heated to a softened state and used to fill a (usually) two-part mold. This was the technique of choice of the Bohemian and Germanic glass industries.

Mosaic Glass. In glassmaking, a product created from preformed, multicolored units. Both the units and the finished products are referred to as mosaic glass. There are many varieties of units and categories of finished products, and most of them have individual popular names, including *millefiore* (medieval Italian for "thousand flowers"), stratified, "ribbon glass," and "filigree glass."

Polychrome. "Polychrome" typically means having more than one color. In the context of glass beads, polychrome means individually created beads decorated by hand through the application of molten colored glass. (See Lamp Bead.)

Reheating. The reheating of a drawn-glass bead so that it may be reshaped by mass treatment (tumbling) or individual treatment (pinching or constricting a heated tube or reheating and shaping a cane segment. See Gold-Glass Beads).

Rosetta Bead. Any drawn-glass cane bead with an internal pattern of multiple-layer construction. Star beads, specifically, are rosetta beads with starry patterns. Chevron beads, specifically, are star beads with their ends cut or ground down.

Star Bead. See Rosetta Bead.

Stratified. See Mosaic Glass.

Wound Glass. Molten glass is wound around a metallic rod or wire similar to the way thread is wound onto a spool. By forming molten material in this manner, there is no need to drill or perforate the bead as a separate step. Today, we speak of beads from the pre-Christian Era as core-formed beads or pendants. We have dispensed with the term "core-formed" in this book to be consistent throughout.

For complete citations refer to the Bibliography. Short titles are given below only when more than one reference by an author is cited in the Bibliography. Notes designated in the captions are listed by Roman numerals and follow the text notes for each chapter.

INTRODUCTION

1. Erikson, 140. 2. Ibid.

THE BEGINNINGS

1. Alexander Marshak, letter to author, February 1983. References to beads and pendants from Lower Paleolithic sites (c. 100,000 B.C.) exist. Naturally pierced flakes of flint, shells, and fossils suggest beads were made in this era, but the evidence is inconclusive. See Francis, "Earliest Beads in India," p. 18. 2. Pfeiffer, *The Creative Explosion*, pp. 53–63. 3. Ibid., pp. 102, 204; See also Pfeiffer, *The Emergence of Man*, pp. 221–27. 4. Movius, p. 120. 5. Dance, pp. 154–56. 6. Francis, "The Earliest Beads in India," 1: p. 18. 7. Klima, p. 197. 8. Francis, "The Earliest Beads in India," 1: pp.18–19. 9. Hiler, pp. 30–33. 10. Campbell, pp. 427–28. 11. Ibid. 12. Chard, pp. 27, 37; Levin and Potapov, p. 20. 13. Francis, "The Earliest Beads in India," 1: p. 19. 14. Cheng, p. 35. 15. Francis, "A Survey of Beads in Korea," pp. 5–6. 16. Francis, "The Earliest Beads in India," 1: p. 19. 17. Dortch, p. 39. 18. Jernigan, pp. 10–11. 19. Pfeiffer, *The Emergence of Man*, p. 250. 20. Ibid., p. 265; Fagan, p. 74. 21. Francis, "The Earliest Beads in India," 2: p. 14. 22. Fagan, p. 160. 23. Cheng, p. 37.

ANTIQUITY

1. Moore, p. 135. 2. Ogden, p. 17; Pierides, p. 1. 3. Tosi and Piperno, pp. 15–23. 4. Von Saldern, "Mosaic Glass," pp. 9–25. 5. Herrmann, p. 21. 6. Mallowan, p. 159. 7. Maxwell-Hyslop, *passim*; Higgins, *passim*. 8. Mellaart, p. 18. 9. Besborodov and Zadneprovsky, p. 127. 10. Vandiver, p. 239. 11. McNeill, p. 71. 12. Bosse-Griffiths, p. 10. For an illustration, see Vilimkova and Darbois, plate 8. 13. Andrews, *Egyptian Jewellery*, p. 5. 14. Aldred, p. 17. 15. Ibid., pp. 19–21, 30. 16. Andrews, *Egyptian Jewellery*, p. 7; Aldred, p. 36. 17. Mellaart, p. 18. Mellaart's dates, however, differ for the Seventh and Eighth dynasties. Using his chronology, these beads are dated 2387–2365 B.C. The Egyptian chronologies used for this book are from *Art of Ancient Egypt*, by Kazimierz Michalowski (New York: Harry N. Abrams, Inc., 1968). 18. For further information, see Chapter 10 and notes of Chapter 11; see also Beck, "Etched Carnelian Beads," pp. 384–98. 19. Bacon, pp. 251–78. 20. Higgins, pp. 53–71. 21. Ibid., pp. 72–87. 22. Taylour, p. 146. 23. Ibid., pp. 145–146. 24. Tatton-Brown, pp. 16–17, 29; Pierides, pp. 1–7. 25. Follett, pp. 64–65. 26. *Jewellery Through 7,000 Years*, p. 79. 27. Weinberg, *passim*. 28. See Ogden for materials traded within the Roman Empire. 29. Higgins, pp. 175–76. 30. Jamey D. Allen, telephone conversation with author, November 1986; Von Saldern, *Ancient Glass*, pp. 14–15.

31. Glumac, pp. 15–17. 32. Oved, p. 58. 33. Guido, p. 23. 34. Oved. p. 58. 35. Guido, pp. 28–29, 31. 36. Ibid., *passim*.
I. Woolley, pp. 87–88. II. Mallowan and Rose, plate 8; Noveck, p. 16. III. Budge, p. 13. IV. Liu, "Afghan Stone Beads," p. 34. V. Maxwell-Hyslop, pp. 31, 34–36; Mallowan, "Excavations at Brak," pp. 171–76. VI. Seefried, *passim*. VII. Maxwell-Hyslop, pp. 180–197. VIII. Liu, "Iranian Faïence," p. 6. IX. Ogden, pp. 18–19. X. Goldstein, p. 29; Von Saldern, "Mosaic Glass," p. 9. XI. Guido, p. 46.

EUROPE

1. Brown, p. 176. 2. Randall, pp. 105–6; Kuntzsch, p. 85. 3. Kuntzsch, p. 86. 4. See plate 49. 5. Eisen, *Glass*, II: pp. 550–649. 6. Peter Francis, letter to author, January 1986. 7. For information on Byzantine glass beads, see Gregorietti, p. 137. 8. The "Vision of Constantine" is a large, flat bead with a cross engraved on one side of it and four hosts (religious symbols) on both sides. The "Road to Golgotha" is a flat bead made of yellow and red or brown and white threads inlaid on a dark matrix. Eisen, *Glass*, II: pp. 522–23, 531, 535–36. 9. Kuntzsch, p. 97. 10. Randall, pp. 105–6. 11. Gregorietti, p. 199. 12. Barraclough, pp. 92–93. 13. Randall, pp. 87–88. 14. Gregorietti, pp. 129–32. 15. *Jewellery Through 7,000 Years*, p. 129. 16. Kuntzsch, p.92. 17. Randall, pp. 87–88. 18. Haevernick, pp. 180–87. 19. Oved, pp. 66–67. 20. Forbes, 197. 21. This is further complicated for those working in the English language, as most available research is published in German or Russian, or in Scandinavian or central European languages. For references see Callmer and Tempelmann-Maczynska. 22. Important glass beadmaking industries existed at Starja Ladoga, north of Moscow, from the eighth to the tenth century, in Poland after the first half of the tenth century, and at Kiev by the end of the tenth century. Several of these glassworks produced drawn-glass beads, a technique not produced elsewhere in Europe. Apparently, all of these beadmaking activities ceased by at least the thirteenth century, a casualty of the Mongolian invasions. See Kidd, *Glass Bead-Making*, p. 9; Forbes, pp. 197–98; Peter Francis, letter to author, January 1986. 23. Forbes, p. 198. 24. Graham-Campbell and Kidd, pp. 41, 76, 134. 25. *Jewellery Through 7,000 Years*, p. 138. 26. Peter Francis, letter to author, January 1986. 27. Callmer, pp. 7–9. 28. Graham-Campbell and Kidd, pp. 41, 76, 134; Lundstrom, *passim*. 29. Callmer, pp. 33–51. 30. Hall, pp. 87–89, 112. 31. Callmer, *passim*. 32. Stout, pp. 58–60, 76; Callmer, plate IV, no. G030. 33. Peter Francis, letter to author, January 1986.

THE WORLD OF ISLAM

1. Al-Jadir, p. 13. 2. Bibby, p. 164. 3. Peter Francis, letter to author, January 1986. 4. Ibid. 5. Hasson, pp. 109–113. 6. Al Jadir, pp. 14, 33–34; Jenkins and Keene, p. 9. 7. Liu, "Beads in the Sudan," p. 27. 8. Erikson, pp.

164–76. 9. Budge, p. 325. 10. Kunz, p. 64. 11. Jenkins and Keene, p. 27. 12. Critchlow, p. 8. 13. Jenkins and Keene, pp. 26, 30. 14. Ibid., p. 47. 15. Dr. Carl G. Becker, telephone conversation with author, April 1985. 16. Al-Jadir, p. 19. 17. Ibid., p. 31; Hawley, *passim*. 18. Kolbas, pp. 95–113; Hasson, pp. 109–113.
I. Eisen, *Glass*, II: p. 523. II. Muller, p. 23. III. Al-Jadir, p. 108. IV. Hawley, *passim*.

PRAYER BEADS

1. Wilkins, p. 48. 2. Pramod Chandra, *Sculpture of India, 300 B.C.–A.D. 300* (Washington D.C.: National Gallery of Art, 1985), plate 15. 3. Edmunds, p. 254. 4. Ibid., p. 44. 5. Ibid., pp. 47, 62; Howe, p. 22. 6. Wilkins, pp. 80–104. 7. Ibid. 8. Ibid., p. 78. 9. Ibid., p. 50. 10. Michael Gelber, conversation with author, December 1985. 11. Casanowicz, p. 34. 12. Michael Meister, conversation with author, August 1985. 13. Casanowicz, p. 337. 14. Ibid. 15. Francis, *A Survey of Beads in Korea*, p. 29. 16. All information on Japanese Buddhist prayer beads is from Casanowicz, pp. 341–48. 17. Casanowicz, p. 349. 18. Ibid. 19. Ibid., pp. 349–50; Jenkins and Keene, p. 106. 20. Budge, p. 81. 21. Wilkins, p. 30. 22. Ibid., p. 25. 23. Ibid., p. 37. 24. Ibid., p. 34. 25. Ibid., p. 50. 26. Ibid., p. 49. 27. Ibid., p. 60; Casanowicz, p. 354; Evans, p. 118. 28. Kuntzsch, p. 106. 29. For a complete history see Wilkins, pp. 105–175. 30. Ibid., p. 221.
I. *Tibetan Collection*, II: p. 11. II. Wilkins, pp. 174, 184, 224.

EUROPEAN EXPANSION

1. McNeill, pp. 565–67. 2. Harris and Levey, "The Renaissance," in *New Columbia Encyclopedia* (New York: Columbia University Press), pp. 2300–1. 3. The *Portrait of Simonetta Vespucci* by Botticelli is in the Stadelsches Kunstinstitut, Frankfurt. 4. Black, p. 156. 5. Hughes, pp. 81–83. 6. Muller, p. 23. 7. Ibid., plate 26. 8. Gold filigree beads are mentioned in Gregorietti, p. 199; Amber beads in Rowe, p. 51. 9. Cocks, pp. 41–43; Newman, p. 162. 10. Black, pp. 209, 234; Kuntzsch, pp. 131–33. 11. There is a coral parure from the 1830s at the Musée des Arts Decoratifs in Paris reproduced in Gregorietti, p. 225. 12. Evans, p. 172. 13. Black, p. 254. 14. Gregorietti, p. 262. 15. Kidd, *Glass Bead-Making*, p. 17. Beads made of crystal and carnelian were traded by the early Spanish explorers. The Frenchman Jacques Cartier gave tin beads as gifts to Indians in Montreal, Canada, in 1535. See Francis, *Beads and the Discovery of the New World*, pp. 36–37. 16. Francis, *Beads and the Discovery of the New World*, p. 26. 17. Barraclough, p. 154. 18. Francis, "Beads and the Discovery of America," pp. 47–50, 53. Handler et al. pp. 15–18. 19. See writings by Kidd, Karklins, Smith and Good, Allen, Francis, Harris, Liu and Harris, and Hayes. 20. Kidd, *Glass Bead-Making, passim*. 21. Tait, pp. 9–11; Francis, *Venetian Beads*, p. 2. 22. Francis, *Venetian Beads*, p. 2. 23. Kidd, *Glass Bead-Making*, p. 18. 24. Tait, pp. 12, 61–62. 25. There are apparently two recorded instances of the death penalty having been carried out. Kidd, *Glass Bead-*

Making, p. 22. **26.** The Romans made drawn-glass beads by the first century A.D. After the fall of Rome, drawn-glass beads were produced in eastern Europe, western Russia, and Moravia. In western and southern Europe after the fifth century and in eastern Europe after the tenth century, there is little evidence of drawn-glass beads. In India, however, drawn-glass beads were made from the fourth century B.C. to the Middle Ages. It is possible the Venetians learned the technique from the Indians. Francis, "When India Was Beadmaker," p. 24. **27.** Kidd, *Glass Bead-Making*, pp. 22–28; Francis, *Venetian Beads*, pp. 7–8; Jamey D. Allen, letter to author, October 1986. **28.** Francis, *Venetian Beads*, p. 14. **29.** Ibid., p. 1. **30.** Allen, "The Manufacture of Intricate Glass Canes," p. 191. **31.** Kidd, *Glass Bead-Making*, p. 28. **32.** Ibid., pp. 18–20. **33.** Fuel supplies must always have been of serious concern to the Venetian and Murano industries. Kidd, *Glass Bead-Making*, p. 23. **34.** Ibid., pp. 39–41. **35.** Francis, *Czech Bead Story*, pp. 10–16. **36.** Ibid., pp. 9–10. **37.** Karklins, "Early Amsterdam Trade Beads," pp. 36–41. **38.** Karklins, "Dutch Trade Beads," p. 114. **39.** Karklins, "Early Amsterdam Trade Beads," p. 41. **40.** It is not clear whether these differences, in addition to the composition of the glass, were a function of change over time. Karklins ("Dutch Trade Beads," pp. 115–16) suggests that beads manufactured from 1500 to 1700 generally used drawn techniques and soda-lime glass. Potash-lime glass was preferred for beads made from 1687 to 1750, possibly because its lower melting point and greater range of plasticity made it more suitable for the smaller scale lamp work. **41.** Karklins, "Early Amsterdam Trade Beads," p. 41. **42.** Kidd, *Glass Bead-Making*, pp. 33–35, 61, 65. **43.** Feulner. **44.** Trebbins, pp. 3, 8. **45.** Ibid., *passim*. **46.** Ibid., p. 12. **47.** Ibid., pp. 8–12. **48.** Kidd, *Glass Bead-Making*, pp. 29–32. **49.** Ibid., pp. 45–46. **50.** Smith, "Chronology from Glass Beads," pp. 147–52. **51.** The "padre" bead may have been made by the Chinese. Liu, "Chinese Glass Beads," p. 14. **I.** In that market, yellow and black backgrounds make up well over 80 percent of the beads found of this type. Blue, green, white, and red backgrounds, present in approximately equal quantities, provide most of the balance. Varieties with red backgrounds are often *cornaline d'Aleppo* beads with white or yellow cores. Michael Heide, letter to author, December 1985. **II.** Karklins, *Glass Beads*, *passim*. **III.** Allen, "Cane Manufacturer for Mosaic Glass Beads," 1:pp. 6–11. **IV.** Liu, "Carnelian Beads and Their Simulations," pp. 14–18. **V.** Allen, "Cane Manufacturer for Mosaic Glass Beads," 1:pp. 6–11. **VI.** Karklins, "Dutch Trade Beads," pp. 59–74. **VII.** Allen, "The Manufacture of Intricate Glass Canes," pp. 173–91. **VIII.** Ibid., "Chevron-Star Rosetta Beads," 1: pp. 19–24; 2: pp. 24–29. **IX.** Smith and Good, *passim*. **X.** Some elements are similar to earlier Venetian types, particularly the translucent layers. On the other hand, the bead relates to later (1800s) chevrons, especially in its color and layer sequencing, suggesting it should be dated to the 1700s. **XI.** Another example is illustrated in Sorensen, figure CL178. **XII.** The following descriptions by Michael Heide are intended to point out features of various chevrons that are unusual or not clear from the illustration. After examining several million beads from West Africa over the past eighteen years, Heide concluded that all of the beads illus-

trated here are uncommon. He has utilized the term "scarce" to mean he has seen only six to ten examples of the type. "Rare" means two to five have been found, and "unique" means he has seen only one. Unless otherwise mentioned, molded layers have twelve points. (1) Very large (otherwise typical), seven-layer chevron with six facets on each end. First and third layers are a transparent light green color. Length, 7 cm. Rare this large. (2) Same as 1, except first and third layers are black. Length, 2.8 cm. (3) Seven layers with outer layer in translucent green. Length, 3.3 cm. Rare. (4) Seven layers with square cross section. First and seventh layers are transparent and colorless. Two red and two teal blue stripes are embedded in seventh layer. Third layer is translucent teal blue. Related to *Nueva Cadiz* beads. Length 3.5 cm. Rare. (5) Five layers with none of the layers molded into points. Facets at each end yield a "chevron" appearance from the side. First layer is transparent and colorless; second layer is dark brown. Length, 1.6 cm. Unique. (6) Three layers with seven yellow stripes on outer layer. Length, 1.3 cm. Unique. (7) Four layers with six red and six blue stripes on outer layer. Length, 1.6 cm. (8) Five layers. *Left:* first and fifth layers are transparent blue. Length, 1.6 cm. *Right:* first and fifth layers are transparent and colorless. Length, 1.6 cm. Six red and six blue stripes are embedded in outer layer in each bead. (9) Three layers. First and third layers are black; second layer is gray. Eight red and eight white stripes on outer layer. Length, 0.8 cm. Unique. (10) Three layers. First and third layers are transparent cobalt blue. Twelve white stripes on outer layer. (Bluish "stripes" are points from the second white layer, showing through the third blue layer.) Length, 1.1 cm. (11) Five layers with five flattened surfaces along the sides and faceted at each end. First layer is translucent cobalt blue. Second and fourth layers are white. Sixteen points. Length, 2.3 cm. Scarce. (12) Four layers. *Left:* third layer only has twelve points. Length, 1.1 cm., diameter, 1.3 cm. Scarce. *Right:* first and third layers have twelve points. Length, 1.3 cm. (13) Four layers. *Right:* fourth layer is black with twelve white stripes. Length, 1.1 cm. Rare. *Left:* same as first bead, except heat rounded. Length, 1.1 cm. Scarce. (14) Four layers. *Left:* fourth layer is black with six yellow stripes. Length, 0.7, diameter, 0.3. *Right:* fourth layer is translucent green with four compound stripes, black on yellow, alternating with four compound stripes yellow on red. Length, 1.8 cm. Scarce. (15) Two layers. *Right:* second layer grooves are filled with alternating blue and brick red stripes. A yellow stripe is atop each red stripe. Second layer is ten points. Length, 0.7 cm. Scarce. *Left:* same as first bead but beveled at both ends. Length, 1.8 cm. Scarce. (16) Six layers, six scooped facets around midline, six facets each end. Length, 2.5 cm. Rare. (17) Four layers. Outer layer blue with four wide green stripes. Length, 2.5 cm. Rare. (18) Six layers. Second and sixth layer dark translucent green, outer layer ground down to appear striped. Length, 2.8 cm. Rare. (19) First layer grayish blue; second layer powder blue; third layer red orange; fourth layer translucent blue, appearing purple because of red layer below. Length, 1.3 cm. Scarce. (20) First layer red, twelve points. Second layer black, seven petal-shaped lobes.

Fourth layer translucent green. Length, 2.5 cm. Scarce. (21) Five layers. First and third layers dark translucent cobalt blue that appear black. Second and fifth layers bright red. Length, 2.0 cm. (Found in the United States, not Africa.) (22) Six layers. Fourth layer yellow. *Left:* length, 2.0 cm., diameter, 1.6 cm. *Right:* length, 2.8 cm. Each unique. (23) Five layers, six facets each end. Second and fifth layers very dark purplish brown. Third layer red with no typical white layer between red and black. Length, 2.8 cm. Unique. (24) Six layers. First, third, and fifth layers dark brown. Second, fourth, and sixth layers white. Length, 2.3 cm. Unique. (25) Eight layers. First, third, fifth, and seventh layers white. Second layer red. Sixth layer "root-beer" brown with aventurine. Fourth layer translucent teal blue. Third layer twelve points; seventh layer twenty-two points. Length, 3.6 cm. Unique. (26) Six layers. First, third, and fifth layers yellow. Second and sixth layers opaque green. Fourth layer orange red. Length, 2.8 cm. Unique.

AFRICA

1. Peter Francis, letter to author, January 1986. **2.** Trebbin, p. 4. **3.** Hodge, p. 65. **4.** Sieber, p. 123. **5.** de Negri, p. 210. **6.** Hodge, p. 65; Roy Sieber, letter to author, March 1986. **7.** Liu, "The Bead in African Assembled Jewelry," p. 40. **8.** Sieber, p. 123. **9.** Based on information from Sidney Goldstein (formerly of the Corning Museum of Glass) regarding the analysis of several glass beads excavated at Djenne by Susan and Roderick McIntosh. Also, see McIntosh and McIntosh, pp. 1–22. **10.** van Riet Lowe, pp. 1–21. **11.** Hodge, p. 65. **12.** The Bida create glass beads and bangles with the winding, drawing, and trailing techniques employed in Venetian glassmaking (and featuring the traditional bellows-forced draft furnaces). Krobo and Mauritanian glassmakers use an entirely different technique that involves firing powder-glass beads in simple furnaces or ovens without a forced air supply. African powder-glass technology has been divided into two varieties: dry-form and wet-form. Dry-form techniques practiced by the Krobo (plate 112) involve placing finely powdered glass into horizontal or vertical molds. The molds are then heated, and the low-firing temperatures allow the glass particles to fuse without melting. This produces a characteristically soft and grainy matte texture. Wet-form techniques are used to create polychrome beads in Mauritania (plate 108). These beads are made with a wet-inlay technique without a mold. Glass powders made by pulverizing imported monochrome glass beads are mixed with a binder (saliva or gum arabic) to form a moist paste. The colored powder is then spread with a needle over a core bead made from plain bottle glass. Applying the powder glass paste with a needle allows the colors to be treated separately, resulting in a finely detailed bead design. The beads are then heated in a simple oven to create a satinlike finish. This finish probably indicates that wet-form techniques require higher firing temperatures and possibly the beads are polished after being fired. Delaroziere, *passim*; Gumpert, *passim*; Liu, "African-Made Glass Ornaments," pp. 52-53. **13.** Laidler, p. 2. **14.** Harding, pp. 104–6. **15.** Ibid. **16.** Ibid. **17.** Laidler, p. 3. **18.** For the people of the Kalahari, who tend to feel more comfortable not

having conspicuous possessions, beads are used to teach children to give things away. See Pfeiffer, *The Creative Explosion*, p. 65. **19.** For both tribes, beaded jewelry and objects were created to mark courtship and marital status. See Levinsohn, pp. 38–40. **20.** de Negri, pp. 210–16. **21.** Fagg, *Yoruba Sculpture*, p. 88. **22.** Northern, *The Sign of the Beaded Leopard*, pp. 17–23. **23.** Waist beads also played an important role in nineteenth century Asante society: "The most fundamental item of dress for women is a set of waist beads (*toma*)....without them a woman is shamefully naked." McLeod, pp. 143–45. **24.** Fisher, pp. 227–65. **25.** Cole, pp. 29–37. **26.** van der Sleen, *A Handbook on Beads*, p. 85. **27.** Landewijk, pp. 8–14. **28.** Sieber, p. 12. **29.** Cole, p. 30. **30.** Vogel, p. 6.
I. Angela Fisher, conversation with author, April 1984. **II.** Lamb, "Krobo Powder-Glass Beads," pp. 23–27. **III.** Michael Heide, letter to author, November 1985. See also Lamb, "Krobo Powder-Glass Beads," pp. 23–27; Bodom beads are defined by Alastair Lamb as Ghanaian powder-glass beads with a black or or grey core; their source of manufacture continues to be a mystery. In a letter to the author in February 1986, Robert Liu, as a result of his own observations and experiments in reconstructing powder-glass beads, suggests that beads such as those seen in plate 109 (figs. 1–5) were probably not made in Africa. He suggests that the high temperature needed to produce these beads, with their well-crafted trailed decorations made from glass rods, argues against an African origin. Regardless of their non-European appearance, he believes they are probably European simulations of African prototypes. **IV.** Cole, p. 30. **V.** Whereas other East African nomads are hostile to metalsmiths because they do not raise cattle, blacksmiths have become part of Turkana society. They produce, among other things, beads of iron, copper, and aluminum. Fedders and Salvadori, *passim*. **VI.** Cole, p. 30. **VII.** Ibid. **VIII.** Fisher, p. 48. **IX.** All information on the Zulus is from Conner and Pelrine, Levinsohn, and Schoeman. **X.** All information on the Ndebele is from Priebatsch and Knight, and Fisher. **XI.** Fagg, p. 71. **XII.** Ibid, p. 42. **XIII.** Vogel, p. 101. **XIV.** Fisher, pp. 227–65; Suzanne Bach and Albert Gordon, letter to author, September 1984. **XV.** Fisher, p. 265.

THE FAR EAST

1. Current research is beginning to reveal the extensiveness of the Chinese glass bead trade. For further information see Francis, *Chinese Glass Beads*, and Liu, "Asian Glass Ornaments," parts 1 and 2. **2.** Chard, pp. 111, 208. **3.** Lee, p. 9. **4.** Translation systems used in this book are: Pinyin for Chinese, Hepburn for Japanese, and McCune-Reischauer for Korean. **5.** Cheng, pp. 35–40. **6.** Branigan, p. 193. **7.** Chinese glass beads were not made with soda-lime formulas until the Tang dynasty (A.D. 618–907). **8.** Dohrenwend, *Chinese Jades, passim*; "Glass in China," pp. 426–46. **9.** Francis, *Chinese Glass Beads*, pp. 10, 32. **10.** Francis, "Asian Bead Study Tour II," p. 11. **11.** Nelson Gallery–Atkins Museum, p. 73. **12.** Akiyama, p. 216 and plate 124. The use of amber, coral, and crystal for Tang dynasty beads is noted by Schaefer, pp. 248, 265. **13.** *China, Guide to the Collection of the University Museum*, p. 162. **14.** Francis,

Chinese Glass Beads, pp. 12–14. **15.** Ibid., pp. 14–15. **16.** Ibid., p. 33. **17.** Ibid., p. 37. **18.** Ibid., pp. 34–37. **19.** Ibid. **20.** Liu, "Chinese Glass Beads," p. 14. **21.** Most glass beads in the Qing dynasty were made by a mandrel-winding technique. See Liu, "Chinese Glass Beads," pp. 14–15. Other techniques observed by Francis, Harris, and Liu include: tube-drawing (a technique possibly dating back to the Tang dynasty), molding, pressing, hot-pinching and blowing, and various methods classified as lapidary (grinding and drilling). **22.** All information on Chinese court beads is from Cammann, pp. 341–48. **23.** Ibid. Manchurian Buddhist necklaces had three rather than two counter strings, plus a unique series of pendants that hung down the back. After passing through a flat stone plaque called "black cloud," the cord terminated in a large pendant called a "dewdrop." Dewdrops also terminated the counter strings. The four dewdrops are known as the "disciple beads" or the "regents of the four heavens," representing the emperor, father, mother, and teacher to whom an individual owed reverence and obedience. All these elements differentiated Manchurian beads from Tibetan beads. **24.** Ibid. From the *Huang-ch'ao lichi t'u-shih*, a volume of dynastic law published in 1766, we know that the emperor's court beads were to consist of 108 large freshwater pearls from Manchuria, and all the accessories—the Buddha heads, the memory beads, the black cloud, and the dewdrops—were to be made of precious and semi-precious jewels, including lapis lazuli, amber, coral and turquoise. **25.** Doris Dohrenwend, letter to author, July 1986; Kunz, p. 83. **26.** Kunz, p. 84. **27.** Nephrite is a silicate of magnesia, while jadeite is a silicate of alumina. Nephrite is fibrous and very tough, jadeite slightly harder but more crystalline and so less tough. **28.** Sullivan, p. 40. **29.** Francis, *A Survey of Beads in Korea*, pp. 5–6, 9. **30.** Kunz, p. 265. The literal translation of *kogok* is "curved jade," and of *magatama*, "curved jade" or "curved bead." Several explanations have been advanced for the mysterious shape of the *kogok* and *magatama*, including stylized representations of animal claws or fangs (items frequently associated with medicine bags and shamanism). **31.** Kunz, p. 265. Chard, p. 189. **32.** Blair, p. 356. **33.** Francis, *A Survey of Beads in Korea*, p. 35. **34.** Francis, *A Survey of Beads in Korea*, pp. 10–21. **35.** Yoshimizu, pp. 98–102. **36.** Stout, pp. 58–60. **37.** Francis, *A Survey of Beads in Korea*, pp. 64, 13–16, 27. **38.** Ibid., p. 21. **39.** Chang-su Houchins, letter to author, July 1986. **40.** Francis, *A Survey of Beads in Korea*, pp. 26–28. **41.** Suk, Joo-sun, p. 161, entry no. 47. **42.** Francis, *A Survey of Beads in Korea*, pp. 31–34. **43.** Okamoto, *passim*. **44.** Chard, p. 131. **45.** Blair, pp. 42–45. **46.** Ibid., pp. 51–52, 57. **47.** Ibid., p. 48. **48.** Ibid., pp. 49–51. **49.** Ibid., pp. 67–69. **50.** Included are beads of crystal, glass, amber, agate, gold, silver, gilt copper, jasper, jadeite, obsidian, stone, pearl, coral, ivory, wood, nuts, and seeds. Ibid., pp. 98–103. **51.** Blair, pp. 94–98, 375; plate 77. **52.** Ibid., p. 131. **53.** Ibid., p. 132. **54.** Ibid., p. 152. **55.** Ibid., p. 181. **56.** Arakawa, pp. 187–89. **57.** Arakawa, p. 191. **58.** A journal kept by Matsura Seizan, lord of the Hirado domain in northern Kyushu, is a valuable source of information on the thematic content of late Edo *inro* ensembles. **59.** *Ojime* were also made of porcelain, lacquer, amber, cloi-

sonné, and stones, including jade, carnelian, malachite, and quartz. **60.** Okada, p. 34. **61.** As explained by Mikoshiba and Bushell, p. 60: "The marvel of the sequential portrayal possible in the *ojime* depends not only on fine miniscule craftsmanship, but also on an optical illusion whereby the length of the circumference as a straight line is remarkable as compared with the small bulk of the sphere."
I. For a more complete description of these beads, see Dohrenwend, "Glass in China"; Liu, "Ancient Chinese Glass Beads"; Francis, *Chinese Glass Beads*; and White, *Tombs of Old Lo-Yang*. **II.** Liu, "Glass Ojime," pp. 24–28. **III.** The *netsuke-ojime-inro* ensemble in this illustration is somewhat atypical, because the compartments comprising the *inro* have been concealed by a sheath of rich gold lacquer and married metalwork. However, the *ojime* still slides up and down to loosen or tighten the compartments. **IV.** Shogun, p. 80.

INDIA

1. Brijbhushan, p. 3; Latif, p. 42. **2.** Francis, "Minor Indian Beadmakers," p. 18. **3.** Michael Meister, conversation with author, August 1985. **4.** Latif, p. 42. **5.** Brijbhushan, p. 5. **6.** Latif, p. 42. **7.** Francis, "The Earliest Beads in India," 1: pp. 18–19; 2: pp. 14–15. **8.** Kenoyer, pp. 18–19. **9.** Ibid. **10.** Possehl, p. 39. **11.** Chandra, *Studies in the Development of Ornaments*, pp. 57–110. **12.** Ibid. **13.** Ibid, p. 160. **14.** Reade, figure 1; Beck, "Etched Carnelian Beads," pp. 384–98. **15.** Francis, *Indian Agate Beads*, p. 9. **16.** Chandra, *Indo-Greek Jewellery*, pp. 55–58. **17.** Ogden, p. 90. **18.** Ibid., p. 109. **19.** Francis, *Indian Agate Beads*, p. 11. **20.** Ibid. **21.** Ibid. **22.** Francis, *Glass Beads of India*, pp. 2–4. **23.** Ibid. **24.** Ibid., p. 2. **25.** Ibid., p. 3. **26.** Ibid., pp. 3–4. **27.** Ibid., p. 4; Lamb, "A Note on Glass Beads from the Malay Peninsula," *passim*. **28.** van der Sleen, *A Handbook on Beads*, p. 13. **29.** Francis, *Glass Beads of India*, p. 4. **30.** Other countries (Yemen, China, and Iran) have agate and carnelian sources and manufacturers, but neither the size of the stone deposits nor length of their exploitation seriously rivaled the Indian industry. Francis, "When India Was Beadmaker to the World," p. 33. **31.** Ibid. **32.** Handler et al, p. 15. **33.** Brijbhushan, p. 14. **34.** Latif, p. 45. **35.** Brijbhushan, pp. 20–21. **36.** Latif, p. 47. **37.** Brijbhushan, p. 18. **38.** The Venetians made drawn-glass beads as did the Indians. However, there is no evidence that they were using the same techniques. Indeed, the evidence strongly suggests Indians were using their own *lada* technique, similar to a technique used today in Papanaidupet. Francis, "Some Thoughts on Glass Beadmaking," p. 196. **39.** Francis, "When India Was Beadmaker to the World," p. 34. **40.** Francis, *Glass Beads of India*, p. 6. In 1879–80, India imported 1,800,000 pounds of foreign glass beads: 78 percent from Venice and 8 percent each from China and Bohemia. **41.** Latif, pp. 88–90. **42.** Francis, *Indian Agate Beads*, p. 35. **43.** Possehl, pp. 40–46. **44.** Most carnelian has no red in it until it is heat-treated. At Ratanpur, the iron is natural to the stone; at Idar-Oberstein, the stones were soaked in an iron solution before heat treatment. Peter Francis, Letter to author, January 1986. **45.** Francis, *Glass Beads of India*, pp. 8–20.
I. See Central Asia chapter for further information on etched carnelian beads. **II.** van der

Sleen, *A Handbook on Beads, passim.* **III.** These beads have been identified through correspondence between the Corning Museum of Glass and van der Sleen, February–March 1957. The beads, according to van der Sleen, are similar to excavated examples from Brahmapuri, Bahmani layer (15th century A.D.). **IV.** Barbier, *passim.* **V.** Ibid. **VI.** Maureen Zarember, conversation with author, December 1982.

CENTRAL ASIA

1. Barraclough, p. 70. **2.** Klimburg-Salter, pp. 112–13. **3.** See The Far East chapter. **4.** Belenitsky, pp. 93–101. plates 57–58. **5.** Newark Museum, I, pp. 41–42; Newark Museum, II, p. 13. **6.** Jeweled sculptures of Buddha, a form derived from northern India, reflect the influences of the Mahayana sect of Buddhism, which created the Bodhisattvas, the Buddha's earthly representatives worthy of Nirvana who stayed on earth to help mankind. To the Bodhisattva, jewelry denoted his worldly connections. **7.** Klimburg-Salter, *passim*; Reynolds, p. 15; and Zwalf, p. 10. **8.** Zwalf, pp. 9–12. **9.** See Prayer Beads chapter. **10.** The Tibetan trading class was small, but most Tibetans were born traders and engaged in bartering among themselves. The nobility, many of whom owned large provincial farms, had commercial agents who managed the sale of their estate produce and were also sent abroad to buy luxury items. **11.** Most Tibetan villages sported gaily painted wooden doors and window trim. During religious festivals, private homes and monasteries were decked with colorful awnings, banners, and flowers. Reynolds, p. 17. **12.** See Zwalf pp. 79, 137; Newark II, p. 92. **13.** Ebbinghouse, book review of *Himalayan Kingdoms,* 97. Diamonds, rubies and emeralds were often inexpensively simulated. On the other hand, pearls, strung with large coral and *dZi* beads, were frequently high quality imitations; they used to be sold in Lhasa for nearly the price of real ones. **14.** Pogue, p. 79. **15.** Weinstein, p. 234. **16.** Laufer, p. 5. **17.** Pogue, p. 24. **18.** Thupten Pheloye, conversation with author, November 1983. **19.** Pal, p. 10. This coexistence appears to have ancient origins and ranges from the location of shrines to the portrayal of images. **20.** Waldschmidt, p. 11; Anderson, p. 32. **21.** Gabriel, "Himalayan Portraits," p. 59; Barker, p. 115. **22.** Gabriel, "The Tilari," p. 34. **23.** Masson and Sarianidi, p. 35. **24.** Ibid., p. 58; Bacon, p. 267. **25.** Pogue, p. 75. There are numerous references at this time to children buried with beads. See Masson and Sarianidi, pp. 64–65. **26.** Masson and Sarianidi, pp. 80, 89. **27.** Ibid., pp. 115–16. **28.** Ibid., p. 119. **29.** Ibid., p. 125. **30.** Fitzgibbon and Hale, "Jewelry of the Ancient Lapis Route," p. 78. **31.** Masson and Sarianidi, pp. 168–69. **32.** Ibid., pp. 145–46. **33.** Barraclough, p. 60; McNeill, p. 104. **34.** Chard, p. 153. **35.** Masson and Sarianidi, p. 151. Mid-second to first millennium B.C. Bronze Age sites, such as Kokcha on the northern steppes of Turkmenistan, yielded beads of bronze, sardonyx, and faience. At Muminabad in the Samarkand oasis, a single burial contained over 1,000 beads. In the Kirghizia Valley, one grave yielded 1300 bronze, faience, and antimony beads, many of which had been sewn onto clothing. **36.** Chard, p. 152. **37.** Forbes, p. 163. **38.** Jettmar, p. 97; Levin and Potapov, n.p. **39.** Peter Francis, letter to author, January 1986. **40.** Forbes, p. 163.

41. Neuburg, p. 29. **42.** Rockhill, p. 24. **43.** Lance, p. 19. **44.** Casady, p. 78; Fitzgibbon and Hale, "Jewelry of the Turkic Tribes," p. 77. **45.** Lance, p. 19.

I. Although originally given to the Ngor Monastery in Tibet, the necklace was retrieved by the Lama Kinga after the Chinese takeover of Tibet and carried out of the country. Ivory Friedus, letter to author, June 1984. **II.** Zwalf, pp. 131, 136; Gabriel, "Himalayan Portraits," *passim.* **III.** Newark Museum, vol. II, p. 11. **IV.** The following descriptions were provided by David Ebbinghouse. *Left to right:* (1) This is an example of a bead that has been artificially treated to bring out the lines in the stone by the application of white lines that follow the natural banding. (2) White lines do not follow natural lines in the agate, but take forms similar to the previous example. However, the natural eyelike forms in the agate are incorporated into the design and become part of the pattern. (3) The patterns are similar to example 2 but one end of the bead did not take the blackening process and the white line curves around the end of this zone (suggesting that the white lines were applied subsequent to the blackening process). (4) *Top:* entirely blackened bead with applied white stripes. *Bottom:* central area blackened and bordered with white stripes. The ends are left untreated. (5) *Top:* it appears that both light and dark stripes have been applied, but both are very watery and transparent. *Bottom:* the bead appears to have been completely darkened and white stripes applied, but the blackening is very light brown and the white stripes have taken unevenly. (6) Bead was completely blackened with white lines applied subsequently. This very plump shape is similar to natural agate beads from the Namazga culture of about 2000 B.C. (7) These beads have been both blackened and whitened. Beads of this pattern are very highly prized by Tibetans today and are frequently displayed in a traditional ensemble (plates 214 and 220). (8) The steps turn in opposite directions in each bead. A highly prized bead. (9) These are considered more precious than eyed-patterns by Tibetans, possibly because they are rarer than the longer beads. (10) The "Earth-Door, Sky-Door" bead has a square on one side, and a circle on the other. (11) Although not considered to be a pure *dZi* by most Tibetans, this bead has extremely uncommon markings and a better than usual shape for a *phum dZi.* Tibetans consider it in the *dZi* family, but not nearly as powerful an amulet. The figure and cartouche are puzzling, but suggest connections to ancient Persia during Sasanian times. **V.** The following classification of the *dZi* beads shown in plate 217 follows the system described in note XI: *Top to bottom:* (1) Nine-eyed "pure" *dZi.* At present, although it is an "etched" bead, none of the existing techniques as originally described by Beck explain its manufacturing process. This bead needs its own technical category. (2) Variety A: a combination of types I and II. The end bands are left untreated. Dark bands are applied over a whitened area, leaving narrower white bands. (3) Type II? (4) Natural agate. **VI.** Ebbinghouse and Winsten, "Tibetan *dZi* Beads I," p. 24. **VII.** Ibid. **VIII.** Thupten Pheloye, conversation with author, November 1983. **IX.** Ebbinghouse and Winsten, "Tibetan *dZi* Beads," vol. I, pp. 24–25. **X.** Similar beads—white chalcedony with dark brown geometric patterns that could be

dZi predecessors—have been excavated from sites in India, Afghanistan, and Turkmenistan that date back to 1500–1000 B.C. Francis, "Followup: dZi Beads," pp. 55–56. **XI.** The following classification system of "etching" (a misnomer) agate beads is based on the original work of Horace Beck with additions as noted by David Ebbinghouse and Michael Winsten in "Tibetan dZi Beads," vol. I: pp. 19–25; and Jamey Allen, conversation with author, October 1986. *Type I:* white design on natural stone background. An alkali (usually potash or white lead) is painted onto the bead's surface and then the bead is fired. This permanently whitens the area of the bead covered with the alkali. This whitening is not merely a glaze; depending on how porous the stone is, it often penetrates it. *Type II:* black design on whitened background. The entire bead is whitened, and then a design is painted with another chemical, often copper nitrate. The bead is fired again, producing a dark design on a white background (Bead Chart 604a-c). Note: There may be no type II. The colors may originally have been carnelian with white patterns that changed color after exposure to fire, (in a cremation, for example.) *Type III:* black design on natural stone background. Sometimes a dark design is applied to the natural stone. *Variety A:* a combination of types I and II. Part of the bead is first whitened, leaving part of the bead unwhitened. The black design is etched over the whitened part of the bead. *Variety B:* a combination of types I and III. Both black and white patterns appear on the same bead, but do not overlap, like variety A. None of these methods appear to describe the manufacture of "pure" *dZi* (see top bead, plate 217). Ebbinghouse and Winsten believe that they were made by black and white being added side by side, and suggest placing pure *dZi* as a subclass of type II. Jamey Allen believes the beads are artificially darkened, with the white designs subsequently added. Allen suggests the possibility of type IV or variety C. **XII.** Newark Museum Tibetan Collection, vol. IV: pp. 68–69; Ebbinghouse and Winsten, "Tibetan *dZi* beads," pp. 36–38. Ebbinghouse hypothesizes that the beads might date to between 1500 and 500 B.C., possibly an offshoot of the Harrapan/Sumerian bead tradition. Also, he does not believe that all *dZi* are of the same age or origins, based on the fact that the markings tend to become stylized with a relatively small repertoire of stable design patterns. David Ebbinghouse, letter to author, July 1986. **XIII.** Ebbinghouse and Winsten, "Tibetan *dZi* Beads," vol. I, pp. 19–24. "Pure" *dZi* beads must be made of genuine etched agate with a very shiny or glossy surface free of alkali from the etching process. It should also have a desirable pattern such as the nine-eyed pattern, or a circle and a square, symbolizing "Earth Door and Sky Door." Shape is very important—the bead should be plump and healthy looking. If they are too thin ("anemic looking") or not round in cross section, they are less desirable. Deep colors increase the value of *dZi*; colors should be true black or deep rich brown. Opacity is also a consideration: when the bead is held up to the light, it should not be translucent. Finally, "pure" *dZi* should not have pattern flaws (caused by differences in the underlying agate structure, which results in uneven whitening). The beads should be in good condition with no chips.

S.E. ASIA AND SOUTH PACIFIC

1. Holt, p. 4; Fraser-Lu, n.p. **2.** Lamb, "Some Observations on Stone and Glass Beads," *passim*. **3.** Rodgers, pp. 21–22. **4.** Ibid., pp. 41–43. **5.** Legarda, p. 64; Dunsmore, Introduction. **6.** Maxwell, p. 136. **7.** Dunsmore, Introduction. **8.** Chongkol, p. 82. **9.** Francis, "Thailand," p. 44. **10.** Ibid. **11.** Ibid.; White, p. 76; Francis, p. 44 and letter to author, January 1986. **12.** Chongkol, pp. 82–83. **13.** Casal, p. 46. **14.** Rawson, *passim*; Rodgers, pp. 32–34. **15.** Rawson, pp. 203–71. **16.** Lamb, "Some Observations on Stone and Glass Beads," pp. 94–98. **17.** Ibid., *passim*; Dunsmore, p. 5. **18.** Dunsmore, p. 5. **19.** Ibid., p. 3. **20.** Lamb, "A Note on Glass Beads," p. 84. **21.** Rodgers, pp. 117–21; Adams, *passim*. **22.** Fraser-Lu, n.p. **23.** Rodgers, p. 121. **24.** Casal, p. 34. **25.** Ibid., p. 52. The earliest glass bead excavated in the Philippines was spherical in shape and made of blue glass with many bubbles. It dates to c. 400 B.C. and is of a type found throughout Southeast Asia. **26.** Ibid., p. 71. **27.** Legarda, "Pre-Hispanic Gold," p. 94. **28.** Ibid., p. 96. **29.** Lamb, "Some Observations on Stone and Glass Beads," p. 95. **30.** Legarda, p. 61. **31.** Ibid., pp. 61–70. **32.** Rodgers, p. 243. **33.** Ibid., p. 254. **34.** Ibid. **35.** Ibid., p. 246. **36.** Liu, "Formosan Ornaments," pp. 21–27. **37.** Ibid.; Francis, *Chinese Glass Beads*, p. 33. Large polychrome glass beads with distinctive millefiore and dragged trail decoration (Bead Chart 903) are currently being excavated in Indonesia, primarily in East Java sites dating from the Majapahit culture (c. 1375–1525). Although the beads have been dated by Yoshimizu to 1600–1800, Liu ("Asian Glass Ornaments Part 1") Derek Content (telephone conversation with author, September 1985) and Jamey D. Allen, (conversation with author, October 1986) believe they are older. These millefiore beads, while resembling those of the Roman era, differ considerably from Roman examples. Indonesian millefiore have very thin cane layers fused to a coarse, opaque central glass core, while ancient Roman era beads have canes that typically extend to the perforation. (An exception are some face beads.) Liu, "Asian Glass Ornaments, Part 1." It has been suggested that possibly the cane layers on the Indonesian beads were cut locally from pre-formed glass ingots manufactured in the Roman Empire. Their thinness may reflect the judicious use of a rare material that came from far away. Derek Content, letter to author, September 1985. **38.** Rodgers, p. 61; Newton, pp. 4–5. **39.** Ross, pp. 20–26; Burt, pp. 6–7. **I.** Lamb, "A Note on Glass Beads," p. 94. **II.** Lewis, pp. 206, 214–16. **III.** Maxwell, pp. 131–40. **IV.** Dunsmore, p. 13; Rodgers, pp. 118–19. **V.** Rodgers, p. 118. **VI.** Casal, pp. 158–59. **VII.** Chen, pp. 163–69, plate 12. **VIII.** Liu, "Formosan Ornaments," pp. 21–27; and "Asian Glass Ornaments Part 1," pp. 28–31; Chen, pp. 357–66; Miyamoto, pp. 89–91. **IX.** This information was obtained from the collector Province M. Henry and submitted to the registrar of the Smithsonian Institution on March 20, 1965, as "General Comments Concerning Formosan Aboriginal Beads." Also see Blair, p. 204. **X.** Ross, pp. 20–36. **XI.** Ibid., p. 23.

MIDDLE AND S. AMERICA

1. Dr. Richard S. MacNeish, letter to author, 9 January 1984. **2.** Robert Liu, conversation with author, November 1986. **3.** Easby, pp. 14–16; Abel-Vidor, pp. 138–39. **4.** Easby, p. 8. **5.** Emmerich, *Sweat of the Sun*, p. 146. **6.** Ibid., pp. 146–49. **7.** Both may be white, various shades of gray, pea green, grass green, emerald green, or blue green. Both also may be mottled or translucent. The emerald green and blue green shades tend to be jadeite, while nephrite also occurs in yellows, oranges, and purples. **8.** Easby, p. 7. **9.** Ibid., pp. 16–26. A weathered jade boulder had to be broken to gain access to the gemlike quality stone within it. The stone was then ground, sawed, grooved, incised, drilled, and polished. The preliminary shaping of the bead depended on fracturing, grinding, and sawing. Some beads, like the bar bead in plate 256 (front left), were shaped entirely by the sawing technique. Cuts were also made with a wooden instrument or with an agave fiber or cord coated with an abrasive, an ancient technique known as "cord sawing." Sawing with a string, a technique apparently invented by the Olmec, enabled craftsmen to make round or angular cuts that could not be made with rigid tools. The drill point, usually a hollow piece of bird bone or bamboo cane, was filled with sand or emery abrasive. Hollow sections of bamboo cane, *Arundinaria*, locally available to Costa Rican lapidaries, were often used for drilling as well as polishing jade, because the plant contains its own abrasive in the form of tiny silica particles. The beads, many of which have an extraordinary soft, almost velvety luster, were finished by being burnished with wood or by polishing with beeswax or jade powder. Easby, pp. 16–26. **10.** Emmerich, *Sweat of the Sun*, p. xix. **11.** Ibid., pp. xxii, 66–68. **12.** Ibid., p. xxii. **13.** Ibid., p. 98; Lothrop, pp. 158–59. **14.** Stierlin, p. 121; Andre Emmerich, conversation with author, December 1985. **15.** Weaver, p. 466. **16.** Emmerich, *Sweat of the Sun*, pp. 131–32; Stierlin, pp. 112–20. **16.** Kessler, "Beads of the Tairona," pp. 3–5. **17.** Peter Francis, letter to author, January 1986, and Earl and Shari Kessler, "Ecuadorian Beads," pp. 48–52. **18.** Easby, p. 143. **19.** Liu, "Identification: Smallest and Largest Beads," p. 69. **20.** Smith and Good, *passim*; Liu and Harris, pp. 3–8. **21.** Smith and Good, p. 4; quoted from *The True History of the Conquest of New Spain* by Bernal Diaz del Castillo (vol. 2), edited by Genaro Garcias, (London: Hakluyt Society, 1910), original translation by Albert Percival Maudslay. **22.** Davis and Pack, pp. 20, 35. **23.** Liu and Harris, pp. 5, 7–11; Smith and Good, *passim*. **24.** Smith and Good, pp. 10–11. **25.** Liu and Harris, pp. 3–11. For extensive discussions of *Nueva Cádiz* beads, see Liu and Harris, and Smith and Good. **26.** Johnson, pp. 18–19. **I.** Easby, pp. 64–66. Both disk-shaped and elaborately carved bar and tubular jade beads are typical of Costa Rica, while round beads are quite rare. Single, large sculptural beads are believed to have been strung on necklaces of jade disk beads. **II.** Proskouriakoff, p. 18. **III.** Ibid. **IV.** Robicsek, *passim*; Andre Emmerich, conversation with author, December 1985. **V.** Emmerich, *Art Before Columbus*, pp. 59–60. **VI.** Emmerich, *Sweat of the Sun*, pp. xxii, 7–8; Tushingham et al., *passim*; Orchard, pp. 62–63. The technique began in Chavin times. Ancient Peruvian craftsmen cut, embossed, bent, shaped, forged, and punched very thin gold sheets to attain the desired forms. Sheet gold was made by placing melted nuggets between animal hides and beating the hardened metal with a stone hammer. When the process of annealing (reheating metal to restore its ductability) was discovered, it became possible to hammer gold into very thin sheets which were then cut with sharp stone chisels into strips or complex shapes. Beads of clay or charcoal were often covered with a thin layer of gold. **VII.** Tushingham et al., *passim*. Peruvian metallurgists seldom used soldering, preferring methods of joining metal that required only moderate skill and no application of external heat. This meant joining by lacing, stapling, crimping (bending of the edge of one sheet tightly over the edge of another), or inserting the edge of one sheet into slots of another. In joining two pieces of metal together, Chimu metalsmiths expressed an aesthetic observable in the textiles produced by their culture. For example, narrow weavings were joined to form broad textiles without attention to the alignment of design in the attached sections. A similar lack of attention to alignment is seen in the joined sections of Peruvian beads made from thin gold sheets. The gold ball beads in plate 259 show unrefined joints, as does the crimping technique on the mask beads (plate 258). **VIII.** Ibid., p. 14. **IX.** Kessler, "Beads of the Tairona," pp. 3–5. The Tairona wore beads at festivals, and also assigned religious significance to them. The Kogi, modern descendants of the Tairona, recall that their ancestors "danced with objects of red rock to call the summer and green rock to call the rains. Rock crystal beads were used as offerings to the spirits of rain and Water and to Mother Universe." Many Kogi own beads inherited from their Tairona ancestors and still use them for ritual purposes. **X.** Ibid. **XI.** It is possible this, as well as the pottery objects shown in plate 270 are not beads but spindle whorls, weights used in the spinning of fibers into yarn. Rebecca Northern, pp. 14-20.

NORTH AMERICA

1. Jernigan, pp. 10–11. Archaeologists working at Tule Springs, Nevada, have found a bead of white caliche (hardened carbonate) possibly dating to 11,000 B.C.—perhaps the earliest known bead from North America. **2.** Mathews, p. 10. **3.** Francis, *Beads and the Discovery of the New World*, pp. 14–17. **4.** Streuver, p. 62. **5.** Francis, *Beads and the Discovery of the New World*, p. 7. **6.** Jernigan, p. 15. **7.** Francis, *Beads and the Discovery of the New World*, p. 22. **8.** Gillette, *passim*; Orchard, pp. 71–83; Speck and Orchard, *passim*; Grand Rapids Public Museum, pp. 16–22; Brasser, p. 126. **9.** Brasser, p. 26. **10.** Francis, *Beads and the Discovery of the New World*, p. 24. **11.** Ibid., p. 25. **12.** Francis, *Beads and the Discovery of the New World*, p. 33; Smith and Good, *passim*. Other materials were traded in. Carnelian and rock crystal along with glass were brought to the Caribbean and Florida by the Spanish. **13.** Francis, *Beads and the Discovery of the New World*, p. 32. **14.** Orchard, p. 16. **15.** Ibid., p. 102. **16.** Orchard, pp. 17–18. **17.** Good, p. 16. **18.** Conn, *Circles of the World*, p. 141. **19.** Harris, *The Russian Bead*, pp. 1–9. The origin of "Russian" beads remains questionable. See Kidd, "Problems in Glass Trade Bead Research," p. 2. **20.** Francis, *Beads and the Discovery of the New World*, pp. 41–43. **21.** Orchard, pp. 104–162; Gil, Part 1, pp. 42–51; Part 2, p. 44–49; Lyford, *passim*. **22.** Dockstader, p. 20. **23.** Furst and Furst, p. 165. **24.** Brasser, p. 20. **25.** Wildschut and Ewers, p. 1. **26.** Dockstader, p. 45. **27.** Lyford, pp. 67–71.

28. "A great deal of beadwork is being done to enhance the costumes at the powwows. During the last twenty years, I have seen a change from pieces of beadwork imported from Hong Kong to more traditional designs being beaded by the dancers and their families. Beadwork classes are well attended at Indian centers and other places such as museums.... The Native American Church uses many objects which require beading. Some of the most beautiful beading today is being done on the handles of rattles etc. using size 13 and smaller beads (usually faceted) and the 'peyote stitch.' Barbara Robertson, letter to author, May 1986.
I. See Holstein and Erdman; Jacka and Hammack, Pogue, Rosnek and Stacey. **II.** Conn, *Native American Art*, p. 353. **III.** Smith and Good, p. 3. **IV.** The Algonquins, in particular, did not realize that land sales meant they could no longer use their land, one example of the differences between European and Indian concepts of property ownership. **V.** Furst and Furst, pp. 165, 170–172. **VI.** Driscoll, pp. 40–47; Winnipeg Art Gallery, *passim*. **VII.** Conn, p. 141. **VIII.** It should be noted that in plates 294 and 297 figures a and d are appliquéd while the objects in 295 and 296 are woven. The technique of weaving has obviously influenced the stylizing of the floral designs in 295. Nevertheless, there were preferences for geometric forms by tribes further west. **IX.** King, p. 32; Lenssen, *passim*; Conn, *Native American Art*, p. 139. **X.** Conn, *Circles of the World*, pp. 8–9. **XI.** Ibid., p. 29. **XII.** Ibid., p. 28. **XIII.** *Chetro Ketl*, p. 4.

THE SPECIAL BEADS

1. Kunz and Stevenson, p. 404. **2.** Poinar, p. 29. Resin from an extinct pine or conifer tree was, for the past hundred years, considered to be the source of amber. More recent studies, however, suggest a species of *Agathis* (the broadleaf Kauri gum of New Zealand is *Aganthis australis*), a genus found in many warm parts of the world. Forty million years ago—the estimated age of most Baltic amber—the climate of the Baltic was subtropical. Today the climate is temperate, and the *aganthis* forests are long gone. **3.** Fagan, p. 160. **4.** Rice, p. 32. **5.** Allen, "Amber and Its Substitutes, Part 1," pp. 18–20; Rice, pp. 35–36; Charles Picard, p. 340. **6.** Rice, p. 36. **7.** Ogden, p. 116. **8.** Shaw, p. 253. **9.** Ibid., p. 219. **10.** *Elektron*, meaning "golden," may derive from a Phoenician word for the sun. **11.** Ibid., p. 220; Ogden, p. 177. **12.** Kunz, pp. 55–56. **13.** Buffum, p. 77. **14.** Ibid., pp. 17–20. The Etruscans' interest in amber went beyond adornment. Follett mentions that Etruscan goldsmiths, famed for their exquisite filigree and granulated jewelry, ingeniously used amber as flux in the granulation process. Follett, pp. 64–65. **15.** Allen, "Amber and Its Substitutes," p. 16. **16.** Hunger, p. 105. **17.** Baltic amber is also called succinite from its characteristic succinic acid content (3 to 8 percent). A lack of succinic acid usually indicates an origin other than the Baltic formation period. Outside the Baltic, succinite has been found in small quantities at several other locales, including England and Thailand. The ambers from Sicily (simetite), Rumania (rumanite), and Burma (burmite) differ from those of the Baltic as they have little or no succinic acid. In addition, rumanite and burmite are younger than succinite, and were formed during the Miocene period, 10 to 25 million years ago, For further reference, see Allen, "Amber and Its Substitutes," Parts 1

and 2. **18.** Allen, "Amber and Its Substitutes," Part 2, pp. 12–13. **19.** Ibid., p. 12. **20.** Ibid. **21.** Buffum, pp. 9–28. **22.** Allen, "Amber and Its Substitutes, Part 2," p. 12. **23.** Cloudy amber resin was formed within the trees to heal splits and cracks. Although there has been some discussion about the relationship between resin flows and opaqueness, (see Poinar, p. 29) Jamey D. Allen who has studied amber extensively does not believe there is any validity to the comparison. From his studies, Allen theorizes that resin flows exuded on warm days are thin, runny, and clear, while cool weather causes thick and cloudy resin deposits. Jamey D. Allen, conversation with author, September 1986. **24.** While it is complex to determine the presence or lack of succinite acid, to differentiate between true amber and amberlike objects, Jamey D. Allen has devised a simple test using a hot-point such as a darning needle. The hot-point test indicates the object's composition by the manner in which the specimen burns, as well as by its odor. **25.** Ibid., Part 2, pp. 14–15. **26.** Ibid., Part 1, p. 19. **27.** Ibid., Part 2, p. 15; Part 3, p. 20. **28.** Jamey D. Allen, conversation with author, September 1986. **29.** Kunz and Stevenson, p. 5; Streeter, pp. 57–61. **30.** Kunz and Stevenson, p. 36. **31.** Ibid., pp. 51–52; Sitwell, p. 43. **32.** King, p. 267; Kunz and Stevenson, p. 53. **33.** Kunz and Stevenson, p. 145. **34.** Ibid., p. 5. Also see plate opposite 404. **35.** Ibid., p. 10. Ibid., p. 9. **37.** Ibid., p. 449. **38.** Ibid., p. 9. **39.** See illustration in Gregorietti on page 128. **40.** Kunz and Stevenson, pp. 16–18. **41.** Ibid., p. 21. **42.** Addison, p. 56. **43.** Gregorietti, p. 192. **44.** Kuntzsch, p. 119. **45.** Ogden, p. 121. **46.** Kunz and Stevenson, p. 460. **47.** Weinstein, p. 79. **48.** Peter Francis, letter to author, January 1986. **49.** Kunz and Stevenson, pp. 184–85. **50.** Ibid., p. 225. **51.** Weinstein, pp. 83–84. **52.** Kunz and Stevenson, p. 251. **53.** Kunz and Stevenson, p. 258. **54.** Ibid., p. 259. **55.** Ibid., pp. 29–31. **56.** Nadelhoffer, pp. 125, 133. **57.** Sitwell, pp. 45–46; Kunz and Stevenson, pp. 266–68, 281–82. **58.** Kunz and Stevenson, p. 261. **59.** Ibid., pp. 130, 297, and Chapter 3, note 13; Sitwell, p. 48. **60.** Birmingham, p. 148; Sitwell, p. 45; Nadelhoffer, p. 136. **61.** Birmingham, p. 196. **62.** Sitwell, p. 48. Natural pearls have not totally disappeared. Most are antiques, but a small quantity of new ones do appear on the market. The chances of finding a round pearl in a cultivated oyster range from one in ten to one in fifty; in natural pearls the odds lengthen to one or two per thousand. **63.** Ibid., p. 50. **64.** Birmingham, p. 198. **I.** Nadelhoffer, p. 125. **II.** Ibid., pp. 125, 130.

THE MAGICAL EYE BEAD

1. Maloney, pp. 5–16. **2.** Di Stasi, pp. 112–13. **3.** Erikson, pp. 170–72. **4.** Budge, p. 358. **5.** Maloney, p. 143. **6.** Ibid., pp. 7–9. **7.** Schienerl, pp. 28, 52. **8.** Budge, p. 359. **9.** Stillman, p. 91. **10.** Budge, pp. 355–59. **11.** Maloney, p. 234. **12.** Ibid., pp. 144–45, 295–99. **13.** Erikson, p. 176. **14.** Lamb, "Some Observations on Stone and Glass Beads," p. 121. **15.** Eisen, pp. 1–24. **16.** Venclova, p. 16. **17.** Derek Content, conversation with author, August 1986. **18.** Delazoire, p. 25. **19.** This has been observed by the author throughout the researching of this project. S. J. Kennedy, in "Some Aspects of Children's Amulets," and Erikson also mention the importance of the color blue in warding off the evil eye. **20.** Maloney, p. 50. **21.** Kennedy, p. 52. **22.** Budge, p. 354.
I. Eye beads and head pendants are found

together in Mediterranean and European sites dating from about 700–200 B.C. **II.** (1–3) Banded agates from Iran, Syria, or Iraq, late fourth to third millennium B.C. (4) Banded agate from Iran, Syria, or Iraq, third to second millennium B.C. (5) "Etched" carnelian of the Indus Valley or Mesopotamia, third millennium B.C. (6) Western Asian double-eye agate, third to first millennium B.C. (7) Western Asian agate base with glass binder layer and "eye," second to first millennium B.C. (8–9) Western Asian stratified glass imitating banded agate, second to first millennium B.C. (10) Western Asian or Egyptian stratified glass, late second to first millennium B.C. (11) Wound glass with impressed coils and stratified eyes from New Kingdom Egypt, Eighteenth to Nineteenth dynasties (1400–1300 B.C.). (12–14) Wound glass with stratified eyes from New Kingdom Egypt, Eighteenth to Nineteenth dynasties (1400–1300 B.C.). (15–17) Phoenician wound glass with stratified eyes, 700–300 B.C. (18) Phoenician or Egyptian wound glass with composite stratified eyes and raised spots, c. 500 B.C. (19) Egyptian wound glass with eye spots, 600–250 B.C. (20) Phoenician wound glass with spirally wound coils and raised stratified eyes from Carthage or Syro-Lebanese coast, 500–300 B.C. (21) Egyptian wound glass with raised stratified eyes, 500–300 B.C. (22) Wound glass with mosaic glass inserts from Gilan, Iran, 300 B.C. (23) Wound glass with stratified eyes from Persepolis, Iran, 300 B.C. (24–26) Chinese wound glass with stratified eyes, 400–200 B.C. (27) Wound glass with stratified eyes from western Asia, Egypt, and Europe, c. 700 B.C.–A.D. 100. (28) Celtic wound glass with trailed spiral eyes upon vestigial horn, 300 B.C.–A.D. 100. (29–31) Roman wound glass with stratified eyes, 100 B.C.–A.D. 200. (32) Roman (?) mosaic glass canes, no core, from Djenne, Mali, A.D. 1–300 (?). (33) Viking period wound glass with trailed designs and mosaic glass insets, A.D. 800–1000. (34) Wound glass with stratified eyes from Borneo, A.D. 1500 (?). (35) West African powder glass, twentieth century. (36) West African powder-glass *bodom* bead, early twentieth century. (37) Venetian wound glass with polychrome eye, nineteenth century. (38) Venetian drawn glass with polychrome eyes, nineteenth century. (39) Bone from Nepal, nineteenth century. (40) Venetian wound glass with polychrome eyes, nineteenth century. (41) Venetian wound glass with polychrome eyes and designs, nineteenth century. (42) Venetian mosaic glass canes on center core, nineteenth century. (43–44) Venetian wound glass with polychrome eyes, nineteenth century. (45) Wound glass with stratified eyes from Goerce, Turkey, 1893. (1–46) All private collection except as follows: 1–3, 5, 7–14, 18, collection Henry Anavian, New York; 4, 6, collection Derek Content, Houlton, Maine; 19, 20, 26, 38, Corning Museum of Glass, Corning, New York; 23, British Museum, London; 24, 25, Royal Ontario Museum, Toronto; 36, collection Dr. Michael Heide, Portland; 39, collection Ivory Freidus.

THE TWENTIETH CENTURY

1. Kennedy, S.J. "Nyhus Design Glasswear," p. 16. **2.** Cartlidge, p. 40; Heininger, p. 246. **3.** Gordon and Nerenberg, p. 4. **4.** Black, pp. 278, 287–89. **5.** Cartlidge, p. 75. **6.** Ibid., p. 11. **7.** Kennedy and Liu, pp. 18–19. **8.** Black, Introduction.
I. Kennedy, S. J. "Nyhus Design Glasswear," p. 17. **II.** Benesh, pp. 20–22.

Bibliography

Abel-Vidor, Suzanne, et al. "Jade." In *Pre-Columbian Art of Costa Rica*, edited by Elizabeth Kennedy Easby. Detroit and New York: Detroit Institute of the Arts and Harry N. Abrams, 1981.

Adams, Monni. *Threads of Life: A Private Collection of Textiles from Indonesia and Sarawak*. Katonah, N.Y.: The Katonah Gallery, 1981.

Addison, Julia deWolf. *Arts and Crafts in the Middle Ages*. Boston: The Page Company, 1908.

Akiyama, T., et al. *Arts of China, Neolithic Culture to the T'ang Dynasty: Recent Discoveries*. Tokyo: Kodansha International, 1968.

Aldred, Cyril. *Jewels of the Pharaohs*. London: Thames and Hudson, 1971.

Allen, Jamey D. "Amber and Its Substitutes." Parts 1–3. *The Bead Journal* 2–3, nos. 3, 4, 1 (1976): 15–20, 20–31, 11–22.

———. "Cane Manufacture for Mosaic Glass Beads." Parts 1, 2. *Ornament* 5, 6, nos. 4, 1 (1982): 6–11, 13.

———. "Chevron-Star Rosetta Beads." Parts 1–4. *Ornament* 7, nos. 1–4 (1983–84): 24–29, 19–24, 24–27, 24–26.

———. "Correspondence." *Ornament* 6, no. 2 (1982): 60.

———. "The Manufacture of Intricate Glass Canes and a New Perspective on the Relationship Between Chevron-Star Beads and Mosaic-Millefiore Beads." In *Proceedings of the 1982 Glass Trade Bead Conference*, edited by Charles F. Hayes, III. Rochester, N.Y.: Rochester Museum and Science Center, 1983: 173–191.

Al-Jadir, Saad. *Arab and Islamic Silver*. London: Stacey International, 1981.

Andrews, Carol. *Catalogue of Egyptian Antiquities in the British Museum*. Vol. 6, *Jewellery I: From the Earliest Times to the Seventeenth Dynasty*. London: British Museum Publications, 1981.

———. *Egyptian Jewellery, Predynastic to End of Dynastic Period*. London: British Museum Publications, 1976.

Arakawa, Hirokazu. *The Go Collection of Netsuke*. Tokyo: Kodansha International, 1983.

Arkell, A. J. "Cambay and the Bead Trade." *Antiquity* 10 (1936): 292–305.

The Art of William Harper. New York: Kennedy Galleries, 1981.

Bacon, Edward. *Vanished Civilizations*. London: Thames and Hudson, 1963.

Ballet, Dr. "La paure aux epogues paleolithiques anciennes." *Bulletin de la Societie Prehistorique Française* 7, no. 2 (1915).

Barbier, Jean-Paul. *Art du Nagaland*. Geneva: Musée Barbier-Muller, 1982.

Barker, Evelyn, and David Barker. "Ethnic Jewellery of Nepal." *Arts of Asia* 14 (1984): n.p.

Barker, Richard, and Lawrence Smith. *Netsuke, The Miniature Sculpture of Japan*. London: British Museum Publications, 1976.

Barraclough, Geoffrey. *The Times Atlas of World History*. Maplewood, N.J.: Hammond, 1980.

Beads: Their Use by Upper Great Lakes Indians. Grand Rapids, Michigan: Grand Rapids Public Museum, 1977.

Bebbington, Julia M. *Quillwork of the Plains*. Calgary, Alberta: Glenbow Museum, 1982.

Beck, Horace C. "Etched Carnelian Beads." *The Antiquaries Journal* 12 (1933): 384–98.

Beier, Ulli. *Yoruba Beaded Crown: Sacred Regalia of the Olokuku of Okuku*. London: Ethnographia, 1982.

Belenitsky, Aleksandr. *Central Asia*. London: Barrie and Rockliff, The Cresset Press, 1969.

Benesh, Carolyn L. E. "William Harper." *Ornament* 6, no. 2 (1982): 20–22.

Besborodov, M. A., and J. A. Zadneprovsky. "Early Stages of Glassmaking in the USSR." *Slava Antiqua* 12 (1965): n.p.

Bibby, Geoffrey. *Looking for Dilmun*. New York: Alfred A. Knopf, 1970.

Birmingham, Nan. "The Peerless Pearl." *Town and Country* 135 (June 1981): n.p.

Black, J. Anderson. *A History of Jewelry*. New York: Park Lane, 1981.

Blair, Dorothy. *A History of Glass in Japan*. Tokyo and Corning, N.Y.: Kodansha International and the Corning Museum of Glass, 1973.

Bosse-Griffiths, Kate. *Pictures from the Wellcome Collection*. No. 1, *Beadwork*. Swansea, Wales: University College, 1978.

Branigan, K. *The Atlas of Archaeology*. New York: St. Martin's Press, 1982.

Brasser, Ted J. "Pleasing the Spirits: Indian Art Around the Great Lakes." In *Pleasing the Spirits*, edited by Douglas C. Ewing. New York: Ghylen Press, 1982.

Brijbhushan, Jamila. *Masterpieces of Indian Jewellery*. Bombay: D. B. Taraporevala Sons & Co., 1979.

Brown, Peter. *The World of Late Antiquity*. London: Thames and Hudson, 1971.

Budge, E. A. Wallis. *Amulets and Talismans*. New York: Collier, 1970.

Buffum, W. Arnold. *The Tears of the Heliades*. London: Sampson Low, Marston & Company, 1896.

Burt, Ben. *Solomon Islanders: The Kwara'ae*. London: British Museum Publications, 1981.

Callmer, Johan. *Trade Beads and Bead Trade in Scandinavia c. 800–1000 A.D.*, Bonn West Germany, and Lund, Sweden: Rudolf Habelt and C.W.K. Gleerup, 1977.

Cammann, Schuyler V. R. "Ch'ing Dynasty Mandarin Chains." *Ornament* 4, no. 1 (1979): 25–29.

Campbell, Bernard G. *Humankind Emerging*. 2d ed. Boston: Little, Brown and Company, 1979.

Canton-Thompson, Gertrude. "A Commentary of Dr. Laidler's Article on Beads in Africa South of the Zambesi." *Rhodesia Scientific Association Proceedings and Transactions* 34, Pt. 2 (1936): 10–118.

Cartlidge, Barbara. *Twentieth-Century Jewelry*. New York: Harry N. Abrams, 1985.

Casal, Gabriel, and Regalado Trota José, Jr. *The People and Arts of the Philippines*. Los Angeles: Museum of Cultural History, University of California, 1981.

Casanowicz, Immanuel M. *The Collection of Rosaries in the United States National Museum*. Washington, D.C.: Government Printing Office, 1909.

Chandra, Rai Govind. *Indo-Greek Jewellery*. New Delhi: Abhinav Publications, 1979.

———. *Studies in the Development of Ornaments and Jewellery in Proto-Historic India*. Varranasi, India: The Chowkhamba Sanskrit Series Office, 1964.

Chard, Chester. *Northeast Asia in Prehistory*. Madison: University of Wisconsin Press, 1974.

Charles-Picard, Gilbert. *Larousse En-*

Bead Technology." *Ornament* 10, no. 1 (1986): 18–23.

Kessler, Earl, and Shari Kessler. "Beads of the Tairona." *The Bead Journal* 3, no. 3 (1978): 2–5.

_____. "Ecuadorian Beads: Ancient to Modern." *Ornament* 20, no. 2 (1986): 48–52.

Kidd, Kenneth E. *Glass Bead-Making from the Middle Ages to the Early 19th Century.* History and Archaeology series, no. 30. Ottawa, Canada: National Historic Parks and Sites Branch, 1979.

_____. "Problems in Glass Trade Bead Research." In *Proceedings of the 1982 Glass Trade Bead Conference*, edited by Charles F. Hayes, III. Rochester, N.Y.: Rochester Museum and Science Center, 1982.

King, C. W. *The Natural History of Precious Stones and of the Precious Metals.* London: Bell and Daldy, 1870.

Klima, Bohuslav. "The First Ground-Plan of an Upper Paleolithic Loess Settlement in Middle Europe and Its Meaning." In *Courses Toward Urban Life.* Wenner-Gren, N.Y.: Braidwood and Wiley, 1962.

Klimburg-Salter, Deborah. *The Silk Road and the Diamond Path.* Los Angeles: U.C.L.A. Art Council, 1982.

Knight, Natalie, and Suzanne Priebatsch. *Ndebele Images.* Johannesburg: Productions, Ltd., 1983.

Kolbas, Judith G. "A Color Chronology of Islamic Glass." *Journal of Glass Studies* 25 (1983): 95–100.

Kramrisch, Stella. *The Art of Nepal.* New York: The Asia Society, 1964.

Kuntzsch, Ingrid. *A History of Jewels and Jewelery.* New York: St. Martin's Press, 1981.

Kunz, G. F. *The Curious Lore of Precious Stones.* New York: Halcyon House, 1913.

Kunz, George Frederick, and Charles Hugh Stevenson. *The Book of the Pearl. The History, Art, Science, and Industry of the Queen of Gems.* New York: The Century Company, 1908.

Laidler, P. W. "Beads in Africa South of the Zambesi." *Rhodesia Scientific Association Proceedings and Transactions* 34, no. 1 (1934).

Lamb, Alastair. "Krobo Powder-Glass Beads." *African Arts* 9, no. 3 (1976): 23–27.

_____. "A Note on Glass Beads from the Malay Peninsula." *Journal of Glass Studies* 8 (1966): 80–94.

_____. "Some Observations on Stone and Glass Beads in Early Southeast Asia." *Journal of Malaysian Branch of the Royal Asiatic Society* 38, no. 2 (1965): 85–124.

_____. "Some 17th-Century Glass Beads from Ghana, West Africa." *The Bead Journal* 3, nos. 3, 4 (1978): 23–27.

Lance, Ney Rene. "Ornamentation in Af-

ghanistan." In *Bead News: Selection from Ten Years of the Bead Society Newsletter*, edited by Dorthea Casady. Los Angeles: The Bead Society, 1982.

Latif, Momin. *Mughul Jewels.* Brussels: Societé Generale de Banque, 1982.

Laufer, Berthold. *Notes on Turquoise in the East.* Field Museum of Natural History Anthropological series. Vol. 8, no. 1 (1913).

Lee, Sherman E. *The Genius of Japanese Design.* Tokyo: Kodansha International, 1981.

Legarda, Angelita G. "Antique Beads of the Philippine Islands." *Arts of Asia* 7, no. 5 (1977): 61–70.

_____. "Pre-Hispanic Gold in the Philippines." *Arts of Asia* 7, no. 5 (1978): n.p.

Lenssen, Barbara G., Andrew Whiteford, and Susan Brown McGreevey. *Lullabies from the Earth: Cradles of Native North America.* Santa Fe, N.M.: Wheelwright Museum of the American Indian, 1980.

Lesley, Parker. *Renaissance Jewels and Jeweled Objects.* Baltimore: Baltimore Museum of Art, 1968.

Levin, M. G., and L. P. Potapov. *The Peoples of Siberia.* Chicago: University of Chicago Press, 1964.

Levinsohn, Rhoda. "Rural Kwazulu Beadwork." *Ornament* 4, no. 4 (1980): 38–42.

Lewis, Paul, and Elaine Lewis. *Peoples of the Golden Triangle.* London: Thames and Hudson, 1984.

Liu, Robert K. "African-Made Glass Ornaments: Survey and Experimental Results." *Ornament* 8, no. 2 (1984): 52–53.

_____. "African Mold-Made Glass Beads." *The Bead Journal* 1, no. 2 (1974): 8–14.

_____. "Amira Francoise: Living with Beads in the Sudan." *Ornament* 5, no. 4 (1982): 24–27.

_____. "Ancient Chinese Glass Beads." *The Bead Journal* 2, no. 2 (1975): 9–19.

_____. "Asian Glass Ornaments." Parts 1, 2. *Ornament* 8, 9, nos. 4, 1 (1985): 28–31.

_____. "The Bead in African Assembled Jewelry: Its Multiple Manifestations." In *Beauty by Design: The Aesthetics of African Adornment*, edited by Marie-Therese Brincard. New York: The African-American Institute, 1984.

_____. "Chinese Glass Beads and Ornaments." *The Bead Journal* 1, no. 3 (1975): 13–28.

_____. "Dan Frost Bead Collection." *Ornament* 6, no. 3 (1983): 25–30.

_____. "Formosan Ornaments and Clothing." *Ornament* 6, no. 4 (1983): 21–27.

_____. "Glass Ojime." *Ornament* 6, no. 2

(1982): 24–28.

_____. "Identification: Afghani Stone Beads." *Ornament* 7, no. 2 (1983): 34–35.

_____. "Identification: Carnelian Beads and Their Simulations." *Ornament* 8, no. 1 (1984): 14–18.

_____. "Identification: Smallest and Largest Beads." *Ornament* 9, no. 1 (1985): 69.

_____. "Identification: Tzi Beads." *Ornament* 4, no. 4 (1980): 56–59.

_____. "Iranian Faience: Beads/Pendants of Late Periods." *Ornament* 6, no. 2 (1982): 6–7.

_____. "Iridescence and Related Phenomena." *Ornament* 9, no. 3 (1986): 31–36.

Liu, Robert K., and Elizabeth Harris. *Nueva Cádiz and Associated Beads.* Lancaster, Pa.: G. B. Fenstermaker, 1982.

Lothrop, Samuel K. *Cocle: An Archaeological Study of Central Panama.* Peabody Museum Memoirs, Vol. 7, Part 1. Cambridge, Mass.: Harvard University Press, 1937.

Lucas, A. *Ancient Egyptian Materials and Industries.* 4th ed. Revised and enlarged by J. R. Harris. London: Edward Arnold, 1962.

Lundstrom, Agneta. "Beadmaking in Scandinavia in the Early Middle Ages." *Antikvarisk Arkiv* (Sweden) 61 (1976): n.p.

Lyford, Carrie A. *Quill and Beadwork of the Western Sioux.* Boulder, Co.: Johnson Publishing Company, 1982.

Mallowan, M.E.L. "Excavations at Brak and Chagar Bazar." *Iraq* 9 (1947): n.p.

Mallowan, M.E.L., and J. Cruikshank Rose. "Excavations at Tell Arpachiyah, 1933." *Iraq* 2, Part 1 (1935): 1–178.

Maloney, Clarence, ed. *The Evil Eye.* New York: Columbia University Press, 1976.

Marshack, Alexander. *Ice Age Art.* New York: American Museum of Natural History, 1978.

Marshall, F. H. *Catalogue of the Jewellery, Greek, Etruscan, and Roman, in the Department of Antiquities, British Museum.* Reprint from 1911 edition. London: The Trustees of the British Museum, 1969.

Mason, Ronald J. *Rock Island: Historical Indian Archaeology in the Northern Lake Michigan Basin.* Kent, Ohio: Kent State University Press, 1985.

Mason, V. M., and V. I. Sarianidi. *Central Asia: Turkmenia Before the Achaemenids.* London: Thames and Hudson, 1972.

Matheson, Sylvia A. *Persia: An Archaeological Guide.* London: Faber and Faber, 1972.

Mathews, Zena Pearlstone. *Color and Shape in American Indian Art.* New

York: The Metropolitan Museum of Art, 1983.

Maxwell, John. "The Beaded Textiles of Maloh." in *Indonesian Textiles*. Washington, D.C.: Textile Museum, 1979.

Maxwell-Hyslop, K. R. *Western Asiatic Jewellery, c. 3000–612 B.C.* London: Methuen & Company, 1971.

McClelland, E. M. *The Cult of Ifa Among the Yoruba: Folk Practice and the Art*. London: Ethnographica, 1982.

McIntosh, Roderick, and Susan McIntosh. "The Inland Niger Delta Before the Empire of Mali: Evidence from Jenne-Jero." *Journal of African History* 22 (1981): 1–22.

McLeod, M. D. *The Asante*. London: British Museum Publications, 1981.

McNeill, William. *The Rise of the West*. Chicago: University of Chicago Press, 1963.

Mellaart, James. "Egyptian and Near Eastern Chronology: A Dilemma?" *Antiquity* 53 (1979): n.p.

Mikoshiba, Misao, and Raymond Bushell. "The Soken Kisho and Ojime." *Arts of Asia*, July–August 1979: 59–69.

Mille, Polly. "A Historical Explanation of Alaskan Trade Beads." *The Bead Journal* 2, no. 2 (1975): 20–24.

Mills, J. P. *The Lhota Nagas*. London: Macmillan, 1922.

——. *The Ao Nagas*. Oxford: Oxford University Press, 1926.

Miyamoto, Nobuto. "Glass Beads of the Formosan Aborigines." *Minzoku-Gaku Kenkyu, Japan Journal of Ethnography* 21, no. 4 (1957): 89–91.

Moore, Andrew M. T. "A Pre-Neolithic Farmers' Village on the Euphrates." In *Prehistoric Times*, edited by Brian M. Fagan. San Francisco: Freeman and Company, 1979.

Movius, Hallam L., Jr. "The Châtelperronian in French Archaeology: The evidence of Arcy-sur-Cure." *Antiquity* 43 (1969): n.p.

Muller, Priscilla E. *Jewels in Spain: 1500–1800*. New York: The Hispanic Society of America, 1972.

Nadelhoffer, Hans. *Cartier, Jewelers Extraordinary*. New York: Harry N. Abrams, 1984.

National Geographic Society. *Early Civilizations in the Middle East* 154, no. 3 supplement (1978): 326B.

——. *Ethnolinguistic Map of the Peoples of Africa* 140, no. 6 supplement (1971): 737.

——. *The Historic Mediterranean* 162, no. 6 supplement (1982): 694B.

National Museums of Korea. *Special Exhibition of Relics from Tomb No. 98*. Kyongju, Korea: National Museums of Korea, 1975.

Nelson Gallery-Atkins Museum. *Chinese Exhibition*. Kansas City, Mo.: The Exhibition of Archaeological Finds of the Peoples Republic of China, 1975.

Neuberg, F. *Glass in Antiquity*. London: Art Trade Press, 1949.

Newark Museum. *Tibetan Collection*. 3 vols. Newark, N.J.: Newark Museum, 1983.

Newman, Harold. *An Illustrated Dictionary of Jewelry*. London: Thames and Hudson, 1981.

Newton, Douglas. *Massim*. New York: Museum of Primitive Art, 1975.

Northern, Rebecca. "The Birdman Bead." *Americas* 20, no. 3. Washington, D.C.: Organization of American States, 1968: 14–20.

Northern, Tamara. *The Sign of the Beaded Leopard: Beaded Art of the Cameroon*. Storrs, Conn.: The William Benton Museum of Art, University of Connecticut, 1975.

——. *The Art of Cameroon*. Washington, D.C.: Smithsonian Institution, 1984.

Noveck, Madeline. *The Mark of Ancient Man*. New York: The Brooklyn Museum, 1976.

Ogden, Jack. *Jewellery of the Ancient World*. London: Trefoil Books, 1982.

Okada, Barbara. *Japanese Netsuke and Ojime*. Newark, N.J.: The Newark Museum Association, 1976.

Okamoto, T. *Japanese Arts to Jomon Age*. Tokyo: Shibundo, 1983.

Orchard, William C. *Beads and Beadwork of the American Indians*. New York: Museum of the American Indian, Heyes Foundation, 1975.

Oved, Sah. *The Book of Necklaces*. London: Arthur Barker, 1953.

Pekarik, Andrew J. *Japanese Lacquer 1600–1900*. New York: Metropolitan Museum of Art, 1980.

Pfeiffer, John E. *The Creative Explosion*. New York: Harper and Row, 1982.

——. *The Emergence of Man*, 2d ed. New York: Harper and Row, 1972.

Pierides, Angeliki. *Jewellery in the Cyprus Museum*. Department of Antiquities. Nicosia: 1971.

Pliny. *Natural History*. 10 vols. Translated and edited by D. E. Eichholz. Loeb Classical Library. Cambridge, Ma.: Harvard University Press, 1962.

Pogue, Joseph E. *Turquoise*. Memoirs of the National Academy of Sciences 12, Part. 2. Reprint from 1915 edition. Glorieta, N.M.: The Rio Grande Press, 1975.

Poinar, George O., Jr. "Sealed in Amber." *Natural History* 92, no. 6. New York: American Museum of Natural History, 1982.

Possehl, Gregory L. "Cambay Beadmaking." *Expedition* 23, no. 4 (1981): 39–47.

Priebatsch, Suzanne, and Nataline White. "Traditional Ndebele Beadwork." *African Arts* 11, no. 2 (1978).

Proskouriakoff, Tatiana. *Jades from the Cenote of Sacrifice, Chichen Itza, Yucatan*. Peabody Museum Memoirs. Vol. 10, no. 1. Cambridge, Mass.: Harvard University Press, 1974.

Randall, Richard H., Jr. *Objects of Adornment*. Baltimore: Walters Art Gallery, 1984.

Rawson, Philip. *The Art of Southeast Asia*. London: Thames and Hudson, 1967.

Reade, Julian. "Early Etched Beads and the Indus-Mesopotamia Trade." Occasional paper, no. 2. London: British Museum, 1979.

Reynolds, Valrae. *Tibet: A Lost World*. New York: The American Federation of the Arts, 1978.

Rice, Patty C. *Amber, The Golden Gem of the Ages*. New York: Van Nostrand Reinhold, 1980.

Robicsek, Francis. *A Study in Maya Art and History: The Mat Symbol*. New York: Museum of the American Indian, Heye Foundation, 1975.

Rodgers, Susan. *Power and Gold: Jewelry from Indonesia, Malaysia, and the Philippines*. Geneva: Barbier-Muller Museum, 1985.

Rosnek, Carl, and Joseph Stacey. *Skystone and Silver*. Englewood Cliffs, N.J.: Prentice-Hall, 1976.

Ross, Kay. "Shell Ornaments of Malaita." *Expedition* 23, no. 2 (1981).

Rowe, Donald. *The Art of Jewelry 1450–1650*. Chicago: The Martin D'Arcy Gallery of Art, Loyola University, 1975.

Sankalia, H. D. *The Prehistory and Protohistory of India and Pakistan*. Poona, India: Deccan College, 1974.

Schafer, Edward H. *The Golden Peaches of Samarkand, A Study of T'ang Exotics*. Berkeley and Los Angeles: University of California Press, 1963.

Schienerl, Peter W. "The Much-Enduring Eye." *Ornament* 7, no. 4 (1984): 27–28.

Schiro, Anne-Marie. "The Return of Pearls: A Guide for Buyers." *The New York Times*. 5 December 1981.

Schoeman, H. "A Preliminary Report on Traditional Beadwork in the Mkhwamazi Area of the Mtunzini District, Zululand." African *Studies* 27, no. 2 (1968).

Schumann, Walter. *Gemstones of the World*. New York and London: Sterling Publishing and NAG Press, 1977.

Seefried, Monique. *Les Pendentifs en verre sur noyau*. Farnese: Ecole Francaise de Rome, 1982.

Seizman, Matsuura. *Kasshi Yawa (Writings Begun on the Night of the First Day of the Rat, 11th Month)*. 6 vols. 1821–41. Edited by Nakamura Yukihiko and Nakano Mitsutoshi. Tokyo: Heibonsha, 1978.

Shaw, T. E. (Colonel T. E. Lawrence), ed. and trans. *The Odyssey of Homer*.

Translation 1935. New York: Oxford University Press, 1965.

Shaw, Thurstan. *Igbo-Ukwu*. Evanston, Ill.: Northwestern University Press, 1970.

Sherratt, Andrew. *The Cambridge Encyclopedia of Archaeology*. New York: Crown Publishers, 1980.

The Shogun Age Exhibition. Japan: Tokugawa Art Museum, 1983.

Sieber, Roy. *African Textiles and Decorative Arts*. New York: The Museum of Modern Art, 1972.

Sitwell, Nigel. "Pearls—The Queen of Gems." *Smithsonian* 15, no. 10 (1985): 40.

Smith, Marvin T. "The Chevron Trade Bead in North America." *The Bead Journal* 3, no. 2 (1977): 15–17.

———. "Chronology from Glass Beads: The Spanish Period in the Southeast, c. A.D. 1513–1670." In *Proceedings of the 1982 Glass Trade Bead Conference Research Records no. 16*, edited by Charles F. Hayes, III. Rochester, N.Y.: Rochester Museum and Science Center, 1983.

Smith, Marvin T., and Mary Elizabeth Good. *Early Sixteenth-Century Glass Beads in the Spanish Colonial Trade*. Greenwood, Miss.: Cottonlandia Museum Publications, 1982.

Sorensen, Cloyd. "This Enduring Intrigue of the Glass Bead Trade." *Arizona Highways* 47, no. 7 (1971).

Speck, Frank G., and William C. Orchard. *The Penn Wampum Belts*. New York: Museum of the American Indian, Heye Foundation, 1925.

Stierlin, Henri. *Art of the Aztecs*. New York: Rizzoli, 1982.

Stout, Ann M. "The Archaeological Context of Late Roman Period Mosaic Glass Face Beads." *Ornament* 9, no. 4 (1986): 58–61.

Streeter, Edwin W. *Pearls and Pearling Life*. York Street, London: George Bell & Sons, 1886.

Streuver, Stuart, and Felicia Antonelli Holton. *Koster: Americans in Search of Their Prehistoric Past*. Garden City, N.Y.: Anchor Press/Doubleday, 1979.

Suk, Joo-sun. *Personal Ornaments in Yi Dynasty*. Folk Art Research Collection series II. Seoul, Korea: Dankook University Press: The Suk Joo-sun Memorial Museum of Korean Folk Art, 1981.

Sullivan, Michael. *The Arts of China*. Berkeley, Ca.: University of California Press, 1979.

Tait, Hugh. *The Golden Age of Venetian Glass*. London: British Museum Publications, 1979.

Tanner, Clara. *Prehistoric Southwestern Craft Art*. Tuscon, Az.: University of Arizona Press, 1976.

Tatton-Brown, Veronica. *Cyprus B.C. 7,000 Years of History*. London: British Museum Publications, 1979.

Taylor, Lord William. *The Mycenaeans*. London: Thames and Hudson, 1983.

Tempelmann-Maczynska, M. *Die Perlen der romischen Kaiserzeit und der fruhen Phasse der Volkerwanderungszeit im Mitteleuropaischen Barbaricum*. Mainz: Verlag Philipp von Zabern, 1985.

Thompson, R. Campbell. *A Dictionary of Assyrian Chemistry and Geology*. Oxford: Clarendon Press, 1936.

Tigger, Bruce G., ed. "Northeast." *Handbook of North American Indians*. Vol. 15. Washington, D.C.: Smithsonian Institution, 1978.

Tosi, Maurizio, and Marcello Piperno. "Lithic Technology Behind the Ancient Lapis Lazuli Trade." *Expedition* 16, no. 1. University of Pennsylvania, 1973.

Trebbin, Cornelius. *Achate, geschliffen in Idar-Oberstein—Amulette, Schmock und Zahlungsmittel, in Afrika*. Idar-Oberstein, West Germany: Museum Idar-Oberstein, 1985.

Tushingham, A. D., et al. *Studies in Ancient Peruvian Metalworking*. Toronto: Royal Ontario Museum, 1979.

Untracht, Oppi. *Jewelry Concepts and Technology*. Garden City, N.Y.: Doubleday, 1982.

van der Sleen, W. G. N. "Ancient Glass Beads, with special reference to the beads of East and Central Africa and the Indian Ocean." *Journal of the Royal Anthropological Institute of Great Britain and Ireland*. (1958): 88.

———. "Beadmaking in 17th-Century Amsterdam." *Archaeology* 16 (1963): 260–63.

———. *A Handbook on Beads*. Liège, Belgium: Librairie Halbart, 1973.

———. "Trade Wind Beads." *Man*. 1966.

Vandiver, Pamela. "Glass Technology at the Mid-Second-Millennium B.C. Hurrian Site of Nuzi." *Journal of Glass Studies* 25 (1983): 88–89.

van Landewijk, J.E.J.M. "What Was the Original Aggrey Bead?" Parts 1–3. *Ghana Journal of Sociology* 6, 7, nos. 2, 4, 1 (1970–71): n.p.

van Riet Lowe, C. "The Glass Beads of Mapungubwe." *Archaeological Survey*, no. 9 (1955): 1–21.

Venclova, Natalie. "Prehistoric Eye Beads in Central Europe." *Journal of Glass Studies* 25 (1983): n.p.

Vilimkova, Milada, and Dominique Darbois. *Egyptian Jewellery*. London: Paul Hamlyn, 1969.

Vogel, Susan. *For Spirits and Kings: African Art from the Ruth and Paul Tishman Collection*. New York: Harry N. Abrams and the Metropolitan Museum of Art, 1981.

Volker, T. *The Animal in Far Eastern Art*. Leiden: E. J. Brill, 1975.

Von Saldern, Axel. *Ancient Glass in the Museum of Fine Arts*. Boston: Museum of Fine Arts, 1968.

———. "Mosaic Glass from Ḥasanlū, Marlik, and Tell al-Rimah." *The Journal of Glass Studies* 8. Corning, N.Y.: Corning Museum of Glass, 1966.

Waldschmidt, Ernest, and Rose Waldschmidt. *Nepal: Art Treasures from the Himalayas*. New York: Universe Books, 1970.

Warmington, E. H. *The Commerce Between the Roman Empire and India*. Cambridge, England: Cambridge University Press, 1928.

Weaver, Muriel Porter. *The Aztecs, Maya, and Their Predecessors*. New York: Academic Press, 1981.

Webster, L., ed. *Aspects of Production and Style in Dark Ages Metalwork*. Occasional paper no. 34. London: British Museum, 1982.

Weinberg, Gladys Davidson. "Glass Manufacture in Hellenistic Rhodes." *Archaiologikon Deltion* 24 (1969): 1971.

Weinstein, Michael. *The World of Jewel Stones*. New York: Sheridan House, 1967.

White, J. C., et al. *Ban Chiang: Discovery of a Lost Bronze Age*. Philadelphia: University Museum, 1982.

White, William Charles. *Tombs of Old Lo-Yang*. Shanghai: Kelly & Walsh, 1934.

Wild, R. P. "A Method of Beadmaking Practiced in the Gold Coast." *Man* 37 (1937): 96–97.

Wildschut, William, and John C. Ewers. *Crow Indian Beadwork: A Descriptive and Historical Study*. New York: Museum of the American Indian, Heye Foundation, 1959.

Wilkins, Eithene. *The Rose-Garden Game: The Symbolic Background to the European Prayer Beads*. London: Victor Gollancz, 1969.

Willcox, Donald J. *Body Jewelry, International Perspectives*. Chicago: Henry Regnery Company, 1973.

Willett, Frank. *Baubles, Bangles, and Beads: Trade Contacts of Medieval Ifa*. Melville J. Herskovitz Memorial Lecture, no. 13. Edinburgh: Center of African Studies, 1977.

Winnipeg Art Gallery. *The Inuit Amautik: I Like My Hood To Be Full*. Winnipeg, Manitoba: Winnipeg Art Gallery, 1980.

Wooley, Sir Leonard C. *Ur Excavations Vol. 2, The Royal Cemetery*. London and Philadelphia: Publications of the Joint Expedition of the British Museum and of the Museum of the University of Pennsylvania, 1934.

Yoshimizu, T. *Eye of the Dragonfly*. Tokyo: Heibonsha, 1980.

Zwalf, W. *Heritage of Tibet*. London: British Museum Publications, 1981.

Index

period, 52, *52*, 54, *54*, 55, 56, 66, 194, 297 ; later revivals of, 102, 104, 106
Greek Orthodox rosaries, 79
Grotte du Rennes (Fr.), 22
Guayaquil (Ecua.), *258, 259*

Haida Indians (N. Amer.), 279
Hallstatt culture, 62, *63*, 73, *294*
Harappa (Indus Valley), 44, 186–87
Harper, William, *325*
Hasanlū (Iran), 51
Haua Fteah (Lib.), 25
Hausa tribe (W. Afr.), *124*, 129
Hawara (Egypt), *54*
Hedeby (Scan.), 76
Helgö (Scan.), 76
Henry VIII (King of England), 102
Hepu pearl fisheries (China), 298
Hinduism, 181–82, 235 ; in central Asia, 204, 206, *209*, 211, *219* ; prayer beads, 80, *80*, 81, 84
Hopewell culture (N. Amer.), 263
Hudson, Henry, 112
Hudson Bay Company, 274, 275
human bones, teeth : in North American Indian jewelry, 282 ; in the South Pacific, *240* ; in Tibetan ritual objects, 79, *82, 85, 215*
Hungary, 47, 262, *273*
Huns, 71, 73
Huron Indians (N. Amer.), *267, 269*, 289
Hurrian culture (Mesop.), 38, *52*

Ibex bone beads, *25, 26*
Ica culture (Peru), *256*
Ice Age, 22, 26, 27. *See also* Upper Paleolithic period
Idar-Oberstein (Ger.), 77, *113*, 113–14, 124, 199
Ife culture (W. Afr.), 124, 129, 141, *142*
Igbo-Ukwu (Afr.), 129
Ikere (W. Afr.), *142*
Ilorin, 124
Inca culture (S. Amer.), 245, 250, 251, *254*
India (*see also* Indus Valley), 18, 66, 93, 101, 102, 181–99, 307, 308 ; African trade, 107, 114, 124, 125, 129, 140, *184*, 195 ; beadmaking industry, 107, 112, *113*, 114, 199 ; carnelian, 37, 76, *184*, 186, 187, 190, 194, 195, 199 ; and central Asia, 201, 202, 204, 206, *209*, 211, 217, 221 ; Far Eastern trade, 154, 159, 162, 175, 179, 199 ; gold-garnet inlay technique, 70, *70* ; Indo-Hellenistic period and Roman trade, 52, 55, 73, 194 ; Kushan dynasty, 159, 204 ; medieval trade, 195 ; Mogul period, 88, *181*, 187, *189*, 198–99 ; pearls, 296, 297, 298, *300*, 304 ; prayer beads, 80, 84, 88, *185* ; prehistoric periods, 21, 25, 27, 29, 186–87 ; and Southeast Asia, 195, 223, 224, *224, 226*, 229, 235, 239 ; tribal jewelry, *185*, 186, *190–93, 196* ; Venetian trade, 190, 199
Indian Ocean trade, 55, 95, 132, *184*, 194, 195, 238

"Indian reds." *See mutisalah* beads
Indonesia, 106, 112, 162, 223, 225, *229*, 239, 243 ; cultures and bead techniques, 235, 238
Industrial Revolution, 101, 104, 179, 135, 316
Indus Valley cultures, *57*, 181, 186–87, 215, 217 ; beadmaking, *33*, 308 ; western Asian trade, 33, 44, 44–45, 95, *182, 184*, 187
inro (Japanese containers), 153, *170*, 178–79
Inuit (Eskimo) tribes, *264, 272, 273*
Iran, 55, 65, 76, 187, 194, 195 ; Achaemenid period (559–330 B.C.), 51, 52, 54, *57*, 297 ; and central Asia, 212, 215, 217 ; etched carnelian from, *17*, 76 ; faience technique, *57*, 97 ; Far Eastern trade, 54, 154, 159, 175 ; Islamic work, *95*, 97, 99 ; lapis trade, processing, 30, 51, *95* ; Neolithic period, *29*, 34, 37, 38, *45* ; Parthian period, *17*, *52*, 54, *57* ; Sasanian period, *17, 57, 95*, 175, 204. *See also* Persian Empire
Ireland, 59, 62, 80, 90
iridescent (fumed) glass, *315, 320, 325*
iron, 18 ; in Africa, 124, 129, 144 ; European cast-iron jewelry, 104
Iron Age, 18, 62, *62*
Iroquois Indians (N. Amer.), 112, *269*, 271, 289
Islam, 71, 88, 93–99, 101, 204 ; in Africa, *123*, 124, 129, 140, 149, *149, 151* ; astronomy and navigation, 98–99 ; dating problems, 99 ; eye-bead amulets, 97, 308 ; glass beadmaking, 55, *60*, 93, *93, 95, 96*, 99, 195 ; glassmaking, 99 ; designs and patterns, 95, *96*, 97, *97*, 98 ; gold- and silversmithing, 97, *98*, 98–99 ; jewelry, 97, *97*, 98, 99, 104 ; pearls, 95, *97*, 297 ; prayer beads, 80, 81, *83*, 88, 91, 95, 97 ; religion, 88, 93, 95, 97 ; scientific knowledge, 102 ; in Southeast Asia, 235, 238, 239 ;
traders, 76, 93, 95, 124, 129, 140
Isneg tribe (Philip. I.), *233*
Italy (*see also* Venice), 55, 56, 70, 73, 74, 77, 81, 88, 104, 107, 166, 179 ; Renaissance jewelry, 102
ivory, 66, 162, 199 ; in Chinese beads, 166 ; in Eskimo fetishes, *273* ; Islamic trade in, 95, 129, 140 ; in Japanese *ojime*, 153, *166, 169, 170–74, 177*, 179 ; 19th-century trade, 17, 106, *108*, 125 ; in the Upper Paleolithic period, 22, 24–25, 26 ; Viking trade, 76
Ivory Coast (W. Afr.), *121, 146*

Jablonec (Czech.), 323
jade beads, 153, *162*, 221, 239 ; Chinese, *156*, 158, 159, 162, *162, 166* ; Japanese, 179 ; Korean, *162*, 167 ; Middle and South American (pre-Hispanic), *245*, 246, 247, *247–50*, 250, 254
jadeite, 166, 167, 250
Jain prayer beads, 80
Japan, 80, 153, 154, 158, 159, 174–79,

204, 238, *240* ; Asuka period, 175 ; Buddhist rosaries, *82, 84, 85*, 88 ; Edo (Tokugawa) period, *164, 166, 170*, 178–79 ; Heian period, 175 ; Jomon period, 174 ; Meiji period, *163, 166, 170*, 179 ; Momoyama period, 178 ; Muromachi period, 175, 178 ; Nara period, 154, 158, *162, 164*, 175 ; Old Tomb period, *163*, 167, 174–75 ; pearl industry, 179, 304 ; Yayoi period, 167, 174. See also *ojime*
jasper, *29*, 37, *39, 41, 44*, 124, 186, *254*
Java (Indon.), *80*, 162, *184*, 235, 243
Jerusalem, 71, 95
jet (lignite), 76, 77, 84, 167 ; British sources, 55, *59*, 62 ; in 19th-century jewelry, 104 ; in Roman trade, 55, *59*, 62, *62, 63* ; Upper Paleolithic, *24*, 26
Jews, 99, 112, 144, *149*, 297, 308
Jordan River valley, *31*, 34
Judaism, and prayer beads, 84
jug beads (Minoan), *51*
Julius Caesar, 297, 298
Justinian I (Byzantine emperor), 66, 68, *68*, 297
Jutland (Den.), 47, *292*

Kabul (Afghan.), 202
Kabylie (Mor.), *149*
Kalahari Desert (S. Afr.), 122
Kalimantan (Indon.), *227, 229, 229*
Kathmandu (Nep.), 211
Kazakhstan (cent. Asia), 201
Kelabit tribe (Borneo), 229
Kenya (E. Afr.), 124, *133*, 137, 149
Kenyatta, Jomo, *133*
Khirokitia (Cyp.), 47
Khmer culture (Camb.), *224*, 229
Khotan region (cent. Asia), 166
Kiffa (Maur.), 129
Kikuyu tribe (E. Afr.), *133*
Kilwa (E. Afr.), 129, 132, 195
Kinga Rinpoche (Tibetan lama), *204*
Kiowa Indians (N. Amer.), *281*
Kirdi tribe (W. Afr.), *146*
Knossos (Crete), 46, 51
kodama beads (Jap.), *163*
kogok (Korean jade bead), *162*, 167, 174
kombologion (Greek Orthodox rosary), 79
Komin (Japanese *ojime* carver), *177*
Kongju (Kor.), 167
Königsberg (Ger.), *294*
Konyak tribe (India), *196*
Koran, 97, 99
Korea, 55, 166–67, 174, 175, 204 ; archaeological sites, 21, 25, 153, 159 ; Buddhist prayer beads, 84, 85, 154
Krasnyi (Russ.), 25
Krobo tribe (W. Afr.), *124*, 129
kuchinashidama (Japanese bead), *164*
kula ring (Trobriand Is.), 243
Kumasi (Ghana), *146*
Kunga Rinpoche (Tibetan lama), *79*
!Kung San tribe (S. Afr.), 122

Lacquer work, Japanese, *168, 170*
Ladakh (cent. Asia), 201, 206, *207*, 211, 217

Lakota Indians (N. Amer.), 289
Lalique, René Jules, 317, 320
lamp-wound beads, 110–11, 344
Langdale Rosary, 88
Laos, 223
lapis lazuli, 84 ; Afghani mines, trade, 9, 30, 37, 44, 45, 187, 215 ; in Egyptian jewelry, 37, 43 ; in Far Eastern jewelry, 166, 167 ; in Islamic jewelry, 95, 95, 97 ; Neolithic uses, trade, 29, 30, 36, 37, 51, 186 ; in 19th-century European jewelry, 106 ; in Migrations Period jewelry, 72, 73 ; in Sumerian jewelry, 32–33
La Quina (Fr.), 21
La Tène culture, 73, 221
"lazy" stitch, in beadwork, 274, 275, 281
lead-barium glass, 156, 159
Lepenski Vir (Yugo.), 59
Lewis and Clark expedition, 271, 274
Lhasa (Tib.), 210, 212
Libya, 25, 121, 122, 144
Lillie, Jacqueline, 320
Limodra (India), 194
Linnaeus, Carolus, 304
Livingstone, David, 132, 149
Lo-lang (Kor.), 153
Lombards, 66, 73, 107
"love beads," in the 1960s, 325–26
lost-wax process, 124, 137, 141, 146, 192
Lough Gur (Ire.), 59
Luoyang tombs (China), 158, 159

*M*agatama (Japanese jade bead), 162, 167, 174
Magellan, Ferdinand, 101
"magic beads," in Thailand, 229
mala (Buddhist rosary), 79, 82, 84
malachite, 34, 59, 246, 256
Malaita I. (Solomon Is.), 240, 243
Malaysia, 184, 195, 225, 243, 296
Mali (W. Afr.), 55, 121, 122, 124, 129, 195
Maloh tribes (Borneo), 229, 229
Mal'ta (Russ.), 25
"Mandarin chains," 162, 163, 168
mandrel-pressed beads, 112
mandrel-wound beads, 123
Manhattan I., sale of, 275
Manteno culture (Ecua.), 258, 259
Mapungubwe tribe (S. Afr.), 125
Margarita I. (Venez.), 258, 302
Marlborough, Duchess of (neé Consuela Vanderbilt), 300
Marquesa Is. (S. Pacific), 240
married metalwork, 169, 175, 179, 325, 326, 344
Marseilles (Massilia) (Fr.), 77, 292
marudama beads (Japan), 163, 164
marvering, 344
mathematics, and Islamic patterns, 95, 97–98
Mauritania, 54, 123, 129, 312
Maya culture (Cent. Amer.), 245, 245, 246, 247, 248, 251, 254, 259 ; jade beads, 248–50
Mecca (Arabia), 88, 95
meditation, and prayer beads, 81, 85

Mediterranean region, 110, 159, 167, 201 ; Bronze Age trade, 46, 47, 48, 51 ; coral from, 90, 104 ; Neolithic trade, 30 ; and silk route trade, 202, 204 ; in the Upper Paleolithic, 21, 22
Mehrgarh (India), 186
melon beads, 37, 59, 63, 159, 164, 209, 221, 224, 229
Merovingians, 68, 73, 74
Mesolithic era, 27
Mesopotamia, 29, 30, 36, 37–38, 45, 95, 182, 186, 187, 215, 217. *See also* Sumer ; Ur
metal alloys, in beads, 324, 325, 326. *See also* married metalwork
Métis people (Can.), 285, 287
Mexico, 245, 246, 259, 298, 302. *See also* Aztec culture ; Maya culture ; Mixtec culture ; Olmec culture
Mezhirichi (Russ.), 292
Middle Ages : in Africa, 122, 124, 140, 141 ; amber trade, 77, 293 ; glass-making in, 74, 77, 107, 110 ; in India, 185 ; jewelry, 77 ; pearls, 297–98 ; prayer beads, 77, 79, 86, 87, 88, 90
Middle America, 245–46. *See also* individual cultures
Migrations Period, 65–77, 204
Mikimoto, Kokichi, 179, 304, 323–34
millefiore glass. *See* mosaic glass
Minoan culture, 41, 46, 46, 47, 47, 51, 59
Mississippi River valley, 263, 271, 302, 304
Mixtec culture (Mex.), 246, 250, 259, 259
Mogadishu (E. Afr.), 132
Mohenjo-daro (India), 44, 45, 186, 187
mold-cast glass, 344
molded glass, 112, 344
Mongol tribes, 99, 107, 221
Mongolia, 201, 202, 206, 210, 215, 219–20, 220
Monte Albán (Mex.), 254, 302
Montezuma (Aztec emperor), 247, 250, 254, 258
Montreal (Can.), 266 ; Treaty of, 267
Moravia, 106, 107, 111–12, 113
Morocco, 97, 144, 149, 151
Morris, William, 316–17
mosaic glass beads, 112, 344 ; Byzantine, 66, 68, 70 ; eye beads, 312 ; Hellenistic and Roman, 54, 56, 60 ; Indian copies, 199 ; Islamic trade, 93 ; Korean, 167 ; manufacturing techniques, 112 ; Mesopotamian, 34 ; Migrations Period, 74 ; in Southeast Asia, 238 ; in the 20th century, 326 ; Venetian, 111, 112, 141 ; Viking, 74, 76, 77
mother-of-pearl, 233, 297
"mummy beads," 42
Mundigak (Afghan.), 44
Murano (It.), 107, 110, 111, 112
mutisalah beads ("Indian reds"), 174, 184, 224, 226, 229, 235, 239
Mycenae, 30, 45, 46, 46, 46, 59, 292

*N*agaland (India), 186, 190–92, 196
Natufian culture (west. Asia), 31, 34
navigation, 55, 98–99, 101, 194

Ndebele tribe (S. Afr.), 135, 136, 140, 149
Neanderthal man, 21, 25–26
Neolithic period, 29–30 ; in Africa, 122 ; in central Asia, 212, 215 ; in Europe, 59 ; eye beads, 307, 308 ; in the Far East, 167, 174 ; in India, 29, 186 ; in Middle and South America, 245 ; in Southeast Asia, 224, 239 ; in western Asia and the Mediterranean, 29–36
Nepal, 10, 201, 201, 202, 204, 206, 209, 210, 211–12, 219
nephrite, 166, 167, 250
Netherlands, 111 ; and African trade, 132 ; chevron beads, 117 ; glass bead-making, 106, 107, 112–113, 117, 258 ; and Japanese trade, 178 ; and North American Indian trade, 266, 271, 275 ; and S.E. Asian trade, 235, 240
netsuke (Japanese ornaments), 153, 166, 170, 176, 178, 179
Newari metalsmiths (cent. Asia), 210, 211–12
New Guinea, 230, 235
New Mexico, 254, 263, 288, 289
New Zealand, 296
Niger (W. Afr.), 129
Nigeria (W. Afr.), 13, 121, 122, 123, 124, 129
Niger River (W. Afr.), 129, 140
Nile River, 38, 132
Nippur (Mesop.), 187
Nishapur (Iran), 95
Nok culture (W. Afr.), 124
North Africa, 66, 71, 73, 129, 312 ; Berber jewelry, 141, 144, 149, 151
North America, 101, 102 ; fur trade, 271, 274 ; pearl fisheries, 302–3
North American Indians, 17, 245, 261–89 ; bead materials, 263, 266 ; bead-work techniques, 115, 261–62, 268, 269, 273, 274, 275, 275, 277, 284 ; cultural groups, 261 ; environment and aesthetics, 277, 279, 284 ; European influences, 261–63, 264, 269, 271, 273, 274–75, 284, 285, 287, 289 ; and glass beads, introduction of, 18, 106, 112–13, 114, 162, 261–63, 271, 274–75 ; and Oriental rug designs, 262, 277, 289 ; pearls, 263, 302 ; tobacco use, 268, 286 ; 20th-century craftsmen, 325 ; Upper Paleolithic, 25. *See also* individual tribes, cultural groupings
Northwest Coast Indians, 261, 263, 264, 274, 275, 279
Nueva Cádiz beads, 110, 114, 258
Nyhus, Jane, 315

*O*bsidian, 34, 36
Odyssey (Homer), 292
ojime (Japanese slide fasteners), 153, 153, 158, 164, 166, 168–73, 176, 177
Olbia (Russ.), 70
Olbia (Sard.), 55
Olmec culture (Mex.), 246, 248, 249, 251, 254
Oman (Arabia), 98, 99, 195
onyx, 95, 106, 186, 194, 195 ; Philippine banded, 239, 242
opus interrasile technique, 69, 69

PHOTOGRAPHY CREDITS

All photographs were taken by Togashi or were provided by the museums credited in the captions, unless listed below. Plate numbers follow the photographers' names.

Ping Amranand: 206, 219–21, 223, p. 11. Dirk Bakker: 252. Lee Boultin: 21. Brown Brothers: 323, 325. Mark Carleton and Dr. Michael Heide: 91, 101, 109 (1–5), 329 (36). Michael Cavanagh and Keith Montague: 62–63. Amos Chan: 341. Crawley, Wilkinson Associates, Ltd.: 318–19. Lois S. Dubin: 121–22, 315. Courtesy of David Ebbinghouse: 216. Andre Emmerich Gallery: 261. Ray Errett: 31, 33–36, 52, 85, 109 (6), 158, 162–68, 194, 228, 329 (19–20, 26, 35), 330. Mary Evan Picture Library/Photo Researchers, Inc.: 321. Angela Fisher: 102, 105, 110–11, 114, 116–18, 120, 123–24, 149–50. Fernand Fonssagrives: 336. Courtesy of Dr. Melvin Fowler, University of Wisconsin, Milwaukee: 273. Courtesy Ivory Freidus: 213, 218. Michael Ginn: 113. Michael B. Glass: 143, 204, 337, 340. Barry Howard: 7, 145. Eeva Inkeri: 232, 240. Howard Jones: 313. Courtesy of Steven Kossak: 225. Victor Krantz: 241–43, 245–46. Jack Kulawik: 331. Francois LeClair: 311. Alexander Marshack: 1–5. Michael Meleski: Bead Shape Table (pp. 342–43). Bruno Piazza: 131, 147, 195, 226–27, 237–39. Norman Priebatsch: 130. William Robertson: 152–57, 159, 329 (24–25). Manu Sassoonian: 197. Heini Schneebeli: 200, 207, 215. Courtesy of Verena Sieber-Fuchs: 332–33, 338. Jerry L. Thompson, courtesy of The Metropolitan Museum of Art: p. 12. Malcolm Varon: 138. Paul Weltchek: 77.

BEAD CHART CREDITS

The following museums provided beads and/or photographs for the Bead Chart. Bead Chart numbers are listed after each museum.

American Museum of Natural History, New York City: 1000a–f, 1001, 1006–1007, 1009–1017. Ashmolean Museum, Oxford University, England: 30. The Bead Museum, Prescott, Arizona: 903a, 908, 913–16. British Museum, London, England: 6–24, 37, 235, 236, 237a–c, 238–39, 244, 298, 319, 374, 376–82, 384–86, 387a–d, 388a–c, 389a–c, 393, 403, 404, 406, 408, 350–52, 357, 412, 413a–b, 414–20, 422–24, 426–30, 432–37, 439–44, 463–64. Corning Museum of Glass, Corning, New York: 383, 397, 398–402, 455, 465, 614a–f, 803, 814, 817–19, 821, 834–37, 843, 901. Dumbarton Oaks Museum, Washington, D.C.: 483. Hegau Museum, Singen, West Germany: 3. Herakleion Museum, Crete: 375. Hispanic Society of America, New York City: 532. Illinois State Museum, Springfield: 1002–1005. Indiana University Museum, Bloomington: 404, 410, 484–85. Instituto Nacional de Seguros, Costa Rica: 1105. Israel Museum, Jerusalem: 200–205. McCord Museum, McGill University, Montreal: 1002. Metropolitan Museum of Art, New York City: 246, 438, 509–10, 533, 622. Moravske Museum, Brno, Czechoslovakia: 1–2. National Museum of Copenhagen, Denmark: 29a–e. Peabody Museum of Ethnology and Archaeology, Cambridge, Massachusetts: 4. Royal Ontario Museum, Toronto, Ontario: 800–802, 804–13, 815–16. San Juan Archaeological Research Center and Library, Bloomfield, New Mexico: 1008. Trondheim Royal Norwegian Scientific Society Museum: 33a–e. University Museum, University of Pennsylvania, Philadelphia: 1210–11. Walters Art Gallery, Baltimore, Maryland: 31.

The following photographers and collectors provided photographs for the Bead Chart.

Dirk Bakker: 1105. Mark Carleton and Dr. Michael Heide: 40–43, 82–84, 98a–c, 102a–f, 103a–b, 104, 105a–c, 108a–c, 109, 1207–1209. Michael Cavanagh and Keith Montague: 405, 406, 484–85. Crawley, Wilkinson Associates, Ltd.: 129a–d, 130. Andre Emmerich Gallery: 1102. Ray Errett: 383, 397, 398–402, 455, 465, 614a–f, 803, 814, 817–19, 821, 834–37, 843. Mia Fonssagrives-Solow: 1315. Michael B. Glass: 1316. Barry Howard: 297, 1000a–f, 1001, 1006, 1007, 1009–1017. Eeva Inkeri: 904, 912a–c. Howard Jones: 1008. Jack Kulawik: 1317, 1319–20. Francois LeClair: 1022. Alexander Marshack: 1–5. Michael Meleski: 1029, 1030, 1103. William Robertson: 800–802, 804–13, 815–16. Heini Schneebeli: 705. All other Bead Chart photographs were taken by Togashi.

The following collectors and galleries kindly provided beads to be photographed for the Bead Chart:

Henry Anavian, Sumer Gallery; Robin Beningson, Antiquarian Gallery; Craft Caravan; Derek Content; Lois S. Dubin; Neil Dwire; Edward Merrin Gallery; Andre Emmerich Gallery; Connie Emmerich; Abram Epstein; Ivory Freidus; Audrey Friedman, Primavera Gallery; Cynthia Gofre, Bamboula; Anita Gumpert; Dr. Michael Heide; Wolf Hunger, Sac Frères; J. Camp Gallery; Suzanne Donnelly Jenkins; Arthur King; Margaret and Joe Knopfelmacher; Ravi Kumar; Gabrielle Liese, The Bead Museum; Karl Mann; Peter and Louise Mroczkowski; Louise Parrish; Ruth and John Picard; Sylvia Pines, Uniquities; Albert Summerfield; Esther Twersky; Sashi Wagner, Midori Gallery; Charles Whitmore; Maureen Zarember, Tambaran Gallery.

BEAD SHAPE CHART

All beads from the collections of Henry Anavian and Lois S. Dubin.